HATE SPEECH ON CAMPUS

Dear Bonnie:
   Thanks for your
warm, wise & winning (!)
[I love Alliterations !!]
help. It was
genuinely much
Appreciated.

Hate Speech on Campus

CASES, CASE STUDIES, AND COMMENTARY

Edited by

MILTON HEUMANN
and THOMAS W. CHURCH

with David P. Redlawsk

NORTHEASTERN UNIVERSITY PRESS
BOSTON

Northeastern University Press

Library of Congress Cataloging-in-Publication Data

Hate speech on campus : cases, case studies, and commentary / edited
  by Milton Heumann and Thomas W. Church with David P. Redlawsk.
     p. cm.
    ISBN 1–55553–291–8 (acid-free paper). — ISBN 1–55553–292–6 (pbk.
    : acid-free paper)
    1. Hate speech—United States. 2. Freedom of speech—United
  States. I. Heumann, Milton. II. Church, Thomas W., 1945– .
  III. Redlawsk, David P.
  KF9345.A7H38   1997
  342.73′0853—dc20
  [347.302853]   96–9871

Designed by Amy Bernstein

Printed and bound by Thomson-Shore, Inc., in Dexter, Michigan. The paper is Glatfelter Supple Opaque Recycled, an acid-free sheet.

MANUFACTURED IN THE UNITED STATES OF AMERICA

00 99 98   4 3 2

CONTENTS

COMMENTARY

PREFACE

This book brings together material on an issue that is currently troubling most university campuses in the United States and, indeed, much of the developed world: the problem of how to deal with a distressing increase in hate speech on college and university campuses. At our own universities, we have found that students are intrinsically interested in this subject and tend to hold strong (if not always well considered) views regarding it. The subject is enormously complicated; the more one delves into the legal, practical, and political context of the problem, the less amenable it seems to simple solution. Students tend to see many social issues in terms of right and wrong, just and unjust. Yet the attempt to formulate an efficacious response to the growing incidence of campus hate speech is perhaps a definitional example of those conflicts that involve right vs. right, just vs. just. Gaining a clear appreciation of the enormously difficult trade-offs such issues raise in legal, social, and political life is the first step toward becoming an educated citizen.

This book is designed to be used in university classes devoted to a variety of subjects: American politics, civil rights and liberties, law and courts, race relations, and educational policy. We have brought together materials of three types, all of which offer different perspectives on the problem at hand: judicial opinions, original case studies of recent efforts to deal with the hate speech problem on American campuses, and commentary bearing on the issue. In selecting this material, we followed several rules. First, we tried to select materials that are interesting and engaging to students. We have used this material in our own classes, and found that students find it interesting and accessible. We cannot promise that all the readings are easy going—predigested summaries and watered-down excerpts cannot do justice to the complexity of the problem under examination, or to the intellectual abilities of the students.

Second, we attempted to provide a wide variety of competing viewpoints. We admit to ambiguous feelings regarding the issues raised in these materials and have not attempted to impose or even suggest an orthodoxy. Where court decisions were accompanied by dissenting opinions that focused on issues of relevance to the issue of hate speech, we included them. We tried to find the most articulate and comprehensive representatives of the various positions on these issues in the commentary section, and endeavored to select cases and commentary in which different judges and writers speak to each other and address each other's arguments. We selected case studies that include a wide variety of contexts within which to assess the effort to deal with campus hate speech, and—unlike our conscious effort to find strong proponents of specific positions in the case and commentary materials—we attempted to ensure that the case studies were written in as neutral a fashion as possible.

Third, while the material we have selected is necessarily compressed and edited, we endeavored to avoid a sin we have frequently found in materials such as these: that of overediting and the resulting "snippity" nature of the excerpts. Many of the excerpts in this book are long by the usual standards of such anthologies. We consciously chose to provide fewer selections in order to allow the arguments to emerge naturally and completely, and to give full voice to opposing views. This is particularly evident with respect to several of the court cases—especially the crucial recent decision by the Supreme Court in *R.A.V.* v. *City of St. Paul*—and in the commentary section. We should note that we eliminated most of the footnotes and case citations from selections in the cases and commentary sections in order to conserve space. The case studies have not been previously published, so we have retained those footnotes.

Finally, we tried to make this volume self-contained. This effort is most relevant to the cases chosen in the first section of the book. Where specific legal doctrines are discussed but not defined in the decisions, we have explained them in the introduction or in footnotes. The cases chosen do not represent a "mini-course" on free speech doctrine, but they do provide a reasonably clear basis from which to discuss the legal environment constraining university efforts to deal with hate speech. If this book is used as a supplement in a case-based constitutional law or civil liberties course, there may be some duplication in the cases we selected. However, many of the cases here are unlikely candidates for a broad-gauged course, and even if there is duplication, it is likely that the excerpts contained here are more substantial and focused than those found in most case books.

A word about our collaboration is in order. As old friends and colleagues, we have argued about the fascinating interplay of principle, politics, and educational philosophy surrounding campus hate speech for at least a decade. (The arrangement of the authors' names on our previous book followed alphabetical order; that order is reversed here for no more compelling reason than to provide a degree of symmetry in our continuing collaborations.) We have traded cases and commentary on hate speech for use in our respective undergraduate and graduate courses for almost as long as we have known each other. In the spring of 1991, we both scheduled graduate seminars on this subject at our respective universities. Because of the distance between our schools, the classes met together only once, but that meeting turned out to be a wonderfully stimulating all-day session at which students presented papers describing a specific campus hate speech case study and debated the issues involved. Several of the case studies in this volume began as papers presented in that seminar.

David Redlawsk, a graduate student in that seminar, has been more of a collaborator than a contributor to this endeavor, and his very substantial efforts in choosing, thinking about, and editing the materials (as well as gently prodding and persuading the two of us) are reflected in the fact that his name appears on the title page of this volume. We wish to thank the students at both Rutgers University and the University at Albany/SUNY who contributed case studies, arguments, and support to this project. We also wish to thank both undergraduate and graduate students we taught in classes held before and since that joint seminar, who have acted as guinea pigs for the materials included in this volume and who have had to suffer through innumerable examples of cases and commentary that did not work pedagogically. Special thanks to David Lorello, a Rutgers undergraduate, and Lance Cassak, a friend and colleague, both keen students of hate speech and speech codes, whose mastery of the hate speech literature proved invaluable in the final preparation of this manuscript. Finally, as always, we wish to thank our families, who put up with our absences and disputations with the good grace that we have grown to expect, but that we probably do not deserve.

HATE SPEECH ON CAMPUS

GENERAL INTRODUCTION

Contours of the Problem

The introduction of speech codes on many campuses is a truly remarkable development. These speech codes address a perceived growing problem of intolerance at the nation's colleges and universities by prohibiting religious or ethnic epithets and racist or sexist language, and by specifying punishments for students who continue to use them. The speech code adopted at the University of Michigan exemplifies such codes by prohibiting "any behavior, verbal or physical, that stigmatizes or victimizes an individual on the basis of race, ethnicity, religion, national origin, sexual orientation, creed, ancestry, age, marital status, handicap, or Vietnam-veteran status."[1]

There is little doubt that there has been an explosion of speech codes at colleges and universities throughout the United States. As many as 70 percent of the more than 3,500 institutions of higher learning in America may have some sort of code designed to place restrictions on speech deemed offensive.[2] Even if many of these codes are little enforced, as some have suggested,[3] their very existence suggests that attention must be paid to this phenomenon. At one time, perhaps, such codes were limited to private, often church-related, institutions. But, over the past several years, state-owned universities have jumped on the speech code bandwagon.[4] While some might argue that no college should be playing the role of speech code enforcer, at least private college codes do not carry with them the color of state action and the resulting requirement to operate within the dictates of the First and Fourteenth Amendments to the U.S. Constitution. Given the long antipathy of the courts to state-supported suppression of free speech, why have so many state universities taken up the speech code cause? One answer may be the desire of such schools to increase their diversity, to bring in students who traditionally were not part of the campus. These "good works" are then defended by "good words" on the part of campus administrators, faculty, and students.

"Good words" are imported by advocates on both sides of this divide. Proponents of codes speak of protecting vulnerable minority groups, of fostering a sense of community, of guaranteeing an environment in which learning can take place.[5] Opponents respond with visions of marketplaces of ideas, of free exchange of thoughts and opinions, of good ideas driving out bad ideas, of the dangers of picking and choosing what is to be allowed and what is to be proscribed.[6]

Without a doubt, however, these codes are animated by a genuine concern to "do the right thing," to ensure that vulnerable members of the university community are not subjected to words that harm. Yet, these codes seem to collide directly with First Amendment speech values. Those of us concerned with civil liberties have studied how the Supreme Court has over time allowed a larger "breathing space" for speech in general, and has struck down almost all content-based limits on most kinds of speech. Thus, to find, in our own university backyards, codes that punish speech based on its content is surprising and, to many, tremendously disturbing.

Intriguing ironies characterize the emergence of these codes as well.[7] Take just two examples. Oftentimes, as students did during the 1960s, proponents of codes limiting speech may well have advocated greater openness on campus. In fact, as Michael Kinsley points out, speech "codes have their roots in the early 1970s, when they were a response to left-wing student activism."[8] At that time, academic conservatives thought that the student activists failed to respect the higher "standard of civility" necessary for the maintenance of academic community. Codes were thought to help preserve a civil discourse. This concern for civility, however, was not completely neutral; many of the faculty members disagreed with the changes that the activists were demanding. Now, as then, advocates of the codes seem undisturbed about making these political choices, relying on their own conceptions of academic propriety, and of good and evil.

Another irony: the codes emphasize that words harass, causing pain and/or making learning difficult. Yet the codes often arise as part of the ascendancy of certain "politically correct" (and we do not mean to use this term pejoratively here) programs on campuses—various multicultural programs, courses, requirements, and the like. Those who depart from the values embedded in these programs may be the object of the very kind of harassment that the codes are intended to punish. They may be contemptuously labeled as "racist," or their university activities may be subject to protests.[9] In the eyes of the code promoters, though, these are the proverbial "bad guys" getting their due, not the sympathetic and vulnerable insular minorities who need and deserve immunity from assaultive language.

Debating Codes and the Emergence of a "New" Civil Liberties

To those familiar with the evolution of First Amendment law and the priority universities give to the unfettered examination of ideas, codes which limit speech are often contemptuously dismissed. They seem so far removed from core First Amendment values that their very existence stands as an affront to this bedrock of our constitutional and educational schema.

Those who oppose speech codes do not deny the harm that can result from hate speech, but instead argue that the restraint of free speech may ultimately produce even greater harm. This restraint, it is argued, becomes particularly problematic at the university. Given its historical commitment to academic freedom and its symbolic status as the embodiment of free thought, the university, more than any other institution, must not act as a censor. Also, by protecting even racist speech, the university, according to Charles Lawrence, "reinforces our society's commitment to tolerance as a value."[10] Of course, tolerance cuts both ways in this context: hate speech codes punish only intolerant words and expressions. To what degree must an open society tolerate the advocacy of intolerance?[11]

The argument for speech codes relies heavily upon sociological premises. For instance, the status of women and minority groups on campus is often rather tenuous, and code supporters argue that the resources of American colleges and universities have become available to these (previously disenfranchised) groups only recently and that speech codes, like the changes in the curriculum that have preceded them, help provide a more comfortable place for these groups within the university community. The rise of campus hate speech is, at least in part, the result of a backlash against the gains that have been made by these groups in changing admissions procedures and the curriculum. Given this phenomenon, the proponents of codes argue that these "marginalized" groups are caught in a bind; as their assertiveness increases with their numbers, they are forced to deal with an increasing number of attacks. Speech codes, according to this argument, are meant to get these groups out of this bind and secure a place for them in the academy.

Proponents of codes argue that they are constitutional, once the First Amendment's protections of free speech are balanced against the Fourteenth Amendment's guarantees of equal protection. They also cite developments protecting against harassment in employment settings.[12] Singularly, or in combination, these and other arguments are marshaled to defend the codes as permissible within our Constitution's parameters, and as desirable from a moral and social perspective.

The complexity of the issues that surround the appropriateness of the codes is also reflected in the divisiveness these codes have caused traditional civil liberties organizations—organizations that rarely hesitated in the past to align themselves with unpopular groups when they felt First Amendment values were at stake. The national ACLU, for example, after heated debate, ultimately came out in opposition to the codes.[13] Debates in local chapters were also long and fractious. In these debates, matters concerning what might be called "new civil liberties" emerged. These new civil liberties may be productively—albeit indirectly—defined as those matters that historically would have elicited clear, widespread, and homogeneous reaction from staunch civil libertarians, but that now lead to splits within the groups that formerly were united by their pro–civil liberties stance.

There is no better example of these kinds of debates than the one that occurred in the Civil Liberties Union of Massachusetts.[14] At this debate, the board was evenly split between "First Amendment absolutists" and those who emphasized the "equal protection under the law" of the Fourteenth Amendment. First Amendment absolutists at this debate argued that the very foundation of the ACLU was the protection of free speech. Those who favored speech codes argued, on the other hand, that it was not only an abstract debate about the value of free speech, but also a matter of *whose* speech was being protected. Hate speech on campuses created a hostile environment for ethnic minorities and women on campuses. Finally, a vote was taken on a statement that condemned speech codes while extolling multicultural reforms in education. It passed 16 to 14—hardly a decisive victory for the First Amendment absolutists.

The national ACLU briefing paper addressing "Hate Speech on Campus" tries to maintain this delicate balance within the organization as well. It argues that codes that punish bigoted speech treat only the symptom and not the underlying disease of bigotry: "The ACLU believes that instead of opting for gestures that only *appear* to cure the disease, universities ought to do the hard work of recruiting to increase faculty and student diversity, counseling to raise awareness about bigotry and its history, and changing curricula to institutionalize more inclusive approaches to all subject matter."[15]

The planned Nazi demonstration in Skokie, Illinois led to similar conflicts among First Amendment champions. In his article "Jews and the Law: The Skokie Free Speech Controversy," Donald Downs argues that the "affirmative action" speech principle currently being used by proponents of speech codes began during the Skokie debate. Those who opposed the Nazis marching in Skokie presaged the current debate by arguing that "in order to achieve true equality, speech and opportunity policy must favor those who bear less social and political power."[16]

More recently, the effort in some jurisdictions to suppress pornography because of the offensiveness of the message has generated similar disputes. Indeed, Catharine MacKinnon, a leader in this effort to restrict pornography, reportedly referred to this movement as "our Skokie."[17] Like proponents of speech codes, feminist opponents of pornography argue that the behavior they seek to restrict harms certain identifiable classes of victims. In the pornography debate, however, opponents of pornography make a larger argument that pornography harms not only the specific women depicted in the material, but all women. In order to overcome this harm, these feminists propose statutes that allow women to seek damages against the producers of pornography.[18] Opposing this group are those feminists who agree that pornography causes harm, but seek less restrictive, nonjuridical means to demonstrate its unacceptability.[19] Like those who oppose speech codes, they fear that the campaign against pornography, as a campaign against free speech, may eventually threaten women's own right to free sexual expression.

The fact that traditional civil liberties organizations have had to struggle for responses to the issues raised in the new civil liberties—speech codes, Nazi demonstrations in Jewish communities, restrictions on pornography— suggests that simple, some would say "knee-jerk," civil liberties responses are being challenged by a "new civil liberties," one that arrays competing claims alongside traditional First Amendment values. Ultimately, this "new civil liberties" has fractured traditional liberal coalitions, severed old ties within the civil rights movement, and created new, often unusual, legal bedfellows. Thomas Grey captures the essence of this split when he writes about "the once-differentiated conglomerate of ideals and practices that once might have been called civil rights and civil liberties. Now it is civil rights vs. civil liberties."[20]

Defending Codes

Traditional Legal Positions

The arguments for the defense of limits on speech run the gamut from traditional positions for limits to more novel approaches, with varying amounts of precedential support marshaled to advance these positions. The usual effort is to encompass hate speech codes within one of the traditional exceptions to the general rules of free speech that have been carved out by the Supreme Court: "fighting words," "group libel," "time, manner, and place regulations." These doctrinal issues are discussed at length in the first part of this book, "Cases."

Special Nature of Universities

A related defense of codes focuses on the climate and special nature of a university community. One strand of this defense argues that community values can appropriately limit speech—that is, some things, such as obscenity and racial epithets, are simply beyond what a community must or should tolerate. Advocates maintain that certain kinds of speech—particularly sexist, homophobic, and racist—fall within this legitimately proscribable domain.

The second argument about the way speech in a university requires special protection emphasizes the effects of negative language on the learning environment of those within the group being mocked or attacked. The notion here is that a "hostile environment" makes learning impossible, and that for those negatively affected, a kind of Fourteenth Amendment denial of equal opportunity to learn is being carried out. Charles Jones, for example, links this argument to the *Brown* decision; in so doing, he draws a strict standard: "[W]here the harm occasioned by group vilifying ethno-violence exceeds the value to society from the exercise of such speech, universities must act to protect the learning environment so that it facilitates, rather than retards, the progress of members of the student minority groups toward the goals of equal citizenship."[21]

The Employment Analogy

Similar arguments about the type of environment necessary to perform (or "learn" in the case of a university) have been made in the employment setting. There, the United States Supreme Court has in fact legitimated the "hostile environment" argument, and accepted the thesis that some kinds of visual and verbal communication are proscribable because their presence makes job performance impossible.[22] Of course, universities and employment settings can be distinguished;[23] but when we reviewed the landscape of materials on both sides of the codes we found the employment analogy to be both powerful and underrepresented in the defenses universities utilized in defense of codes.

The "Increase the Penalty for Hate-Motivated Crime" Argument

While some continue to defend speech codes as they have developed over the past five to ten years, others have begun to look to the most recent Supreme Court decisions as providing a new approach to the problem. The combination of the *Mitchell* and *R.A.V.* cases,[24] along with the lower court decisions striking down codes at public institutions like the Universities of Michigan and Wisconsin, have led to a move away from creating new categories of offenses to cover hate speech, and toward proposals to increase penalties for existing violations if those committing offenses were motivated by bias. A university may already provide sanctions for physical attacks; and when the attacks are accompanied by evidence that the victim was chosen because of group membership, or in some other way that indicates bias, the university may increase the penalty that would otherwise apply to the case.

While *Mitchell* and *R.A.V.* may not clearly sanction such an approach to bias crimes, commentators like Delgado and Stefancic[25] believe that these rulings show a new way to control hate speech. They argue that prosecutions for offenses always implicate the motivation of the suspect. To add intentional selection of the victim on account of the victim's race, color, gender, sexual preference, and so on, into the equation is therefore reasonable and constitutional. In so doing, they believe that the problem of regulating speech is avoided, since it is not speech, but action, that is being punished. Interestingly, Nadine Strossen, head of the ACLU, agrees with this approach, believing that it does not create limitations on speech, but instead adds a legitimate punishment based on motive. She argues that enhanced penalties do not create "hate-speech crimes" but instead "target acts that are more accurately described as 'discriminatory crimes,' and thus may be punished consistent with the First Amendment so long as the laws are narrowly drawn and carefully applied." A defendant's words can be relevant as long as "they are directly related to the underlying crime and probative of his discriminatory intent."[26]

Others, however, argue that even though the use of motive fits well within traditional criminal law, investigating whether the motive in any particular violation is suffused with "hate" is a risky business. Paul Robinson asks: "How can we tell when an offense was in fact motivated by hatred? Even if we can show hate motivation, how can we tell whether the hatred is for the group or for this person in particular, or some combination of the two? . . . If some combination of hatred for the group and the individual is requisite, what proportion of the hate motivation must be hate for the group rather than the individual?"[27]

Nat Hentoff also vehemently disagrees with Strossen's view on increased penalties for hate speech, asking why only particular groups are singled out for this special protection. Writing about *Wisconsin* v. *Mitchell* prior to the Supreme Court's decision, Hentoff argues that the act of aggravated battery was being "justly punished, but the speech purportedly accompanying the act is also being punished."[28] While supporters of penalty enhancement argue that bias crimes require harsher penalties as a message to protected groups, Hentoff asks:

> But what message is sent to all the others in the community who are attacked for no reason other than the criminal's lust for money?

Are the injuries they suffer—however painful physically and psychologically—of less importance to the community?

Whatever happened to [the ACLU's] support of equal protection under the law?[29]

Overview of Book

The material in this book falls into three categories. First, we present excerpts
from the relevant United States Supreme Court cases dealing with free expression. We try to include those cases with the most ringing endorsements for
the values of a free marketplace of ideas to those such as *Chaplinsky*'s prohibition on "fighting words" and *Beauharnais*'s prohibition on "group libel."
Headnotes preceding each of the cases are designed to call attention to the
ways in which the case is especially relevant to the current debates about
campus speech codes. We think the cases collectively arm the reader with a
rich array of legal options that can be applied to form one's own opinion as
to what a constitutionally acceptable code might contain. What makes this so
exciting, of course, is that these matters are currently being heatedly debated,
and, by going directly to the cases, readers can arrive at their own conclusions
about rules appropriately and inappropriately included in university codes.

Second, we include four case studies (and a court case) of speech code
conflicts on college campuses. Two of the settings—Michigan and Wisconsin—are public universities; three others—Duke, Brown, and Dartmouth—are
private universities. These studies, undertaken by four young scholars working
under our supervision, collectively yield a fascinating picture of the controversies that prompted the decision to adopt codes and/or alternate approaches, of
the development of codes or these other strategies, and of the subsequent
history of speech disputes on the respective campuses.

Finally, we include several excerpts of commentary about free speech in
general and university codes in particular. Having examined many of the relevant case precedents, and having seen real-life efforts to deal with the movement on college campuses, along with the case studies, it is our hope that
readers will be intrigued, as we were, by the use to which these cases and
arguments are put on both sides of the debate. We have tried to present sam-
ples of materials across the ideological continuum.

These three bodies of material in and of themselves constitute a kind of
grand case study of an ongoing issue that goes to the heart of our constitutional schema and raises important questions about the nature of our academic
communities. We are certain the debate about campus speech codes will in-
trigue students in the same way that it captivated us and those who worked
with us on the case studies. Moreover, we hope the materials and case studies

serve to inspire students to undertake similar studies on their own campuses. Indeed, in a very preliminary way, we have begun to think of ways to solicit these kinds of studies from readers of this volume, and perhaps include some of these new studies in a second edition.

In 1943, in *West Virginia* v. *Barnette,* the Court struck down state legislation requiring students to salute the flag. Justice Frankfurter dissented, making plain both his distaste for the state legislation and his belief that the states had the right to pass this kind of insensitive and painful law. Writing about the West Virginia flag salute statute, Justice Frankfurter observed: "The tendency of focusing attention on constitutionality is to make constitutionality synonymous with wisdom, to regard a law as all right if it is constitutional. Such an attitude is a great enemy of liberalism. Particularly in legislation affecting freedom of thought and freedom of speech much which would offend a free-spirited society is constitutional. . . . Reliance for the most precious interests of civilization, therefore, must be found outside of their vindication in courts of law."[30]

Unraveling what is wise and what is constitutional, what is permitted and what is prohibited, and what is properly in the legislative domain and what is the prerogative of the courts, is no easier now than it was half a century ago. By bringing this rich set of materials together, we hope that students can work through these problems and, by their own labors, bring some new wisdom to this difficult exercise in doing the right thing in the right way.

Notes

1. *Doe* v. *University of Michigan,* 721 F. Supp. 856 (E.D. Mich. 1989). The code was later held to be unconstitutional. See *Doe,* at 131. The debate surrounding hate speech on campuses often arises in a "politically correct" ambiance, which is present at many of our colleges. Associated debates, consideration of which would lead us too far astray in this book, but which are nonetheless important and fascinating, involve curriculum and multiculturalism, and restrictions on or reactions to the statements of faculty, as in the case of Leonard Jeffries or William Shockley. See, for example, Paul Berman, ed., *Debating PC* (New York: Dell Publishing Co., 1992); *Levin* v. *Harleston,* 770 F. Supp. 895 (E.D. N.Y. 1991); and *Jefferies* v. *Harleston,* 52 F.3d 9 (2d Cir. 1995). Though space constraints preclude systematically addressing matters of multiculturalism and faculty speech, obviously much of our material is informed by, and informs, these issues.

2. Carnegie Foundation estimate, reported in D. F. McGowan and R. K. Tangri, *A Libertarian Critique of University Restrictions of Offensive Speech,* 79 California Law Review 825, note 26, at 830. See also Samuel Walker, *Hate Speech* (Lincoln: University of Nebraska Press, 1974), at 127.

3. "Campus Codes that Ban Hate Speech Are Rarely Used to Penalize Students," *Chronicle of Higher Education,* 12 February 1992, at A35. Ironically, when codes are

in fact used, they can punish those for whom they were designed to offer protection. Henry Louis Gates notes that "other commentators have argued that speech codes have been used most frequently by white majorities against minorities, turning on its head the usual assumptions that the codes are used by politically correct members of minority groups against the majority." "Critical Race Theory and the First Amendment," in *Speaking of Race, Speaking of Sex* (New York: New York University Press, 1994), at 127. Nadine Strossen makes a similar point in her excerpt in the third section of this book, "Commentary."

4. A recent survey of 384 public colleges and universities by the Freedom Forum's First Amendment Center found that 36 percent had rules punishing verbal abuse based upon group membership, while 28 percent had restrictions barring "offensive or outrageous" speech. Reported by the Associated Press in the *Home News* (New Brunswick, N.J.), 24 April 1994, at A11.

5. Examples of these arguments concerning campus speech codes and racist speech in general can be found in Mari Matsuda, *Public Response to Racist Speech: Considering the Victim's Story,* 87 Michigan Law Review 2320 (1989); Richard Perry and Patricia Williams, "Freedom of Hate Speech," in *Debating P.C.,* ed. Paul Berman (New York: Laurel, 1992), at 225; and Richard Delgado, *Words That Wound: A Tort Action for Racial Insults, Epithets, and Name-Calling,* 17 Harvard Civil Rights & Civil Liberties Review 133 (1982); and many others.

6. A good example of this position is in Nat Hentoff, *Free Speech for Me but Not for Thee* (New York: Harper Collins, 1992). For a more recent scholarly effort exploring the limits of First Amendment jurisprudence, see Cass Sunstein, *Democracy and the Problem of Free Speech* (New York: The Free Press, 1993).

7. For a more detailed discussion of the history of hate speech issues, see S. Walker, *Hate Speech: The History of an American Controversy* (Lincoln: University of Nebraska Press, 1993), as well as J. Levin and J. McDevitt, *Hate Crimes: The Rising Tide of Bigotry and Bloodshed* (New York: Plenum Publishing, 1993). For a skeptical view on the efficacy of hate crime legislation, see J. Jacobs, *Should Hate Be a Crime?,* The Public Interest 133 (Fall 1993), at 3. Moreover, Walker argues that the controversy over proscribing hate speech arises in the United States because of the First Amendment and the libertarian tradition that has arisen around it. Walker points to statutes, codes, etc. in other countries that proscribe similar language and that are taken for granted as being good policy and perfectly proper or even necessary to a well-ordered society. See Walker at 1, 4–5, 16, 49, 62, 78, 138, 159. For further discussion of other nations' attempts to deal with racist speech, see Rodney Smolla, *Free Speech in an Open Society* (New York: Alfred Knopf, 1992), at 354–58.

8. Michael Kinsley in New Republic, cited in Cathy N. Davison, *PH Stands for Political Hypocrisy,* Academe, September–October 1991.

9. Rather than recount some of these, by now, oft-repeated stories, we direct the reader to any number of "anti-pc" manifestoes, such as Allan Bloom, *The Closing of the American Mind* (New York: Simon and Schuster, 1987); Roger Kimball, *Tenured Radicals* (New York: Harper & Row, 1990); and Dinesh D'Souza, *Illiberal Education* (New York: The Free Press, 1991).

10. Charles R. Lawrence III, "The Debates Over Placing Limits on Racist Speech Must not Ignore the Damage It Does to Its Victims," *Chronicle of Higher Education,* 25 October 1989.

11. See Lee C. Bollinger, *The Tolerant Society* (New York: Oxford University Press, 1986), esp. at 43–75.

12. In *Meritor Savings Bank, FSB* v. *Vinson,* 477 U.S. 57 (1986), for example, the Supreme Court ruled that sexual harassment in the workplace created a "hostile work environment" that violates Title VII of the Civil Rights Act of 1964.

13. But, see Nadine Strossen, *Hate Crimes, Should They Carry Enhanced Penalties? Yes: Discriminatory Crimes,* ABA Journal (May 1993), at 44, on the national ACLU's support of increased penalties for crimes motivated by bias.

14. Village Voice, 19 June 1990.

15. ACLU Briefing Paper, Number 16, *Hate Speech on Campus.*

16. Donald Downs, *Jews and the Law: The Skokie Free Speech Controversy.* Paper presented at the Conference on Jews and the Law in the United States, University of Wisconsin–Madison, 14–17 November 1991. See also the discussion of "outsider jurisprudence" in Steven Shiffrin, *Racist Speech, Outsider Jurisprudence and the Meaning of America,* 80 Cornell Law Review 1 (1994), at 43.

17. Donald Downs, *op. cit.,* note 16.

18. Although this movement has achieved little success in America, the Canadian Supreme Court set a precedent by accepting the argument that pornography harms women. Tamar Lewin, "Canada Court Says Pornography Harms Women," *New York Times,* 12 March 1993.

19. Isabel Wilerson, "Foes of Pornography and Bigotry Join Forces," *New York Times,* 12 March 1993.

20. Unpublished memo cited by Charles Jones, *Equality, Dignity and Harm: The Constitutionality of Regulating American Campus Ethnoviolence,* 37 Wayne Law Review 3 (1991), at 1383.

21. Charles H. Jones, *op. cit.,* at 1396.

22. See *Meritor Savings* v. *Vinson,* 477 U.S. 57 (1986), and *Harris* v. *Forklift Systems,* 114 S.Ct. 367 (1993). Excerpts from *Harris* appears in the second section of this book, "Case Studies."

23. This distinction is becoming more and more tenuous, however, as universities adopt formal codes prohibiting relationships between faculty members and students. "U. of Virginia Considers Wide Ban on Intimate Teacher-Student Ties," *New York Times,* 4 April 1993, at I22.

24. *Wisconsin* v. *Mitchell,* 113 S.Ct. 2194 (1993), and *R.A.V.* v. *City of St. Paul, Minnesota,* 112 S.Ct. 2538 (1992). *R.A.V.* is discussed in some detail in the following section.

25. R. Delgado and J. Stefancic, "Overcoming Legal Barriers to Regulating Hate Speech on Campus," *Chronicle of Higher Education,* 11 August 1993, at B1.

26. Strossen, *Hate Crimes,* at 44.

27. Paul H. Robinson, *Hate Crimes: Crimes of Motive, Character, or Group Terror?,* 1992/93 Annual Survey of American Law 4, New York University School of Law, at 613.

28. Nat Hentoff, *Hate Crimes, Should They Carry Enhanced Penalties? No: Equality Among Victims,* ABA Journal, May 1993, at 45.

29. *Ibid.*

30. *West Virginia State Board of Education* v. *Barnette,* 319 U.S. 624 (1943).

CASES

INTRODUCTION

"Congress shall make no law . . . abridging the freedom of speech." These ten, seemingly unambiguous, words in the First Amendment to the United States Constitution have provoked more conflict on the Supreme Court than almost any other clause in the document. Efforts on college and university campuses to address the troubling problems brought about by hate speech inevitably run up against an assertion that campus hate speech regulations—no matter how well-intentioned and carefully formulated—cannot be squared with this dictate of the First Amendment. Hate speech, despite its potentially harmful qualities, is assuredly speech. Perhaps Mr. Justice Black was correct in his frequent assertion that when the framers of the Amendment said "no law" could abridge the freedom of speech, they meant *no* law!

The legal problems that confront campus hate speech codes cannot be addressed so simply, at least not in terms of the current position of the Supreme Court regarding the meaning of the First Amendment. As we will see, the definitions of "the freedom of speech," of what constitutes an "abridgment" of this freedom, and even of what activities are encompassed under the term "speech," are far from clear. This chapter sets out the legal framework that courts must use to assess the constitutional validity of efforts to regulate, punish, or otherwise control hate speech on college and university campuses.

One point regarding legal doctrine[1] needs to be made with regard to the cases and analysis that follow. The United States Constitution is first and foremost a blueprint for the organization and structure of government, and virtually all the restrictions or prohibitions found in the document are addressed to government officials. For example, nearly every case in this chapter involves a constitutional challenge to the actions of some employee or official of local, state, or national government. This is true in most areas of constitutional law. The Supreme Court has fashioned a general rule, the "state action doctrine," which restricts most constitutional protections to actions of the government. This means that the Constitution primarily protects individuals against *governmental* violation of such basic rights as freedom of speech, freedom of religion, and equal protection of the laws. We all know that private individuals and organizations can do much to restrict an individual's ability to speak freely, practice his or her religion, or be treated equally. Most legal protections of individual rights against such acts come not from the Constitution, but from legislation—in particular, from the civil rights laws passed over the years by Congress and state legislatures.[2]

In the context of campus speech codes, the state action doctrine implies that the First Amendment limits the actions of administrators at state-supported colleges and universities. Employees at governmentally sponsored institutions act under color of state law, and their actions must therefore conform to constitutional guidelines. Speech codes made and enforced at private institutions generally do not constitute state action, and therefore are not directly subject to constitutional restrictions. This much being said, an alleged inconsistency with the U.S. Constitution can be a potent political argument against adoption of a hate speech ordinance at a private university.[3] Federal or state statutes, though, *could* require private colleges and universities to comply with constitutional free speech standards as a precondition for receiving governmental aid, research grants, tax benefits, and the like.[4]

The Constitutional Presumption of Free, "Uninhibited, Robust, and Wide-open" Speech

There is some debate as to the original intention of the framers of the Bill of Rights regarding the First Amendment's prohibition of Congress's "abridging the freedom of speech." At the very least, these men intended the words to prohibit the application of "prior restraints" on speech—that is, governmental censorship and other forms of vetting speech before it is uttered or printed. However, it is also reasonably clear that many, if not most, of the framers of the First Amendment regarded as quite proper governmental punishment of certain types of dangerous or harmful speech *after* it was uttered. For example, even prominent libertarians of the day believed that antigovernmental speech, or speech that is libelous or "licentious," could and should be punished by the government. In the words of John Locke, the English political theorist whose views influenced the Constitution's framers: ". . . [N]o opinions contrary to human society, or to those moral rules which are necessary to the preservation of civil society, are to be tolerated by the magistrate."[5]

James Madison, the primary architect of the Constitution, held substantially more libertarian views. His proposed language for the free speech guarantee that ultimately became the First Amendment contained a broad prohibition of any governmental control of the people's right "to speak, to write, or to publish their sentiments." But those views were not widely shared in the early days of the Republic. In the intervening 200 years, constitutional history has moved free speech doctrine to, and in many areas beyond, the Madisonian position. It would take a very adventurous magistrate to refuse a substantial degree of legal toleration of the expression of opinions contrary to "human society" or "moral rules" today.

While the proper scope of the freedom of speech guarantee in the Bill of Rights was debated throughout the nineteenth century—beginning with the controversy surrounding passage and enforcement of the Sedition Act of 1798—the Supreme Court had little opportunity to authoritatively enunciate the meaning of "the freedom of speech" until well into the twentieth century. The paucity of free speech cases reaching the U.S. Supreme Court was due in part to the Court's 1833 decision in *Barron* v. *Baltimore*,[6] which restricted the scope of the Bill of Rights to prohibitions on the actions of Congress and the national government. Actions of state officials, after *Barron*, were not subject to federal constitutional restrictions. Given the limited scope of the national government's dealings with individual citizens prior to the middle of the twentieth century, this limitation put most governmental conflicts with individual liberties outside the protections of the national constitution and the federal courts.[7]

Passage of the Fourteenth Amendment in the wake of the Civil War would ultimately change all of this and revolutionize the legal relationship of the federal government—especially the federal courts—and the states. This process of growing national protection of civil rights and liberties from the adverse actions of state and local officials, however, took nearly a century to be completed. The Equal Protection Clause of the Fourteenth Amendment served as the key constitutional provision used by African-Americans and other racial and ethnic minorities in their quest for civil rights and equality of treatment by state governmental officials. The amendment's Due Process Clause, which states that "No state shall deny any person life, liberty, or property without due process of law," became the fountainhead for protection of individual liberties, such as freedom of speech and religion, against incursions by state governments.[8] It is now accepted constitutional doctrine that the Due Process Clause of the Fourteenth Amendment "absorbs" or "incorporates" most important individual liberties found in the Bill of Rights—among them, freedom of speech—and protects them against actions by state governmental officials.[9] In the cases included here, therefore, it is largely immaterial whether the challenged governmental action was performed by state or federal officials.

It was not until the first decades of the twentieth century that the free speech protections inherent in the First and Fourteenth Amendments began to take shape. World War I and the subsequent "Red Scare" led both federal and state governments to place significant restrictions on the speech and association of those espousing causes believed to be dangerous to the war effort or to the body politic. Cases arising from these activities provided the first opportunity for the Supreme Court to come to terms with just what "the freedom of speech" is, and what constitutes an abridgment of that freedom.

During and immediately after World War I, both federal and state legislatures enacted a variety of statutes designed to insure that the Republic remained safe from the agitation of anarchists, communists, and other assorted malcontents who urged America to stay out of the war or to change its system of government. The Supreme Court's first major attempt to define the contours of freedom of speech came in cases involving federal statutes, most notably the Espionage Act of 1917. These early cases also included the first explicit statement by the Court that the constitutional guarantees of freedom of speech and of the press "are among the fundamental personal rights and 'liberties' protected by the due process clause of the Fourteenth Amendment from impairment by the States."[10]

First Amendment free speech doctrine is exceedingly complex. A full discussion of its historical development and present contours could easily encompass volumes of text and several university courses. The specific problem of hate speech on university campuses restricts our focus somewhat, however. Perhaps the most useful conceptualization of the current meaning of freedom of speech for our purposes is that of a broad general rule specifying the overall scope of the freedom of speech protected by the First and the Fourteenth Amendments, together with a series of exceptions to the rule. The broad rule is a presumption *against* the validity of governmental attempts to prohibit, punish, or (to a lesser degree) regulate expression—particularly expression relating to questions of relevance to government and public policy. This rule is based on "a profound national commitment to the principle that debate on public issues should be uninhibited, robust, and wide-open."[11]

The exceptions to this rule are of three broad types. The first relates to several specific categories of speech or expression that have been defined by the court as falling outside the scope of constitutional protection. Some of these forms of unprotected speech raise few problems to even the most ardent advocate of free expression; bribery and perjury, for example, are undoubtedly forms of speech, yet few would argue that these criminal offenses are constitutionally protected. Over time, the Supreme Court has developed a list of more problematic kinds of speech that are either partially or completely outside the Constitution's protective shield. Some of these exceptions are largely irrelevant to our present concern. For example, obscene speech[12] is not protected by the Constitution, although the Supreme Court has had an extremely difficult time drawing the line between what is obscene and what is not. Commercial speech, such as product advertisements and the like, is protected only to a limited degree.[13] As we shall see, however, some of the other asserted exceptions to the rule of free expression—such as advocacy of illegal action, offensive speech, or "fighting words"—are directly relevant to university campuses facing problems of hate speech.

The second type of exception to the general rule of protection of speech concerns the circumstances where expression takes place—regardless of its content or import. In particular contexts, some forms of expression can interfere with legitimate governmental functions. For example, cities may wish to regulate marches to ensure the free movement of traffic,[14] or to prohibit sound trucks that cause nighttime disturbances in residential neighborhoods;[15] schools are legitimately concerned about expressive behavior that interferes with teaching and learning;[16] and courts might prohibit demonstrations that have the potential of undermining or compromising the integrity of the judicial process.[17] The courts have tended to be fairly lenient in allowing these so-called "time, manner, and place" regulations of speech, as long as the government is not trying to regulate the content of the ideas being expressed. However, once government establishes a "public forum"—that is, a place or other context for the expression of views—it may not pick and choose among the views expressed. Indeed, the requirement of content neutrality has become something of a litmus test for *any* attempt by government to regulate expression.[18]

The final type of exception comes from efforts to protect employees against unequal treatment in the workplace. These efforts are grounded in federal civil rights legislation rather than in the Constitution. A concern with avoiding harassment based on race or sex has led the courts to prohibit employers from maintaining workplaces that constitute a "hostile environment."[19] The elements of these hostile environments, however, are frequently related to speech and expression. The courts have not yet established constitutional guidelines for defining the hostile environment prohibitions, but, at least at present, it would appear that some forms of expression that lead to a hostile environment in the workplace are not protected by the Constitution.

The readings for this chapter are drawn exclusively from court decisions; most are opinions by justices of the United States Supreme Court. The readings are arranged in accordance with the broad framework set out above: the first three readings focus on the general rule or presumption of freedom of expression and its scope. Cases in the next sections focus on a variety of exceptions or modifications to that rule, based on particular types of speech, or contexts in which speech or expression take place. Finally, two cases pull many of these doctrines together in the context of two hate speech cases—one involving a march of American Nazi Party demonstrators in Skokie, Illinois, and the other involving an attempt by the city of St. Paul, Minnesota, to punish several persons for burning a cross on an African-American family's front lawn.[20]

These cases should help a university community assess the constitutional landscape surrounding any proposed effort to regulate, punish, or prohibit hate speech on campus. However, these cases present factual situations that are different from a university contemplating some form of hate speech regulation. Most did not arise in the context of a university at all, and the specific expression involved in the cases is frequently quite different from what is being addressed today on university campuses. Some of the cases are the product of an earlier era of constitutional law in which First Amendment standards were relatively lax; thus they may have limited current applicability. The principles laid down in these cases are clearly relevant to our present concern; the reader will have to determine just how viable these various approaches are, and how applicable to the specific situation facing universities today.

The General Rule of Constitutional Protection, and its Exceptions

As indicated above, the Supreme Court has imposed a very high level of protection of speech when government officials attempt to curtail it. The first reading in this section is an excerpt from the famous concurring opinion by Justice Brandeis in *Whitney* v. *California*. This opinion sets out in eloquent terms the reasoning behind the preference for freedom of speech and the broad constitutional rule that supports it. The next two cases—*Tinker* v. *Des Moines* and *Texas* v. *Johnson*—provide a useful general introduction to the following broad themes raised throughout this chapter: the presumption in favor of free expression, the requirement for governmental neutrality regarding the content of speech, the complex issues raised regarding free expression in an educational setting, and the ambiguity in constitutional protection afforded to "symbolic speech," that is, conduct (rather than words) that expresses ideas.

Freedom of speech, as these cases suggest, occupies an important place in American constitutional law. The Supreme Court, however, has not elevated it to an absolute; rather, there are types of speech and circumstances surrounding its delivery that are subject to governmental regulation, even prohibition and punishment. The major exceptions to the general presumption in favor of free expression that are relevant to our present undertaking are discussed in the following sections.

Incitement to Subversive Activity and Other Illegal Acts

Most Americans would probably regard incitement to riot and similar forms of expression as outside the protections of the First Amendment, for the same reasons that bribery or solicitation of crime is unprotected, even though it is crime that intimately involves speech. The traditional definition of incitement to riot, however, is quite circumscribed. The offense requires intent on the part of the speaker to produce a riot, and a setting in which there is a reasonable likelihood that riotous behavior will take place. The free speech issues become more complex when the speech involved merely advocates some form of illegal action, without the immediacy of a potential riot, and sometimes without even the element of intent on the part of the speaker. To what degree should this more abstract advocacy of illegality qualify as an exception to the general rule of free speech protection?

The extent of constitutional protection for speech that advocates illegal action has been a perennial issue in constitutional adjudication, beginning with the heated controversy surrounding the Sedition Act of 1798. The Supreme Court's first systematic discussions of the meaning of the freedom of speech protected by the First and Fourteenth Amendments were in the context of cases arising during and immediately following World War I, in which defendants were charged with advocating insubordination in the armed forces or obstruction of the draft,[21] seeking to cause "disloyalty, mutiny, and refusal of duty in the military"[22] or advocating "the duty, necessity, and propriety of overthrowing and overturning organized government by force, violence, and unlawful means."[23]

These cases gave rise to the famous "clear and present danger" test of the constitutionality of governmental efforts to punish speech. This formulation was first articulated by Justice Holmes in *Schenck* v. *United States:* "[The] question in every case is whether the words used are used in such circumstances and are of such a nature as to create a clear and present danger that they will bring about the substantive evils that Congress has a right to prevent. It is a question of proximity and degree."[24] This test for the validity of governmental efforts to punish speech suggests that the feared societal danger or "evil" arising from the speech must be substantial and immediate before the speech itself can be punished. The test thus appears to be protective of speech, far more protective than the predominant conceptualization at the time—the "bad tendency" test that held that speech could be punished if it simply had a tendency to bring about illegal or undesirable consequences.[25] Readers should assess for themselves whether the elements of "proximity and degree" were in fact present in the behavior of the defendants in the *Schenck* case.

The clear and present danger test remained a major tool of the courts in dealing with allegedly dangerous speech throughout much of the twentieth century, although its meaning remained elastic. After the "Red Scare," the next spate of free speech cases involving advocacy of illegal actions arose in the years immediately following World War II, when the fear was of Communist subversion of American institutions. The chief proponent of this alleged danger was Senator Joseph McCarthy of Wisconsin. A version of the clear and present danger test was applied by the federal courts in these cases, although its resemblance to the original Holmesian test was attenuated.[26]

The most recent definition of the constitutional limits on the punishment of speech advocating illegal behavior came in 1969, in *Brandenburg* v. *Ohio*,[27] a case involving an attempt by Ohio authorities to punish participants at a rally of the Ku Klux Klan. Interestingly, the opinion was unsigned; it was "per curiam," or "by the court," a treatment that is usually reserved for relatively unimportant rulings. Tucked into this seemingly minor case, however, under the guise of a mere restatement of existing constitutional doctrine, is a major declaration of the limits of governmental punishment of speech that advocates illegal action. According to the court, the principle fashioned by previous cases is: ". . . the constitutional guarantees of free speech and free press do not permit a State to forbid or proscribe advocacy of the use of force or of law violation except where such advocacy is directed to inciting or producing imminent lawless action and is likely to incite or produce such action."[28]

The *Brandenburg* test is substantially more protective of advocacy of illegality than any previously announced standard. It is, in fact, almost identical to the standards necessary to convict a defendant on the criminal charge of incitement to riot. Because of this very high level of immunity given to speech advocating various forms of illegal behavior, *Brandenburg* has been recently criticized as being *too* protective of truly dangerous speech, such as publication of detailed instructions for the construction of bombs.[29]

"Fighting Words" and the Related Problem of the Hostile Audience

The previous section focused on speech that advocated some form of illegal behavior. A different type of constitutionally regulated speech involves the verbal equivalent of a physical assault on the person to whom the speech is directed. Certain racial, ethnic, and gender-based epithets fall into this category. In a brief opinion in *Chaplinsky* v. *New Hampshire*,[30] a 1942 case involving a member of a religious group proselytizing on a sidewalk, the Supreme Court specifically exempted from constitutional protection these so-called "fighting words." The court defined fighting words to be "those words which by their very utterance inflict injury or tend to incite an immediate breach of the peace."[31] The court's rationale for exempting fighting words from constitutional protection appears to be based on both the infliction of injury on the target of the speech and the danger that fighting words will lead to a breach of the peace.

Chaplinksy's fighting-words exception has been relied upon in a number of efforts to regulate hate speech. Epithets are perhaps the definitional form of hate speech, and certainly might serve as a starting point for campus regulations. Proponents of using *Chaplinsky* for this purpose, however, need also to read a subsequent fighting-words case, *Gooding* v. *Wilson*. *Gooding* involved punishment of speech that would seem to be at the core of the meaning of fighting words. Yet the Supreme Court overturned the conviction on the basis of vagueness and "overbreadth" in the statute upon which the conviction was grounded.[32] Readers will need to consider whether the *Gooding* case dilutes the current validity of *Chaplinsky*, as suggested in the dissent.

The exemption of fighting words from constitutional protection is grounded in part on the potentially violent response of the individual to whom the words are directed. A somewhat different problem arises when a speaker is addressing a larger audience with words and ideas that they disagree with, and that could potentially lead to violence against the speaker. This is the "hostile audience" problem and it, too, finds relevance on the university campus. The problem is tricky. On the one hand, law enforcement officials have a legitimate interest in preventing violence, protecting the speaker, and avoiding a riot. On the other hand, it is apparent that muzzling a speaker upon the threat of violence by a disgruntled listener would constitute a "heckler's veto" of the expression of unpopular ideas. Civil rights advocates in the South in the 1960s, for example, could have been effectively silenced because of audience reaction against their position. The most extensive Supreme Court discussion of this problem took place in *Feiner* v. *New York*.[33]

Offensive and Hurtful Speech

Justice Murphy in *Chaplinsky* suggested a number of categories of speech, the punishment of which raised no First Amendment problems: "the lewd and obscene, the profane, the libelous, and the insulting or 'fighting word'—those words which by their very utterance inflict injury or tend to incite an immediate breach of the peace." Justice Murphy did not use the word "offensive" in this categorization, perhaps because it was too broad or vague for his purposes, but some notion of offensiveness to the listener underlies all the specific examples he gives. Offensive expressions, such as obscenity, profanity, libelous statements, and racial or other epithets, "by their very utterance inflict injury." The injury is mental (or, perhaps, reputational) rather than physical; but contrary to the schoolyard ditty ("sticks and stones can break my bones, but words can never hurt me"), words can wound. And it is precisely this kind of injury that many universities are trying to prevent by regulating hate speech on their campuses.[34]

The problem, of course, is that the term "offensive" can be applied to a wide variety of expressions. This is perhaps why Justice Murphy chose to set down a series of narrower types of speech rather than use the broader and more inclusive category. Different groups in American society—based on age, social class, ethnic group, religion, or occupation—have very different standards for what is offensive and what is not, in both speech and deed. As Justice Harlan was moved to write in *Cohen* v. *California*: "One man's vulgarity is another's lyric."[35] Furthermore, efforts to prohibit offensive speech frequently move into the realm of ideas, that most sensitive of First Amendment values. An atheist's assertion in a religion class that "God is dead" is likely to be deeply offensive to a fundamentalist Christian. An assertion that the Holocaust never happened would be especially repugnant and hurtful to concentration camp victims and their families. Efforts to show a relationship between race and intelligence are inevitably hurtful to those whose own mental abilities are thereby called into question. Yet these offensive statements certainly involve the expression of ideas, however wrongheaded or odious we may believe them to be. How far may courts go in protecting listeners from this kind of offense?

The leading case on this issue, and one that contains much of relevance to the entire hate speech debate, is *Cohen* v. *California*. The case involved a defendant who wore into a Los Angeles courthouse a jacket emblazoned with the words "Fuck the Draft." The defendant, who testified that he was attempting to inform the public of the depth of his feelings regarding the Vietnam War and the draft, was convicted of "maliciously and willfully disturb[ing] the peace or quiet of any neighborhood or person" by "offensive conduct." The Supreme Court overturned the conviction, in words reminiscent of Justice Brandeis's *Whitney* concurrence.

Another of the exceptions to First Amendment protection suggested in *Chaplinsky* is libel—the civil (and, less frequently, criminal) offense concerning words that injure a person's reputation. The use of libel law to quell criticism of public officials can raise serious First Amendment problems, an issue that was comprehensively addressed by the Supreme Court in the landmark case of *New York Times* v. *Sullivan*.[36] These issues have limited application to the problem of campus hate speech. However, a variant on individual libel addresses alleged harm to the reputation of a group, so-called "group libel," a concept that has been used as a justification for university speech code provisions as well as other hate speech regulation. Group libel found its way into the First Amendment lexicon in the 1952 Supreme Court decision in *Beauharnais* v. *Illinois*,[37] a case in which the Supreme Court upheld the punishment of a group of white citizens who published an inflammatory pamphlet aimed at black residents of Chicago.[38] As with other asserted exceptions to First Amendment protection, the group libel concept has come under recent criticism.[39]

Time, Manner, and Place Regulations

A very broad category of approved exemptions from First Amendment prohibitions on regulation of speech relate to governmental efforts to regulate not what is said or expressed, but when, where, and how the expression takes place. Some places have been locations for speech and other forms of expressive conduct from time immemorial—for instance, streets and parks, and the "seat of government." Other locations or contexts become public forums through more recent practice or the positive action of public officials. For example, a university might allow speeches or demonstrations to take place in a particular location on campus, or could construct kiosks for display of posters and other campus announcements. The critical concept in many of these cases is that of the *public forum*, a place where public expression takes place, either through tradition or permission, that is thereby protected by the First Amendment. In locations that are not regarded by the courts as public forums, the government is generally permitted broad latitude to regulate or even prohibit expressive activities. For example, the Supreme Court upheld a prohibition of demonstrations on the grounds of a county jail and in front of a courthouse on the theory that security (in the former) and preservation of the sanctity of the judicial process (in the latter) must prevail over First Amendment interests.[40] A critical underpinning of these restrictions, however, is their "content neutrality"; government officials cannot allow some views but not others to be expressed in these places.

It is one thing to determine that government may not pick and choose among the views presented on a public forum. But what of a uniform, nondiscriminatory policy that forbids *all* speech or expressive activity? The courts have been moving in the direction of ensuring at least some minimum access to a public forum for expression of views. For example, while a municipality might well determine that street demonstrations could not be held on certain streets, or at certain times of the day, or on certain days of the week, the courts would be less likely to approve an ordinance that forbade all marches, parades, speeches, and demonstrations on all streets at all times. This would appear to be particularly true regarding places where speech-related activities have traditionally taken place, such as in public parks, in front of public buildings like the state capitol, or on streets and sidewalks. The Court has in fact stated that time, place, and manner regulations of speech must "leave open ample alternative channels for communication of . . . information."[41] Just how "ample" these "alternative channels" of communication must be, however, is something decided by the courts on a case-by-case basis.[42]

Taken with others of a more recent vintage, these cases resulted in the development of a basic constitutional rule governing such regulation: "Expression, whether oral or written or symbolized by conduct, is subject to reasonable time, place, and manner restrictions. We have often noted that restrictions of this kind are valid provided that they are justified without reference to the content of the regulated speech, that they are narrowly tailored to serve a significant governmental interest, and that they leave open ample alternative channels for communication of information."[43] *Healey* v. *James,* reprinted in this chapter, applies this standard to the university context.

Speech Creating a "Hostile Environment"

One final potential exception to the general rule of free expression arises from federal statute. The relevant statutory provision is Title VII of the Civil Rights Act of 1964. Title VII defines as "unlawful employment practices" employer discrimination "against any individual with respect to his compensation, terms, conditions, or privileges of employment, because of such individual's race, color, religion, sex, or national origin."[44]

In an important interpretation of this provision of the Civil Rights Act, the U.S. Supreme Court held, in *Meritor Savings Bank* v. *Vinson,*[45] that this provision prohibits "sexual harassment" that produces a "hostile environment." *Meritor* involved a female bank employee who was subjected to a barrage of abusive behavior from her supervisor, including continuing and unwelcome demands for sexual favors, abusive language, fondling, and even forcible rape. To violate the statute, the Court determined that the offending behavior must be sufficiently severe or pervasive to alter conditions of the victim's employment and create an abusive working environment. There was little question that this threshold was met in the *Meritor* case.

The notion of a hostile environment, based on the race, sex, religion, or ethnic heritage of the victim, has been adopted by several universities as a basis for hate speech regulations. However, it is not clear from the cases just how far the definition of a hostile environment can move into realms of otherwise protected expression. There is little question that physical abuse or even abusive language directed at an individual employee would command little constitutional protection. But other forms of expression that make employees feel uncomfortable or offended can certainly contribute to their perception of a hostile environment, while at the same time raising free speech concerns.[46] Furthermore, the hostile environment cases deal explicitly with the workplace, and it is not clear how relevant they are to a university setting involving students rather than employees, and an educational institution rather than a place of employment.

We include one recent case involving a hostile work environment, *Harris* v. *Forklift Systems*, to indicate the Supreme Court's current position on the hostile environment issue regarding employment. There are clear parallels between this case and some variants of the type of behavior the colleges and universities are attempting to address in their speech codes. There are obvious differences, as well.

Hate Speech

The final two cases in this chapter bring together most of the doctrines discussed previously, in the context of municipal efforts to prohibit speech or other expressive activity specifically directed against racial and ethnic minorities.[47] The first of these cases, *Collin* v. *Smith*, involved an effort by members of the American Nazi Party to conduct a march and demonstration in Skokie, Illinois, a city populated by a substantial number of Jewish survivors of the German concentration camps of World War II. The town relied on several of the exceptions to First Amendment protection discussed above—fighting words, group libel, and the hostile audience—to justify its refusal to allow the march to take place. The case did not reach the United States Supreme Court on most of the free speech issues, so we have reprinted excerpts from the opinions of the United States Court of Appeals for the Fifth Circuit.

The final case involves the United States Supreme Court's most recent and most comprehensive pronouncement on hate speech. This case, *R.A.V.* v. *City of St. Paul,* involves a municipal ordinance that criminalized the placement on public or private property of "a symbol, object, appellation, characterization, or graffiti, including, but not limited to, a burning cross or Nazi swastika, which one knows or has reasonable grounds to know arouses anger, alarm, or resentment in others on the basis of race, color, creed, religion, or gender. . . ."[48] This case, while clearly of substantial importance in sorting out free speech issues in university hate speech regulation, presents an extraordinarily diverse and difficult set of opinions. As has been increasingly common on the Supreme Court over the past several decades, the justices failed to agree on even the issues presented in the case, let alone how they should be decided. As a result, the *R.A.V.* decision presents something of a cacophony of voices, led by Justice Scalia, whose opinion of the court is, at best, obscure. While the St. Paul ordinance found little support on the Court, the nature of its constitutional transgressions does not emerge clearly from the opinions of the justices. Students will need to sort through the various opinions and determine for themselves the application of the case to the campus speech problem.

Notes

1. Throughout this section, we will speak of legal, or constitutional, "doctrine." A legal doctrine is simply a theory regarding how the Constitution should be interpreted, a general rule that attempts to clarify the meaning of the Constitution so it can be more easily and predictably applied to specific cases.

2. These laws protect such important values as freedom from private discrimination on the basis of race, sex, religion, or ethnic group, in such matters as employment, housing, and education.

3. There is debate concerning whether private universities should follow constitutional free speech guarantees on a voluntary basis. See Randall Kennedy, "Should Private Universities Voluntarily Bind Themselves to the First Amendment? No!" *Chronicle of Higher Education,* 21 September 1994, at B1. In *Corry et al.* v. *Stanford,* Superior Court, State of California, County of Santa Clara, Case #740309, decided February 27, 1995, the California Court declared a private university's speech code unconstitutional.

4. Statutory restrictions often apply to colleges and universities because of their frequent acceptance of substantial amounts of federal financial aid, in the forms of research and other grants, and student financial aid. In *Grove City College* v. *Bell,* 465 U.S. 555 (1984), the Court ruled that discrimination claims were limited to the sections of the college that received federal financial aid—in this case, the admissions office. Subsequent congressional legislation overturned the Court's Grove City interpretation of the limits of Title IX of the Federal Education Act. See David M. O'Brien, *Civil Rights and Civil Liberties* (New York: W. W. Norton and Co., 1991), at 1455.

Also, private schools are frequently reluctant to apply rules and regulations that would be unconstitutional at a state-supported institution. Some of these arguments are apparent in the case studies of speech codes at Duke, Brown, and Dartmouth (all private institutions), found in the Case Studies section of this text. Indeed, Congressman Henry Hyde introduced the Collegiate Speech Act of 1991, designed to make First Amendment protections applicable to all private universities receiving federal aid. For a more detailed discussion of the rather strange bedfellows this effort created, see Nat Hentoff, "A Congressman Moves to Protect Free Speech and Colleges," *The Village Voice,* 9 April 1991.

5. John Locke, "A Letter Concerning Toleration," in *The Works of John Locke,* Vol. 4, 11th ed. (London: W. Otridge, 1905–1907), at 45–46.

6. 7 Pet. (32 U.S.) 243 (1833).

7. There were exceptions, of course. Perhaps the most celebrated was congressional passage of the Sedition Act of 1798, which imposed federal criminal sanctions for "a false, scandalous writing against the government of the United States." The act expired in 1801. See James M. Smith, *Freedom's Fetters; the Alien and Sedition Laws and American Civil Liberties* (Ithaca, N.Y.: Cornell University Press, 1956). There were also free speech conflicts arising out of federal governmental restrictions on speech and the press during the Civil War.

8. It is also the source of protection for the procedural rights (such as the rights to counsel, to search warrants, and to freedom from cruel and unusual punishments) afforded criminal defendants in state courts.

9. There is a vast literature on the issue of which substantive rights are protected by the Due Process Clause, how judges are to determine what those rights are, and the relationship of the Bill of Rights protections in the federal constitution to those rights protected by the Due Process Clause. For a summary, see Laurence Tribe, *American Constitutional Law,* 2d ed. (Mineola, N.Y.: Foundation Press, 1988).

10. *Gitlow* v. *New York*, 268 U.S. 652, at 673 (1925). These cases did not, however, enunciate a particularly expansive notion of those free speech guarantees.

11. *New York Times* v. *Sullivan*, 376 U.S. 254 (1969), at 270.

12. Obscene speech is defined as expression that contains explicit depictions of sexual behavior, is "patently offensive" to community standards, and is without artistic, scientific, or other value to society. *Roth* v. *United States*, 354 U.S. 476 (1957), and *Miller* v. *California*, 413 U.S. 15 (1973), spell out the constitutional requirements in this area.

13. See, e.g., *Central Hudson Gas* v. *Public Service Commission*, 447 U.S. 557 (1980).

14. *Cox* v. *Louisiana I*, 379 U.S. 536 (1965).

15. *Kovacs* v. *Cooper*, 336 U.S. 77 (1949).

16. *Bethel School District* v. *Fraser*, 478 U.S. 675 (1986); compare *Tinker* v. *Des Moines School District*, 393 U.S. 503 (1969).

17. *Cox* v. *Louisiana II*, 379 U.S. 559 (1965); compare *U.S.* v. *Grace*, 461 U.S. 171 (1983).

18. Governmental efforts to regulate the content of speech must be necessary to achieve an extraordinarily important governmental purpose—a "compelling state interest"—and they must be essential to achieve that purpose. As applied, this test of constitutional validity is seldom, if ever, passed. The result is that content-based regulation of expression is almost always invalidated. See *Texas* v. *Johnson*, 491 U.S. 397 (1989).

19. See *Meritor Savings Bank, FBD* v. *Vinson*, 477 U.S. 57 (1986), and *Harris* v. *Forklift Systems Inc.,* 114 S.Ct. 367 (1993).

20. A recent third case, *Wisconsin* v. *Mitchell,* 113 S.Ct. 2194 (1993), also touches upon hate crime issues. It upheld the constitutionality of enhanced state criminal penalties for crimes in which specified forms of prejudice animated the offender.

21. *Schenck* v. *United States*, 249 U.S. 47 (1919).

22. *Frohwek* v. *United States*, 249 U.S. 205 (1919); *Debs* v. *United States*, 249 U.S. 211 (1919).

23. *Gitlow* v. *New York*, 268 U.S. 652 (1925); *Whitney* v. *California,* 274 U.S. 357 (1927).

24. 249 U.S. 47 (1919), at 55.

25. *Gitlow* v. *New York,* 268 U.S. 652 (1925).

26. The first reformulation of the test came in *Dennis* v. *United States,* a case that involved prosecution of the national leadership of the Communist Party of the United States. In upholding the convictions, the Supreme Court adopted a version of clear and present danger set out by Judge Learned Hand in the court below: "In each case [courts] must ask whether the gravity of the 'evil,' discounted by its improbability, justifies such invasion of free speech as is necessary to avoid the danger." 341 U.S. 494 (1951), at 510. The immediacy requirement in Holmes's original test disappears in this formulation.

27. 395 U.S. 444 (1969).

28. *Brandenburg* v. *Ohio,* 395 U.S. 444 (1969), at 447.

29. There are publications by anti-abortion groups that give detailed instructions for construction of incendiary devices to be used at abortion clinics, or for the use of ventilating ducts to make the clinics unusable. Similar detailed instructions for explosive devices were published by antiwar activists during the Vietnam era. See *United States* v. *Progressive, Inc.,* 467 F. Supp. 990 (W.D. Wis. 1979).

30. 315 U.S. 568 (1942).

31. *Chaplinsky* v. *New Hampshire*, 315 U.S. 568 (1942), at 572.

32. These two related concepts—vagueness and overbreadth—should also be borne in mind in the hate speech context; they refer to the necessity of statutes that have the potential of infringing on free speech to be drawn very narrowly and clearly so that only unprotected speech can be punished. If statutes are not so drawn, if a potential speaker has to guess as to whether what he wants to say will be illegal, such laws have the potential of discouraging (or "chilling") protected speech. The Court has determined that such vague or overbroad statutes are unconstitutional. These concepts are discussed in more length in *R.A.V.* v. *City of St. Paul*, 112 S.Ct. 2538 (1992). This case is excerpted below.

33. 340 U.S. 315 (1951). More recent cases addressing the hostile audience problem include *Edwards* v. *South Carolina*, 372 U.S. 229 (1963), and *Gregory* v. *Chicago*, 394 U.S. 111 (1969).

34. An emphasis on the harm that can be caused by words and other forms of expressive conduct can be found in a conceptualization of pornography that was put forward by feminist lawyers in the 1980s. Rather than focusing on explicit depiction of sexual acts and deviation from community standards of decency, this definition focuses on "the graphic sexually explicit subordination of women, whether in pictures or in words." This form of pornography was criminalized in several American and Canadian jurisdictions. A widely cited opinion by the U.S. Court of Appeals for the Seventh Circuit overturned the statute on First Amendment grounds: "The ordinance discriminates on the ground of the content of the speech. Speech treating women in the approved way—in sexual encounters "premised on equality"—is lawful no matter how sexually explicit. Speech treating women in the disapproved way—as submissive in matters sexual or as enjoying humiliation—is unlawful no matter how significant the literary, artistic, or political qualities of the work taken as a whole. The state may not ordain preferred viewpoints in this way. The Constitution forbids the state to declare one perspective right and silence opponents." *American Booksellers Ass'n.* v. *Hudnut,* 771 F. 2d. 323 (7th Cir. 1985). The Canadian Supreme Court, in contrast, has

recently upheld statutory restrictions proscribing pornography as harmful. See "Canada Court Says Pornography Harms Women," *New York Times,* 28 February 1992, and *Butler* v. *Regina*, 2 W.W.R. 577 (Can.), 1992.

35. *Cohen* v. *California*, 403 U.S. 15 (1971), at 25.

36. Libel is not generally recognized to be constitutionally protected speech, although the Supreme Court in *New York Times* v. *Sullivan*, 376 U.S. 254 (1964), extended First Amendment protection to even false and damaging statements about a public figure. In that case, the Court held that public officials could not obtain compensation even for falsely published information unless they could prove "actual malice," that is, that the information was published with knowledge of its falsity, or with reckless disregard for whether it was true or false. This case is not included in the discussion because of its distant application to the problems raised by hate speech on university campuses. For a wonderful discussion of *Sullivan,* see Anthony Lewis, *Make No Law* (New York: Vintage Books, 1992). This case has been extended to "public figures," people in the public eye, as well. See *Curtis Publishing Co.* v. *Butts* and *Associated Press* v. *Walker*, 388 U.S. 130 (1967); but compare *Gertz* v. *Robert Welch, Inc.*, 418 U.S. 323 (1974).

37. 343 U.S. 250 (1952).

38. A variant on the libel theme involves the "intentional infliction of emotional harm," a basis for a civil lawsuit for damages. Obviously, many instances of hate speech are specifically intended to insult and, ultimately, to hurt their targets emotionally, and one potential approach to dealing with such efforts is to address this problem directly, either through individual lawsuits or by regulations prohibiting speech aimed at causing emotional hurt. The leading case on this issue is *Hustler Magazine* v. *Falwell*, 485 U.S. 46 (1985). This case involved a crude parody directed at a public figure, the fundamentalist televangelist Jerry Falwell. In this context, the Court held that First Amendment interests trumped the individual damage done to Mr. Falwell. The Court has not addressed whether the rule might be different in cases involving individuals who are not public figures.

39. See, for example, discussion of *Beauharnais* in *Collin* v. *Smith*, excerpted below.

40. *Adderley* v. *Florida*, 385 U.S. 39 (1966); *Cox* v. *Louisiana*, 379 U.S. 559 (1965). Interestingly, the Supreme Court in the same term overturned a conviction of several demonstrators who staged a sit-in at a segregated library in Louisiana. See *Brown* v. *Louisiana*, 383 U.S. 131 (1966).

41. *Clark* v. *Community for Creative Non-Violence,* 468 U.S. 293 (1984).

42. This is not an area of law in which the Supreme Court has been entirely consistent, or where the guiding principles are clear. See *Note, The Public Forum: Minimum Access Equal Access, and the First Amendment*, 28 Stanford Law Review 117 (1975).

43. *Clark* v. *Community for Creative Non-Violence*, at 7.

44. 42 U.S.C. s 20003–2(a)(1).

45. 477 U.S. 57 (1986).

46. For example, the posting of nude pictures of women on an office door or over a watercooler may result in female employees feeling uncomfortable; and racist slogans or ethnically oriented jokes or cartoons, posted in a work setting, can result in similar offense and insecurity. To what degree may such expressions be regulated in an office setting, when they are arguably protected on the street or in the public forum?

47. A case on college codes at the University of Michigan is presented later in this book. See *Doe* v. *University of Michigan,* 721 F. Supp. 852 (E.D. Mich. 1989). See also *UMW Post, Inc.* v. *Board of Regents of the University of Wisconsin,* 1991 WL 206819 (E.D. Wisc.). A California Superior Court judge recently struck down a narrower speech code at Stanford University. See *Corry et al.* v. *Stanford,* Superior Court, State of California, County of Santa Clara, Case #740309, 27 February 1995.

48. *R.A.V.* v. *City of St. Paul,* 112 S.Ct. 2538 (1992), excerpted below.

THE PRESUMPTION IN FAVOR
OF FREE EXPRESSION

Whitney v. *California*
274 U.S. 357

*As a member of a breakaway "radical" faction of the Socialist Party, Whitney
was one of the founding members of the Communist Labor Party of the United
States in 1919. She was an active leader in its California branch. The party
platform pledged its support for the principles found in the* Communist Mani-
festo, *a document that urged workers around the world to participate in national strikes, propaganda efforts, and ultimately a "class war" to bring about
a "Communist Commonwealth" based on a "Dictatorship of the Proletariat."
She was convicted of violating California's Criminal Syndicalism Act, a statute that forbade being a knowing member of or organizing a group that sub-
scribed to "any doctrine or precept advocating, teaching, or aiding and abet-
ting the commission of crime, sabotage . . . , or unlawful acts of force and
violence or unlawful methods of terrorism as a means of accomplishing a
change in industrial ownership or control or effecting any political change."
Her appeals to California appellate courts were denied. Her appeal to the
U.S. Supreme Court was based on a variety of constitutional claims, one of
which was that the California statute violated the First and Fourteenth
Amendments. The Supreme Court affirmed the conviction. Justice Brandeis,
joined by Justice Holmes, concurred in the Court's decision that Whitney's
convictions should be upheld, but wrote the following concurring opinion.*

Mr. Justice Brandeis, concurring.

Miss Whitney was convicted of the felony of assisting in organizing, in the
year 1919, the Communist Labor Party of California, of being a member of
it, and of assembling with it. These acts are held to constitute a crime, because
the party was formed to teach criminal syndicalism. The statute which made
these acts a crime restricted the right of free speech and of assembly thereto-
fore existing. The claim is that the statute, as applied, denied to Miss Whitney
the liberty guaranteed by the Fourteenth Amendment. The felony which the
statute created is a crime very unlike the old felony of conspiracy or the old
misdemeanor of unlawful assembly. The mere act of assisting in forming a
society for teaching syndicalism, of becoming a member of it, or assembling

with others for that purpose is given the dynamic quality of crime. There is guilt although the society may not contemplate immediate promulgation of the doctrine. Thus the accused is to be punished, not for attempt, incitement, or conspiracy, but for a step in preparation, which, if it threatens the public order at all, does so only remotely. The novelty in the prohibition introduced is that the statute aims, not at the practice of criminal syndicalism, nor even directly at the preaching of it, but at association with those who propose to preach it.

Despite arguments to the contrary which had seemed to me persuasive, it is settled that the due process clause of the Fourteenth Amendment applies to matters of substantive law as well as to matters of procedure. Thus all fundamental rights comprised within the term liberty are protected by the federal Constitution from invasion by the states. The right of free speech, the right to teach, and the right of assembly are, of course, fundamental rights. These may not be denied or abridged. But, although the rights of free speech and assembly are fundamental, they are not in their nature absolute. Their exercise is subject to restriction, if the particular restriction proposed is required in order to protect the state from destruction or from serious injury, political, economic, or moral. That the necessity which is essential to a valid restriction does not exist unless speech would produce, or is intended to produce, a clear and imminent danger of some substantive evil which the state constitutionally may seek to prevent has been settled. See *Schenck*. . . .

This court has not yet fixed the standard by which to determine when a danger shall be deemed clear; how remote the danger may be and yet be deemed present; and what degree of evil shall be deemed sufficiently substantial to justify resort to abridgment of free speech and assembly as the means of protection. To reach sound conclusions on these matters, we must bear in mind why a state is, ordinarily, denied the power to prohibit dissemination of social, economic, and political doctrine which a vast majority of its citizens believes to be false and fraught with evil consequence.

Those who won our independence believed that the final end of the state was to make men free to develop their faculties, and that in its government the deliberative forces should prevail over the arbitrary. They valued liberty both as an end and as a means. They believed liberty to be the secret of happiness and courage to be the secret of liberty. They believed that freedom to think as you will and to speak as you think are means indispensable to the discovery and spread of political truth; that without free speech and assembly discussion would be futile; that with them, discussion affords ordinarily adequate protection against the dissemination of noxious doctrine; that the greatest menace to freedom is an inert people; that public discussion is a political duty; and that this should be a fundamental principle of the American government. They recognized the risks to which all human institutions are subject. But they knew that order cannot be secured merely through fear of punishment for its infraction; that it is hazardous to discourage thought, hope, and imagination; that fear breeds repression; that repression breeds hate; that hate menaces stable government; that the path of safety lies in the opportunity to discuss freely supposed grievances and proposed remedies; and that the fitting remedy for evil counsels is good ones. Believing in the power of reason as applied through public discussion, they eschewed silence coerced by law—the argument of force in its worst form. Recognizing the occasional tyrannies of governing majorities, they amended the Constitution so that free speech and assembly should be guaranteed.

Fear of serious injury cannot alone justify suppression of free speech and assembly. Men feared witches and burnt women. It is the function of speech to free men from the bondage of irrational fears. To justify suppression of free speech there must be reasonable ground to fear that serious evil will result if free speech is practiced. There must be reasonable ground to believe that the danger apprehended is imminent. There must be reasonable ground to believe that the evil to be prevented is a serious one. Every denunciation of existing law tends in some measure to increase the probability that there will be violation of it. Condoning of a breach enhances the probability. Expressions of approval add to the probability. Propagation of the criminal state of mind by teaching syndicalism increases it. Advocacy of law-breaking heightens it still further. But even advocacy of violation, however reprehensible morally, is not a justification for denying free speech where the advocacy falls short of incitement and there is nothing to indicate that the advocacy would be immediately acted on. The wide difference between advocacy and incitement, between preparation and attempt, between assembling and conspiracy, must be borne in mind. In order to support a finding of clear and present danger it must be shown either that immediate serious violence was to be expected or was advocated, or that the past conduct furnished reason to believe that such advocacy was then contemplated.

Those who won our independence by revolution were not cowards. They did not fear political change. They did not exalt order at the cost of liberty. To courageous, self-reliant men, with confidence in the power of free and fearless reasoning applied through the processes of popular government, no danger flowing from speech can be deemed clear and present, unless the incidence of the evil apprehended is so imminent that it may befall before there is opportunity for full discussion. If there be time to expose through discussion the falsehood and fallacies, to avert the evil by the processes of education, the remedy to be applied is more speech, not enforced silence. Only an emergency can justify repression. Such must be the rule if authority is to be reconciled with freedom. Such, in my opinion, is the command of the Constitution. It is therefore always open to Americans to challenge a law abridging free speech and assembly by showing that there was no emergency justifying it.

Moreover, even imminent danger cannot justify resort to prohibition of these functions essential to effective democracy, unless the evil apprehended is relatively serious. Prohibition of free speech and assembly is a measure so stringent that it would be inappropriate as the means for averting a relatively trivial harm to society. A police measure may be unconstitutional merely because the remedy, although effective as means of protection, is unduly harsh or oppressive. Thus, a state might, in the exercise of its police power, make any trespass upon the land of another a crime, regardless of the results or of the intent or purpose of the trespasser. It might, also, punish an attempt, a conspiracy, or an incitement to commit the trespass. But it is hardly conceivable that this court would hold constitutional a statute which punished as a felony the mere voluntary assembly with a society formed to teach that pedestrians had the moral right to cross uninclosed, unposted, waste lands and to advocate their doing so, even if there was imminent danger that advocacy would lead to a trespass. The fact that speech is likely to result in some violence or in destruction of property is not enough to justify its suppression. There must be the probability of serious injury to the State. Among free men, the deterrents ordinarily to be applied to prevent crime are education and punishment for violations of the law, not abridgment of the rights of free speech and assembly. . . .

Whether in 1919, when Miss Whitney did the things complained of, there was in California such clear and present danger of serious evil, might have been made the important issue in the case. She might have required that the issue be determined either by the court or the jury. She claimed below that the statute as applied to her violated the federal Constitution; but she did not claim that it was void because there was no clear and present danger of serious evil, nor did she request that the existence of these conditions of a valid measure thus restricting the rights of free speech and assembly be passed upon by the court or a jury. On the other hand, there was evidence on which the court or jury might have found that such danger existed. I am unable to assent to the suggestion in the opinion of the court that assembling with a political party, formed to advocate the desirability of a proletarian revolution by mass action at some date necessarily far in the future, is not a right within the protection of the Fourteenth Amendment. In the present case, however, there was other testimony which tended to establish the existence of a conspiracy, on the part of members of the International Workers of the World, to commit present serious crimes, and likewise to show that such a conspiracy would be furthered by the activity of the society of which Miss Whitney was a member. Under these circumstances the judgment of the State court cannot be disturbed. . . .

Discussion Questions

1. There are two general classes of argument to support free speech. The first posits free speech as an essential means to the end of good government, social progress, and the discovery of truth. John Stuart Mill is a proponent of this school of thought (see third section, "Commentary"), which we might term the "utilitarian" defense of freedom of expression. The other position argues that free expression is essential to the full development of the human spirit, is a natural right of all humans, and is good in and of itself—regardless of any utilitarian purposes it might serve in political, social, or scientific realms. We might call this position the "natural rights/ self-actualization" defense of free speech. Which justification for free speech does Justice Brandeis emphasize? Does the nature of the justification of freedom of expression have any potential impact on how that freedom is applied in real-world situations?
2. In light of Justice Brandeis's strong statement in favor of freedom of expression, why did he concur in the majority's decision to uphold Whitney's conviction for criminal syndicalism?
3. Is there "food for thought" in this opinion that might give pause to proponents of campus speech codes? How persuasive do you find the arguments?

Tinker v. Des Moines
393 U.S. 503 (1969)

John Tinker, 15, was a student at a public high school in Des Moines, Iowa. Mary Beth Tinker, his 13-year-old sister, attended junior high school. After meeting with a group of adults and students, they decided to publicize their objections to the Vietnam War by wearing black armbands to school. School authorities became aware of the plan and adopted a policy that any student wearing an armband would be asked to remove it; if the student refused, the student would be suspended until he or she returned to school without the armband. The Tinker children wore armbands and were suspended from school.

Mr. Justice Fortas delivered the opinion of the Court.

I

First Amendment rights, applied in light of the special characteristics of the school environment, are available to teachers and students. It can hardly be argued that either students or teachers shed their constitutional rights to freedom of speech or expression at the schoolhouse gate. This has been the unmistakable holding of this Court for almost 50 years. . . .

On the other hand, the Court has repeatedly emphasized the need for affirming the comprehensive authority of the States and of school officials, consistent with fundamental constitutional safeguards, to prescribe and control conduct in the schools. Our problem lies in the area where students in the exercise of First Amendment rights collide with the rules of the school authorities.

II

The problem posed by the present case does not relate to regulation of the length of skirts or the type of clothing, to hair style, or deportment. It does not concern aggressive, disruptive action, or even group demonstrations. Our problem involves direct, primary First Amendment rights akin to "pure speech."

The school officials banned and sought to punish petitioners for a silent, passive expression of opinion, unaccompanied by any disorder or disturbance on the part of petitioners. There is here no evidence whatever of petitioners' interference, actual or nascent, with the schools' work or of collision with the rights of other students to be secure and to be let alone. Accordingly, this case does not concern speech or action that intrudes upon the work of the schools or the rights of other students.

Only a few of the 18,000 students in the school system wore the black armbands. Only five students were suspended for wearing them. There is no indication that the work of the schools or any class was disrupted. Outside the classrooms, a few students made hostile remarks to the children wearing armbands, but there were no threats or acts of violence on school premises.

The District Court concluded that the action of the school authorities was reasonable because it was based upon their fear of a disturbance from the wearing of the armbands. But, in our system, undifferentiated fear or apprehension of disturbance is not enough to overcome the right to freedom of expression. Any departure from absolute regimentation may cause trouble. Any variation from the majority's opinion may inspire fear. Any word spoken, in class, in the lunchroom, or on the campus, that deviates from the views of another person may start an argument or cause a disturbance. But our Constitution says we must take this risk, and our history says that it is this sort of hazardous freedom—this kind of openness—that is the basis of our national strength and of the independence and vigor of Americans who grow up and live in this relatively permissive, often disputatious, society.

In order for the State in the person of school officials to justify prohibition of a particular expression of opinion, it must be able to show that its action was caused by something more than a mere desire to avoid the discomfort and unpleasantness that always accompany an unpopular viewpoint. Certainly where there is no finding and no showing that engaging in the forbidden conduct would "materially and substantially interfere with the requirements of appropriate discipline in the operation of the school," the prohibition cannot be sustained.

In the present case, the District Court made no such finding, and our independent examination of the record fails to yield evidence that the school authorities had reason to anticipate that the wearing of the armbands would substantially interfere with the work of the school or impinge upon the rights of other students. Even an official memorandum prepared after the suspension that listed the reasons for the ban on wearing the armbands made no reference to the anticipation of such disruption.

On the contrary, the action of the school authorities appears to have been based upon an urgent wish to avoid the controversy which might result from the expression, even by the silent symbol of armbands, of opposition to this Nation's part in the conflagration in Vietnam. . . . It is also relevant that the school authorities did not purport to prohibit the wearing of all symbols of political or controversial significance. The record shows that students in some of the schools wore buttons relating to national political campaigns, and some even wore the Iron Cross, traditionally a symbol of Nazism. The order prohibiting the wearing of armbands did not extend to these. Instead, a particular symbol—black armbands worn to exhibit opposition to this Nation's involvement in Vietnam—was singled out for prohibition. Clearly, the prohibition of expression of one particular opinion, at least without evidence that it is necessary to avoid material and substantial interference with schoolwork or discipline, is not constitutionally permissible.

In our system, state-operated schools may not be enclaves of totalitarianism.

School officials do not possess absolute authority over their students. Students in school as well as out of school are "persons" under our Constitution. They are possessed of fundamental rights which the State must respect, just as they themselves must respect their obligations to the State. In our system, students may not be regarded as closed-circuit recipients of only that which the State chooses to communicate. They may not be confined to the expression of those sentiments that are officially approved. In the absence of a specific showing of constitutionally valid reasons to regulate their speech, students are entitled to freedom of expression of their views. . . .

The principle of these cases is not confined to the supervised and ordained discussion which takes place in the classroom. The principal use to which the schools are dedicated is to accommodate students during prescribed hours for the purpose of certain types of activities. Among those activities is personal intercommunication among the students. This is not only an inevitable part of the process of attending school; it is also an important part of the educational process. A student's rights, therefore, do not embrace merely the classroom hours. When he is in the cafeteria, or on the playing field, or on the campus during the authorized hours, he may express his opinions, even on controversial subjects like the conflict in Vietnam, if he does so without "materially and substantially interfer(ing) with the requirements of appropriate discipline in the operation of the school" and without colliding with the rights of others. But conduct by the student, in class or out of it, which for any reason—whether it stems from time, place, or type of behavior—materially disrupts classwork or involves substantial disorder or invasion of the rights of others is, of course, not immunized by the constitutional guarantee of freedom of speech.

Under our Constitution, free speech is not a right that is given only to be so circumscribed that it exists in principle but not in fact. Freedom of expression would not truly exist if the right could be exercised only in an area that a benevolent government has provided as a safe haven for crackpots. The Constitution says that Congress (and the States) may not abridge the right to free speech. This provision means what it says. We properly read it to permit reasonable regulation of speech-connected activities in carefully restricted circumstances. But we do not confine the permissible exercise of First Amendment rights to a telephone booth or the four corners of a pamphlet, or to supervised and ordained discussion in a school classroom.

If a regulation were adopted by school officials forbidding discussion of the Vietnam conflict, or the expression by any student of opposition to it anywhere on school property except as part of a prescribed classroom exercise, it would be obvious that the regulation would violate the constitutional rights of students, at least if it could not be justified by a showing that the students' activities would materially and substantially disrupt the work and discipline of the school. In the circumstances of the present case, the prohibition of the silent, passive "witness of the armbands," as one of the children called it, is no less offensive to the Constitution's guarantees.

As we have discussed, the record does not demonstrate any facts which might reasonably have led school authorities to forecast substantial disruption of or material interference with school activities, and no disturbances or disorders on the school premises in fact occurred. These petitioners merely went about their ordained rounds in school. Their deviation consisted only in wearing on their sleeve a band of black cloth, not more than two inches wide. They wore it to exhibit their disapproval of the Vietnam hostilities and their advocacy of a truce, to make their views known, and, by their example, to influence others to adopt them. They neither interrupted school activities nor sought to intrude in the school affairs or the lives of others. They caused discussion outside of the classrooms, but no interference with work and no disorder. In the circumstances, our Constitution does not permit officials of the State to deny their form of expression. . . .

Reversed and remanded.

Mr. Justice Black, dissenting.

The Court's holding in this case ushers in what I deem to be an entirely new era in which the power to control pupils by the elected "officials of state supported public schools . . . in the United States is in ultimate effect transferred to the Supreme Court." . . .

As I read the Court's opinion it relies upon the following grounds for holding unconstitutional the judgment of the Des Moines school officials and the two courts below. First, the Court concludes that the wearing of armbands is "symbolic speech" which is "akin to 'pure speech' " and therefore protected by the First and Fourteenth Amendments. Secondly, the Court decides that the public schools are an appropriate place to exercise "symbolic speech" as long as normal school functions are not "unreasonably" disrupted. Finally, the Court arrogates to itself, rather than to the State's elected officials charged with running the schools, the decision as to which school disciplinary regulations are "reasonable."

Assuming that the Court is correct in holding that the conduct of wearing armbands for the purpose of conveying political ideas is protected by the First Amendment, the crucial remaining questions are whether students and teachers may use the schools at their whim as a platform for the exercise of free speech—"symbolic" or "pure"—and whether the courts will allocate to themselves the function of deciding how the pupils' school day will be spent. While I have always believed that under the First and Fourteenth Amendments neither the State nor the Federal Government has any authority to regulate or censor the content of speech, I have never believed that any person has a right to give speeches or engage in demonstrations where he pleases and when he pleases. This Court has already rejected such a notion.

While the record does not show that any of these armband students shouted, used profane language, or were violent in any manner, detailed testimony by some of them shows their armbands caused comments, warnings by other students, the poking of fun at them, and a warning by an older football player that other, nonprotesting students had better let them alone. There is also evidence that a teacher of mathematics had his lesson period practically "wrecked" chiefly by disputes with Mary Beth Tinker, who wore her armband for her "demonstration." Even a causal reading of the record shows that this armband did divert students' minds from their regular lessons, and that talk, comments, etc., made John Tinker "self-conscious" in attending school with his armband. While the absence of obscene remarks or boisterous and loud disorder perhaps justifies the Court's statement that the few armband students did not actually "disrupt" the classwork, I think the record overwhelmingly shows that the armbands did exactly what the elected school officials and principals foresaw they would, that is, took the students' minds off their class-work and diverted them to thoughts about the highly emotional subject of the Vietnam war.

I deny . . . that it has been the "unmistakable holding of this Court for almost 50 years" that "students" and "teachers" take with them into the "schoolhouse gate" constitutional rights to "freedom of speech or expression." . . . The truth is that a teacher of kindergarten, grammar school, or high school pupils no more carries into a school with him a complete right to freedom of speech and expression than an anti-Catholic or anti-Semite carries with him a complete freedom of speech and religion into a Catholic church or Jewish synagogue. Nor does a person carry with him into the United States Senate or House, or into the Supreme Court, or any other court, a complete constitutional right to go into those places contrary to their rules and speak his mind on any subject he pleases. It is a myth to say that any person has a constitutional right to say what he pleases, where he pleases, and when he pleases. Our Court has decided precisely the opposite. . . .

This case, . . . wholly without constitutional reasons in my judgment, sub-jects all the public schools in the country to the whims and caprices of their loudest-mouthed, but maybe not their brightest, students. I, for one, am not fully persuaded that school pupils are wise enough, even with this Court's expert help from Washington, to run the 23,390 public school systems in our 50 States. I wish, therefore, wholly to disclaim any purpose on my part to hold that the Federal Constitution compels the teachers, parents, and elected school officials to surrender control of the American public school system to public school students. I dissent.

Discussion Questions

1. Justice Fortas, while speaking in broad terms, emphasizes a number of specific factual elements of this case that led to the Court's final decision: that no classes were disrupted, that the expression of views was silent and passive, and that other symbols (such as political campaign buttons and iron crosses) were allowed by school authorities. Which, if any, of these specific factual attributes of this case do you think were essential to the Court's ruling? Can you posit a different factual situation in which the Court might have upheld the prohibition on expression? What if the school had been located on an army base where parents of many of the children were serving in Vietnam?

2. The Court sets out the specific finding that must be made in a school context to justify restriction of students' freedom of expression: "In order for the State in the person of school officials to justify prohibition of a particular expression of opinion, it must be able to show that its action was caused by something more than a mere desire to avoid the discomfort and unpleasantness that always accompany an unpopular viewpoint. Certainly where there is no finding and no showing that engaging in the forbidden conduct would 'materially and substantially interfere with the requirements of appropriate discipline in the operation of the school,' the prohibition cannot be sustained." Does the Court's formulation allow school officials more leeway to restrict speech than, say, police officers in a public park? Should standards be different in the two places? Do you think the Court would (or should) assess the case differently if it involved elementary school students? Students at a public university?

3. This case involves "symbolic speech," that is, expression of ideas through conduct rather than words. Does the majority opinion treat this expressive conduct differently than it treats "pure speech?" Should it? What if the students wore buttons that read "Stop the U.S. Army's murders in Vietnam"? What if the buttons read "Fuck the Draft" (see *Cohen* v. *California,* below)?

Texas v. *Johnson*
491 U.S. 397 (1989)

Mr. Justice Brennan delivered the opinion of the Court.

After publicly burning an American flag as a means of political protest, Gregory Lee Johnson was convicted of desecrating a flag in violation of Texas law. This case presents the question whether his conviction is consistent with the First Amendment. We hold that it is not.

I

While the Republican National Convention was taking place in Dallas in 1984, respondent Johnson participated in a political demonstration dubbed the "Republican War Chest Tour." . . . The demonstration ended in front of Dallas City Hall, where Johnson unfurled the American flag, doused it with kerosene, and set it on fire. While the flag burned, the protesters chanted, "America, the red, white, and blue, we spit on you." After the demonstrators dispersed, a witness to the flag burning collected the flag's remains and buried them in his backyard. No one was physically injured or threatened with injury, though several witnesses testified that they had been seriously offended by the flag burning.

Of the approximately 100 demonstrators, Johnson alone was charged with a crime. The only criminal offense with which he was charged was the desecration of a venerated object in violation of Texas Penal Code. After a trial, he was convicted, sentenced to one year in prison, and fined $2,000. The Court of Appeals for the Fifth District of Texas at Dallas affirmed Johnson's conviction, but the Texas Court of Criminal Appeals reversed, holding that the State could not, consistent with the First Amendment, punish Johnson for burning the flag in these circumstances. . . . We granted certiorari, and now affirm.

II

Johnson was convicted of flag desecration for burning the flag rather than for uttering insulting words. This fact somewhat complicates our consideration of his conviction under the First Amendment. We must first determine whether

Johnson's burning of the flag constituted expressive conduct, permitting him to invoke the First Amendment in challenging his conviction. If his conduct was expressive, we next decide whether the State's regulation is related to the suppression of free expression. If the State's regulation is not related to expression, then the less stringent standard we announced in *United States* v. *O'Brien* for regulations of noncommunicative conduct controls. [In *O'Brien*, the Court held that when speech and expression are combined into a form of "symbolic speech," regulation of that speech is permissible "if it is within the constitutional power of the Government; if it furthers an important or substantial governmental interest; if the governmental interest is unrelated to the suppression of free expression; and if the incidental restriction on alleged First Amendment freedoms is no greater than is essential to the furtherance of that interest."] If it is, then we are outside of *O'Brien*'s test, and we must ask whether this interest justifies Johnson's conviction under a more demanding standard. A third possibility is that the State's asserted interest is simply not implicated on these facts, and in that event the interest drops out of the picture. . . .

The First Amendment literally forbids the abridgment only of "speech," but we have long recognized that its protection does not end at the spoken or written word. While we have rejected "the view that an apparently limitless variety of conduct can be labeled 'speech' whenever the person engaging in the conduct intends thereby to express an idea," we have acknowledged that conduct may be "sufficiently imbued with elements of communication to fall within the scope of the First and Fourteenth Amendments."

In deciding whether particular conduct possesses sufficient communicative elements to bring the First Amendment into play, we have asked whether "[a]n intent to convey a particularized message was present, and [whether] the likelihood was great that the message would be understood by those who viewed it." Hence, we have recognized the expressive nature of students' wearing of black armbands to protest American military involvement in Vietnam [*Tinker*]; of a sit-in by blacks in a "whites only" area to protest segregation; of the wearing of American military uniforms in a dramatic presentation criticizing American involvement in Vietnam; and of picketing about a wide variety of causes.

Especially pertinent to this case are our decisions recognizing the communicative nature of conduct relating to flags. Attaching a peace sign to the flag; refusing to salute the flag; and displaying a red flag, we have held, all may find shelter under the First Amendment. . . . Pregnant with expressive content, the flag as readily signifies this Nation as does the combination of letters found in "America." We have not automatically concluded, however, that any action taken with respect to our flag is expressive. Instead, in characterizing such action for First Amendment purposes, we have considered the context in which it occurred. . . .

Johnson burned an American flag as part—indeed, as the culmination—of a political demonstration that coincided with the convening of the Republican Party and its renomination of Ronald Reagan for President. The expressive, overtly political nature of this conduct was both intentional and overwhelmingly apparent. . . .

III

The government generally has a freer hand in restricting expressive conduct than it has in restricting the written or spoken word. It may not, however, proscribe particular conduct because it has expressive elements. "[W]hat might be termed the more generalized guarantee of freedom of expression makes the communicative nature of conduct an inadequate basis for singling out that conduct for proscription. A law directed at the communicative nature of conduct must, like a law directed at speech itself, be justified by the substantial showing of need that the First Amendment requires." It is, in short, not simply the verbal or nonverbal nature of the expression, but the governmental interest at stake, that helps to determine whether a restriction on that expression is valid.

Thus, although we have recognized that where " 'speech' and 'nonspeech' elements are combined in the same course of conduct, a sufficiently important governmental interest in regulating the nonspeech element can justify incidental limitations on First Amendment freedoms," we have limited the applicability of *O'Brien*'s relatively lenient standard to those cases in which "the governmental interest is unrelated to the suppression of free expression." . . .

In order to decide whether *O'Brien*'s test applies here, therefore, we must decide whether Texas has asserted an interest in support of Johnson's conviction that is unrelated to the suppression of expression. If we find that an interest asserted by the State is simply not implicated on the facts before us, we need not ask whether *O'Brien*'s test applies. The State offers two separate interests to justify this conviction: preventing breaches of the peace and preserving the flag as a symbol of nationhood and national unity. We hold that the first interest is not implicated on this record and that the second is related to the suppression of expression.

A

Texas claims that its interest in preventing breaches of the peace justifies Johnson's conviction for flag desecration. However, no disturbance of the peace actually occurred or threatened to occur because of Johnson's burning of the flag. Although the State stresses the disruptive behavior of the protesters during their march toward City Hall, it admits that "no actual breach of the peace occurred at the time of the flag burning or in response to the flag burning." The State's emphasis on the protesters' disorderly actions prior to arriving at City Hall is not only somewhat surprising given that no charges were brought on the basis of this conduct, but it also fails to show that a disturbance of the peace was a likely reaction to Johnson's conduct. The only evidence offered by the State at trial to show the reaction to Johnson's actions was the testimony of several persons who had been seriously offended by the flag burning.

The State's position, therefore, amounts to a claim that an audience that takes serious offense at a particular expression is necessarily likely to disturb the peace and that the expression may be prohibited on this basis. Our precedents do not countenance such a presumption. On the contrary, they recognize that a principal "function of free speech under our system of government is to invite dispute. It may indeed best serve its high purpose when it induces a condition of unrest, creates dissatisfaction with conditions as they are, or even stirs people to anger." It would be odd indeed to conclude both that "if it is the speaker's opinion that gives offense, that consequence is a reason for according it constitutional protection," and that the Government may ban the expression of certain disagreeable ideas on the unsupported presumption that their very disagreeableness will provoke violence.

Thus, we have not permitted the government to assume that every expression of a provocative idea will incite a riot, but have instead required careful consideration of the actual circumstances surrounding such expression, asking whether the expression "is directed to inciting or producing imminent lawless action and is likely to incite or produce such action" [*Brandenburg*]. To accept *Texas*'s arguments that it need only demonstrate "the potential for a breach of the peace," and that every flag burning necessarily possesses that potential, would be to eviscerate our holding in *Brandenburg*. This we decline to do.

Nor does Johnson's expressive conduct fall within that small class of "fighting words" that are "likely to provoke the average person to retaliation, and thereby cause a breach of the peace" [*Chaplinsky*]. No reasonable onlooker would have regarded Johnson's generalized expression of dissatisfaction with the policies of the Federal Government as a direct personal insult or an invitation to exchange fisticuffs.

We thus conclude that the State's interest in maintaining order is not implicated on these facts. The State need not worry that our holding will disable it from preserving the peace. We do not suggest that the First Amendment forbids a State to prevent "imminent lawless action" [*Brandenburg*]. . . .

B

The State also asserts an interest in preserving the flag as a symbol of nationhood and national unity. In *Spence,* we acknowledged that the government's interest in preserving the flag's special symbolic value "is directly related to expression in the context of activity" such as affixing a peace symbol to a flag. We are equally persuaded that this interest is related to expression in the case of Johnson's burning of the flag. The State, apparently, is concerned that such conduct will lead people to believe either that the flag does not stand for nationhood and national unity, but instead reflects other, less positive concepts, or that the concepts reflected in the flag do not in fact exist, that is, that we do not enjoy unity as a Nation. These concerns blossom only when a person's treatment of the flag communicates some message, and thus are related "to the suppression of free expression" within the meaning of *O'Brien.* We are thus outside of *O'Brien*'s test altogether.

IV

It remains to consider whether the State's interest in preserving the flag as a symbol of nationhood and national unity justifies Johnson's conviction.

As in *Spence,* "[W]e are confronted with a case of prosecution for the expression of an idea through activity" and, "[a]ccordingly, we must examine with particular care the interests advanced by [petitioner] to support its prosecution." Johnson was not, we add, prosecuted for the expression of just any idea; he was prosecuted for his expression of dissatisfaction with the policies of this country, expression situated at the core of our First Amendment values.

Moreover, Johnson was prosecuted because he knew that his politically charged expression would cause "serious offense." If he had burned the flag as a means of disposing of it because it was dirty or torn, he would not have been convicted of flag desecration under this Texas law. . . . Texas concedes as much: "[It] reaches only those severe acts of physical abuse of the flag carried out in a way likely to be offensive. The statute mandates intentional or knowing abuse, that is, the kind of mistreatment that is not innocent, but rather is intentionally designed to seriously offend other individuals."

Whether Johnson's treatment of the flag violated Texas law thus depended on the likely communicative impact of his expressive conduct. . . . We must therefore subject the State's asserted interest in preserving the special symbolic character of the flag to "the most exacting scrutiny."

Texas argues that its interest in preserving the flag as a symbol of nationhood and national unity survives this close analysis. Quoting extensively from the writings of this Court chronicling the flag's historic and symbolic role in our society, the State emphasizes the "special place" reserved for the flag in our Nation. The State's argument is not that it has an interest simply in maintaining the flag as a symbol of something, no matter what it symbolizes; indeed, if that were the State's position, it would be difficult to see how that interest is endangered by highly symbolic conduct such as Johnson's. Rather, the State's claim is that it has an interest in preserving the flag as a symbol of nationhood and national unity, a symbol with a determinate range of meanings. According to Texas, if one physically treats the flag in a way that would tend to cast doubt on either the idea that nationhood and national unity are the flag's referents or that national unity actually exists, the message conveyed thereby is a harmful one and therefore may be prohibited.

If there is a bedrock principle underlying the First Amendment, it is that the government may not prohibit the expression of an idea simply because society finds the idea itself offensive or disagreeable.

We have not recognized an exception to this principle even where our flag has been involved. . . . In holding in *Barnette* that the Constitution did not leave this course open to the government, Justice Jackson described one of our society's defining principles in words deserving of their frequent repetition: "If there is any fixed star in our constitutional constellation, it is that no official, high or petty, can prescribe what shall be orthodox in politics, nationalism, religion, or other matters of opinion or force citizens to confess by word or act their faith therein." . . . In short, nothing in our precedents suggests that a State may foster its own view of the flag by prohibiting expressive conduct relating to it. . . .

There is, moreover, no indication—either in the text of the Constitution or in our cases interpreting it—that a separate juridical category exists for the American flag alone. Indeed, we would not be surprised to learn that the persons who framed our Constitution and wrote the Amendment that we now construe were not known for their reverence for the Union Jack. The First Amendment does not guarantee that other concepts virtually sacred to our Nation as a whole—such as the principle that discrimination on the basis of race is odious and destructive—will go unquestioned in the marketplace of ideas. See [*Brandenburg*]. We decline, therefore, to create for the flag an exception to the joust of principles protected by the First Amendment. . . .

The way to preserve the flag's special role is not to punish those who feel differently about these matters. It is to persuade them that they are wrong [citing Justice Brandeis in *Whitney*]. And, precisely because it is our flag that is involved, one's response to the flag burner may exploit the uniquely persuasive power of the flag itself. We can imagine no more appropriate response to burning a flag than waving one's own, no better way to counter a flag burner's message than by saluting the flag that burns, no surer means of preserving the dignity even of the flag that burned than by—as one witness here did—according its remains a respectful burial. We do not consecrate the flag by punishing its desecration, for in doing so we dilute the freedom that this cherished emblem represents.

V

Johnson was convicted for engaging in expressive conduct. The State's interest in preventing breaches of the peace does not support his conviction because Johnson's conduct did not threaten to disturb the peace. Nor does the State's interest in preserving the flag as a symbol of nationhood and national unity justify his criminal conviction for engaging in political expression. The judgment of the Texas Court of Criminal Appeals is therefore Affirmed.

Chief Justice Rehnquist, with whom Justice White and Justice O'Connor join, dissenting.

In holding this Texas statute unconstitutional, the Court ignores Justice Holmes's familiar aphorism that "a page of history is worth a volume of logic." For more than 200 years, the American flag has occupied a unique position as the symbol of our Nation, a uniqueness that justifies a governmental prohibition against flag burning in the way respondent Johnson did here. . . .

I cannot agree that the First Amendment invalidates the Act of Congress, and the laws of 48 of the 50 States, which make criminal the public burning of the flag. . . .

But the Court insists that the Texas statute prohibiting the public burning of the American flag infringes on respondent Johnson's freedom of expression. Such freedom, of course, is not absolute. See [*Schenck*]. In [*Chaplinsky*], a unanimous Court said:

> Allowing the broadest scope to the language and purpose of the Fourteenth Amendment, it is well understood that the right of free speech is not absolute at all times and under all circumstances. There are certain well-defined and nar-

rowly limited classes of speech, the prevention and punishment of which have never been thought to raise any Constitutional problem. These include the lewd and obscene, the profane, the libelous, and the insulting or "fighting" words— those which by their very utterance inflict injury or tend to incite an immediate breach of the peace. It has been well observed that such utterances are no essential part of any exposition of ideas, and are of such slight social value as a step to truth that any benefit that may be derived from them is clearly outweighed by the social interest in order and morality.

The Court upheld Chaplinsky's conviction under a state statute that made it unlawful to "address any offensive, derisive, or annoying word to any person who is lawfully in any street or other public place." Chaplinsky had told a local marshal, "You are a God damned racketeer" and a "damned Fascist and the whole government of Rochester are Fascists or agents of Fascists."

Here it may equally well be said that the public burning of the American flag by Johnson was no essential part of any exposition of ideas, and at the same time it had a tendency to incite a breach of the peace. Johnson was free to make any verbal denunciation of the flag that he wished; indeed, he was free to burn the flag in private. He could publicly burn other symbols of the Government or effigies of political leaders. He did lead a march through the streets of Dallas, and conducted a rally in front of the Dallas City Hall. He engaged in a "die-in" to protest nuclear weapons. He shouted out various slogans during the march, including: "Reagan, Mondale, which will it be? Either one means World War III"; "Ronald Reagan, killer of the hour, perfect example of U.S. power"; and "Red, white and blue, we spit on you, you stand for plunder, you will go under." For none of these acts was he arrested or prosecuted; it was only when he proceeded to burn publicly an American flag stolen from its rightful owner that he violated the Texas statute.

The Court could not, and did not, say that Chaplinsky's utterances were not expressive phrases—they clearly and succinctly conveyed an extremely low opinion of the addressee. The same may be said of Johnson's public burning of the flag in this case; it obviously did convey Johnson's bitter dislike of his country. But his act, like Chaplinsky's provocative words, conveyed nothing that could not have been conveyed and was not conveyed just as forcefully in a dozen different ways. As with "fighting words," so with flag burning, for purposes of the First Amendment: It is "no essential part of any exposition of ideas, and [is] of such slight social value as a step to truth that any benefit that may be derived from [it] is clearly outweighed" by the public interest in avoiding a probable breach of the peace. The highest courts of several States have upheld state statutes prohibiting the public burning of the flag on the grounds that it is so inherently inflammatory that it may cause a breach of public order.

The result of the Texas statute is obviously to deny one in Johnson's frame of mind one of many means of "symbolic speech." Far from being a case of "one picture being worth a thousand words," flag burning is the equivalent of an inarticulate grunt or roar that, it seems fair to say, is most likely to be indulged in not to express any particular idea, but to antagonize others. . . . The Texas statute deprived Johnson of only one rather inarticulate symbolic form of protest—a form of protest that was profoundly offensive to many— and left him with a full panoply of other symbols and every conceivable form of verbal expression to express his deep disapproval of national policy. Thus, in no way can it be said that Texas is punishing him because his hearers—or any other group of people—were profoundly opposed to the message that he sought to convey. Such opposition is no proper basis for restricting speech or expression under the First Amendment. It was Johnson's use of this particular symbol, and not the idea that he sought to convey by it or by his many other expressions, for which he was punished.

Our Constitution wisely places limits on powers of legislative majorities to act, but the declaration of such limits by this Court "is, at all times, a question of much delicacy, which ought seldom, if ever, to be decided in the affirmative, in a doubtful case." Uncritical extension of constitutional protection to the burning of the flag risks the frustration of the very purpose for which organized governments are instituted. The Court decides that the American flag is just another symbol, about which not only must opinions pro and con be tolerated, but for which the most minimal public respect may not be enjoined. The government may conscript men into the Armed Forces where they must fight and perhaps die for the flag, but the government may not prohibit the public burning of the banner under which they fight. I would uphold the Texas statute as applied in this case.

[A separate dissent was filed by Justice Stevens.]

Discussion Questions

1. Texas put forward a desire to avoid a breach of the peace as a rationale for Johnson's conviction. The Court argues that no actual disturbance either occurred or was threatened. Do you think the decision would (or should) have been different if a group of Vietnam vets had threatened physical abuse of Johnson and his fellow demonstrators? Should the rights of speakers depend on the threatened negative reaction of listeners? (See *Feiner* v. *New York*, below.)

2. Do you agree with the dissenters that Johnson's burning of the flag was

not expression but an "inarticulate grunt"? that his message could have been conveyed just as effectively through words? Does it make sense to protect the chanting of "Red, white and blue, we spit on you," while incriminating flag burning? Why or why not?

3. How would you apply this case to an effort by a public university to prohibit a planned cross burning and white supremacy rally on campus?

INCITEMENT TO SUBVERSIVE ACTIVITY
AND OTHER ILLEGAL ACTS

Schenck v. United States
249 U.S. 47 (1919)

Schenck was general secretary of the Socialist Party of the United States. The party printed 15,000 leaflets (described in the opinion) to be distributed to men who were eligible to be drafted into military service during World War I. For his role in the preparation and distribution of the leaflets, Schenck was convicted under the Espionage Act of 1917, under the provisions that incriminated "causing and attempting to cause insubordination in the military and naval forces of the United States," and with "obstructing the recruiting and enlistment service of the United States."

Mr. Justice Holmes delivered the opinion of the Court.

. . . The document in question upon its first printed side recited the first section of the Thirteenth Amendment, said that the idea embodied in it was violated by the conscription act and that a conscript is little better than a convict. In impassioned language it intimated that conscription was despotism in its worst form and a monstrous wrong against humanity in the interest of Wall Street's chosen few. It said, "Do not submit to intimidation," but in form at least confined itself to peaceful measures such as a petition for the repeal of the act. The other and later printed side of the sheet was headed "Assert Your Rights." It stated reasons for alleging that anyone violated the Constitution when he refused to recognize "your right to assert your opposition to the draft," and went on, "If you do not assert and support your rights, you are helping to deny or disparage rights which it is the solemn duty of all citizens and residents of the United States to retain." It described the arguments on the other side as coming from cunning politicians and a mercenary capitalist press, and even silent consent to the conscription law as helping to support an infamous conspiracy. It denied the power to send our citizens away to foreign shores to shoot up the people of other lands, and added that words could not express the condemnation such cold-blooded ruthlessness deserves, &c., &c., winding up, "You must do your share to maintain, support, and uphold the rights of the people of this country." Of course the document would not have been sent unless it had been intended to have some effect, and we do not see what effect it could be expected to have upon persons subject to the draft except to influence them to obstruct the carrying of it out. The defendants do not deny that the jury might find against them on this point.

But it is said, suppose that that was the tendency of this circular, it is protected by the First Amendment to the Constitution. . . . We admit that in many places and in ordinary times the defendants in saying all that was said in the circular would have been within their constitutional rights. But the character of every act depends upon the circumstances in which it is done. The most stringent protection of free speech would not protect a man in falsely shouting fire in a theater and causing a panic. . . . The question in every case is whether the words used are used in such circumstances and are of such a nature as to create a clear and present danger that they will bring about the substantive evils that Congress has a right to prevent. It is a question of proximity and degree. When a nation is at war many things that might be said in time of peace are such a hindrance to its effort that their utterance will not be endured so long as men fight and that no Court could regard them as protected by any constitutional right. It seems to be admitted that if an actual obstruction of the recruiting service were proved, liability for words that produced that effect might be enforced. The statute of 1917 punishes conspiracies to obstruct as well as actual obstruction. If the act (speaking, or circulating a paper), its tendency, and the intent with which it is done are the same, we perceive no ground for saying that success alone warrants making the act a crime. . . .

Judgments affirmed.

Discussion Questions

1. This opinion is famous for setting out the much-cited "clear and present danger" test, requiring both "proximity and degree" to social harm before speech can be punished. This test is also applied in Justice Brandeis's concurrence in *Whitney* (above). Review Brandeis's opinion in that case and determine whether you think the clear and present danger test was actually applied by Justice Holmes in *Schenck*.
2. Justice Holmes states, "If the act (speaking, or circulating a paper), its tendency, and the intent with which it is done are all the same, we perceive no ground for saying that success alone warrants making the act a crime." What does the tendency of an act and the intent with which it is done have to do with clear and present danger?

Brandenburg v. *Ohio*
395 U.S. 444 (1969)

Per Curiam.

The appellant, a leader of a Ku Klux Klan group, was convicted under the Ohio Criminal Syndicalism statute for "advocat(ing) . . . the duty, necessity, or propriety of crime, sabotage, violence, or unlawful methods of terrorism as a means of accomplishing industrial or political reform" and for "voluntarily assembl(ing) with any society, group, or assemblage of persons formed to teach or advocate the doctrines of criminal syndicalism." He was fined $1,000 and sentenced to 1 to 10 years' imprisonment. The appellant challenged the constitutionality of the criminal syndicalism statute under the First and Fourteenth Amendments to the United States Constitution, but the intermediate appellate court of Ohio affirmed his conviction without opinion. The Supreme Court of Ohio dismissed his appeal, sua sponte, "for the reason that no substantial constitutional question exists herein." It did not file an opinion or explain its conclusions. Appeal was taken to this Court, and we noted probable jurisdiction. We reverse.

The record shows that a man, identified at trial as the appellant, telephoned an announcer-reporter on the staff of a Cincinnati television station and invited him to come to a Ku Klux Klan "rally" to be held at a farm in Hamilton County. With the cooperation of the organizers, the reporter and a cameraman attended the meeting and filmed the events. Portions of the films were later broadcast on the local station and on a national network.

The prosecution's case rested on the films and on testimony identifying the appellant as the person who communicated with the reporter and who spoke at the rally. The State also introduced into evidence several articles appearing in the film, including a pistol, a rifle, a shotgun, ammunition, a Bible, and a red hood worn by the speaker in the films.

One film showed 12 hooded figures, some of whom carried firearms. They were gathered around a large wooden cross, which they burned. No one was present other than the participants and the newsmen who made the film. Most of the words uttered during the scene were incomprehensible when the film was projected, but scattered phrases could be understood that were derogatory of Negroes and, in one instance, of Jews. Another scene on the same film showed the appellant, in Klan regalia, making a speech. The speech, in full, was as follows:

This is an organizers' meeting. We have had quite a few members here today which are—we have hundreds, hundreds of members throughout the State of Ohio. I can quote from a newspaper clipping from the Columbus, Ohio, Dispatch, five weeks ago Sunday morning. The Klan has more members in the State of Ohio than does any other organization. We're not a revengent organization, but if our President, our Congress, our Supreme Court, continues to suppress the white, Caucasian race, it's possible that there might have to be some revenge-ance taken.

We are marching on Congress July the Fourth, four hundred thousand strong. From there we are dividing into two groups, one group to march on St. Augustine, Florida, the other group to march into Mississippi. Thank you.

The second film showed six hooded figures one of whom, later identified as the appellant, repeated a speech very similar to that recorded on the first film. The reference to the possibility of "revengeance" was omitted, and one sentence was added: "Personally, I believe the nigger should be returned to Africa, the Jew returned to Israel." Though some of the figures in the films carried weapons, the speaker did not.

The Ohio Criminal Syndicalism Statute was enacted in 1919. From 1917 to 1920, identical or quite similar laws were adopted by 20 States and two territories. In 1927, this Court sustained the constitutionality of California's Criminal Syndicalism Act, the text of which is quite similar to that of the laws of Ohio [*Whitney* v. *California*]. The Court upheld the statute on the ground that, without more, "advocating" violent means to effect political and economic change involves such danger to the security of the State that the State may outlaw it. But *Whitney* has been thoroughly discredited by later decisions. These later decisions have fashioned the principle that the constitutional guarantees of free speech and free press do not permit a State to forbid or proscribe advocacy of the use of force or of law violation except where such advocacy is directed to inciting or producing imminent lawless action and is likely to incite or produce such action. As we said in *Noto* v. *United States*, "the mere abstract teaching . . . of the moral propriety or even moral necessity for a resort to force and violence, is not the same as preparing a group for violent action and steeling it to such action." A statute which fails to draw this distinction impermissibly intrudes upon the freedoms guaranteed by the First and Fourteenth Amendments. It sweeps within its condemnation speech which our Constitution has immunized from governmental control.

Measured by this test, Ohio's Criminal Syndicalism Act cannot be sustained. The Act punishes persons who "advocate or teach the duty, necessity, or propriety [of violence] as a means of accomplishing industrial or political reform"; or who publish or circulate or display any book or paper containing such advocacy; or who "justify" the commission of violent acts "with intent to exemplify, spread, or advocate the propriety of the doctrines of criminal syndicalism"; or who "voluntarily assemble" with a group formed "to teach or advocate the doctrines of criminal syndicalism." Neither the indictment nor the trial judge's instructions to the jury in any way refined the statute's bald definition of the crime in terms of mere advocacy not distinguished from incitement to imminent lawless action.

Accordingly, we are here confronted with a statute which, by its own words and as applied, purports to punish mere advocacy and to forbid, on pain of criminal punishment, assembly with others merely to advocate the described type of action. Such a statute falls within the condemnation of the First and Fourteenth Amendments. The contrary teaching of *Whitney* v. *California* cannot be supported, and that decision is therefore overruled.

Discussion Questions

1. What is the general standard that emerges from this case for punishment of speech advocating law violation? Would Schenck's conviction be upheld under this standard? How does it relate to Brandeis's opinion in *Whitney*?

2. Some commentators have argued that the Court went *too* far in *Brandenburg*, that some forms of speech short of incitement to riot should be punishable consistent with the First Amendment. How would you apply this test to a manual on bomb construction or assassination published by a paramilitary or terrorist group? What of publication of a "how to" manual for construction of a nuclear weapon? (See *United States* v. *Progressive, Inc.*, 467 F. Supp. 990 [W.D. Wis. 1979].) What of a campus speaker who declares "open season on Blacks" and urges students to assault minority students to coerce them into withdrawing from the university?

"FIGHTING WORDS" AND THE RELATED PROBLEM OF THE HOSTILE AUDIENCE

Chaplinsky v. *New Hampshire*
315 U.S. 568 (1942)

Mr. Justice Murphy delivered the opinion of the Court.

Appellant, a member of the sect known as Jehovah's Witnesses, was convicted in the municipal court of Rochester, New Hampshire, for violation of Chapter 378, Section 2, of the Public Laws of New Hampshire: "No person shall address any offensive, derisive, or annoying word to any other person who is lawfully in any street or other public place, nor call him by any offensive or derisive name, nor make any noise or exclamation in his presence and hearing with intent to deride, offend, or annoy him, or to prevent him from pursuing his lawful business or occupation."

The complaint charged that appellant "with force and arms, in a certain public place in said city of Rochester, to wit, on the public sidewalk . . . , did unlawfully repeat, the words following, addressed to the complainant, that is to say, 'You are a God damned racketeer' and 'a damned Fascist and the whole government of Rochester are Fascists or agents of Fascists' the same being offensive, derisive, and annoying words and names." . . .

There is no substantial dispute over the facts. Chaplinsky was distributing the literature of his sect on the streets of Rochester on a busy Saturday afternoon. Members of the local citizenry complained to the City Marshal, Bowering, that Chaplinsky was denouncing all religion as a "racket." Bowering told them that Chaplinsky was lawfully engaged, and then warned Chaplinsky that the crowd was getting restless. Some time later a disturbance occurred and the traffic officer on duty at the busy intersection started with Chaplinsky for the police station, but did not inform him that he was under arrest or that he was going to be arrested. On the way they encountered Marshal Bowering who had been advised that a riot was under way and was therefore hurrying to the scene. Bowering repeated his earlier warning to Chaplinsky who then addressed to Bowering the words set forth in the complaint. . . .

Appellant here pitches his argument on the due process clause of the Fourteenth Amendment. Allowing the broadest scope to the language and purpose of the Fourteenth Amendment, it is well understood that the right of free speech is not absolute at all times and under all circumstances. There are certain well-defined and narrowly limited classes of speech, the prevention and punishment of which has never been thought to raise any Constitutional problem. These include the lewd and obscene, the profane, the libelous, and the insulting or "fighting" words—those which by their very utterance inflict injury or tend to incite an immediate breach of the peace. It has been well observed that such utterances are no essential part of any exposition of ideas, and are of such slight social value as a step to truth that any benefit that may be derived from them is clearly outweighed by the social interest in order and morality. "Resort to epithets or personal abuse is not in any proper sense communication of information or opinion safeguarded by the Constitution, and its punishment as a criminal act would raise no question under that in-strument."

The state statute here challenged comes to us authoritatively construed by the highest court of New Hampshire. It has two provisions—the first relates to words or names addressed to another in a public place; the second refers to noises and exclamations. . . .

On the authority of its earlier decisions, the state court declared that the statute's purpose was to preserve the public peace, no words being "forbidden except such as have a direct tendency to cause acts of violence by the person to whom, individually, the remark is addressed." It was further said: "The word 'offensive' is not to be defined in terms of what a particular addressee thinks. . . . The test is what men of common intelligence would understand would be words likely to cause an average addressee to fight. . . . The English language has a number of words and expressions which by general consent are 'fighting words' when said without a disarming smile. . . . Such words, as ordinary men know, are likely to cause a fight. So are threatening, profane, or obscene revilings. Derisive and annoying words can be taken as coming within the purview of the statute as heretofore interpreted only when they have this characteristic of plainly tending to excite the addressee to a breach of the peace. . . . The statute, as construed, does no more than prohibit the face-to-face words plainly likely to cause a breach of the peace by the addressee, words whose speaking constitute a breach of the peace by the speaker—including 'classical fighting words,' words in current use less 'classical' but equally likely to cause violence, and other disorderly words, including profan-ity, obscenity, and threats."

We are unable to say that the limited scope of the statute as thus construed contravenes the constitutional right of free expression. It is a statute narrowly drawn and limited to define and punish specific conduct lying within the do-main of state power, the use in a public place of words likely to cause a breach of the peace. This conclusion necessarily disposes of appellant's contention that the statute is so vague and indefinite as to render a conviction thereunder a violation of due process. A statute punishing verbal acts, carefully drawn so as not unduly to impair liberty of expression, is not too vague for a criminal law.

Appellant need not therefore have been a prophet to understand what the statute condemned. Nor can we say that the application of the statute to the facts disclosed by the record substantially or unreasonably impinges upon the privilege of free speech. Argument is unnecessary to demonstrate that the appellations "damn racketeer" and "damn Fascist" are epithets likely to provoke the average person to retaliation, and thereby cause a breach of the peace. The refusal of the state court to admit evidence of provocation and evidence bearing on the truth or falsity of the utterances is open to no Constitutional objection. Whether the facts sought to be proved by such evidence constitute a defense to the charge or may be shown in mitigation are questions for the state court to determine. Our function is fulfilled by a determination that the challenged statute, on its face and as applied, does not contravene the Fourteenth Amendment.

Affirmed.

Discussion Questions

1. The *Chaplinsky* case is famous for its establishment of a "fighting words" exception from First Amendment protection. It is perhaps the major case relied upon by universities seeking to regulate hate speech. However, the exact meaning of the term "fighting words" is ambiguous in the decision, a situation that has caused confusion in subsequent cases and commentary. There are two different formulations of the concept in the *Chaplinsky* decision: (1) words "which by their very utterance inflict injury or tend to incite an immediate breach of the peace"; and (2) words that "have a direct tendency to cause acts of violence by the person to whom, individually, the remark is addressed."

   What different elements of fighting words emerge from these definitions? Which are necessary, and which are sufficient, conditions for expression to fit within the category? In thinking about these issues, consider the following hypothetical situations, asking yourself whether they involve unprotected "fighting words" that might be punished by a state university administration, consistent with the First Amendment:

   a. Use of the word "nigger" by a speaker at a campus Ku Klux Klan rally attended only by members of the Klan

b. Use of the word "faggot" in an inflammatory editorial published by a student newspaper sponsored by a campus right-wing political group

c. Use of the word "Jew-boy" by an anti-Semitic student speaking to a mixed campus audience

d. A cross burning held on campus as part of a Ku Klux Klan rally open to all students

e. The hanging of a swastika flag on a dormitory door or from a dorm window

f. Use of the word "bitch" as an insult by a football player to a diminutive female student

Answers to these questions require sorting out the following competing elements in the notion of fighting words:

a. Whether the threat of direct, macho-like violence is essential (something that may be missing in all of the hypotheticals, especially f)

b. Whether fighting words are restricted to individual, "in-your-face," spoken insults, or whether they also apply when uttered (or, perhaps, published or displayed) to a larger audience (of relevance to all but f)

c. Whether fighting "words" can include symbols and other forms of nonverbal communication (relevant to d and e)

d. The role of injury in the notion of fighting words (relevant to all hypotheticals)

2. Contrast the following two hypothetical statements addressed to a black freshman at an elite university in light of *Chaplinsky*:

a. LeVon, if you find yourself struggling in your classes here, you should realize it isn't your fault. It's simply that you're the beneficiary of a disruptive policy of affirmative action that places underqualified, underprepared, and often undertalented black students in demanding educational environments like this one. The policy's egalitarian aims may be well-intentioned, but given the fact that aptitude tests place African-Americans almost a full standard deviation below the mean, and even controlling for socioeconomic disparities, they are also profoundly misguided. The truth is, you probably don't belong here, and your college experience will be a long downhill slide.

b. Out of my face, jungle bunny.[1]

Which of the two statements is likely to be the most hurtful? Which would fall within the fighting words exception of *Chaplinsky*? What, if anything, does this tell you about the utility of the fighting words concept to the problem of campus hate speech?

Gooding v. *Wilson*
405 U.S. 518 (1972)

The defendant was one of a group of persons who, on August 18, 1966, pick- eted the building in which the 12th Corps Headquarters of the United States Army was located, carrying signs opposing the war in Vietnam. When the inductees arrived at the building, these persons began to block the door so that the inductees could not enter. They were requested by police officers to move from the door, but refused to do so. The officers attempted to remove them from the door, and a scuffle ensued. . . . Count 3 of the indictment al- leged that the accused "did without provocation use to and of M. G. Redding and in his presence, the following abusive language and opprobrious words, tending to cause a breach of the peace: 'White son of a bitch, I'll kill you. You son of a bitch, I'll choke you to death.' " Count 4 alleged that the defendant "did without provocation use to and of T. L. Raborn, and in his presence, the following abusive language and opprobrious words, tending to cause a breach of the peace: 'You son of a bitch, if you ever put your hands on me again, I'll cut you all to pieces.' " [From footnote by the Court.]

Mr. Justice Brennan delivered the opinion of the Court.

Appellee was convicted in Superior Court, Fulton County, Georgia, on two counts of using opprobrious words and abusive language in violation of Geor- gia Code Ann. s 26–6303, which provides: "Any person who shall, without provocation, use to or of another, and in his presence . . . opprobrious words or abusive language, tending to cause a breach of the peace . . . shall be guilty of a misdemeanor."

Section 26–6303 punishes only spoken words. It can therefore withstand appellee's attack upon its facial constitutionality only if, as authoritatively construed by the Georgia courts, it is not susceptible of application to speech, although vulgar or offensive, that is protected by the First and Fourteenth Amendments [*Cohen* v. *California*].

Although a statute may be neither vague, overbroad, nor otherwise invalid as applied to the conduct charged against a particular defendant, he is permit- ted to raise its vagueness or unconstitutional overbreadth as applied to others. And if the law is found deficient in one of these respects, it may not be applied to him either, until and unless a satisfactory limiting construction is placed on the statute. The statute, in effect, is stricken down on its face. This result is deemed justified since the otherwise continued existence of the statute in unnarrowed form would tend to suppress constitutionally protected rights. "The constitutional guarantees of freedom of speech forbid the States to punish the use of words or language not within narrowly limited classes of speech" [*Chaplinsky*]. Even as to such a class, however, . . . the statute must be carefully drawn or be authoritatively construed to punish only unprotected speech and not be susceptible of application to protected expression. Because First Amendment freedoms need breathing space to survive, government may regulate in the area only with narrow specificity.

Appellant does not challenge these principles but contends that the Georgia statute is narrowly drawn to apply only to a constitutionally unprotected class of words—"fighting words"—"those which by their very utterance inflict injury or tend to incite an immediate breach of the peace" [*Chaplinsky*]. . . .

Appellant argues that the Georgia appellate courts have by construction limited the proscription of s 26–6303 to "fighting" words, as the New Hampshire Supreme Court limited the New Hampshire statute. We have, however, made our own examination of the Georgia cases, both those cited and others discovered in research. That examination brings us to the conclusion, in agreement with the courts below, that the Georgia appellate decisions have not construed 26–6303 to be limited in application, as in *Chaplinsky*, to words that "have a direct tendency to cause acts of violence by the person to whom, individually, the remark is addressed."

The dictionary definitions of "opprobrious" and "abusive" give them greater reach than "fighting" words. *Webster's Third New International Dictionary* (1961) defines "opprobrious" as "conveying or intended to convey disgrace," and "abusive" as including "harsh insulting language." Georgia appellate decisions have construed 26–6303 to apply to utterances that, although within these definitions, are not "fighting" words as *Chaplinsky* defines them. . . .

Because earlier appellate decisions applied 26–6303 to utterances where there was no likelihood that the person addressed would make an immediate violent response, it is clear that the standard allowing juries to determine guilt "measured by common understanding and practice" does not limit the application of 26–6303 to "fighting" words defined by *Chaplinsky*. Rather, that broad standard effectively "licenses the jury to create its own standard in each case." Accordingly, we agree with the conclusion of the District Court, "[T]he fault of the statute is that it leaves wide open the standard of responsibility, so that it is easily susceptible to improper application." Unlike the construction of the New Hampshire statute by the New Hampshire Supreme Court, the Georgia appellate courts have not construed 26–6303 so as to avoid all constitutional difficulties.

Affirmed.

Mr. Justice Blackmun, with whom the Chief Justice joins, dissenting.

It seems strange, indeed, that in this day a man may say to a police officer, who is attempting to restore access to a public building, "White son of a bitch, I'll kill you" and "You son of a bitch, I'll choke you to death," and say to an accompanying officer, "You son of a bitch, if you ever put your hands on me again, I'll cut you all to pieces," and yet constitutionally cannot be prosecuted and convicted under a state statute that makes it a misdemeanor to "use to or of another, and in his presence . . . opprobrious words or abusive language, tending to cause a breach of the peace. . . ." This, however, is precisely what the Court pronounces as the law today.

The Supreme Court of Georgia, when the conviction was appealed, unanimously held the other way. Surely any adult who can read—and I do not exclude this appellee-defendant from that category—should reasonably expect no other conclusion. The words of Georgia Code s 26–6303 are clear. They are also concise. They are not, in my view, overbroad or incapable of being understood. Except perhaps for the "big" word "opprobrious"—and no point is made of its bigness—any Georgia schoolboy would expect that this defendant's fighting and provocative words to the officers were covered by s 26–6303. Common sense permits no other conclusion. This is demonstrated by the fact that the appellee, and this Court, attack the statute, not as it applies to the appellee, but as it conceivably might apply to others who might utter other words.

The Court reaches its result by saying that the Georgia statute has been interpreted by the State's courts so as to be applicable in practice to otherwise constitutionally protected speech. It follows, says the Court, that the statute is overbroad and therefore is facially unconstitutional and to be struck down in its entirety. Thus Georgia apparently is to be left with no valid statute on its books to meet Wilson's bullying tactic. This result, achieved by what is indeed a very strict construction, will be totally incomprehensible to the State of Georgia, to its courts, and to its citizens. . . .

For me, *Chaplinsky* v. *New Hampshire* was good law when it was decided and deserves to remain as good law now. A unanimous Court, including among its members Chief Justice Stone and Justices Black, Reed, Douglas, and Murphy, obviously thought it was good law. But I feel that by decisions such as this one and, indeed, *Cohen* v. *California,* the Court, despite its protestations to the contrary, is merely paying lip service to *Chaplinsky.* As the appellee states in a footnote to his brief, "Although there is no doubt that the state can punish 'fighting words' this appears to be about all that is left of the decision in *Chaplinsky.*" If this is what the overbreadth doctrine means, and if this is what it produces, it urgently needs re-examination. The Court has painted itself into a corner from which it, and the States, can extricate themselves only with difficulty.

Discussion Questions

1. Does this decision seem consistent with *Chaplinsky?* Or does it, as the dissent suggests, cast into doubt the validity of *Chaplinsky*'s fighting words doctrine?

2. Is the court saying that the defendant's words, spoken while being arrested, were constitutionally protected? Or could the defendant be punished for uttering those words under a different, presumably more specific, statute? If so, what might such a statute look like?

Feiner v. *New York*
340 U.S. 315 (1951)

Mr. Chief Justice Vinson delivered the opinion of the Court.

Petitioner was convicted of the offense of disorderly conduct, a misdemeanor under the New York penal laws . . . and was sentenced to thirty days in the county penitentiary. . . .

On the evening of March 8, 1949, petitioner Irving Feiner was addressing an open-air meeting at the corner of South McBride and Harrison Streets in the City of Syracuse. At approximately 6:30 P.M., the police received a telephone complaint concerning the meeting, and two officers were detailed to investigate. One of these officers went to the scene immediately, the other arriving some twelve minutes later. They found a crowd of about seventy-five or eighty people, both Negro and white, filling the sidewalk and spreading out into the street. Petitioner, . . . standing on a large wooden box on the sidewalk, was addressing the crowd through a loud-speaker system attached to an automobile. Although the purpose of his speech was to urge his listeners to attend a meeting to be held that night in the Syracuse Hotel, in its course he was making derogatory remarks concerning President Truman, the American Legion, the Mayor of Syracuse, and other local political officials. . . . The police officers made no effort to interfere with petitioner's speech, but were first concerned with the effect of the crowd on both pedestrian and vehicular traffic. They observed the situation from the opposite side of the street, noting that some pedestrians were forced to walk in the street to avoid the crowd. Since traffic was passing at the time, the officers attempted to get the people listening to petitioner back on the sidewalk. The crowd was restless and there was some pushing, shoving, and milling around. One of the officers telephoned the police station from a nearby store, and then both policemen crossed the street and mingled with the crowd without any intention of arresting the speaker.

At this time, petitioner was speaking in a "loud, high-pitched voice." He gave the impression that he was endeavoring to arouse the Negro people against the whites, urging that they rise up in arms and fight for equal rights. The statements before such a mixed audience "stirred up a little excitement." Some of the onlookers made remarks to the police about their inability to handle the crowd and at least one threatened violence if the police did not act. There were others who appeared to be favoring petitioner's arguments. Because of the feeling that existed in the crowd both for and against the speaker, the officers finally "stepped in to prevent it from resulting in a fight." One of the officers approached the petitioner, not for the purpose of arresting him, but to get him to break up the crowd. He asked petitioner to get down . . . off the box, but the latter refused to accede to his request and continued talking. The officer waited for a minute and then demanded that he cease talking. Although the officer had thus twice requested petitioner to stop over the course of several minutes, petitioner not only ignored him but continued talking. During all this time, the crowd was pressing closer around petitioner and the officer. Finally, the officer told petitioner he was under arrest and ordered him to get down from the box, reaching up to grab him. Petitioner stepped down, announcing over the microphone that "the law has arrived, and I suppose they will take over now." In all, the officer had asked petitioner to get down off the box three times over a space of four or five minutes. Petitioner had been speaking for over a half hour.

On these facts, petitioner was specifically charged with violation of s 722 of the Penal Law of New York ["Any person who with intent to provoke a breach of the peace, or whereby a breach of the peace may be occasioned, commits any of the following acts shall be deemed to have committed the offense of disorderly conduct: 1. Uses offensive, disorderly, threatening, abusive, or insulting language, conduct or behavior; 2. Acts in such a manner as to annoy, disturb, interfere with, obstruct, or be offensive to others; 3. Congregates with others on a public street and refuses to move on when ordered by the police"]. The bill of particulars . . . gave in detail the facts upon which the prosecution relied to support the charge of disorderly conduct. . . . "By ignoring and refusing to heed and obey reasonable police orders issued at the time and place mentioned in the Information to regulate and control said crowd and to prevent a breach or breaches of the peace and to prevent injury to pedestrians . . . attempting to use said walk, and being forced into the highway adjacent to the place in question, and prevent injury to the public generally."

We are not faced here with blind condonation by a state court of arbitrary police action. Petitioner was accorded a full, fair trial. The trial judge heard testimony supporting and contradicting the judgment of the police officers that a clear danger of disorder was threatened. After weighing this contradictory evidence, the trial judge reached the conclusion that the police officers were justified in taking action . . . to prevent a breach of the peace. The exercise of the police officers' proper discretionary power to prevent a breach of the peace was thus approved by the trial court and later by two courts on review. The courts below recognized petitioner's right to hold a street meeting at this locality, to make use of loud-speaking equipment in giving his speech, and to make derogatory remarks concerning public officials and the American Legion. They found that the officers in making the arrest were motivated solely by a proper concern for the preservation of order and protection of the general welfare, and that there was no evidence which could lend color to a claim that the acts of the police were a cover for suppression of petitioner's views and opinions. Petitioner was thus neither arrested nor convicted for the . . . making or the content of his speech. Rather, it was the reaction which it actually engendered.

The language of *Cantwell* v. *Connecticut* is appropriate here. "The offense known as breach of the peace embraces a great variety of conduct destroying or menacing public order and tranquillity. It includes not only violent acts but acts and words likely to produce violence in others. No one would have the hardihood to suggest that the principle of freedom of speech sanctions incitement to riot or that religious liberty connotes the privilege to exhort others to physical attack upon those belonging to another sect. When clear and present danger of riot, disorder, interference with traffic upon the public streets, or other immediate threat to public safety, peace, or order, appears, the power of the State to prevent or punish is obvious." The findings of the New York courts as to the condition of the crowd and the refusal of petitioner to obey the police requests, supported as they are by the record of this case, are persuasive that the conviction of petitioner for violation of public peace, order, and authority does not exceed the bounds of proper state police action. This Court respects, as it must, the interest of the community in maintaining peace and order on its streets. We cannot say that the preservation of that interest here encroaches on the constitutional rights of this petitioner.

We are well aware that the ordinary murmurings and objections of a hostile audience cannot be allowed to silence a speaker, and are also mindful of the possible danger of giving overzealous police officials complete discretion to break up otherwise lawful public meetings. "A State may not unduly suppress free communication of views, religious or other, under the guise of conserving desirable conditions" [*Cantwell*]. But we are not faced here with such a situation. It is one thing to say that the police cannot be used as an instrument for the suppression of unpopular views, and another to say that, when as here the speaker passes the bounds of argument or persuasion and undertakes incitement to riot, they are powerless to prevent a breach of the peace. Nor in this case can we condemn the considered judgment of three . . . New York courts approving the means which the police, faced with a crisis, used in the exercise of their power and duty to preserve peace and order. The findings of the state courts as to the existing situation and the imminence of greater disorder coupled with petitioner's deliberate defiance of the police officers convince us that we should not reverse this conviction in the name of free speech.

Affirmed.

Mr. Justice Black, dissenting.

The record before us convinces me that petitioner, a young college student, has been sentenced to the penitentiary for the unpopular views he expressed on matters of public interest while lawfully making a street-corner . . . speech in Syracuse, New York. Today's decision, however, indicates that we must blind ourselves to this fact because the trial judge fully accepted the testimony of the prosecution witnesses on all important points. Many times in the past this Court has said that despite findings below, we will examine the evidence for ourselves to ascertain whether federally protected rights have been denied; otherwise review here would fail of its purpose in safeguarding constitutional guarantees. Even a partial . . . abandonment of this rule marks a dark day for civil liberties in our Nation.

But still more has been lost today. Even accepting every "finding of fact" below, I . . . think this conviction makes a mockery of the free speech guarantees of the First and Fourteenth Amendments. The end result of the affirmance here is to approve a simple and readily available technique by which cities and states can with impunity subject all speeches, political or otherwise, on streets or elsewhere, to the supervision and censorship of the local police. I will have no part or parcel in this holding which I view as a long step toward totalitarian authority. . . .

The Court's opinion apparently rests on this reasoning: The policeman, under the circumstances detailed, could reasonably conclude that serious fighting or even riot was imminent; therefore he could stop petitioner's speech to prevent a breach of peace; accordingly, it was "disorderly conduct" for petitioner to continue speaking in disobedience of the officer's request. As to the existence of a dangerous situation on the street corner, it seems farfetched to suggest that the "facts" show any imminent threat of riot or uncontrollable disorder. It . . . is neither unusual nor unexpected that some people at public street meetings mutter, mill about, push, shove, or disagree, even violently, with the speaker. Indeed, it is rare where controversial topics are discussed that an outdoor crowd does not do some or all of these things. Nor does one isolated threat to assault the speaker forebode disorder. Especially should the danger be discounted where, as here, the person threatening was a man whose wife and two small children accompanied him and who, so far as the record shows, was never close enough to petitioner to carry out the threat.

Moreover, assuming that the "facts" did indicate a critical situation, I reject the implication of the Court's opinion that the police had no obligation to protect petitioner's . . . constitutional right to talk. The police of course have power to prevent breaches of the peace. But if, in the name of preserving order, they ever can interfere with a lawful public speaker, they first must make all reasonable efforts to protect him. Here the policemen did not even pretend to try to protect petitioner. According to the officers' testimony, the crowd was restless but there is . . . no showing of any attempt to quiet it; pedestrians were forced to walk into the street, but there was no effort to clear a path on the sidewalk; one person threatened to assault petitioner but the officers did nothing to discourage this when even a word might have sufficed. Their duty was to protect petitioner's right to talk, even to the extent of arresting the man who threatened to interfere. Instead, they shirked that duty and acted only to suppress the right to speak.

Finally, I cannot agree with the Court's statement that petitioner's disregard of the policeman's unexplained request amounted to such "deliberate defiance" as would justify an arrest or conviction for disorderly conduct. On the contrary, I think that the policeman's action was a "deliberate defiance" of ordinary official duty as well as of the constitutional right of free speech. For at least where time allows, courtesy and explanation of commands are basic elements of good official conduct in a democratic society. Here petitioner was "asked" then "told" then "commanded" to stop speaking, but a man making a lawful address is certainly not required to be silent merely . . . because an officer directs it. Petitioner was entitled to know why he should cease doing a lawful act. Not once was he told. I understand that people in authoritarian countries must obey arbitrary orders. I had hoped that there was no such duty in the United States.

In my judgment, today's holding means that as a practical matter, minority speakers can be silenced in any city. Hereafter, despite the First and Fourteenth Amendments, the policeman's club can take heavy toll of a current administration's public critics. Criticism of public officials will be too dangerous for all but the most . . . courageous. . . . In this case I would reverse the conviction.

Discussion Questions

1. This was a 1951 decision. Do you think this conviction would withstand judicial scrutiny today, in light of *Brandenburg*?
2. Justice Black, in dissent, suggests that the police officer's first duty should have been to protect the speaker from a hostile audience. He argues that the danger of a riot in the circumstances of this case was very low. What if the risks of riot were much greater? Under what circumstances should the police silence a speaker—whose speech is constitutionally protected— because of a hostile audience reaction?
3. Would your view of this case be different if Feiner were an African-American civil rights worker speaking about unjust and "racist" laws to a mixed (and ominously grumbling) crowd in the 1960s South? What if a real riot, brought about by KKK members in the crowd, was seriously threatened?
4. Does *Feiner* support university decisions to keep highly controversial or extremist speakers off university campuses in order to avoid a hostile audience reaction and possible violence?

Note

1. The hypotheticals were quoted directly from Henry Louis Gates Jr., *Let Them Talk*, New Republic 37 (27 September 1993), at 45.

OFFENSIVE AND HURTFUL SPEECH

Cohen v. California
403 U.S. 15 (1971)

Cohen was observed in the Los Angeles County Courthouse wearing a jacket bearing the words "Fuck the Draft." He was arrested and convicted of violating that part of California Penal Code which prohibits "maliciously and willfully disturb[ing] the peace or quiet of any neighborhood or person . . . by . . . offensive conduct."

Mr. Justice Harlan delivered the opinion of the Court.

This case may seem at first blush too inconsequential to find its way into our books, but the issue it presents is of no small constitutional significance. . . .

I

In order to lay hands on the precise issue which this case involves, it is useful first to canvass various matters which this record does not present. The conviction quite clearly rests upon the asserted offensiveness of the words Cohen used to convey his message to the public. The only "conduct" which the State sought to punish is the fact of communication. Thus, we deal here with a conviction resting solely upon "speech," not upon any separately identifiable conduct which allegedly was intended by Cohen to be perceived by others as expressive of particular views but which, on its face, does not necessarily convey any message and hence arguably could be regulated without effectively repressing Cohen's ability to express himself. Further, the State certainly lacks power to punish Cohen for the underlying content of the message the inscription conveyed. At least so long as there is no showing of an intent to incite disobedience to or disruption of the draft, Cohen could not, consistently with the First and Fourteenth Amendments, be punished for asserting the evident position on the inutility or immorality of the draft his jacket reflected.

Appellant's conviction, then, rests squarely upon his exercise of the "freedom of speech" protected from arbitrary governmental interference by the Constitution and can be justified, if at all, only as a valid regulation of the manner in which he exercised that freedom, not as a permissible prohibition on the substantive message it conveys. This does not end the inquiry, of course, for the First and Fourteenth Amendments have never been thought to give absolute protection to every individual to speak whenever or wherever he pleases or to use any form of address in any circumstances that he chooses. In this vein, too, however, we think it important to note that several issues typically associated with such problems are not presented here. In the first place, Cohen was tried under a statute applicable throughout the entire State. Any attempt to support this conviction on the ground that the statute seeks to preserve an appropriately decorous atmosphere in the courthouse where Cohen was arrested must fail in the absence of any language in the statute that would have put appellant on notice that certain kinds of otherwise permissible speech or conduct would nevertheless, under California law, not be tolerated in certain places. No fair reading of the phrase "offensive conduct" can be said sufficiently to inform the ordinary person that distinctions between certain locations are thereby created.

In the second place, as it comes to us, this case cannot be said to fall within those relatively few categories of instances where prior decisions have established the power of government to deal more comprehensively with certain forms of individual expression simply upon a showing that such a form was employed. This is not, for example, an obscenity case. Whatever else may be necessary to give rise to the States' broader power to prohibit obscene expression, such expression must be, in some significant way, erotic. It cannot plausibly be maintained that this vulgar allusion to the Selective Service System would conjure up such psychic stimulation in anyone likely to be confronted with Cohen's crudely defaced jacket. This Court has also held that the States are free to ban the simple use, without a demonstration of additional justifying circumstances, of so-called "fighting words," those personally abusive epithets which, when addressed to the ordinary citizen, are, as a matter of common knowledge, inherently likely to provoke violent reaction [Chaplinsky]. While the four-letter word displayed by Cohen in relation to the draft is not uncommonly employed in a personally provocative fashion, in this instance it was clearly not "directed to the person of the hearer" [Cantwell]. No individual actually or likely to be present could reasonably have regarded the words on appellant's jacket as a direct personal insult. Nor do we have here an instance of the exercise of the State's police power to prevent a speaker from intentionally provoking a given group to hostile reaction [Feiner]. There is, as noted above, no showing that anyone who saw Cohen was in fact violently aroused or that appellant intended such a result.

Finally, in arguments before this Court much has been made of the claim

that Cohen's distasteful mode of expression was thrust upon unwilling or un-
suspecting viewers, and that the State might therefore legitimately act as it
did in order to protect the sensitive from otherwise unavoidable exposure to
appellant's crude form of protest. Of course, the mere presumed presence of
unwitting listeners or viewers does not serve automatically to justify curtailing
all speech capable of giving offense. While this Court has recognized that
government may properly act in many situations to prohibit intrusion into the
privacy of the home of unwelcome views and ideas which cannot be totally
banned from the public dialogue, we have at the same time consistently
stressed that "we are often 'captives' outside the sanctuary of the home and
subject to objectionable speech." The ability of government, consonant with
the Constitution, to shut off discourse solely to protect others from hearing it
is, in other words, dependent upon a showing that substantial privacy interests
are being invaded in an essentially intolerable manner. Any broader view of
this authority would effectively empower a majority to silence dissidents simply as a matter of personal predilections. In this regard, persons confronted
with Cohen's jacket were in a quite different posture than, say, those subjected
to the raucous emissions of sound trucks blaring outside their residences.
Those in the Los Angeles courthouse could effectively avoid further bombard-
ment of their sensibilities simply by averting their eyes. And, while it may be
that one has a more substantial claim to a recognizable privacy interest when
walking through a courthouse corridor than, for example, strolling through
Central Park, surely it is nothing like the interest in being free from unwanted
expression in the confines of one's own home. Given the subtlety and complexity of the factors involved, if Cohen's "speech" was otherwise entitled to
constitutional protection, we do not think the fact that some unwilling "listeners" in a public building may have been briefly exposed to it can serve to
justify this breach of the peace conviction where, as here, there was no evidence that persons powerless to avoid appellant's conduct did in fact object to
it, and where that portion of the statute upon which Cohen's conviction rests
evinces no concern, either on its face or as construed by the California courts,
with the special plight of the captive auditor, but, instead, indiscriminately
sweeps within its prohibitions all "offensive conduct" that disturbs "any
neighborhood or person."

II

Against this background, the issue flushed by this case stands out in bold
relief. It is whether California can excise, as "offensive conduct," one particular scurrilous epithet from the public discourse, either upon the theory of the

court below that its use is inherently likely to cause violent reaction or upon a more general assertion that the States, acting as guardians of public morality, may properly remove this offensive word from the public vocabulary. The rationale of the California court is plainly untenable. At most it reflects an "undifferentiated fear or apprehension of disturbance (which) is not enough to overcome the right to freedom of expression" [*Tinker*]. We have been shown no evidence that substantial numbers of citizens are standing ready to strike out physically at whoever may assault their sensibilities with execrations like that uttered by Cohen. There may be some persons about with such lawless and violent proclivities, but that is an insufficient base upon which to erect, consistently with constitutional values, a governmental power to force persons who wish to ventilate their dissident views into avoiding particular forms of expression. The argument amounts to little more than the self-defeating proposition that to avoid physical censorship of one who has not sought to provoke such a response by a hypothetical coterie of the violent and lawless, the States may more appropriately effectuate that censorship themselves.

Admittedly, it is not so obvious that the First and Fourteenth Amendments must be taken to disable the States from punishing public utterance of this unseemly expletive in order to maintain what they regard as a suitable level of discourse within the body politic. We think, however, that examination and reflection will reveal the shortcomings of a contrary viewpoint.

At the outset, we cannot overemphasize that, in our judgment, most situations where the State has a justifiable interest in regulating speech will fall within one or more of the various established exceptions, discussed above but not applicable here, to the usual rule that governmental bodies may not prescribe the form or content of individual expression. Equally important to our conclusion is the constitutional backdrop against which our decision must be made. The constitutional right of free expression is powerful medicine in a society as diverse and populous as ours. It is designed and intended to remove governmental restraints from the arena of public discussion, putting the decision as to what views shall be voiced largely into the hands of each of us, in the hope that use of such freedom will ultimately produce a more capable citizenry and more perfect polity and in the belief that no other approach would comport with the premise of individual dignity and choice upon which our political system rests.

To many, the immediate consequence of this freedom may often appear to be only verbal tumult, discord, and even offensive utterance. These are, however, within established limits, in truth necessary side effects of the broader enduring values which the process of open debate permits us to achieve. That the air may at times seem filled with verbal cacophony is, in this sense, not a sign of weakness but of strength. We cannot lose sight of the fact that, in what otherwise might seem a trifling and annoying instance of individual distasteful abuse of a privilege, these fundamental societal values are truly implicated. That is why "[w]holly neutral futilities . . . come under the protection of free speech as fully as do Keats' poems or Donne's sermons," and why "so long as the means are peaceful, the communication need not meet standards of acceptability."

Against this perception of the constitutional policies involved, we discern certain more particularized considerations that peculiarly call for reversal of this conviction. First, the principle contended for by the State seems inherently boundless. How is one to distinguish this from any other offensive word? Surely the State has no right to cleanse public debate to the point where it is grammatically palatable to the most squeamish among us. Yet no readily ascertainable general principle exists for stopping short of that result were we to affirm the judgment below. For, while the particular four-letter word being litigated here is perhaps more distasteful than most others of its genre, it is nevertheless often true that one man's vulgarity is another's lyric. Indeed, we think it is largely because governmental officials cannot make principled distinctions in this area that the Constitution leaves matters of taste and style so largely to the individual. Additionally, we cannot overlook the fact, because it is well illustrated by the episode involved here, that much linguistic expression serves a dual communicative function: it conveys not only ideas capable of relatively precise, detached explication, but otherwise inexpressible emotions as well. In fact, words are often chosen as much for their emotive as their cognitive force. We cannot sanction the view that the Constitution, while solicitous of the cognitive content of individual speech has little or no regard for that emotive function which practically speaking, may often be the more important element of the overall message sought to be communicated. Indeed, as Mr. Justice Frankfurter has said, "[O]ne of the prerogatives of American citizenship is the right to criticize public men and measures—and that means not only informed and responsible criticism but the freedom to speak foolishly and without moderation."

Finally, and in the same vein, we cannot indulge the facile assumption that one can forbid particular words without also running a substantial risk of suppressing ideas in the process. Indeed, governments might soon seize upon the censorship of particular words as a convenient guise for banning the expression of unpopular views. We have been able, as noted above, to discern little social benefit that might result from running the risk of opening the door to such grave results. It is, in sum, our judgment that, absent a more particularized and compelling reason for its actions, the State may not, consistently with the First and Fourteenth Amendments, make the simple public display here involved of this single four-letter expletive a criminal offense. Because that is the only arguably sustainable rationale for the conviction here at issue, the judgment below must be reversed.

Reversed.

Mr. Justice Blackmun, with whom the Chief Justice and Mr. Justice Black join . . .

Cohen's absurd and immature antic, in my view, was mainly conduct and little speech. Further, the case appears to me to be well within the sphere of [*Chaplinsky*], where Mr. Justice Murphy, a known champion of First Amendment freedoms, wrote for a unanimous bench. As a consequence, this Court's agonizing over First Amendment values seems misplaced and unnecessary. . . .

Discussion Questions

1. Justice Harlan emphasizes the fact that the statute in question was not directed specifically at offensive or disrespectful dress or behavior in a courtroom. Might the case have been decided differently if the relevant statute were a relatively narrow provision aimed at achieving a minimum amount of decorum in a courtroom? Could a similar rule apply to university classrooms? To campuses in general?

2. The words on Cohen's jacket were not directed at any specific individual or group. Might he be punished under *Chaplinsky*'s "fighting words" exception if he replaced "the draft" with a slur directed at a minority group? If so, under what circumstances?

3. Reexamine *Chaplinsky* (and the discussion questions asked after that case) in light of *Cohen*. The *Chaplinsky* Court defined fighting words, in part, as words "which by their very utterance inflict injury. . . ." What, if anything, is the difference between words that injure and words that are offensive? Does *Cohen* essentially eliminate the possibility of constitutionally punishing the speaker of words that injure or offend those who hear them? What about face-to-face insults of the type likely to result in fisticuffs?

4. Justice Harlan argues that vulgar or offensive language may sometimes communicate ideas and emotions more clearly and expressively than more polished (and socially acceptable) prose, and that by exempting certain words from social discourse, we necessarily restrict the expression of ideas.

Surely "Down with the draft," or even "Damn the draft," fails to convey quite the same message as Cohen's jacket. The same argument can be made regarding racial slurs and other expressions of contempt for groups or individuals in society, however. A racial epithet, for example, communicates a message of hatred and intolerance more eloquently than a discourse on alleged genetic differences between the races. Can Justice Harlan's argument be used to insulate these traditional "fighting words" from governmental regulation or proscription? Should the constitutional considerations be different if the epithet is uttered in a face-to-face confrontation?

Beauharnais v. Illinois
343 U.S. 250 (1952)

Mr. Justice Frankfurter delivered the opinion of the Court.

The petitioner was convicted upon information in the Municipal Court of Chicago of violating s 224a of Division 1 of the Illinois Criminal Code. He was fined $200. The section provides: "It shall be unlawful for any person, firm or corporation to manufacture, sell, or offer for sale, advertise or publish, present or exhibit in any public place in this state any lithograph, moving picture, play, drama or sketch, which publication or exhibition portrays depravity, criminality, unchastity, or lack of virtue of a class of citizens, of any race, color, creed or religion which said publication or exhibition exposes the citizens of any race, color, creed or religion to contempt, derision, or obloquy or which is productive of breach of the peace or riots. . . ."

Beauharnais challenged the statute as violating the liberty of speech and of the press guaranteed as against the States by the Due Process Clause of the Fourteenth Amendment, and as too vague, under the restrictions implicit in the same Clause, to support conviction for crime. The Illinois courts rejected these contentions and sustained defendant's conviction. We granted certiorari in view of the serious questions raised concerning the limitations imposed by the Fourteenth Amendment on the power of a State to punish utterances promoting friction among racial and religious groups. . . .

The lithograph complained of was a leaflet setting forth a petition calling on the Mayor and City Council of Chicago "to halt the further encroachment, harassment and invasion of white people, their property, neighborhoods, and persons, by the Negro. . . ." Below was a call for "[o]ne million self-respecting white people in Chicago to unite. . . ." with the statement added that "[i]f persuasion and the need to prevent the white race from becoming mongrelized by the Negro will not unite us, then the aggressions . . . rapes, robberies, knives, guns, and marijuana of the Negro, surely will." This, with more language, similar if not so violent, concluded with an attached application for membership in the White Circle League of America, Inc.

The testimony at the trial was substantially undisputed. From it the jury could find that Beauharnais was president of the White Circle League; that, at a meeting on January 6, 1950, he passed out bundles of the lithographs in question, together with other literature, to volunteers for distribution on downtown Chicago street corners the following day; that he carefully organized that distribution, giving detailed instructions for it; and that the leaflets were in fact distributed on January 7 in accordance with his plan and instructions. . . . Upon this evidence and these instructions, the jury brought in the conviction here for review. . . .

The Illinois Supreme Court tells us that s 224a "is a form of criminal libel law." The defendant, the trial court, and the Supreme Court consistently treated it as such. The defendant offered evidence tending to prove the truth of parts of the utterance, and the courts below considered and disposed of this offer in terms of ordinary criminal libel precedents. Section 224a does not deal with the defense of truth, but by the Illinois Constitution, "in all trials for libel, both civil and criminal, the truth, when published with good motives and for justifiable ends, shall be a sufficient defense." Similarly, the action of the trial court in deciding as a matter of law the libelous character of the utterance, leaving to the jury only the question of publication, follows the settled rule in prosecutions for libel in Illinois and other States. Moreover, the Supreme Court's characterization of the words prohibited by the statute as those "liable to cause violence and disorder" paraphrases the traditional justification for punishing libels criminally, namely their "tendency to cause breach of the peace."

Illinois did not have to look beyond her own borders or await the tragic experience of the last three to conclude that willful purveyors of falsehood concerning racial and religious groups promote strife and tend powerfully to obstruct the manifold adjustments required for free, ordered life in a metropolitan, polyglot community. From the murder of the abolitionist Lovejoy in 1837 to the Cicero riots of 1951, Illinois has been the scene of exacerbated tension between races, often flaring into violence and destruction. In many of these outbreaks, utterances of the character here in question, so the Illinois legislature could conclude, played a significant part. . . .

In the face of this history and its frequent obligato of extreme racial and religious propaganda, we would deny experience to say that the Illinois legislature was without reason in seeking ways to curb false or malicious defamation of racial and religious groups, made in public places and by means calculated to have a powerful emotional impact on those to whom it was presented. "There are limits to the exercise of these liberties (of speech and of the press). The danger in these times from the coercive activities of those who in the delusion of racial or religious conceit would incite violence and breaches of the peace in order to deprive others of their equal right to the exercise of their liberties, is emphasized by events familiar to all. These and other transgressions of those limits the states appropriately may punish." . . .

It may be argued, and weightily, that this legislation will not help matters; that tension and on occasion violence between racial and religious groups must be traced to causes more deeply embedded in our society than the rantings of modern Know-Nothings. Only those lacking responsible humility will have a confident solution for problems as intractable as the frictions attributable to differences of race, color, or religion. This being so, it would be out of bounds for the judiciary to deny the legislature a choice of policy, provided it is not unrelated to the problem and not forbidden by some explicit limitation on the State's power. . . .

Long ago this Court recognized that the economic rights of an individual may depend for the effectiveness of their enforcement on rights in the group, even though not formally corporate, to which he belongs. Such group-protection on behalf of the individual may, for all we know, be a need not confined to the part that a trade union plays in effectuating rights abstractly recognized as belonging to its members. It is not within our competence to confirm or deny claims of social scientists as to the dependence of the individual on the position of his racial or religious group in the community. It would, however, be arrant dogmatism, quite outside the scope of our authority in passing on the powers of a State, for us to deny that the Illinois legislature may warrantably believe that a man's job and his educational opportunities and the dignity accorded him may depend as much on the reputation of the racial and religious group to which he willy-nilly belongs, as on his own merits. This being so, we are precluded from saying that speech concededly punishable when immediately directed at individuals cannot be outlawed if directed at groups with whose position and esteem in society the affiliated individual may be inextricably involved. We are warned that the choice open to the Illinois legislature here may be abused, that the law may be discriminatorily enforced; prohibiting libel of a creed or of a racial group, we are told, is but a step from prohibiting libel of a political party.

Every power may be abused, but the possibility of abuse is a poor reason for denying Illinois the power to adopt measures against criminal libels sanctioned by centuries of Anglo-American law. "While this Court sits" it retains and exercises authority to nullify action which encroaches on freedom of utterance under the guise of punishing libel. Of course discussion cannot be denied and the right, as well as the duty, of criticism must not be stifled. . . .

Libelous utterances not being within the area of constitutionally protected speech, it is unnecessary, either for us or for the State courts, to consider the issues behind the phrase "clear and present danger." Certainly no one would contend that obscene speech, for example, may be punished only upon a showing of such circumstances. Libel, as we have seen, is in the same class. We find no warrant in the Constitution for denying to Illinois the power to pass the law here under attack. But it bears repeating—although it should not—that our finding that the law is not constitutionally objectionable carries no implication of approval of the wisdom of the legislation or of its efficacy. These questions may raise doubts in our minds as well as in others. It is not for us, however, to make the legislative judgment. We are not at liberty to erect those doubts into fundamental law.

Affirmed.

Mr. Justice Black, with whom Mr. Justice Douglas concurs, dissenting.

. . . The Court's holding here and the constitutional doctrine behind it leave the rights of assembly, petition, speech, and press almost completely at the mercy of state legislative, executive, and judicial agencies. I say "almost" because state curtailment of these freedoms may still be invalidated if a majority of this Court conclude that a particular infringement is "without reason," or is "a willful and purposeless restriction unrelated to the peace and well-being of the State." But lest this encouragement should give too much hope as to how and when this Court might protect these basic freedoms from state invasion, we are cautioned that state legislatures must be left free to "experiment" and to make "legislative judgments." We are told that mistakes may be made during the legislative process of curbing public opinion. In such event the Court fortunately does not leave those mistakenly curbed, or any of us for that matter, unadvised. Consolation can be sought and must be found in the philosophical reflection that state legislative error in stifling speech and press "is the price to be paid for the trial-and-error inherent in legislative efforts to deal with obstinate social issues." My own belief is that no legislature is charged with the duty or vested with the power to decide what public issues Americans can discuss. In a free country that is the individual's choice, not the state's. State experimentation in curbing freedom of expression is startling and frightening doctrine in a country dedicated to self-government by its people. I reject the holding that either state or nation can punish people for having their say in matters of public concern.

The Court condones this expansive state censorship by painstakingly analogizing it to the law of criminal libel. As a result of this refined analysis, the Illinois statute emerges labeled a "group libel law." This label may make the Court's holding more palatable for those who sustain it, but the sugar-coating does not make the censorship less deadly. However tagged, the Illinois law is not that criminal libel which has been "defined, limited, and constitutionally recognized time out of mind." For as "constitutionally recognized" that crime has provided for punishment of false, malicious, scurrilous charges against individuals, not against huge groups. This limited scope of the law of criminal libel is of no small importance. It has confined state punishment of speech and expression to the narrowest of areas involving nothing more than purely private feuds. Every expansion of the law of criminal libel so as to punish discussions of matters of public concern means a corresponding invasion of the area dedicated to free expression by the First Amendment.

The Court's reliance on [*Chaplinsky*] is also misplaced. New Hampshire had a state law making it an offense to direct insulting words at an individual on a public street. Chaplinsky had violated that law by calling a man vile names "face-to-face." We pointed out in that context that the use of such "fighting" words was not an essential part of exposition of ideas. Whether the words used in their context here are "fighting" words in the same sense is doubtful, but whether so or not they are not addressed to or about individuals. Moreover, the leaflet used here was also the means adopted by an assembled group to enlist interest in their efforts to have legislation enacted. And the fighting words were but a part of arguments on questions of wide public interest and importance. Freedom of petition, assembly, speech, and press could be greatly abridged by a practice of meticulously scrutinizing every editorial, speech, sermon, or other printed matter to extract two or three naughty words on which to hang charges of "group libel." The *Chaplinsky* case makes no such broad inroads on First Amendment freedoms. Nothing Mr. Justice Murphy wrote for the Court in that case or in any other case justifies any such inference.

Unless I misread history the majority is giving libel a more expansive scope and more respectable status than it was ever accorded even in the Star Chamber. For here it is held to be punishable to give publicity to any picture, moving picture, play, drama, or sketch, or any printed matter which a judge may find unduly offensive to any race, color, creed, or religion. In other words, in arguing for or against the enactment of laws that may differently affect huge groups, it is now very dangerous indeed to say something critical of one of the groups. And any "person, firm, or corporation" can be tried for this crime. "Person, firm, or corporation" certainly includes a book publisher, newspaper, radio or television station, candidate, or even a preacher.

It is easy enough to say that none of this latter group has been proceeded against under the Illinois Act. And they have not—yet. But emotions bubble and tempers flare in racial and religious controversies, the kind here involved. It would not be easy for any court, in good conscience, to narrow this Act so as to exclude from it any of those I have mentioned.

This Act sets up a system of state censorship which is at war with the kind of free government envisioned by those who forced adoption of our Bill of Rights. The motives behind the state law may have been to do good. But the same can be said about most laws making opinions punishable as crimes. History indicates that urges to do good have led to the burning of books and even to the burning of "witches."

No rationalization on a purely legal level can conceal the fact that state laws like this one present a constant overhanging threat to freedom of speech, press, and religion. Today Beauharnais is punished for publicly expressing strong views in favor of segregation. Ironically enough, Beauharnais, convicted of crime in Chicago, would probably be given a hero's reception in many other localities, if not in some parts of Chicago itself. Moreover, the same kind of state law that makes Beauharnais a criminal for advocating segregation in Illinois can be utilized to send people to jail in other states for advocating equality and nonsegregation. What Beauharnais said in his leaflet is mild compared with usual arguments on both sides of racial controversies.

We are told that freedom of petition and discussion are in no danger "while this Court sits." This case raises considerable doubt. Since those who peacefully petition for changes in the law are not to be protected "while this Court sits," who is? I do not agree that the Constitution leaves freedom of petition, assembly, speech, press or worship at the mercy of a case-by-case, day-by-day majority of this Court. I had supposed that our people could rely for their freedom on the Constitution's commands, rather than on the grace of this Court on an individual case basis. To say that a legislative body can, with this Court's approval, make it a crime to petition for and publicly discuss proposed legislation seems as farfetched to me as it would be to say that a valid law could be enacted to punish a candidate for President for telling the people his views. I think the First Amendment, with the Fourteenth, "absolutely" forbids such laws without any "ifs" or "buts" or "whereases." Whatever the danger, if any, in such public discussions, it is a danger the Founders deemed outweighed by the danger incident to the stifling of thought and speech. The Court does not act on this view of the Founders. It calculates what it deems to be the danger of public discussion, holds the scales are tipped on the side of state suppression, and upholds state censorship. This method of decision offers little protection to First Amendment liberties "while this Court sits."

If there be minority groups who hail this holding as their victory, they might consider the possible relevancy of this ancient remark: "Another such victory and I am undone."

Discussion Questions

1. The majority argue that derogatory statements made against a racial, ethnic, or religious group are analogous to libel on an individual level. Libel usually refers to false statements made about an individual that damage that person's reputation and standing in the community. The dissenters, on the other hand, argue that negative statements made against social groups are not like libel, but are analogous to statements made on issues of public concern. Libel is not protected by the Constitution (with some important exceptions; see *New York Times* v. *United States*); statements on issues of public concern are protected by the First Amendment. Which position regarding group libel do you agree with?

2. *Beauharnais* was decided in 1952, before the Supreme Court's rulings in cases such as *Cohen*, *Brandenburg*, and *Tinker*. To what degree is the Court's assessment of the constitutional validity of the "group libel" concept still valid in light of these later cases? (See discussion of this issue in the Skokie case, *Collins* v. *Smith*, excerpted below.)

3. To what degree is the statute in question susceptible to the sins of "overbreadth" or "vagueness," applied by the Court in *Gooding* v. *Wilson*?

4. In light of the above, do you think the group libel concept might serve as a useful model for university campuses seeking a way to deal with hate speech?

TIME, MANNER, AND PLACE REGULATIONS

Healey v. *James*

408 U.S. 169 (1972)

Mr. Justice Powell delivered the opinion of the Court.

This case, arising out of a denial by a state college of official recognition to a group of students who desired to form a local chapter of Students for a Democratic Society (SDS), presents this Court with questions requiring the application of well-established First Amendment principles. While the factual background of this particular case raises these constitutional issues in a manner not heretofore passed on by the Court, and only infrequently presented to lower federal courts, our decision today is governed by existing precedent.

As the case involves delicate issues concerning the academic community, we approach our task with special caution, recognizing the mutual interest of students, faculty members, and administrators in an environment free from disruptive interference with the educational process. We also are mindful of the equally significant interest in the widest latitude for free expression and debate consonant with the maintenance of order. Where these interests appear to compete, the First Amendment, made binding on the States by the Fourteenth Amendment, strikes the required balance.

I

[On many campuses, SDS had been at the forefront of building seizures, vandalism, and other forms of "radical action" to protest the Vietnam War. The president of Central Connecticut State College (CCSC) denied formal recognition to the group on several grounds: "He found that the organization's philosophy was antithetical to the school's policies, and that the group's independence was doubtful. He concluded that approval should not be granted to any group that 'openly repudiates' the College's dedication to academic freedom." Denial of official recognition meant that its members could not place announcements regarding meetings and other activities in the student newspaper or on campus bulletin boards, and they could not use campus facilities to hold meetings.

After the Federal District Court ordered that the University hold a hearing to examine several factual issues regarding the denial of authorization, the President reaffirmed his prior decision, again arguing that the group would be a "disruptive influence" at CCSC and that recognition would be "contrary to the orderly process of change" on the campus. The Federal District Court and Court of Appeals validated this decision against the students' charges that it violated the First and Fourteenth Amendments.]

II

At the outset we note that state colleges and universities are not enclaves immune from the sweep of the First Amendment. "It can hardly be argued that either students or teachers shed their constitutional rights to freedom of speech or expression at the schoolhouse gate" [*Tinker*]. Of course, as Mr. Justice Fortas made clear in *Tinker,* First Amendment rights must always be applied "in light of the special characteristics of the . . . environment" in the particular case. And, where state-operated educational institutions are involved, this Court has long recognized "the need for affirming the comprehensive authority of the States and of school officials, consistent with fundamental constitutional safeguards, to prescribe and control conduct in the schools." Yet, the precedents of this Court leave no room for the view that, because of the acknowledged need for order, First Amendment protections should apply with less force on college compuses than in the community at large. Quite to the contrary, "[T]he vigilant protection of constitutional freedoms is nowhere more vital than in the community of American schools." The college classroom with its surrounding environs is peculiarly the "marketplace of ideas," and we break no new constitutional ground in reaffirming this Nation's dedication to safeguarding academic freedom.

Among the rights protected by the First Amendment is the right of individuals to associate to further their personal beliefs. While the freedom of association is not explicitly set out in the Amendment, it has long been held to be implicit in the freedoms of speech, assembly, and petition. There can be no doubt that denial of official recognition, without justification, to college organizations burdens or abridges that associational right. The primary impediment to free association flowing from nonrecognition is the denial of use of campus facilities for meetings and other appropriate purposes. The practical effect of nonrecognition was demonstrated in this case when, several days after the President's decision was announced, petitioners were not allowed to hold a meeting in the campus coffee shop because they were not an approved group.

Petitioners' associational interests also were circumscribed by the denial of the use of campus bulletin boards and the school newspaper. If an organization is to remain a viable entity in a campus community in which new students enter on a regular basis, it must possess the means of communicating with these students. Moreover, the organization's ability to participate in the intellectual give-and-take of campus debate, and to pursue its stated purposes, is limited by denial of access to the customary media for communicating with the administration, faculty members, and other students. Such impediments cannot be viewed as insubstantial.

Respondents and the courts below appear to have taken the view that denial of official recognition in this case abridged no constitutional rights. The District Court concluded that "President James's discretionary action in denying this application cannot be legitimately magnified and distorted into a constitutionally cognizable interference with the personal ideas or beliefs of any segment of the college students; neither does his action deter in any material way the individual advocacy of their personal beliefs; nor can his action be reasonably construed to be an invasion of, or having a chilling effect on academic freedom."

In that court's view all that was denied petitioners was the "administrative seal of official college respectability." A majority of the Court of Appeals agreed that petitioners had been denied only the "college's stamp of approval." Respondents take that same position here, arguing that petitioners still may meet as a group off campus, that they still may distribute written material off campus, and that they still may meet together informally on campus—as individuals, but not as CCSC–SDS.

We do not agree with the characterization by the courts below of the consequences of nonrecognition. We may concede . . . that the administration "has taken no direct action . . . to restrict the rights of (petitioners) to associate freely. . . ." But the Constitution's protection is not limited to direct interference with fundamental rights. [I]n this case, the group's possible ability to exist outside the campus community does not ameliorate significantly the disabilities imposed by the President's action. We are not free to disregard the practical realities. "Freedoms such as these are protected not only against heavy-handed frontal attack, but also from being stifled by more subtle governmental interference."

The opinions below also assumed that petitioners had the burden of showing entitlement to recognition by the College. While petitioners have not challenged the procedural requirement that they file an application in conformity with the rules of the College, they do question the view of the courts below that final rejection could rest on their failure to convince the administration that their organization was unaffiliated with the National SDS. For reasons to be stated later in this opinion, we do not consider the issue of affiliation to be a controlling one. But, apart from any particular issue, once petitioners had filed an application in conformity with the requirements, the burden was upon the College administration to justify its decision of rejection. It is to be remembered that the effect of the College's denial of recognition was a form of prior restraint, denying to petitioners' organization the range of associational activities described above. While a college has a legitimate interest in preventing disruption on the campus, which under circumstances requiring the safeguarding of that interest may justify such restraint, a "heavy burden" rests on the college to demonstrate the appropriateness of that action.

III

These fundamental errors—discounting the existence of a cognizable First Amendment interest and misplacing the burden of proof—require that the judgments below be reversed. But we are unable to conclude that no basis exists upon which nonrecognition might be appropriate. Indeed, based on a reasonable reading of the ambiguous facts of this case, there appears to be at least one potentially acceptable ground for a denial of recognition. Because of this ambiguous state of the record we conclude that the case should be remanded and, in an effort to provide guidance to the lower courts upon reconsideration, it is appropriate to discuss the several bases of President James's decision. Four possible justifications for nonrecognition, all closely related, might be derived from the record and his statements. Three of those grounds are inadequate to substantiate his decision: a fourth, however, has merit.

A

From the outset the controversy in this case has centered in large measure around the relationship, if any, between petitioners' group and the National SDS. The Student Affairs Committee meetings, as reflected in its minutes, focused considerable attention on this issue; the court-ordered hearing also was directed primarily to this question. Despite assurances from petitioners and their counsel that the local group was in fact independent of the National organization, it is evident that President James was significantly influenced by his apprehension that there was a connection. Aware of the fact that some SDS chapters had been associated with disruptive and violent campus activity, he apparently considered that affiliation itself was sufficient justification for denying recognition.

Although this precise issue has not come before the Court heretofore, the

Court has consistently disapproved governmental action imposing criminal sanctions or denying rights and privileges solely because of a citizen's association with an unpopular organization. In these cases it has been established that "guilt by association alone, without (establishing) that an individual's association poses the threat feared by the Government," is an impermissible basis upon which to deny First Amendment rights. The government has the burden of establishing a knowing affiliation with an organization possessing unlawful aims and goals, and a specific intent to further those illegal aims.

Students for a Democratic Society, as conceded by the College and the lower courts, is loosely organized, having various factions and promoting a number of diverse social and political views only some of which call for unlawful action. Not only did petitioners proclaim their complete independence from this organization, but they also indicated that they shared only some of the beliefs its leaders have expressed. On this record it is clear that the relationship was not an adequate ground for the denial of recognition.

B

Having concluded that petitioners were affiliated with, or at least retained an affinity for, National SDS, President James attributed what he believed to be the philosophy of that organization to the local group. He characterized the petitioning group as adhering to "some of the major tenets of the national organization," including a philosophy of violence and disruption. Understandably, he found that philosophy abhorrent. In an article signed by President James in an alumni periodical, and made a part of the record below, he announced his unwillingness to "sanction an organization that openly advocates the destruction of the very ideals and freedoms upon which the academic life is founded." He further emphasized that the petitioners' philosophies were counter to the official policy of the college.

The mere disagreement of the President with the group's philosophy affords no reason to deny it recognition. As repugnant as these views may have been, especially to one with President James's responsibility, the mere expression of them would not justify the denial of First Amendment rights. Whether petitioners did in fact advocate a philosophy of "destruction" thus becomes immaterial. The College, acting here as the instrumentality of the State, may not restrict speech or association simply because it finds the views expressed by any group to be abhorrent. As Mr. Justice Black put it most simply and clearly: "I do not believe that it can be too often repeated that the freedoms of speech, press, petition, and assembly guaranteed by the First Amendment

must be accorded to the ideas we hate or sooner or later they will be denied
to the ideas we cherish."

C

As the litigation progressed in the District Court, a third rationale for President
James's decision—beyond the questions of affiliation and philosophy— began
to emerge. His second statement, issued after the court-ordered hearing, indicates that he based rejection on a conclusion that this particular group would
be a "disruptive influence at CCSC." This language was underscored in the
second District Court opinion. In fact, the court concluded that the President
had determined that CCSC–SDS' "prospective campus activities were likely
to cause a disruptive influence at CCSC."

If this reason, directed at the organization's activities rather than its philosophy, were factually supported by the record, this Court's prior decisions would
provide a basis for considering the propriety of nonrecognition. The critical
line heretofore drawn for determining the permissibility of regulation is the
line between mere advocacy and advocacy "directed to inciting or producing
imminent lawless action and . . . likely to incite or produce such action"
[*Brandenburg*]. In the context of the "special characteristics of the school
environment," the power of the government to prohibit "lawless action" is
not limited to acts of a criminal nature. Also prohibitable are actions which
"materially and substantially disrupt the work and discipline of the school"
[*Tinker*]. Associational activities need not be tolerated where they infringe
reasonable campus rules, interrupt classes, or substantially interfere with the
opportunity of other students to obtain an education.

The "Student Bill of Rights" at CCSC, upon which great emphasis was
placed by the President, draws precisely this distinction between advocacy and
action. It purports to impose no limitations on the right of college student
organizations "to examine and discuss all questions of interest to them." But
it also states that students have no right (1) "to deprive others of the opportunity to speak or be heard," (2) "to invade the privacy of others," (3) "to
damage the property of others," (4) "to disrupt the regular and essential operation of the college," or (5) "to interfere with the rights of others." The line
between permissible speech and impermissible conduct tracks the constitutional requirement, and if there were an evidential basis to support the conclusion that CCSC–SDS posed a substantial threat of material disruption in violation of that command the President's decision should be affirmed.

The record, however, offers no substantial basis . . . that these particular
individuals acting together would constitute a disruptive force on campus.

Therefore, insofar as nonrecognition flowed from such fears, it constituted little more than the sort of "undifferentiated fear or apprehension of disturbance (which) is not enough to overcome the right to freedom of expression" [*Tinker*].

D

These same references in the record to the group's equivocation regarding how it might respond to "issues of violence" and whether it could ever "envision . . . interrupting a class," suggest a fourth possible reason why recognition might have been denied to these petitioners. These remarks might well have been read as announcing petitioners' unwillingness to be bound by reasonable school rules governing conduct. The College's Statement of Rights, Freedoms, and Responsibilities of Students contains, as we have seen, an explicit statement with respect to campus disruption. The regulation, carefully differentiating between advocacy and action, is a reasonable one, and petitioners have not questioned it directly. Yet their statements raise considerable question whether they intend to abide by the prohibitions contained therein.

As we have already stated in Parts B and C, the critical line for First Amendment purposes must be drawn between advocacy, which is entitled to full protection, and action, which is not. Petitioners may, if they so choose, preach the propriety of amending or even doing away with any or all campus regulations. They may not, however, undertake to flout these rules. Mr. Justice Blackmun, at the time he was a circuit judge on the Eighth Circuit, stated: "We . . . hold that a college has the inherent power to promulgate rules and regulations; that it has the inherent power properly to discipline; that it has power appropriately to protect itself and its property; that it may expect that its students adhere to generally accepted standards of conduct."

Just as in the community at large, reasonable regulations with respect to the time, the place, and the manner in which student groups conduct their speech-related activities must be respected. A college administration may impose a requirement, such as may have been imposed in this case, that a group seeking official recognition affirm in advance its willingness to adhere to reasonable campus law. Such a requirement does not impose an impermissible condition on the students' associational rights. Their freedom to speak out, to assemble, or to petition for changes in school rules is in no sense infringed. It merely constitutes an agreement to conform with reasonable standards respecting conduct. This is a minimal requirement, in the interest of the entire academic community, of any group seeking the privilege of official recognition.

Petitioners have not challenged in this litigation the procedural or substantive aspects of the College's requirements governing applications for official recognition. Although the record is unclear on this point, CCSC may have, among its requirements for recognition, a rule that prospective groups affirm that they intend to comply with reasonable campus regulations. Upon remand it should first be determined whether the College recognition procedures contemplate any such requirement. If so, it should then be ascertained whether petitioners intend to comply. Since we do not have the terms of a specific prior affirmation rule before us, we are not called on to decide whether any particular formulation would or would not prove constitutionally acceptable. Assuming the existence of a valid rule, however, we do conclude that the benefits of participation in the internal life of the college community may be denied to any group that reserves the right to violate any valid campus rules with which it disagrees.

IV

We think the above discussion establishes the appropriate framework for consideration of petitioners' request for campus recognition. Because respondents failed to accord due recognition to First Amendment principles, the judgments below approving respondents' denial of recognition must be reversed. Since we cannot conclude from this record that petitioners were willing to abide by reasonable campus rules and regulations, we order the case remanded for reconsideration. We note, in so holding, that the wide latitude accorded by the Constitution to the freedoms of expression and association is not without its costs in terms of the risk to the maintenance of civility and an ordered society. Indeed, this latitude often has resulted, on the campus and elsewhere, in the infringement of the rights of others. Though we deplore the tendency of some to abuse the very constitutional privileges they invoke, and although the infringement of rights of others certainly should not be tolerated, we reaffirm this Court's dedication to the principles of the Bill of Rights upon which our vigorous and free society is founded.

Reversed and remanded.

Discussion Questions

1. In light of *Healey*, under what circumstances—if any—could a state university constitutionally refuse to recognize a campus chapter of the Ku Klux Klan or the American Nazi Party?
2. There is an indication in the opinion that university administrators have

some latitude to structure rules that protect "the rights of others" and that ensure that the educational process is not disrupted. Might these concerns serve as the basis for certain types of restrictions on campus hate speech? What kind of restrictions? What limitations would you expect to see in these restrictions in order to avoid constitutional difficulties?

SPEECH CREATING A "HOSTILE ENVIRONMENT"

Harris v. *Forklift Systems*
114 S.Ct. 367 (1993)

Justice O'Connor delivered the opinion of the Court.

In this case we consider the definition of a discriminatorily "abusive work environment" (also known as a "hostile work environment") under Title VII of the Civil Rights Act of 1964.

I

Teresa Harris worked as a manager at Forklift Systems, Inc., an equipment rental company, from April 1985 until October 1987. Charles Hardy was Forklift's president.

The Magistrate found that, throughout Harris' time at Forklift, Hardy often insulted her because of her gender and often made her the target of unwanted sexual innuendoes. Hardy told Harris on several occasions, in the presence of other employees, "You're a woman, what do you know" and "We need a man as the rental manager"; at least once, he told her she was "a dumb ass woman." Again in front of others, he suggested that the two of them "go to the Holiday Inn to negotiate [Harris'] raise." Hardy occasionally asked Harris and other female employees to get coins from his front pants pocket. He threw objects on the ground in front of Harris and other women, and asked them to pick the objects up. He made sexual innuendoes about Harris' and other women's clothing.

In mid-August 1987, Harris complained to Hardy about his conduct. Hardy said he was surprised that Harris was offended, claimed he was only joking, and apologized. He also promised he would stop, and based on this assurance Harris stayed on the job. But in early September, Hardy began anew: while Harris was arranging a deal with one of Forklift's customers, he asked her, again in front of other employees, "What did you do, promise the guy . . . some [sex] Saturday night?" On October 1, Harris collected her paycheck and quit.

Harris then sued Forklift, claiming that Hardy's conduct had created an abusive work environment for her because of her gender. The United States District Court for the Middle District of Tennessee, adopting the report and recommendation of the Magistrate, found this to be "a close case," but held that Hardy's conduct did not create an abusive environment. The court found that some of Hardy's comments "offended [Harris], and would offend the reasonable woman," but that they were not "so severe as to be expected to seriously affect [Harris'] psychological well-being. A reasonable woman manager under like circumstances would have been offended by Hardy, but his conduct would not have risen to the level of interfering with that person's work performance. . . . Neither do I believe that [Harris] was subjectively so offended that she suffered injury. . . . Although Hardy may at times have genuinely offended [Harris], I do not believe that he created a working environment so poisoned as to be intimidating or abusive to [Harris]."

. . . We granted certiorari, to resolve a conflict among the Circuits on whether conduct, to be actionable as "abusive work environment" harassment (no quid pro quo harassment issue is present here), must "seriously affect [an employee's] psychological well-being" or lead the plaintiff to "suffe[r] injury."

II

Title VII of the Civil Rights Act of 1964 makes it "an unlawful employment practice for an employer . . . to discriminate against any individual with respect to his compensation, terms, conditions, or privileges of employment, because of such individual's race, color, religion, sex, or national origin." As we made clear in *Meritor Savings Bank* v. *Vinson*, this language "is not limited to 'economic' or 'tangible' discrimination. The phrase 'terms, conditions, or privileges of employment' evinces a congressional intent 'to strike at the entire spectrum of disparate treatment of men and women' in employment," which includes requiring people to work in a discriminatorily hostile or abusive environment. When the workplace is permeated with "discriminatory intimidation, ridicule, and insult," that is "sufficiently severe or pervasive to alter the conditions of the victim's employment and create an abusive working environment," Title VII is violated.

This standard, which we reaffirm today, takes a middle path between making actionable any conduct that is merely offensive and requiring the conduct to cause a tangible psychological injury. As we pointed out in *Meritor*, "mere utterance of an . . . epithet which engenders offensive feelings in an employee" does not sufficiently affect the conditions of employment to implicate Title VII. Conduct that is not severe or pervasive enough to create an objectively hostile or abusive work environment—an environment that a reasonable person would find hostile or abusive—is beyond Title VII's purview. Likewise, if the victim does not subjectively perceive the environment to be abusive, the conduct has not actually altered the conditions of the victim's employment, and there is no Title VII violation.

But Title VII comes into play before the harassing conduct leads to a nervous breakdown. A discriminatorily abusive work environment, even one that does not seriously affect employees' psychological well-being, can and often will detract from employees' job performance, discourage employees from remaining on the job, or keep them from advancing in their careers. Moreover, even without regard to these tangible effects, the very fact that the discriminatory conduct was so severe or pervasive that it created a work environment abusive to employees because of their race, gender, religion, or national origin offends Title VII's broad rule of workplace equality. The appalling conduct alleged in *Meritor*, and the reference in that case to environments "so heavily polluted with discrimination as to destroy completely the emotional and psychological stability of minority group workers," merely present some especially egregious examples of harassment. They do not mark the boundary of what is actionable.

We therefore believe the District Court erred in relying on whether the conduct "seriously affect[ed] plaintiff's psychological well-being" or led her to "suffe[r] injury." Such an inquiry may needlessly focus the factfinder's attention on concrete psychological harm, an element Title VII does not require. Certainly Title VII bars conduct that would seriously affect a reasonable person's psychological well-being, but the statute is not limited to such conduct. So long as the environment would reasonably be perceived, and is perceived, as hostile or abusive, there is no need for it also to be psychologically injurious.

This is not, and by its nature cannot be, a mathematically precise test. . . . But we can say that whether an environment is "hostile" or "abusive" can be determined only by looking at all the circumstances. These may include the frequency of the discriminatory conduct; its severity; whether it is physically threatening or humiliating, or a mere offensive utterance; and whether it unreasonably interferes with an employee's work performance. The effect on the employee's psychological well-being is, of course, relevant to determining whether the plaintiff actually found the environment abusive. But while psychological harm, like any other relevant factor, may be taken into account, no single factor is required.

III

Forklift, while conceding that a requirement that the conduct seriously affect psychological well-being is unfounded, argues that the District Court nonetheless correctly applied the *Meritor* standard. We disagree. Though the District Court did conclude that the work environment was not "intimidating or abusive to [Harris]," it did so only after finding that the conduct was not "so severe as to be expected to seriously affect plaintiff's psychological well-being," and that Harris was not "subjectively so offended that she suffered injury." The District Court's application of these incorrect standards may well have influenced its ultimate conclusion, especially given that the court found this to be a "close case." We therefore reverse the judgment of the Court of Appeals, and remand the case for further proceedings consistent with this opinion.

So ordered.

Discussion Questions

1. The *Harris* case is based on Title VII of the Civil Rights Act of 1964, which was held by the Supreme Court to forbid employers from maintaining a "hostile work environment" based on employees' race, sex, etc. To what extent do you think a university might utilize elements of this ruling to prohibit speech and other forms of expression that constitute a "hostile educational environment"? How? In thinking about this question you should consider:

   a. The differences between a worker/employer relationship and a student/university relationship, and between a place of employment and an educational institution

   b. The circumstances set out by the Court in the first and last paragraphs of section II for determining what constitutes a hostile work environment

2. The *Harris* case involved abuse by an employee's supervisor. What if the abuser had been a coworker with no supervisory relationship to Harris? What, in other words, is the employer's obligation to ensure that no employees act in ways that exhibit hostility to other employees on the basis of race, sex, etc.? If the notion of hostile work environment were exported to a university context, what would be the university's responsibility for ensuring that students have a nonhostile educational environment against acts and statements of faculty (who are protected to a certain degree by academic freedom)? Against the acts and statements of fellow students (over whom the university has no direct supervisory control)?

HATE SPEECH

Collin v. Smith
578 F.2d. 1197 (Seventh Circuit, 1978)

Pell, Circuit Judge.

Plaintiff-appellee, the National Socialist Party of America (NSPA) is a political group described by its leader, plaintiff-appellee . . . Frank Collin, as a Nazi party. Among NSPA's more controversial and generally unacceptable beliefs are that black persons are biologically inferior to white persons, and should be expatriated to Africa as soon as possible; that American Jews have "inordinate . . . political and financial power" in the world and are "in the forefront of the international Communist revolution." NSPA members affect a uniform reminiscent of those worn by members of the German Nazi Party during the Third Reich, and display a swastika thereon and on a red, white, and black flag they frequently carry.

The Village of Skokie, Illinois, a defendant-appellant, is a suburb north of Chicago. It has a large Jewish population, including as many as several thousand survivors of the Nazi holocaust in Europe before and during World War II. Other defendants-appellants are Village officials.

When Collin and NSPA announced plans to march in front of the Village Hall in Skokie on May 1, 1977, Village officials responded by obtaining in state court a preliminary injunction against the demonstration. After state courts refused to stay the injunction pending appeal, the United States Supreme Court ordered a stay. The injunction was subsequently reversed first in part, and then in its entirety. On May 2, 1977, the Village enacted three ordinances to prohibit demonstrations such as the one Collin and NSPA had threatened. This lawsuit seeks declaratory and injunctive relief against enforcement of the ordinances.

Village Ordinance 994 is a comprehensive permit system for all parades or public assemblies of more than 50 persons. It requires permit applicants to obtain $300,000 in public liability insurance and $50,000 in property damage insurance. One of the prerequisites for a permit is a finding by the appropriate official(s) that the assembly "will not portray criminality, depravity or lack of virtue in, or incite violence, hatred, abuse or hostility toward a person or group of persons by reason of reference to religious, racial, ethnic, national or regional affiliation." Another is a finding that the permit activity will not be conducted "for an unlawful purpose." None of this ordinance applies to activities of the Village itself or of a governmental agency, and any provision of the ordinance may be waived by unanimous consent of the Board of Trustees of the Village. To parade or assemble without a permit is a crime, punishable by fines from $5 to $500.

Village Ordinance No. 995 prohibits "[t]he dissemination of any materials within the Village of Skokie which promotes and incites hatred against persons by reason of their race, national origin, or religion, and is intended to do so." "Dissemination of materials" includes " . . . publication or display or distribution of posters, signs, handbills, or writings and public display of markings and clothing of symbolic significance." Violation is a crime punishable by fine of up to $500, or imprisonment of up to six months. Village Ordinance 996 prohibits public demonstrations by members of political parties while wearing "military-style" uniforms, and violation is punishable as in 995.

Collin and NSPA applied for a permit to march on July 4, 1977, which was denied on the ground the application disclosed an intention to violate 996. The Village apparently applies 994 so that an intention to violate 995 or 996 establishes an "unlawful purpose" for the march or assembly. The permit application stated that the march would last about a half hour, and would involve 30 to 50 demonstrators wearing uniforms including swastikas and carrying a party banner with a swastika and placards with statements thereon such as "White Free Speech," "Free Speech for the White Man," and "Free Speech for White America." A single file sidewalk march that would not disrupt traffic was proposed, without speeches or the distribution of handbills or literature. Counsel for the Village advises us that the Village does not maintain that Collin and NSPA will behave other than as described in the permit application(s).

The district court, after considering memoranda, exhibits, depositions, and live testimony, issued a comprehensive and thorough opinion granting relief to Collin and NSPA. The insurance requirements of 994 were invalidated as insuperable obstacles to free speech in Skokie, and . . . were adjudged impermissible prior restraints. Ordinance 995 was determined to be fatally vague and overbroad, and 996 was invalidated as overbroad and patently unjustified.

On its appeal, the Village concedes the invalidity of the insurance requirements as applied to these plaintiffs and of the uniform prohibition of 996.

I

The conflict underlying this litigation has commanded substantial public attention, and engendered considerable and understandable emotion. We would
hopefully surprise no one by confessing personal views that NSPA's beliefs
and goals are repugnant to the core values held generally by residents of this
country and, indeed, to much of what we cherish in civilization. As judges
sworn to defend the Constitution, however, we cannot decide this or any case
on that basis. Ideological tyranny, no matter how worthy its motivation, is
forbidden as much to appointed judges as to elected legislators.

We cannot . . . be unmindful of the horrors associated with the Nazi regime
of the Third Reich, with which to some real and apparently intentional degree
appellees associate themselves. Nor does the record allow us to ignore the
certainty that appellees know full well that, in light of their views and the
historical associations they would bring with them to Skokie, many people
would find their demonstration extremely mentally and emotionally disturbing, or the suspicion that such a result may be relished by appellees.

But our task here is to decide whether the First Amendment protects the
activity in which appellees wish to engage, not to render moral judgment on
their views or tactics. No authorities need be cited to establish the proposition,
which the Village does not dispute, that First Amendment rights are truly
precious and fundamental to our national life. Nor is this truth without relevance to the saddening historical images this case inevitably arouses. It is,
after all, in part the fact that our constitutional system protects minorities
unpopular at a particular time or place from governmental harassment and
intimidation, that distinguishes life in this country from life under the Third
Reich.

Before undertaking specific analysis of the clash between the Village ordinances and appellees' desires to demonstrate in Skokie, it will be helpful to
establish some general principles of pertinence to the decision required of us.
Putting to one side for the moment the question of whether the content of
appellees' views and symbols makes a constitutional difference here, we find
we are unable to deny that the activities in which the appellees wish to engage
are within the ambit of the First Amendment.

These activities involve the "cognate rights" of free speech and free assembly. See [Tinker]. Standing alone, at least, it is "closely akin to 'pure speech'
which, we have repeatedly held, is entitled to comprehensive protection under
the First Amendment" [Tinker]. The same thing can be said of NSPA's intended display of a party flag, and of the messages intended for the placards
party members would carry. See [Cohen]. Likewise, although marching, pa-

rading, and picketing, because they involve conduct implicating significant interests in maintaining public order, are less protected than pure speech, they are nonetheless subject to significant First Amendment protection. Indeed, an orderly and peaceful demonstration, with placards, in the vicinity of a seat of government, is "an exercise of (the) basic constitutional rights of (speech, assembly, and petition) in their most pristine and classic form."

No doubt, the Nazi demonstration could be subjected to reasonable regulation of its time, place, and manner. Although much of the permit system of 994 is of that nature, the provisions attacked here are not. No objection is raised by the Village, in ordinances or in their proofs and arguments in this case, to the suggested time, place, or manner of the demonstration, except the general assertion that in the place of Skokie, in these times, given the content of appellees' views and symbols, the demonstration and its symbols and speech should be prohibited. Because the ordinances turn on the content of the demonstration, they are necessarily not time, place, or manner regulations.

Legislating against the content of First Amendment activity, however, launches the government on a slippery and precarious path: "(A)bove all else, the First Amendment means that government has no power to restrict expression because of its message, its ideas, its subject matter, or its content [*Cohen*]." To permit the continued building of our politics and culture, and to assure self-fulfillment for each individual, our people are guaranteed the right to express any thought, free from government censorship. The essence of this forbidden censorship is content control. Any restriction on expressive activity because of its content would completely undercut the "profound national commitment to the principle that debate on public issues should be uninhibited, robust, and wide-open."

This is not to say, of course, that content legislation is per se invalid. Chief Justice Burger [has pointed] out the established exceptions to such a rule, namely obscenity, fighting words, and, as limited by constitutional requirements, libel. Likewise, in very narrow circumstances, a government may proscribe content on the basis of imminent danger of a grave substantive evil [*Brandenburg*]. But analysis of content restrictions must begin with a healthy respect for the truth that they are the most direct threat to the vitality of First Amendment rights.

II

We first consider ordinance 995, prohibiting the dissemination of materials which would promote hatred towards persons on the basis of their heritage.

The Village would apparently apply this provision to NSPA's display of swastikas, their uniforms, and, perhaps, to the content of their placards.

The ordinance cannot be sustained on the basis of some of the more obvious exceptions to the rule against content control. While some would no doubt be willing to label appellees' views and symbols obscene, the constitutional rule that obscenity is unprotected applies only to material with erotic content [*Cohen*]. Furthermore, although the Village introduced evidence in the district court tending to prove that some individuals, at least, might have difficulty restraining their reactions to the Nazi demonstration, the Village tells us that it does not rely on a fear of responsive violence to justify the ordinance, and does not even suggest that there will be any physical violence if the march is held. This confession takes this case out of the scope of [*Brandenburg*] and [*Feiner*]. The Village does not argue otherwise.

The concession also eliminates any argument based on the fighting words doctrine of [*Chaplinsky*]. The Court in *Chaplinsky* affirmed a conviction under a statute that, as authoritatively construed, applied only to words with a direct tendency to cause violence by the persons to whom, individually, the words were addressed. A conviction for less than words that at least tend to incite an immediate breach of the peace cannot be justified under *Chaplinsky*. The Illinois Supreme Court has squarely ruled that responsive violence fears and the fighting words doctrine could not support the prohibition of appellees' demonstration. Although that decision was in a prior restraint context, and we are here considering only the post facto criminal aspects of 995, the decision does buttress our conclusion that *Chaplinsky* does not cover this case. Again, the Village does not seriously contest this point.

Four basic arguments are advanced by the Village to justify the content restrictions of 995. First, it is said that the content criminalized by 995 is "totally lacking in social content," and that it consists of "false statements of fact" in which there is "no constitutional value." We disagree that, if applied to the proposed demonstration, the ordinance can be said to be limited to "statements of fact," false or otherwise. No handbills are to be distributed; no speeches are planned. To the degree that the symbols in question can be said to assert anything specific, it must be the Nazi ideology, which cannot be treated as a mere false "fact." . . .

In the words of Justice Jackson, "every person must be his own watchman for truth, because the forefathers did not trust any government to separate the true from the false for us." The asserted falseness of Nazi dogma, and, indeed, its general repudiation, simply do not justify its suppression.

The Village's second argument, and the one on which principal reliance is placed, centers on *Beauharnais* v. *Illinois*. There a conviction was upheld under a statute prohibiting, in language substantially (and perhaps not unintentionally) similar to that used in the ordinance here, the dissemination of materials promoting racial or religious hatred. The closely-divided Court stated that the criminal punishment of libel of an individual raised no constitutional problems, relying on [Chaplinsky]. . . .

In our opinion Beauharnais does not support ordinance 995, for two independent reasons. First, the rationale of that decision turns quite plainly on the strong tendency of the prohibited utterances to cause violence and disorder. The Illinois Supreme Court had so limited the statute's application, as the United States Supreme Court noted. The latter Court also pointed out that the tendency to induce breach of the peace was the traditional justification for the criminal libel laws which had always been thought to be immune from the First Amendment. After stating the issue (whether Illinois could extend criminal libel to groups) the Court turned to Illinois' history of racial strife "and its frequent obligato of extreme racial and religious propaganda," and concluded that the Illinois legislature could reasonably connect the strife and the propaganda and criminalize the latter to prevent the former. . . .

It may be questioned, after cases such as [Cohen], [Gooding], and [Brandenburg], whether the tendency to induce violence approach sanctioned implicitly in Beauharnais would pass constitutional muster today. Assuming that it would, however, it does not support ordinance 995, because the Village, as we have indicated, does not assert appellees' possible violence, an audience's possible responsive violence, or possible violence against third parties by those incited by appellees, as justifications for 995. Ordinance 995 would apparently be applied in the absence of any such threat. The rationale of Beauharnais, then, simply does not apply here.

Further, when considering the application of Beauharnais to the present litigation, we cannot be unmindful of the "package" aspects of the ordinances and that the "insulting" words are to be made public only after a 30-day permit application waiting period. Violence occurring under such a circumstance would have such indicia of premeditation as to seem inconsistent with calling into play any remaining vitality of the Beauharnais rationale.

The Village asserts that Beauharnais implicitly sanctions prohibiting the use of First Amendment rights to invoke racial or religious hatred even without reference to fears of violence. In the light of our discussion of Beauharnais's premises, we do not find the case susceptible of this interpretation. Even if it were, however, we agree with the district court that decisions in the quarter-century since Beauharnais have abrogated the Chaplinsky dictum, made one of the premises of Beauharnais, that the punishment of libel "has never been thought to raise any Constitutional problem." [New York Times v. Sulli-

van and subsequent cases] are indisputable evidence that libel does indeed now raise serious and knotty First Amendment problems, sufficient as a matter of constitutional law to require the substantial rewriting of both criminal and civil state libel laws.

The Eighth Circuit, and Judge Wright of the District of Columbia Circuit, have expressed doubt, which we share, that *Beauharnais* remains good law at all after the constitutional libel cases. We agree at least this far: If 995 is to be sustained, it must be done on the basis of the Village's interest asserted, and the conduct to which 995 applies, not on the basis of blind obeisance to uncertain implications from an opinion issued years before the Supreme Court itself rewrote the rules.

The Village's third argument is that it has a policy of fair housing, which the dissemination of racially defamatory material could undercut. We reject this argument without extended discussion. That the effective exercise of First Amendment rights may undercut a given government's policy on some issue is, indeed, one of the purposes of those rights. No distinction is constitutionally admissible that turns on the intrinsic justice of the particular policy in issue.

The Village's fourth argument is that the Nazi march, involving as it does the display of uniforms and swastikas, will create a substantive evil that it has a right to prohibit: the infliction of psychic trauma on resident holocaust survivors and other Jewish residents. The Village points out that Illinois recognizes the "new tort" of intentional infliction of severe emotional distress, the coverage of which may well include personally directed racial slurs. Assuming that specific individuals could proceed in tort under this theory to recover damages provably occasioned by the proposed march, and that a First Amendment defense would not bar the action, it is nonetheless quite a different matter to criminalize protected First Amendment conduct in anticipation of such results.

It would be grossly insensitive to deny, as we do not, that the proposed demonstration would seriously disturb, emotionally and mentally, at least some, and probably many of the Village's residents. The problem with engrafting an exception on the First Amendment for such situations is that they are indistinguishable in principle from speech that "invite(s) dispute . . . induces a condition of unrest, creates dissatisfaction with conditions as they are, or even stirs people to anger." Yet these are among the "high purposes" of the First Amendment. It is perfectly clear that a state may not "make criminal the peaceful expression of unpopular views." Likewise, "mere public intolerance or animosity cannot be the basis for abridgment of these constitutional freedoms." Where, as here, a crime is made of a silent march, attended only by symbols and not by extrinsic conduct offensive in itself, we think the words of the Court [in *Street* v. *New York*] are very much on point: "[A]ny shock effect . . . must be attributed to the content of the ideas expressed. It is firmly settled that under our Constitution the public expression of ideas may not be prohibited merely because the ideas are themselves offensive to some of their hearers."

It is said that the proposed march is not speech, or even "speech plus," but rather an invasion, intensely menacing no matter how peacefully conducted. The Village's expert psychiatric witness, in fact, testified that the effect of the march would be much the same regardless of whether uniforms and swastikas were displayed, due to the intrusion of self-proclaimed Nazis into what he characterized as predominately Jewish "turf." There is room under the First Amendment for the government to protect targeted listeners from offensive speech, but only when the speaker intrudes on the privacy of the home, or a captive audience cannot practically avoid exposure. . . .

This case does not involve intrusion into people's homes. There need be no captive audience, as Village residents may, if they wish, simply avoid the Village Hall for thirty minutes on a Sunday afternoon, which no doubt would be their normal course of conduct on a day when the Village Hall was not open in the regular course of business. Absent such intrusion or captivity, there is no justifiable substantial privacy interest to save 995 from constitutional infirmity, when it attempts, by fiat, to declare the entire Village, at all times, a privacy zone that may be sanitized from the offensiveness of Nazi ideology and symbols.

We conclude that 995 may not be applied to criminalize the conduct of the proposed demonstration. Because it is susceptible to such an application, we also conclude that it suffers from substantial overbreadth, even if some of the purposes 995 is said to serve might constitutionally be protectible by an appropriate and narrower ordinance. The latter conclusion is also supported by the fact that the ordinance could conceivably be applied to criminalize dissemination of *The Merchant of Venice* or a vigorous discussion of the merits of reverse racial discrimination in Skokie. Although there is reason to think, as the district court concluded, that the ordinance is fatally vague as well, because it turns in part on subjective reactions to prohibited conduct, we do not deem it necessary to rest our decision on that ground. . . .

[The court goes on to invalidate the insurance requirements imposed by the Village for large marches and demonstrations.]

The preparation and issuance of this opinion has not been an easy task, or one which we have relished. Recognizing the implication that often seems to follow over-protestation, we nevertheless feel compelled once again to express our repugnance at the doctrines which the appellees desire to profess publicly. Indeed, it is a source of extreme regret that after several thousand years of attempting to strengthen the often thin coating of civilization with which humankind has attempted to hide brutal animal-like instincts, there would still be those who would resort to hatred and vilification of fellow human beings because of their racial background or their religious beliefs, or for that matter, because of any reason at all.

Retaining meaning in civil rights, particularly those many of the founding fathers believed sufficiently important as to delay the approval of the Constitution until they could be included in the Bill of Rights, seldom seems to be accomplished by the easy cases, however, and it was not so here.

Although we would have thought it unnecessary to say so, it apparently deserves emphasis in the light of the dissent's reference to this court apologizing as to the result, that our *regret* at the use appellees plan to make of their rights is not in any sense an *apology* for upholding the First Amendment. The result we have reached is dictated by the fundamental proposition that if these civil rights are to remain vital for all, they must protect not only those society deems acceptable, but also those whose ideas it quite justifiably rejects and despises.

The judgment of the district court is affirmed.

Discussion Questions

1. As in previous First Amendment cases you have read, context seems particularly important in this case. To what extent do you think any of the following hypothetical *changes* to the factual situation would have altered the Court's decision in this case?

     a. Collin and the NSPA wished to
        • march with several thousand members through Skokie's streets
        • deliver an anti-Semitic speech in a park directly in front of the city's major Jewish synagogue
        • deliver the speech during Saturday morning services
     b. The local chapter of the Jewish Defense League has threatened to "Stop this Nazi disgrace, no matter what it takes to do so."

2. This ruling has been seen as particularly problematic for advocates of campus hate speech codes. Can you make a persuasive case that the Skokie situation is fundamentally different from the situation on public university

campuses, and that more regulation of hate speech should be permissible in universities than in local communities? Alternatively, is there not an argument that universities—as places of open inquiry and the "search for truth"—should be even more open to free expression of ideas than society at large?

3. Do you agree with this decision? Why or why not? If you disagree, what kinds of constitutional arguments could you make to support the Village of Skokie's actions? Are there other actions the village might have taken that could have addressed the situation with fewer constitutional problems?

R.A.V. v. *City of St. Paul*
505 U.S. 377 (1992)

Mr. Justice Scalia delivered the opinion of the Court.

In the predawn hours of June 21, 1990, petitioner and several other teenagers allegedly assembled a crudely-made cross by taping together broken chair legs. They then allegedly burned the cross inside the fenced yard of a black family that lived across the street from the house where petitioner was staying. Although this conduct could have been punished under any of a number of laws, one of the two provisions under which respondent city of St. Paul chose to charge petitioner (then a juvenile) was the St. Paul Bias-Motivated Crime Ordinance, which provides: "Whoever places on public or private property a symbol, object, appellation, characterization or graffiti, including, but not limited to, a burning cross or Nazi swastika, which one knows or has reasonable grounds to know arouses anger, alarm or resentment in others on the basis of race, color, creed, religion or gender commits disorderly conduct and shall be guilty of a misdemeanor."

Petitioner moved to dismiss this count on the ground that the St. Paul ordinance was substantially overbroad and impermissibly content-based and therefore facially invalid under the First Amendment. The trial court granted this motion, but the Minnesota Supreme Court reversed. That court rejected petitioner's overbreadth claim because, as construed in prior Minnesota cases, the modifying phrase "arouses anger, alarm or resentment in others" limited the reach of the ordinance to conduct that amounts to "fighting words," i.e., "conduct that itself inflicts injury or tends to incite immediate violence . . ." [*Chaplinsky*], and therefore the ordinance reached only expression "that the First Amendment does not protect." The court also concluded that the ordinance was not impermissibly content-based because, in its view, "the ordinance is a narrowly tailored means toward accomplishing the compelling governmental interest in protecting the community against bias-motivated threats to public safety and order." We granted certiorari.

I

In construing the St. Paul ordinance, we are bound by the construction given to it by the Minnesota court. Accordingly, we accept the Minnesota Supreme Court's authoritative statement that the ordinance reaches only those expressions that constitute "fighting words" within the meaning of *Chaplinsky*. Petitioner and his amici urge us to modify the scope of the *Chaplinsky* formulation, thereby invalidating the ordinance as "substantially overbroad." We find it unnecessary to consider this issue. Assuming, arguendo, that all of the expression reached by the ordinance is proscribable under the "fighting words" doctrine, we nonetheless conclude that the ordinance is facially unconstitutional in that it prohibits otherwise permitted speech solely on the basis of the subjects the speech addresses.

The First Amendment generally prevents government from proscribing speech, or even expressive conduct, see, e.g., *Texas* v. *Johnson*, because of disapproval of the ideas expressed. Content-based regulations are presumptively invalid. From 1791 to the present, however, our society, like other free but civilized societies, has permitted restrictions upon the content of speech in a few limited areas, which are "of such slight social value as a step to truth that any benefit that may be derived from them is clearly outweighed by the social interest in order and morality" [*Chaplinsky*]. We have recognized that "the freedom of speech" referred to by the First Amendment does not include a freedom to disregard these traditional limitations. Our decisions since the 1960s have narrowed the scope of the traditional categorical exceptions for defamation, and for obscenity, but a limited categorical approach has remained an important part of our First Amendment jurisprudence.

We have sometimes said that these categories of expression are "not within the area of constitutionally protected speech," or that the "protection of the First Amendment does not extend" to them. Such statements must be taken in context, however, and are no more literally true than is the occasionally repeated shorthand characterizing obscenity "as not being speech at all." What they mean is that these areas of speech can, consistently with the First Amendment, be regulated because of their constitutionally proscribable content (obscenity, defamation, etc.)—not that they are categories of speech entirely invisible to the Constitution, so that they may be made the vehicles for content discrimination unrelated to their distinctively proscribable content.

Thus, the government may proscribe libel; but it may not make the further content discrimination of proscribing only libel critical of the government. . . .

Our cases surely do not establish the proposition that the First Amendment imposes no obstacle whatsoever to regulation of particular instances of such proscribable expression, so that the government "may regulate [them] freely." That would mean that a city council could enact an ordinance prohibiting only those legally obscene works that contain criticism of the city government or, indeed, that do not include endorsement of the city government. Such a simplistic, all-or-nothing-at-all approach to First Amendment protection is at odds with common sense and with our jurisprudence as well. It is not true that "fighting words" have at most a "de minimis" expressive content, or that their content is in all respects "worthless and undeserving of constitutional protection"; sometimes they are quite expressive indeed. We have not said that they constitute "no part of the expression of ideas," but only that they constitute "no essential part of any exposition of ideas" [*Chaplinsky*].

The proposition that a particular instance of speech can be proscribable on the basis of one feature (e.g., obscenity) but not on the basis of another (e.g., opposition to the city government) is commonplace, and has found application in many contexts. We have long held, for example, that nonverbal expressive activity can be banned because of the action it entails, but not because of the ideas it expresses—so that burning a flag in violation of an ordinance against outdoor fires could be punishable, whereas burning a flag in violation of an ordinance against dishonoring the flag is not [*Johnson*]. Similarly, we have upheld reasonable "time, place, or manner" restrictions, but only if they are "justified without reference to the content of the regulated speech." And just as the power to proscribe particular speech on the basis of a noncontent element (e.g., noise) does not entail the power to proscribe the same speech on the basis of a content element; so also, the power to proscribe it on the basis of one content element (e.g., obscenity) does not entail the power to proscribe it on the basis of other content elements.

In other words, the exclusion of "fighting words" from the scope of the First Amendment simply means that, for purposes of that Amendment, the unprotected features of the words are, despite their verbal character, essentially a "nonspeech" element of communication. Fighting words are thus analogous to a noisy sound truck: Each is, as Justice Frankfurter recognized, a "mode of speech"; both can be used to convey an idea; but neither has, in and of itself, a claim upon the First Amendment. As with the sound truck, however, so also with fighting words: The government may not regulate use based on hostility—or favoritism—towards the underlying message expressed.

The concurrences describe us as setting forth a new First Amendment principle that prohibition of constitutionally proscribable speech cannot be "un-derinclusiv[e]"—a First Amendment "absolutism" whereby "within a partic-ular 'proscribable' category of expression, . . . a government must either proscribe all speech or no speech at all." That easy target is of the con-currences' own invention. In our view, the First Amendment imposes not an "underinclusiveness" limitation but a "content discrimination" limitation upon a State's prohibition of proscribable speech. There is no problem what-ever, for example, with a State's prohibiting obscenity (and other forms of proscribable expression) only in certain media or markets, for although that prohibition would be "underinclusive," it would not discriminate on the basis of content.

Even the prohibition against content discrimination that we assert the First Amendment requires is not absolute. It applies differently in the context of proscribable speech than in the area of fully protected speech. The rationale of the general prohibition, after all, is that content discrimination "rais[es] the specter that the Government may effectively drive certain ideas or viewpoints from the marketplace." But content discrimination among various instances of a class of proscribable speech often does not pose this threat.

When the basis for the content discrimination consists entirely of the very reason the entire class of speech at issue is proscribable, no significant danger of idea or viewpoint discrimination exists. Such a reason, having been ad-judged neutral enough to support exclusion of the entire class of speech from First Amendment protection, is also neutral enough to form the basis of dis-tinction within the class. To illustrate: A State might choose to prohibit only that obscenity which is the most patently offensive in its prurience—i.e., that which involves the most lascivious displays of sexual activity. But it may not prohibit, for example, only that obscenity which includes offensive political messages. And the Federal Government can criminalize only those threats of violence that are directed against the President—since the reasons why threats of violence are outside the First Amendment (protecting individuals from the fear of violence, from the disruption that fear engenders, and from the possi-bility that the threatened violence will occur) have special force when applied to the person of the President. But the Federal Government may not criminal-ize only those threats against the President that mention his policy on aid to inner cities. And to take a final example (one mentioned by Justice Stevens), a State may choose to regulate price advertising in one industry but not in others, because of the risk of fraud (one of the characteristics of commercial speech that justifies depriving it of full First Amendment protection). But a State may not prohibit only that commercial advertising that depicts men in a demeaning fashion.

Another valid basis for according differential treatment to even a content-defined subclass of proscribable speech is that the subclass happens to be associated with particular "secondary effects" of the speech, so that the regulation is "justified without reference to the content of the . . . speech." A State could, for example, permit all obscene live performances except those involving minors. Moreover, since words can in some circumstances violate laws directed not against speech but against conduct (a law against treason, for example, is violated by telling the enemy the nation's defense secrets), a particular content-based subcategory of a proscribable class of speech can be swept up incidentally within the reach of a statute directed at conduct rather than speech. Thus, for example, sexually derogatory "fighting words," among other words, may produce a violation of Title VII's general prohibition against sexual discrimination in employment practices. Where the government does not target conduct on the basis of its expressive content, acts are not shielded from regulation merely because they express a discriminatory idea or philosophy.

These bases for distinction refute the proposition that the selectivity of the restriction is "even arguably" conditioned upon the sovereign's agreement with what a speaker may intend to say. There may be other such bases as well. Indeed, to validate such selectivity (where totally proscribable speech is at issue) it may not even be necessary to identify any particular "neutral" basis, so long as the nature of the content discrimination is such that there is no realistic possibility that official suppression of ideas is afoot. (We cannot think of any First Amendment interest that would stand in the way of a State's prohibiting only those obscene motion pictures with blue-eyed actresses.) Save for that limitation, the regulation of "fighting words," like the regulation of noisy speech, may address some offensive instances and leave other, equally offensive, instances alone.

II

Applying these principles to the St. Paul ordinance, we conclude that, even as narrowly construed by the Minnesota Supreme Court, the ordinance is facially unconstitutional. Although the phrase in the ordinance, "arouses anger, alarm or resentment in others," has been limited by the Minnesota Supreme Court's construction to reach only those symbols or displays that amount to "fighting words," the remaining, unmodified terms make clear that the ordinance applies only to "fighting words" that insult, or provoke violence, "on the basis of race, color, creed, religion or gender." Displays containing abusive invective, no matter how vicious or severe, are permissible unless they are addressed to one of the specified disfavored topics. Those who wish to use "fighting words" in connection with other ideas—to express hostility, for example, on the basis of political affiliation, union membership, or homosexuality—are not covered. The First Amendment does not permit St. Paul to impose special prohibitions on those speakers who express views on disfavored subjects.

In its practical operation, moreover, the ordinance goes even beyond mere content discrimination, to actual viewpoint discrimination. Displays containing some words—odious racial epithets, for example—would be prohibited to proponents of all views. But "fighting words" that do not themselves invoke race, color, creed, religion, or gender—aspersions upon a person's mother, for example—would seemingly be usable ad libitum in the placards of those arguing in favor of racial, color, etc. tolerance and equality, but could not be used by that speaker's opponents. One could hold up a sign saying, for example, that all "anti-Catholic bigots" are misbegotten; but not that all "papists" are, for that would insult and provoke violence "on the basis of religion." St. Paul has no such authority to license one side of a debate to fight freestyle, while requiring the other to follow Marquis of Queensbury Rules.

What we have here, it must be emphasized, is not a prohibition of fighting words that are directed at certain persons or groups (which would be facially valid if it met the requirements of the Equal Protection Clause); but rather, a prohibition of fighting words that contain (as the Minnesota Supreme Court repeatedly emphasized) messages of "bias-motivated" hatred and in particular, as applied to this case, messages "based on virulent notions of racial supremacy." One must wholeheartedly agree with the Minnesota Supreme Court that "[i]t is the responsibility, even the obligation, of diverse communities to confront such notions in whatever form they appear," but the manner of that confrontation cannot consist of selective limitations upon speech. St. Paul's brief asserts that a general "fighting words" law would not meet the city's needs because only a content-specific measure can communicate to minority groups that the "group hatred" aspect of such speech "is not condoned by the majority." The point of the First Amendment is that majority preferences must be expressed in some fashion other than silencing speech on the basis of its content.

Despite the fact that the Minnesota Supreme Court and St. Paul acknowledge that the ordinance is directed at expression of group hatred, Justice Stevens suggests that this "fundamentally misreads" the ordinance. It is directed, he claims, not to speech of a particular content, but to particular "injur[ies]" that are "qualitatively different" from other injuries. This is word-play. What makes the anger, fear, sense of dishonor, etc. produced by violation of this ordinance distinct from the anger, fear, sense of dishonor, etc. produced by other fighting words is nothing other than the fact that it is caused by a distinctive idea, conveyed by a distinctive message. The First Amendment cannot be evaded that easily. It is obvious that the symbols which will arouse "anger, alarm or resentment in others on the basis of race, color, creed, religion or gender" are those symbols that communicate a message of hostility based on one of these characteristics. St. Paul concedes in its brief that the ordinance applies only to "racial, religious, or gender-specific symbols" such as "a burning cross, Nazi swastika, or other instrumentality of like import." Indeed, St. Paul argued in the Juvenile Court that "[t]he burning of a cross does express a message and it is, in fact, the content of that message which the St. Paul Ordinance attempts to legislate." . . .

Let there be no mistake about our belief that burning a cross in someone's front yard is reprehensible. But St. Paul has sufficient means at its disposal to prevent such behavior without adding the First Amendment to the fire.

The judgment of the Minnesota Supreme Court is reversed, and the case is remanded for proceedings not inconsistent with this opinion.

It is so ordered.

Justice White, with whom Justice Blackmun and Justice O'Connor join, and with whom Justice Stevens joins except as to Part I(A), concurring in the judgment.

I agree with the majority that the judgment of the Minnesota Supreme Court should be reversed. However, our agreement ends there.

This case could easily be decided within the contours of established First Amendment law by holding, as petitioner argues, that the St. Paul ordinance is fatally overbroad because it criminalizes not only unprotected expression but expression protected by the First Amendment. See Part II. Instead, "find-[ing] it unnecessary" to consider the questions upon which we granted review, the Court holds the ordinance facially unconstitutional on a ground that was never presented to the Minnesota Supreme Court, a ground that has not been briefed by the parties before this Court, a ground that requires serious departures from the teaching of prior cases. . . .

[In] the present case, the majority casts aside long-established First Amendment doctrine without the benefit of briefing and adopts an untried theory. This is hardly a judicious way of proceeding, and the Court's reasoning in reaching its result is transparently wrong.

I

A

This Court's decisions have plainly stated that expression falling within certain limited categories so lacks the values the First Amendment was designed to protect that the Constitution affords no protection to that expression [*Chaplinsky*]. . . .

Today, however, the Court announces that earlier Courts did not mean their repeated statements that certain categories of expression are "not within the area of constitutionally protected speech." The present Court submits that such clear statements "must be taken in context" and are not "literally true."

To the contrary, those statements meant precisely what they said: The categorical approach is a firmly entrenched part of our First Amendment jurisprudence. . . .

To borrow a phrase, "Such a simplistic, all-or-nothing-at-all approach to First Amendment protection is at odds with common sense and with our jurisprudence as well." It is inconsistent to hold that the government may proscribe an entire category of speech because the content of that speech is evil, but that the government may not treat a subset of that category differently without violating the First Amendment; the content of the subset is by definition worthless and undeserving of constitutional protection.

The majority's observation that fighting words are "quite expressive indeed" is no answer. Fighting words are not a means of exchanging views, rallying supporters, or registering a protest; they are directed against individuals to provoke violence or to inflict injury [*Chaplinsky*]. Therefore, a ban on all fighting words or on a subset of the fighting words category would restrict only the social evil of hate speech, without creating the danger of driving viewpoints from the marketplace. . . .

[Part IB is omitted.]

II

Although I disagree with the Court's analysis, I do agree with its conclusion: The St. Paul ordinance is unconstitutional. However, I would decide the case on overbreadth grounds. . . .

In construing the St. Paul ordinance, the Minnesota Supreme Court drew upon the definition of fighting words that appears in *Chaplinsky*—words "which by their very utterance inflict injury or tend to incite an immediate breach of the peace." However, the Minnesota court was far from clear in identifying the "injur[ies]" inflicted by the expression that St. Paul sought to regulate. Indeed, the Minnesota court emphasized (tracking the language of the ordinance) that "the ordinance censors only those displays that one knows or should know will create anger, alarm or resentment based on racial, ethnic, gender or religious bias." I therefore understand the court to have ruled that St. Paul may constitutionally prohibit expression that "by its very utterance" causes "anger, alarm or resentment."

Our fighting words cases have made clear, however, that such generalized reactions are not sufficient to strip expression of its constitutional protection. The mere fact that expressive activity causes hurt feelings, offense, or resentment does not render the expression unprotected [*Texas* v. *Johnson, Cohen* v. *California*].

In the First Amendment context, "[c]riminal statutes must be scrutinized with particular care; those that make unlawful a substantial amount of constitutionally protected conduct may be held facially invalid even if they also have legitimate application." The St. Paul antibias ordinance is such a law. Although the ordinance reaches conduct that is unprotected, it also makes criminal expressive conduct that causes only hurt feelings, offense, or resentment, and is protected by the First Amendment. The ordinance is therefore fatally overbroad and invalid on its face.

III

Today, the Court has disregarded two established principles of First Amendment law without providing a coherent replacement theory. Its decision is an arid, doctrinaire interpretation, driven by the frequently irresistible impulse of judges to tinker with the First Amendment. The decision is mischievous at best and will surely confuse the lower courts. I join the judgment, but not the folly of the opinion.

Justice Stevens, with whom Justice White and Justice Blackmun join as to Part I, concurring in the judgment.

Conduct that creates special risks or causes special harms may be prohibited by special rules. Lighting a fire near an ammunition dump or a gasoline storage tank is especially dangerous; such behavior may be punished more severely than burning trash in a vacant lot. Threatening someone because of her race or religious beliefs may cause particularly severe trauma or touch off a riot, and threatening a high public official may cause substantial social disruption; such threats may be punished more severely than threats against someone based on, say, his support of a particular athletic team. There are legitimate, reasonable, and neutral justifications for such special rules.

This case involves the constitutionality of one such ordinance. Because the regulated conduct has some communicative content—a message of racial, religious, or gender hostility—the ordinance raises two quite different First Amendment questions. Is the ordinance "overbroad" because it prohibits too much speech? If not, is it "underbroad" because it does not prohibit enough speech?

In answering these questions, my colleagues today wrestle with two broad principles: first, that certain "categories of expression [including 'fighting words'] are 'not within the area of constitutionally protected speech' "; and second, that "[c]ontent-based regulations [of expression] are presumptively invalid." Although in past opinions the Court has repeated both of these maxims, it has—quite rightly—adhered to neither with the absolutism suggested by my colleagues. Thus, while I agree that the St. Paul ordinance is unconstitutionally overbroad for the reasons stated in Part II of Justice White's opinion, I write separately to suggest how the allure of absolute principles has skewed the analysis of both the majority and concurring opinions.

I

Fifty years ago, the Court articulated a categorical approach to First Amendment jurisprudence. "There are certain well-defined and narrowly limited classes of speech, the prevention and punishment of which have never been thought to raise any Constitutional problem. . . . It has been well observed that such utterances are no essential part of any exposition of ideas, and are of such slight social value as a step to truth that any benefit that may be derived from them is clearly outweighed by the social interest in order and morality" [*Chaplinsky*]. We have, as Justice White observes, often described such categories of expression as "not within the area of constitutionally protected speech."

The Court today revises this categorical approach. It is not, the Court rules, that certain "categories" of expression are "unprotected," but rather that certain "elements" of expression are wholly "proscribable." To the Court, an expressive act, like a chemical compound, consists of more than one element. Although the act may be regulated because it contains a proscribable element, it may not be regulated on the basis of another (nonproscribable) element it also contains. Thus, obscene antigovernment speech may be regulated because it is obscene, but not because it is antigovernment. It is this revision of the categorical approach that allows the Court to assume that the St. Paul ordinance proscribes only fighting words, while at the same time concluding that the ordinance is invalid because it imposes a content-based regulation on expressive activity.

As an initial matter, the Court's revision of the categorical approach seems to me something of an adventure in a doctrinal wonderland, for the concept of "obscene anti-government" speech is fantastical. The category of the obscene is very narrow; to be obscene, expression must be found by the trier of fact to "appea[l] to the prurient interest, . . . depic[t] or describ[e], in a patently offensive way, sexual conduct, [and] taken as a whole, lac[k] serious literary, artistic, political, or scientific value." "Obscene antigovernment" speech, then, is a contradiction in terms: If expression is antigovernment, it does not "lac[k] serious . . . political . . . value" and cannot be obscene.

The Court attempts to bolster its argument by likening its novel analysis to that applied to restrictions on the time, place, or manner of expression or on expressive conduct. It is true that loud speech in favor of the Republican Party can be regulated because it is loud, but not because it is pro-Republican; and it is true that the public burning of the American flag can be regulated because it involves public burning and not because it involves the flag. But these analogies are inapposite. In each of these examples, the two elements (e.g., loudness and pro-Republican orientation) can coexist; in the case of "obscene antigovernment" speech, however, the presence of one element ("obscenity") by definition means the absence of the other. To my mind, it is unwise and unsound to craft a new doctrine based on such highly speculative hypotheticals.

I am, however, even more troubled by the second step of the Court's analysis—namely, its conclusion that the St. Paul ordinance is an unconstitutional content-based regulation of speech. Drawing on broadly worded dicta, the Court establishes a near-absolute ban on content-based regulations of expression and holds that the First Amendment prohibits the regulation of fighting words by subject matter. Thus, while the Court rejects the "all-or-nothing-at-all" nature of the categorical approach, it promptly embraces an absolutism of its own: within a particular "proscribable" category of expression, the Court holds, a government must either proscribe all speech or no speech at all. This aspect of the Court's ruling fundamentally misunderstands the role and constitutional status of content-based regulations on speech, conflicts with the very nature of First Amendment jurisprudence, and disrupts well-settled principles of First Amendment law. . . .

Our First Amendment decisions have created a rough hierarchy in the constitutional protection of speech. Core political speech occupies the highest, most protected position; commercial speech and nonobscene, sexually explicit speech are regarded as a sort of second-class expression; obscenity and fighting words receive the least protection of all. Assuming that the Court is correct that this last class of speech is not wholly "unprotected," it certainly does not follow that fighting words and obscenity receive the same sort of protection afforded core political speech. Yet in ruling that proscribable speech cannot be regulated based on subject matter, the Court does just that. Perversely, this gives fighting words greater protection than is afforded commercial speech. If Congress can prohibit false advertising directed at airline passengers without also prohibiting false advertising directed at bus passengers and if a city can prohibit political advertisements in its buses while allowing other advertisements, it is ironic to hold that a city cannot regulate fighting words based on "race, color, creed, religion or gender" while leaving unregulated fighting words based on "union membership or homosexuality." The Court today turns First Amendment law on its head: Communication that was once entirely unprotected (and that still can be wholly proscribed) is now entitled to greater protection than commercial speech—and possibly greater protection than core political speech. . . .

In sum, the central premise of the Court's ruling—that "[c]ontent-based regulations are presumptively invalid"—has simplistic appeal, but lacks support in our First Amendment jurisprudence. To make matters worse, the Court today extends this overstated claim to reach categories of hitherto unprotected speech and, in doing so, wreaks havoc in an area of settled law. Finally, although the Court recognizes exceptions to its new principle, those exceptions undermine its very conclusion that the St. Paul ordinance is unconstitutional. Stated directly, the majority's position cannot withstand scrutiny. . . .

[Part II is omitted.]

III

As the foregoing suggests, I disagree with both the Court's and part of Justice White's analysis of the constitutionality of the St. Paul ordinance. Unlike the Court, I do not believe that all content-based regulations are equally infirm and presumptively invalid; unlike Justice White, I do not believe that fighting words are wholly unprotected by the First Amendment. To the contrary, I believe our decisions establish a more complex and subtle analysis, one that considers the content and context of the regulated speech, and the nature and scope of the restriction on speech. Applying this analysis and assuming arguendo (as the Court does) that the St. Paul ordinance is not overbroad, I conclude that such a selective, subject-matter regulation on proscribable speech is constitutional. . . .

Contrary to the suggestion of the majority, the St. Paul ordinance does not regulate expression based on viewpoint. The Court contends that the ordinance requires proponents of racial intolerance to "follow the Marquis of Queensbury Rules" while allowing advocates of racial tolerance to "fight freestyle." The law does no such thing. . . .

The St. Paul ordinance is evenhanded. In a battle between advocates of tolerance and advocates of intolerance, the ordinance does not prevent either side from hurling fighting words at the other on the basis of their conflicting ideas, but it does bar both sides from hurling such words on the basis of the target's "race, color, creed, religion or gender." To extend the Court's pugilistic metaphor, the St. Paul ordinance simply bans punches "below the belt"—by either party. It does not, therefore, favor one side of any debate.

Finally, it is noteworthy that the St. Paul ordinance is, as construed by the Court today, quite narrow. The St. Paul ordinance does not ban all "hate speech," nor does it ban, say, all cross-burnings or all swastika displays. Rather it only bans a subcategory of the already narrow category of fighting words. Such a limited ordinance leaves open and protected a vast range of expression on the subjects of racial, religious, and gender equality. As construed by the Court today, the ordinance certainly does not "raise the specter that the Government may effectively drive certain ideas or viewpoints from the marketplace." Petitioner is free to burn a cross to announce a rally or to express his views about racial supremacy, he may do so on private property or public land, at day or at night, so long as the burning is not so threatening and so directed at an individual as to "by its very [execution] inflict injury." Such a limited proscription scarcely offends the First Amendment.

In sum, the St. Paul ordinance (as construed by the Court) regulates expressive activity that is wholly proscribable and does so not on the basis of viewpoint, but rather in recognition of the different harms caused by such activity. Taken together, these several considerations persuade me that the St. Paul ordinance is not an unconstitutional content-based regulation of speech. Thus, were the ordinance not overbroad, I would vote to uphold it.

Discussion Questions

1. The constitutional defect of the St. Paul ordinance, according to Justice Scalia, would appear to be its "picking and choosing" of fighting words to be criminalized—even though fighting words as a general category are not protected by the Constitution.

    a. Do you agree with Justice Scalia that the ordinance is "content based," or with the justices who argue to the contrary?

b. What, if anything, might St. Paul do to remedy the defects in the ordinance and still maintain its general thrust?

2. Do you agree with Justice White that the problem with the ordinance is its "overbreadth"? What might be done to address this problem? Is the overbreadth problem more susceptible to solution than the defects identified in Justice Scalia's opinion?

3. This case has been interpreted by some commentators as sounding a "death knell" to efforts to address hate speech on university campuses. Do you agree?

CASE STUDIES

INTRODUCTION

One prominent scholar has described the problem of hate speech as perhaps the most difficult free speech issue of all.[1] As the materials that follow demonstrate, introducing the issue onto a college campus makes it even more difficult. Four case studies and one case vividly described in a court opinion are reported in this volume.[2] These include schools that have experienced particularly visible free speech conflicts as well as schools—public and private—that have grappled with different approaches to balancing speech rights and community considerations. Obviously, a handful of selected case studies cannot perfectly reflect the range of intriguing speech matters that have confronted universities, nor do we claim that our sample of cases captures even most of these issues. Instead, our purposes are far more modest: to take a first step toward cataloguing these disputes on several campuses, and to use these studies to illustrate some, though surely not all, of the issues implicated in today's speech debates on many of our campuses. As we indicated in the introduction to this book, it is our hope that this volume of material—along with these five illustrative cases—will provide an impetus to perform additional research and investigation of the home campuses of our readers.

The four case studies are comparable in format. In each, emphasis is given to description, not normative critique; the focus is on what happened on each campus, not on how things should have been resolved as a matter of policy or law. From time to time, the personal values of the authors do intrude on the analysis. When this happened, we tried to make the "editorializing" as clear as possible, while also keeping it to a minimum. The authors of the case studies, as well as the editors of the overall volume, begin with a strong attachment to traditional First Amendment values, but they also recognize the competing complexities that colleges confront, and even when the First Amendment "trumps" in these college disputes, it is plain that the victory, though not hollow, is at the expense of other worthwhile values and concerns.

There are many interesting themes implicit and explicit in these case studies. First, is the public/private distinction. The Bill of Rights, as a general proposition, applies to public, not private, institutions.[3] Yet there is a perversity of sorts in our cases—namely, that the two public universities (Michigan and Wisconsin) putatively took the most Draconian anti–First Amendment approaches, two of the private universities (Dartmouth and Duke) had no code at all, and the code of the third (Brown) was interpreted by University officials as being closer to a conventional regulation of action than to a proscription of pure speech.[4]

A second theme of these cases is the intriguing issue of whether codes are in fact adopted to do something substantial about hateful speech, or whether they are symbolic attempts to *appear* to care.[5] By passing the speech code, only to have it overturned later by the courts, the college becomes free to say that "its hands are tied" and there is nothing further it can do consistent with legal rulings; or, alternatively, it can eschew its earlier commitment to a code and once again champion a conviction to conventional First Amendment values. In either case, the college appears to have fought for the proscription of harmful speech, and can advertise that value regardless of how the formal position fared in the courts. Relatedly, there is some belief among college officials that codes contribute effectively to the recruitment of minority students because codes can provide concrete evidence of a school's commitment to creating a nonhostile environment for all of its students. There may be, then, many reasons for initially adopting a code, one of which may be a genuine belief that the code can and will effectively work, but other code proponents may be more interested in the symbolic value of the code than in its actual implementation and effectiveness.[6]

A third dimension along which codes vary is their location on an action/pure speech dimension. No schools countenance obvious, explicit harassing actions or behavior; codes of conduct or conventional statutes prohibit these. It is when speech—not action per se—is prohibited that the waters get more muddied. Again, even within the "speech" variable, there is clearly a continuum of characterizations of speech. The easiest speech to restrict is that which is inextricably linked to action. For example, after the Michigan code was struck down by the courts, the successor code linked the prohibited speech to action through the fighting words doctrine. This occurred at Wisconsin as well. Words could be prohibited if they were understood to lead immediately to a breach of peace. Moving along the continuum are words that, when uttered, constitute already prohibited forms of speech—for instance, slander and harassment. Although what constitutes each is not as easily decipherable, systematic harassment—even with words—and slanderous statements can be seen as outside the protection of the First Amendment. Moving even further along the continuum are words that collectively constitute a "hostile environment." As discussed earlier, and as exemplified in *Meritor Savings* and *Forklift Systems*,[7] the Supreme Court, in employment settings, has accepted the notion that a "hostile environment" constitutes proscribable "sexual harass-ment." Speech code proponents sometimes import this logic to defend limits on speech on campus. For example, Brown University's president invoked the logic of the workplace cases to justify Brown's emphasis on the need for a civil community, and thus the limits it imposed on language, which collec-tively constituted a "hostile environment" for selected sets of students. A bit further along the continuum is the "First v. Fourteenth" Amendments argu-ment, a close cousin to the "hostile environment" position. We labeled this view as part of the "new civil liberties" in our introduction. Basically it states that the First Amendment has no primacy in our constitutional schema and that it is natural to balance its protections against those of the Fourteenth Amendment. When speech conflicts with equality of opportunity (here equal opportunity to learn), equality "trumps" speech, assuming all else is equal. Free speech may be important, advocates of this new position argue, but it is an empty protection if all members of the college community do not have equal opportunities to engage freely in it. And, these proponents argue, in a college in which "words that wound" are protected, the fact that the words deeply offend particular vulnerable groups makes learning and participation for members in these groups impossible without codes. A genuine market-place of ideas cannot exist unless codes introduce civility into campus com-munication. Without this civility, vulnerable groups cannot meaningfully par-ticipate in the discourse that the First Amendment envisions. Thus, in the imperfect world of the "real" college, a choice between the primacy of the First and the Fourteenth Amendments sometimes becomes necessary, and some feel that creating a civilized college community dictates that, when in doubt, the Fourteenth Amendment ought to prevail.[8]

Another set of dimensions along which codes vary are the "to whom" and "where" considerations. Do the codes apply in public spaces in the classroom, public spaces in dorms, dorms at night, and so on? Similarly, should the codes apply to students alone, to faculty, to staff? The case studies deal with both actual incidents implicating many of these concerns, and hypothetical efforts by universities (see, for example, both Michigan's and Wisconsin's attempts) to answer these "who" and "where" questions. And the scope of these real and imagined applications most certainly put to the test the kinds of "First Amendment *v.* other values" matters noted above.

A major theme lurking in the case studies goes to the issue of who sup-ported these codes, who opposed them, and why each felt as he or she did. Some, for example, view supporters as pursuing a "PC" kind of agenda—that is, attempting to legislate what is and is not "politically correct." Others see supporters as being interested in minority recruitment, and in offering meaningful protections to those successfully recruited. On the other side of the issue, opponents range from those concerned that the codes really are disingenuous symbolic steps—steps taken, as discussed above, to appear to be doing "something" while not expecting or wanting much to change—to those who genuinely believe the codes ought to fail in light of standard First Amendment prescriptions. At Duke, for example, the voices of law professors trumpeting values succeeded in derailing the effort to pass a speech code. At many other universities (for example, Michigan and Wisconsin), opposition, when mounted, was unsuccessful. In traditional constitutional discussions, political and legal elites are conceived of as the "keepers of the creed," as individuals steeped in the importance of preserving fundamental rights even if unattractive individuals or groups are availing themselves of these rights. In a case such as the one at Duke when the "keepers of the creed" raised their voices in opposition to a challenge to traditional First Amendment values, the literature's predictions were borne out. However, what is just as interesting or more interesting, is when the proverbial "dogs didn't bark"—that is, when the "keepers of the creed" did not rally to fend off an assault on traditional values. There are many explanations for their behavior, but their relative silence, and in many instances, ineffectiveness, remain both puzzling and fascinating.

The specific case studies included here run the gamut from schools that adopted specific speech codes (Michigan, Wisconsin, and Brown) to those who considered codes but ultimately opted not to have them (Dartmouth and Duke). Each case study attempts to understand the particular school's final decision, but with such a small sample size, we remain reluctant to offer any sweeping generalizations about the correlates of codes versus no codes, or of particular provisions in codes. Each case study tackles the issues in a different way. At Brown, a specific incident triggered the story that is explored in the paper; the Duke study looks more generally at a university's attempts to balance speech with other laudable objectives; at Michigan and Wisconsin, we encounter perhaps the two most specific codes in the country, and trace their fortunes as they were considered in court; and at Dartmouth, we encounter a particularly polarized world, and a university's attempts to confront it consistent with the sensitivity it desires to show to minorities and its commitment to First Amendment values. Collectively, the cases give readers a feel for the concerns about speech on our nation's campuses and the ways in which universities have addressed these concerns. Most importantly, they tell a story about law in action, about values in conflict, and about trying to do the right thing while respecting constitutional provisions. And since these are debates about institutions that are familiar to all of us—our schools—the debates ought to resonate loudly and force the readers to begin coming to grips with how they feel such rules could be made and implemented.

Notes

1. Rodney Smolla, *Free Speech in an Open Society* (New York: Alfred Knopf, 1992), at 151–54.

2. The four case studies are products of original research. For a fifth case—that of the University of Michigan—we rely primarily on the Federal District Court opinion. The reasons for this choice are explained prior to presentation of the opinion.

3. In 1991, U.S. Representative Henry Hyde of Illinois introduced a bill that would have made the First Amendment apply to private colleges. The proposed law would have applied the requirements of the First Amendment to private colleges and universities. The bill was not acted upon by the House.

4. For discussion of a relatively narrowly drawn code at a private university (Stanford) see Thomas Grey, *Civil Rights vs. Civil Liberties: The Case of Discriminating Verbal Harassment,* 8 Social Philosophy and Policy 81 (1991). This code was struck down in *Corry et al.* v. *Stanford University,* Superior Court, State of California, County of Santa Clara, 27 February 1995.

5. The "nonuse" or "nonenforcement" of some codes has not gone unnoticed by observers. See Samuel Walker, *Hate Speech* (Lincoln: University of Nebraska Press, 1994), at 23 and 146.

6. Another cynical interpretation of the posture of university administrators suggests their professing support for codes and the values they represent, but also claiming that because of the First Amendment the school's "hands are tied."

7. *Meritor Savings Bank, FSB* v. *Vinson,* 477 U.S. 57 (1986), and *Harris* v. *Forklift Systems, Inc.,* 126 L. Ed. 2d. 295 (1993).

8. See Thomas Grey, *op. cit.,* for a similar discussion of individual liberties and group rights.

BLUE CHILL AT THE
UNIVERSITY OF MICHIGAN

In 1988, the University of Michigan instituted a speech code in response to growing unrest on campus. The code was declared unconstitutional by a Federal District Court in 1989, and no limits on speech have been subsequently adopted.

The Michigan speech code was far-reaching and dramatic. It applied to words uttered both outside and inside the classroom and to words spoken generally, not simply to words uttered "face-to-face," which are more easily regulated under case law.[1] It protected individuals from verbal stigmatization based on predictable attributes—race, ethnicity, sex, and so on—but also added a number of less common attributes for protection—for example, marital status and "Vietnam-era veteran status." In short, the Michigan Code was sweeping, novel in terms of its inclusiveness, and, most importantly, a package that stood in sharp conflict with traditional First Amendment jurisprudence.[2]

For this case study, we present the Federal District Court opinion, Doe v. University of Michigan, *the decision in which the code was declared unconstitutional. Two reasons led to our decision to provide the case instead of the case studies that were written for each of the other four campuses. First, though Michigan's code was more sweeping than Wisconsin's (one of the campuses for which we do present a case study), much of the two codes and of their subsequent history is similar. Second, and relatedly, the specific details of the Michigan Code are wonderfully presented in* Doe, *and the "value added" of a separate case study is not great. Thus,* Doe *functions as our Michigan case study, and along with the discussion of Wisconsin, a clear sense of the responses of these two midwestern public institutions is presented.*

Opinion in the Case of
Doe v. University of Michigan
721 F. Supp. 852 (E.D. Mich. 1989)

Cohn, District Judge.

> [T]aking stock of the legal system's own limitations, we must realize that judges, being human, will not only make mistakes but will sometimes succumb to the pressures exerted by the government to allow restraints [on speech] that ought not to be allowed. To guard against these possibilities we must give judges as little room to maneuver as possible and, again, extend the boundary of the realm of protected speech into the hinterlands of speech in order to minimize the potential harm from judicial miscalculation and misdeeds.

—*L. Bollinger*, The Tolerant Society *78 (1986)*

Introduction

It is an unfortunate fact of our constitutional system that the ideals of freedom and equality are often in conflict. The difficult and sometimes painful task of our political and legal institutions is to mediate the appropriate balance between these two competing values. Recently, the University of Michigan at Ann Arbor (the University), a state-chartered university, adopted a Policy on Discrimination and Discriminatory Harassment of Students in the University Environment (the Policy) in an attempt to curb what the University's governing Board of Regents (Regents) viewed as a rising tide of racial intolerance and harassment on campus. The Policy prohibited individuals, under the penalty of sanctions, from "stigmatizing or victimizing" individuals or groups on the basis of race, ethnicity, religion, sex, sexual orientation, creed, national origin, ancestry, age, marital status, handicap, or Vietnam-era veteran status. However laudable or appropriate an effort this may have been, the Court found that the Policy swept within its scope a significant amount of "verbal conduct" or "verbal behavior" which is unquestionably protected speech under the First Amendment. Accordingly, the Court granted plaintiff John Doe's (Doe) prayer for a permanent injunction as to those parts of the Policy restricting speech activity, but denied the injunction as to the Policy's regulation of physical conduct. The reasons follow.

Facts Generally

According to the University, in the last three years incidents of racism and racial harassment appeared to become increasingly frequent at the University. For example, on January 27, 1987, unknown persons distributed a flier declaring "open season" on blacks, which it referred to as "saucer lips, porch monkeys, and jigaboos." On February 4, 1987, a student disc jockey at an on-campus radio station allowed racist jokes to be broadcast. At a demonstration protesting these incidents, a Ku Klux Klan uniform was displayed from a dormitory window. These events and others prompted the University's president on February 19, 1987 to issue a statement expressing outrage and reaffirming the University's commitment to maintaining a racially, ethnically, and culturally diverse campus. The University was unable to identify any of the perpetrators. It is unknown whether the culprits were students. Likewise, there was no evidence to suggest that these were anything other than isolated and purposeless acts.

On March 5, 1987, the Chairperson of the State House of Representatives Appropriations Subcommittee on Higher Education held a public hearing on the problem of racism at the University in Ann Arbor. Forty-eight speakers addressed the subcommittee and an audience of about 600. The speakers were uniformly critical of the University's response to racial incidents and accused it of generally ignoring the problems of minority students. At the close of the hearing, the Chairperson was quoted as stating, "Michigan legislators will not tolerate racism on the campus of a state institution. . . . Racism has no place in this day and age. . . . [The subcommittee] will make our decision [on appropriations for the University] during their budget discussions of the next few weeks. . . . Some things have to change. The committee members want to meet with [the University's president]. Holding up funds as a club may be part of our response, but that will predicate on how the university responds."

Following the hearing, the United Coalition Against Racism (UCAR), a campus anti-discrimination group, announced that it intended to file a class action civil rights suit against the University "for not maintaining or creating a non-racist, non-violent atmosphere" on campus. Following discussions with a national civil rights leader in March of 1987, the University adopted a six-point action plan to remedy the racial problems on campus. This included the adoption of "[a]n anti-racial harassment policy . . . as a component of the University's rules and regulations with appropriate sanctions specified."

. . . In December 1987, the University President resigned and a former University president was temporarily appointed to the post until a permanent successor was chosen. On December 14, 1987, the Acting President circulated a confidential memorandum to the University's executive officers detailing a proposal for an anti-discrimination disciplinary policy. The proposed policy prohibited "[h]arassment of anyone through word or deed or any other behavior which discriminates on the basis of inappropriate criteria." The Acting President recognized at the time that the proposed policy would engender serious First Amendment problems, but reasoned,

> [J]ust as an individual cannot shout "Fire!" in a crowded theater and then claim immunity from prosecution for causing a riot on the basis of exercising his rights of free speech, so a great many American universities have taken the position that students at a university cannot by speaking or writing discriminatory remarks which seriously offend many individuals beyond the immediate victim, and which, therefore detract from the necessary educational climate of a campus, claim immunity from a campus disciplinary proceeding. I believe that position to be valid.

. . . At the January 15, 1988 meeting of the Regents, the Acting President informed the Board that he had been working on a proposed policy on student discipline dealing with racial harassment. . . . Adoption of a policy, he noted, "would enable the University to take the position that it was willing to do something about this issue." The Acting President conceded that any proposed policy would implicate serious civil liberties questions, but he expressed a commitment to pursue the problem nevertheless.

Following the January meeting, the Acting President appointed the Director of the University Office of Affirmative Action (Director) to draft a policy. The proposed policy went through twelve drafts. Throughout this process, the Director consulted with a lawyer in the Office of University Counsel and perhaps several University of Michigan Law School professors. . . . At the April 14, 1988 Regents meeting, the Policy was unanimously adopted. It became effective on May 31, 1988, and was set to expire on December 31, 1989, unless reenacted.

The University of Michigan Policy on Discrimination and Discriminatory Harassment

The Terms of the Policy

The Policy established a three-tiered system whereby the degree of regulation was dependent on the location of the conduct at issue. The broadest range of speech and dialogue was "tolerated" in variously described public parts of the campus. Only an act of physical violence or destruction of property was considered sanctionable in these settings. Publications sponsored by the University such as the *Michigan Daily* and the *Michigan Review* were not subject to regulation. The conduct of students living in University housing is primarily governed by the standard provisions of individual leases, however the Policy appeared to apply in this setting as well. The Policy by its terms applied specifically to "[e]ducational and academic centers, such as classroom buildings, libraries, research laboratories, recreation and study centers." In these areas, persons were subject to discipline for:

1. Any behavior, verbal or physical, that stigmatizes or victimizes an individual on the basis of race, ethnicity, religion, sex, sexual orientation, creed, national origin, ancestry, age, marital status, handicap, or Vietnam-era veteran status, and that
   a. Involves an express or implied threat to an individual's academic efforts, employment, participation in University sponsored extra-curricular activities, or personal safety; or
   b. Has the purpose or reasonably foreseeable effect of interfering with an individual's academic efforts, employment, participation in University sponsored extra-curricular activities, or personal safety; or
   c. Creates an intimidating, hostile, or demeaning environment for educational pursuits, employment, or participation in University sponsored extra-curricular activities.
2. Sexual advances, requests for sexual favors, and verbal or physical conduct that stigmatizes or victimizes an individual on the basis of sex or sexual orientation where such behavior:
   a. Involves an express or implied threat to an individual's academic efforts, employment, participation in University sponsored extra-curricular activities, or personal safety; or
   b. Has the purpose or reasonably foreseeable effect of interfering with an individual's academic efforts, employment, participation in University sponsored extra-curricular activities, or personal safety; or
   c. Creates an intimidating, hostile, or demeaning environment for educational pursuits, employment, or participation in University sponsored extra-curricular activities.

On August 22, 1989, the University publicly announced, without prior notice to the Court or Doe, that it was withdrawing section 1(c) on the grounds that "a need exists for further explanation and clarification of [that section] of the policy." No reason was given why the analogous provision in paragraph 2(c) was allowed to stand.

The Policy by its terms recognizes that certain speech which might be considered in violation may not be sanctionable, stating: "The Office of the General Counsel will rule on any claim that conduct which is the subject of a formal hearing is constitutionally protected by the First Amendment."

Hearing Procedures

Any member of the University community could initiate the process leading to sanctions by either filing a formal complaint with an appropriate University office or by seeking informal counseling with described University officials and support centers. The Policy states that it is the preference of the University to employ informal mechanisms for mediation and resolution of complaints whenever possible and in fact most complainants have chosen to proceed informally. University officers are authorized to act as mediators and employ educational sanctions, community service, disciplinary warnings, and restitution in attempting to reach a settlement acceptable to both the victim and the perpetrator. None of the records relating to enforcement of the Policy is to be included in a student's academic files, and the records so generated are to be maintained in accordance with applicable privacy laws.

Where a negotiated settlement proves impossible, a formal complaint would be filed with the Administrator of Complaints of Discriminatory Behavior in the Office of Vice-President of Student Services (Policy Administrator). The Policy Administrator would then undertake an independent investigation of the alleged incident to determine whether there is sufficient evidence of a violation to warrant the initiation of a formal hearing. If a hearing were necessary, a panel consisting of four students and one tenured faculty member would be convened to pass on the merits. The accused student would then be notified that a complaint had been filed against him or her, the specific charges, the identity of the complaining witness, and the facts of the complaint and investigation. At the hearing, the Policy Administrator would be responsible for presenting the charges against the accused student. Both the accused student and the complainant have the right to call and cross-examine witnesses and give testimony. The accused student has the right to have an attorney present at the hearing, but the attorney could not participate fully in the hearing unless suspension or expulsion were likely sanctions. If a majority of the hearing panel found by clear and convincing evidence that the Policy had been violated, they were to recommend an appropriate sanction. If the accused student is dissatisfied with the panel's decision, he or she has the right to have an appellate tribunal consisting of two students and the vice-president for Student Services independently review the conviction and sanction.

Sanctions

The Policy provides for progressive discipline based on the severity of the violation. . . . Depending on the intent of the accused student, the effect of the conduct, and whether the accused student is a repeat offender, one or more of the following sanctions may be imposed: (1) formal reprimand; (2) community service; (3) class attendance; (4) restitution; (5) removal from University housing; (6) suspension from specific courses and activities; (7) suspension; (8) expulsion. The sanctions of suspension and expulsion could only be imposed for violent or dangerous acts, repeated offenses, or a willful failure to comply with a lesser sanction. The University President could set aside or lessen any sanction.

Interpretive Guide

Shortly after the promulgation of the policy in the fall of 1988, the University Office of Affirmative Action issued an interpretive guide (Guide) entitled What Students Should Know about Discrimination and Discriminatory Harassment by Students in the University Environment. The Guide purported to be an authoritative interpretation of the Policy and provided examples of sanctionable conduct. These included:

- A flier containing racist threats distributed in a residence hall.
- Racist graffiti written on the door of an Asian student's study carrel.
- A male student makes remarks in class like "Women just aren't as good in this field as men," thus creating a hostile learning atmosphere for female classmates.
- Students in a residence hall have a floor party and invite everyone on their floor except one person because they think she might be a lesbian.
- A black student is confronted and racially insulted by two white students in a cafeteria.
- Male students leave pornographic pictures and jokes on the desk of a female graduate student.
- Two men demand that their roommate in the residence hall move out and be tested for AIDS.

In addition, the Guide contained a separate section entitled "You are a harasser when . . ." which contains the following examples of discriminatory conduct:

- You exclude someone from a study group because that person is of a different race, sex, or ethnic origin than you are.
- You tell jokes about gay men and lesbians.
- Your student organization sponsors entertainment that includes a comedian who slurs Hispanics.

- You display a confederate flag on the door of your room in the residence hall.
- You laugh at a joke about someone in your class who stutters.
- You make obscene telephone calls or send racist notes or computer messages.
- You comment in a derogatory way about a particular person or group's physical appearance or sexual orientation, or their cultural origins, or religious beliefs.

It was not clear whether each of these actions would subject a student to sanctions, although the title of the section suggests that they would. It was also unclear why these additional examples were listed separately from those in the section entitled "What Is Discriminatory Harassment?"

According to the University, the Guide was withdrawn at an unknown date in the winter of 1989, because "the information in it was not accurate." The withdrawal had not been announced publicly as of the date this case was filed.

Standing

Doe is a psychology graduate student. His specialty is the field of biopsychology, which he describes as the interdisciplinary study of the biological bases of individual differences in personality traits and mental abilities. Doe said that certain controversial theories positing biologically-based differences between sexes and races might be perceived as "sexist" and "racist" by some students, and he feared that discussion of such theories might be sanctionable under the Policy. He asserted that his right to freely and openly discuss these theories was impermissibly chilled, and he requested that the Policy be declared unconstitutional and enjoined on the grounds of vagueness and overbreadth.

The University in response questioned Doe's standing to challenge the Policy, saying that it has never been applied to sanction classroom discussion of legitimate ideas and that Doe did not demonstrate a credible threat of enforcement as to himself. The University also asserts that Doe could not base his claim on the free speech interests of unspecified third parties. These arguments served only to diminish the credibility of the University's argument on the merits because it appeared that it sought to avoid coming to grips with the constitutionality of the Policy.

Article III of the Constitution limits the judicial power of federal courts to live cases and controversies. Traditionally, federal courts have interpreted this limitation to bar a party from maintaining a lawsuit unless the party had a sufficient stake in the outcome "as to assure that concrete adverseness which sharpens the presentation of issues upon which the Court so largely depends for illumination of difficult constitutional questions." . . .

It is well settled that an individual has standing to challenge the constitutionality of a penal statute if he or she can demonstrate a realistic and credible threat of enforcement. The mere possibility that a person might be subject to the sanctions of a statute is insufficient. Rather, the threat of enforcement must be specific and direct and against a particular party. It is not necessary, however, that an individual first be exposed to prosecution in order to have standing to challenge a statute which is claimed to deter the exercise of constitutional rights.

Were the Court to look only at the plain language of the Policy, it might have to agree with the University that Doe could not have realistically alleged a genuine and credible threat of enforcement. . . . The slate was not so clean, however. The Court had before it not only the terms of the Policy, but also its legislative history, the Guide, and experiences gleaned from a year of enforcement. The record clearly shows that there existed a realistic and credible threat that Doe could be sanctioned were he to discuss certain biopsychological theories.

The legislative history demonstrated that the Policy was originally conceived as a remedy for racially insensitive and derogatory remarks which students found offensive. The Acting President's December 14, 1987 memorandum to the University's Executive Officers stated that the proposed anti-harassment policy would sanction any "remarks which seriously offend many individuals beyond the immediate victim, and which, therefore, detract from the necessary educational climate of a campus." . . . [A]s late as February 2, 1988, the University attorney who researched the law and assisted in the drafting of the Policy wrote a memorandum in which he conceded that merely offensive speech was constitutionally protected, but declared that "[w]e cannot be frustrated by the reluctance of the courts and the common law to recognize the personal damage that is caused by discriminatory speech, nor should our policy attempt to conform to traditional methods of identifying harmful speech. Rather the University should identify and prohibit that speech that causes damage to individuals within the community." The record before the Court thus indicated that the drafters of the policy intended that speech need only be offensive to be sanctionable.

The Guide also suggested that the kinds of ideas Doe wished to discuss would be sanctionable. The Guide was the University's authoritative interpretation of the Policy. It explicitly stated that an example of sanctionable conduct would include: "A male student makes remarks in class like 'Women just aren't as good in this field as men,' thus creating a hostile learning atmosphere for female classmates."

Doe said in an affidavit that he would like to discuss questions relating to sex and race differences in his capacity as a teaching assistant in Psychology 430, Comparative Animal Behavior. He went on to say: "An appropriate topic for discussion in the discussion groups is sexual differences between male and female mammals, including humans. [One] . . . hypothesis regarding sex differences in mental abilities is that men as a group do better than women in some spatially related mental tasks partly because of a biological difference. This may partly explain, for example, why many more men than women chose to enter the engineering profession." Doe also said that some students and teachers regarded such theories as "sexist" and he feared that he might be charged with a violation of the Policy if he were to discuss them. In light of the statements in the Guide, such fears could not be dismissed as speculative and conjectural. The ideas discussed in Doe's field of study bear sufficient similarity to ideas denounced as "harassing" in the Guide to constitute a realistic and specific threat of prosecution. . . .

Finally, the record of the University's enforcement of the Policy over the past year suggested that students in the classroom and research setting who offended others by discussing ideas deemed controversial could be and were subject to discipline. . . . As will be discussed below, the Policy was enforced so broadly and indiscriminately, that plaintiff's fears of prosecution were entirely reasonable. Accordingly, the Court found that Doe had standing to challenge the policy.

Vagueness and Overbreadth

Doe initially moved for a preliminary injunction against the Policy on the grounds that it was unconstitutionally vague and overbroad and that it chilled speech and conduct protected by the First Amendment. The University in response said that the Policy has never been applied to reach protected speech and a preliminary injunction should therefore be denied. . . .

Scope of Permissible Regulation

Before inquiring whether the policy is impermissibly vague and overbroad, it would be helpful to first distinguish between verbal conduct and verbal acts that are generally protected by the First Amendment and those that are not. It is the latter class of behavior that the University may legitimately regulate.

Although the line is sometimes difficult to draw with precision, the Court must distinguish at the outset between the First Amendment protection of so-called "pure speech" and mere conduct. As to the latter, it can be safely said that most extreme and blatant forms of discriminatory conduct are not protected by the First Amendment, and indeed are punishable by a variety of state and federal criminal laws and subject to civil actions. Discrimination in employment, education, and government benefits on the basis of race, sex, ethnicity, and religion are prohibited by the [C]onstitution and both state and federal statutes. In addition, the state provides criminal penalties and civil remedies for assault and battery. Federal law imposes civil and criminal sanctions against persons depriving or conspiring to deprive others of rights guaranteed by the United States [C]onstitution.

Many forms of sexually abusive and harassing conduct are also sanctionable. These would include abduction, rape, and other forms of criminal sexual conduct. The dissemination of legally obscene materials is also a crime under state law. In addition, a civil remedy exists for women who are subjected to demands for sexual favors by employers as an express or implied quid pro quo for employment benefits. Minorities or women who are exposed to such extreme and pervasive workplace harassment as to create a hostile or offensive working environment are also entitled to civil damages. The First Amendment presents no obstacle to the establishment of internal University sanctions as to any of these categories of conduct, over and above any remedies already supplied by state or federal law.

While the University's power to regulate so-called pure speech is far more restricted [*O'Brien*], certain categories can be generally described as unprotected by the First Amendment. It is clear that so-called "fighting words" are not entitled to First Amendment protection [*Chaplinsky*]. These would include "the lewd and obscene, the profane, the libelous, and the insulting or 'fighting words'—those which by their very utterance inflict injury or tend to incite an immediate breach of the peace." Under certain circumstances racial and ethnic epithets, slurs, and insults might fall within this description and could constitutionally be prohibited by the University. In addition, such speech may also be sufficient to state a claim for common law intentional infliction of emotional distress. Credible threats of violence or property damage made with the specific intent to harass or intimidate the victim because of his race, sex, religion, or national origin is punishable both criminally and civilly under state law. Similarly, speech which has the effect of inciting imminent lawless action and which is likely to incite such action may also be lawfully punished [*Brandenburg*]. Civil damages are available for speech which creates a hostile or abusive working environment on the basis of race or sex [see *Harris* v. *Forklift Systems,* supra.]. Legally obscene speech is unprotected by the First Amendment, as are materials involving the sexual exploitation of children.

Similarly, speech which is "vulgar," "offensive," and "shocking" is not entitled to absolute constitutional protection in all circumstances. Certain kinds of libel and slander are also not protected, including possibly group libel [*Beauharnais*]. Finally, the University may subject all speech and conduct to reasonable and nondiscriminatory time, place, and manner restrictions which are narrowly tailored and which leave open ample alternative means of communication. If the Policy had the effect of only regulating in these areas, it is unlikely that any constitutional problem would have arisen.

What the University could not do, however, was establish an anti-discrimination policy which had the effect of prohibiting certain speech because it disagreed with ideas or messages sought to be conveyed [*Texas* v. *Johnson*]. As the Supreme Court stated in *West Virginia State Board of Education* v. *Barnette:* "If there is any star fixed in our constitutional constellation, it is that no official, high or petty, can prescribe what shall be orthodox in politics, nationalism, religion, or other matters of opinion or force citizens to confess by word or act their faith therein." Nor could the University proscribe speech simply because it was found to be offensive, even gravely so, by large numbers of people [*Texas* v. *Johnson; Collin* v. *Smith*]. As the Supreme Court noted in *Street* v. *New York:* "It is firmly settled that under our Constitution the public expression of ideas may not be prohibited merely because the ideas are themselves offensive to some of their hearers." These principles acquire a special significance in the university setting, where the free and unfettered interplay of competing views is essential to the institution's educational mission. With these general rules in mind, the Court can now consider whether the Policy sweeps within its scope speech which is otherwise protected by the First Amendment.

Overbreadth

1.

Doe claimed that the Policy was invalid because it was facially overbroad. It is fundamental that statutes regulating First Amendment activities must be narrowly drawn to address only the specific evil at hand. "Because First Amendment freedoms need breathing space to survive, government may regulate in the area only with narrow specificity." A law regulating speech will be deemed overbroad if it sweeps within its ambit a substantial amount of protected speech along with that which it may legitimately regulate.

The Supreme Court has consistently held that statutes punishing speech or conduct solely on the grounds that they are unseemly or offensive are unconstitutionally overbroad. . . . In *Gooding* v. *Wilson* the Supreme Court struck down a Georgia statute which made it a misdemeanor for "[a]ny person [to], without provocation, use to or of another, and in his presence . . . opprobrious words or abusive language, tending to cause a breach of the peace." The Supreme Court found that this statute was overbroad as well, because it punished speech which did not rise to the level of "fighting words," as defined in [*Chaplinsky*]. . . . In *Papish* v. *Board of Curators of the University of Missouri,* the Supreme Court ordered the reinstatement of a university student expelled for distributing an underground newspaper sporting the headline "Motherfucker acquitted" on the grounds that "the mere dissemination of ideas—no matter how offensive to good taste—on a state university campus may not be shut off in the name alone of conventions of decency." Although the Supreme Court acknowledged that reasonable restrictions on the time, place, and manner of distribution might have been permissible, "the opinions below show clearly that [plaintiff] was dismissed because of the disapproved content of the newspaper." Most recently, in *Texas* v. *Johnson,* the Supreme Court invalidated a Texas statute prohibiting burning of the American flag on the grounds that there was no showing that the prohibited conduct was likely to incite a breach of the peace. These cases stand generally for the proposition that the state may not prohibit broad classes of speech, some of which may indeed be legitimately regulable, if in so doing a substantial amount of constitutionally protected conduct is also prohibited. This was the fundamental infirmity of the Policy.

2.

The University repeatedly argued that the Policy did not apply to speech that is protected by the First Amendment. It urged the Court to disregard the Guide as "inaccurate" and look instead to "the manner in which the Policy has been interpreted and applied by those charged with its enforcement." However, as applied by the University over the past year, the Policy was consistently applied to reach protected speech.

On December 7, 1988, a complaint was filed against a graduate student in the School of Social Work alleging that he harassed students based on sexual orientation and sex. The basis for the sexual orientation charge was apparently that in a research class, the student openly stated his belief that homosexuality was a disease and that he intended to develop a counseling plan for changing gay clients to straight. He also related to other students that he had been counseling several of his gay patients accordingly. The student apparently had several heated discussions with his classmates over the validity and morality of his theory and program. On January 11, 1989, the Interim Policy Administrator wrote to the student informing him that following an investigation of the complaints, there was sufficient evidence to warrant a formal hearing on the charges of sex and sexual orientation harassment. [The letter stated in part: "One type of complaint alleges that you have engaged in discrimination and/ or discriminatory harassment on the basis of sexual orientation. Specifically the complaints allege the following: 1. You have made harassing statements in class and in classroom buildings to other students and/or faculty that are intimidating, hostile, and demeaning on the basis of sexual orientation. Specifically ——— complains that you have stated repeatedly that homosexuality is an illness that needs to be 'cured.' 2. You have made several anti-gay comments to other students, specifically to ——— stating that homosexuality is abnormal and unnatural." Although the Policy required identification of the complainants, these names were withheld from the Court to protect their privacy.] A formal hearing on the charges was held on January 28, 1989. The hearing panel unanimously found that the student was guilty of sexual harassment but refused to convict him of harassment on the basis of sexual orientation. The panel stated: "In a divided decision the hearing panel finds that the evidence available to the panel indicates that ——— did not harass students on the basis of sexual orientation under the strict definition of 'The University of Michigan Policy on Discrimination and Discriminatory Harassment by Students in the University Environment.' In accordance with First Amendment rights to free speech and the University's policy of academic freedom, ——— did not violate the policy by discussing either the origins or 'curability' of homosexuality in the School of Social Work."

Although the student was not sanctioned over the allegations of sexual orientation harassment, the fact remains that the Policy Administrator—the authoritative voice of the University on these matters—saw no First Amendment problem in forcing the student to a hearing to answer for allegedly harassing statements made in the course of academic discussion and research. Moreover, there is no indication that had the hearing panel convicted rather than acquitted the student, the University would have interceded to protect the interests of academic freedom and freedom of speech.

A second case, which was informally resolved, also demonstrated that the University did not exempt statements made in the course of classroom academic discussions from the sanctions of the Policy. On September 28, 1988, a complaint was filed against a student in an entrepreneurship class in the School of Business Administration for reading an allegedly homophobic limerick during a scheduled class public-speaking exercise which ridiculed a well known athlete for his presumed sexual orientation. The Policy Administrator was able to persuade the perpetrator to attend an educational "gay rap" session, write a letter of apology to the *Michigan Daily,* and apologize to his class and the matter was dropped. No discussion of the possibility that the limerick was protected speech appears in the file or in the Administrator's notes.

A third incident involved a comment made in the orientation session of a preclinical dentistry class. The class was widely regarded as one of the most difficult for second year dentistry students. To allay fears and concerns at the outset, the class was broken up into small sections to informally discuss anticipated problems. During the ensuing discussion, a student stated that "he had heard that minorities had a difficult time in the course and that he had heard that they were not treated fairly." A minority professor teaching the class filed a complaint on the grounds that the comment was unfair and hurt her chances for tenure. Following the filing of the complaint, the student was "counseled" about the existence of the Policy and agreed to write a letter apologizing for making the comment without adequately verifying the allegation, which he said he had heard from his roommate, a black former dentistry student.

The manner in which these three complaints were handled demonstrated that the University considered serious comments made in the context of classroom discussion to be sanctionable under the Policy. The innocent intent of the speaker was apparently immaterial to whether a complaint would be pursued. Moreover, the Administrator generally failed to consider whether a comment was protected by the First Amendment before informing the accused student that a complaint had been filed. The Administrator instead attempted to persuade the accused student to accept "voluntary" sanctions. Behind this persuasion was, of course, the subtle threat that failure to accept such sanctions might result in a formal hearing. There is no evidence in the record that the Administrator ever declined to pursue a complaint through attempted mediation because the alleged harassing conduct was protected by the First Amendment. Nor is there evidence that the Administrator ever informed an accused harasser during mediation negotiations that the complained of conduct might be protected. The Administrator's manner of enforcing the Policy was constitutionally indistinguishable from a full blown prosecution. The University could not seriously argue that the policy was never interpreted to reach protected conduct. It is clear that the policy was overbroad both on its face and as applied.

Vagueness

Doe also urges that the Policy be struck down on the grounds that it is impermissibly vague. A statute is unconstitutionally vague when "men of common intelligence must necessarily guess at its meaning." A statute must give adequate warning of the conduct which is to be prohibited and must set out explicit standards for those who apply it. "No one may be required at the peril of life, liberty, or property to speculate as to the meaning of penal statutes. All are entitled to be informed as to what the State commands or forbids." These considerations apply with particular force where the challenged statute acts to inhibit freedoms affirmatively protected by the [C]onstitution. However, the chilling effect caused by an overly vague statute must be both real and substantial, and a narrowing construction must be unavailable before a court will set it aside.

Looking at the plain language of the Policy, it was simply impossible to discern any limitation on its scope or any conceptual distinction between protected and unprotected conduct. The structure of the Policy was in two parts; one relates to cause and the other to effect. Both cause and effect must be present to state a prima facie violation of the Policy. The operative words in the cause section required that language must "stigmatize" or "victimize" an individual. However, both of these terms are general and elude precise definition. Moreover, it is clear that the fact that a statement may victimize or stigmatize an individual does not, in and of itself, strip it of protection under the accepted First Amendment tests.

The first of the "effects clauses" stated that in order to be sanctionable, the stigmatizing and victimizing statements had to "involve an express or implied threat to an individual's academic efforts, employment, participation in University sponsored extra-curricular activities, or personal safety." It is not clear what kind of conduct would constitute a "threat" to an individual's academic efforts. It might refer to an unspecified threat of future retaliation by the speaker. Or it might equally plausibly refer to the threat to a victim's academic success because the stigmatizing and victimizing speech is so inherently distracting. Certainly the former would be unprotected speech. However, it is not clear whether the latter would.

Moving to the second "effect clause," a stigmatizing or victimizing comment is sanctionable if it has the purpose or reasonably foreseeable effect of interfering with an individual's academic efforts, etc. Again, the question is what conduct will be held to "interfere" with an individual's academic efforts. The language of the policy alone gives no inherent guidance. The one interpretive resource the University provided was withdrawn as "inaccurate," an implicit admission that even the University itself was unsure of the precise scope and meaning of the Policy.

During the oral argument, the Court asked the University's counsel how he would distinguish between speech which was merely offensive, which he conceded was protected, and speech which "stigmatizes or victimizes" on the basis of an invidious factor. Counsel replied "very carefully." The response, while refreshingly candid, illustrated the plain fact that the University never articulated any principled way to distinguish sanctionable from protected speech. Students of common understanding were necessarily forced to guess at whether a comment about a controversial issue would later be found to be sanctionable under the Policy. The terms of the Policy were so vague that its enforcement would violate the due process clause.

Conclusion

A.

The foregoing constitutes the Court's findings of fact and conclusions of law. However, at this juncture, a few additional observations of a general nature would seem to be in order. . . . While the Court is sympathetic to the University's obligation to ensure equal educational opportunities for all of its students, such efforts must not be at the expense of free speech. Unfortunately, this was precisely what the University did. From the Acting President's December 14 memorandum forward to the adoption of the Policy and continuing through the August 25 hearing, there is no evidence in the record that any officials at the University ever seriously attempted to reconcile their efforts to combat discrimination with the requirements of the First Amendment. The apparent willingness to dilute the values of free speech is ironic in light of the University's previous statements of policy on this matter. In 1977, the Regents adopted the "Statement on Freedom of Speech and Artistic Expression: The Rights and Obligations of Speakers, Performers, Audience Members, and Protesters at the University of Michigan" (Statement) which "reaffirm[ed] formally [the University's] deep and lasting commitment to freedom of speech and artistic expression." The Statement provides in part that "freedom of speech must not ordinarily be restricted, governed, or curtailed in any way by content except where the law, as interpreted by the Supreme Court of Michigan or the Supreme Court of the United States, holds that such an expression does not fall within constitutionally protected free speech. In all instances, the University authorities should act with maximum constraint, even in the face of obvious bad taste or provocation. The belief that some opinion is pernicious, false, or in any other way detestable cannot be grounds for its suppression." The Statement was redrafted by the University's Civil Liberties Board in 1988. The new Statement, substantially identical to the old, was formally re-enacted by the Regents at their July 1988 meeting.

Needless to say, the philosophy expressed in the Statement is diametrically opposed to that reflected in the Acting President's December 14 memorandum. Apparently, no one involved in the drafting process noted the apparent inconsistency with the Regents' views as expressed in the Statement.

Throughout the case, the University's counsel strenuously urged that First Amendment concerns held a top priority in the development and administration of the Policy. Counsel repeatedly argued that the University interpreted the Policy to reach conduct such as racial slurs and epithets in the classroom directed at an individual victim. However, as the Court observed in its August 25, 1989 bench opinion, "[W]hat we have heard here this morning . . . from University counsel is a revisionist view of the Policy on Discrimination and Discriminatory Harassment by Students in the University Environment, and it is a view and interpretation of the Policy that was not in the minds of the legislators when it was adopted. And there is nothing in the record that has been presented to the Court which suggests that this was an appropriate interpretation of the policy." Not only has the administrative enforcement of the Policy been wholly inconsistent with counsel's interpretation, but withdrawal of the Guide, and the eleventh hour suspension of section 1(c), suggest that the University had no idea what the limits of the Policy were and it was essentially making up the rules as it went along.

B.

In his famous treatise on constitutional law, Thomas Cooley, Justice of the Michigan Supreme Court and Professor of Law at the University's Law School, came out as an early and forceful proponent of an expansive interpretation of the First Amendment. He reasoned that even if speech "exceed[s] all the proper bounds of moderation, the consolation must be that the evil likely to spring from the violent discussion will probably be less, and its correction by public sentiment more speedy, than if the terrors of the law were brought to bear to prevent the discussion." This observation appears as compelling today as when it was first written over one hundred and twenty years ago.

Discussion Questions

1. The interpretive guide distributed shortly after the code was promulgated included as sanctionable behavior the following: "Two men demand that their roommate in the residence hall move out and be tested for AIDS." On what basis does this constitute a form of "harassment" forbidden by the code? That these men should not "discriminate" against possible or

potential AIDS victims? If the roommate were an openly practicing homosexual, would a request that he be moved to another room by his heterosexual roommates constitute sanctionable harassment?

2. The Michigan code lists a specific set of criteria upon which students may not engage in "harassment": race, sex, religion, sexual orientation, etc. What is the justification for singling out these particular human characteristics for special protection? Is harassment on the basis of mental capacity ("You are too stupid to be studying at this university") or physical appearance ("You are an ugly cow") or body type ("fat slob," "flat as a board") any less hurtful to the victim? Should these categories be added to the list? How should it be determined which kinds of insults are sanctionable and which are not?

3. The "guidelines for implementation" state that the comment "Women simply aren't as good in this field as men" is a form of verbal harassment. Should an examination or discussion of physical or mental differences across races or between the sexes be excluded from classroom discussion? From faculty or student research projects? If so, on what basis? And does this determination have implications for research and study of other controversial topics? If not, how does one separate the academic study of these questions from racial- or gender-based harassment?

4. What is the fundamental problem with the Michigan speech code, at least in the eyes of the court? Do you read the court as saying that this particular code is invalid but that another code might pass muster? Or, as a practical matter, do you think the court is saying that any effort to stop hate speech by way of a campus speech code is doomed to failure?

5. The speech code at Michigan appears to have been prompted, to some degree, by legislative pressure and the threat of a lawsuit. Should the court's decision be a complete answer to the legislative pressure?

Notes

1. See *Chaplinsky*, above.

2. For a more detailed assessment of the Michigan code see Samuel Walker, *Hate Speech* (Lincoln: University of Nebraska Press, 1994), at 127.

BROWN UNIVERSITY'S ANTI-HARASSMENT CODE: THE CASE OF DOUGLAS A. HANN

Thomas R. Hower
Rutgers University

Spring, 1989
I issue a solemn warning that it is the policy of my administration
to take action against those who incite hatred. It is my intention
to prosecute vigorously and to expel immediately such individual
or individuals for any attempt to inject and promote racism and
thus insult the dignity of our students as citizens of Brown.

—*Vartan Gregorian*
  President, Brown University[1]

January 24, 1991
The Undergraduate Disciplinary Council's expulsion of Douglas A. Hann
for the drunken perpetration of homophobic, anti-Semitic and racially motivated "action" is upheld by Brown University's President Gregorian.

—*Brown University Student Newspaper* [2]

Summer, 1991
If freedom of thought on campus is to be protected, the universities themselves must summon up the clarity of purpose to defend the principles of
liberty on which the academic mission must rest.

—*Benno Schmidt, Jr.*
  former President, Yale University[3]

The Facts in the Case of Douglas A. Hann

On November 19, 1990, Brown University's Undergraduate Disciplinary
Council voted to expel junior Douglas A. Hann from the college. This would
have been an unexceptional occurrence had it not been for the fact that one of
the offenses for which Mr. Hann was expelled was "harassment" based on
certain racist, sexist, homophobic, and anti-Semitic slurs he made months earlier. This was the first test of Brown University's "harassment" offense, a
new addition to the University's Standards of Student Conduct in the student
handbook, as well as the first operation of the new university expulsion pen-

alty. The new offense and penalty were meant to protect students as "citizens of Brown" against offensive affronts to their dignity perpetrated by their more insensitive peers. For others, however, they represent another step in the imposition of "politically correct" sentiments at American colleges and universities.

Brown University in Providence, Rhode Island, is considered one of the country's most elite, most politically liberal, and most socially progressive educational institutions. Founded by New England Baptists in 1764, it draws together some 1,500 talented high school seniors each year, many of whose parents pay in excess of $30,000 a year for this educational privilege. The "harassment" offense was not the school's only liberal feature: Brown's educational philosophy, as represented by its curriculum, also manifests a zealously progressive spirit.

Brown University's curriculum does not require students to take any particular group of classes, usually called distribution requirements or a core curriculum at other colleges. In the American university, these classes have traditionally served to transmit a common body of knowledge about Western Civilization to generations of college students. Brown University maintained a core curriculum until 1969 when it was redesigned by two undergraduates, Ira Magaziner and Elliot Maxwell, based on the educational philosophies of John Dewey. The "New Curriculum" is based on free choice, combining pass/fail grade evaluations with maximum educational experimentation and minimal grade pressure. Symbolically, Brown University's "New Curriculum" represents a break with the traditional institutional transmission of the Western educational canon.

Another manifestation of Brown's social progressiveness are the "Tenets of Community Behavior," a document that articulates the preferred blend of individuality and community in the university context. The Tenets espouse a strong commitment to "the active promotion of racial and religious understanding, and to honest, open, and equitable dealings with racial, religious, sexual, and ethnic differences."[4] Individual freedoms are encouraged, as long as they are not exercised so "self-indulgently that they threaten the rights or freedoms of other individuals or groups."[5] In sum, "community members will be guided by a mutual concern for each other's integrity, needs, and feelings. Such concern demands sensitivity and a sense of responsibility—whether among members of the same sex, or the opposite sex; or among members of different religious groups; or among faculty, staff, and students."[6] To insure the dissemination of this understanding, each student is required to sign a card affirming that they have read the Tenets. The card is kept in the student's permanent file.

Thus it was in keeping with Brown University's path-breaking iconoclasm when it elevated the first nonwhite academic, a Stanford-educated Armenian named Vartan Gregorian from Tabriz, Iran, to an Ivy League presidency in early April, 1989. Years before, Gregorian, then Provost at the University of Pennsylvania, had been passed over for its presidency in a move rumored to have racial overtones. Gregorian left the University of Pennsylvania to head the New York Public Library where he proved to be a talented fund-raiser, closely tied to the highest levels of New York society.

Ironically, Douglas A. Hann and Vartan Gregorian arrived at Brown University within months of each other. Hann, of Pittsburgh, Pennsylvania, was admitted to the university's "time-honored walls"[7] in the fall of 1988. He was recruited as a football prospect and would eventually major in Business Economics and Organizational and Behavioral Management.

Two incidents occurred during Hann's freshman year at Brown which were harbingers for his subsequent educational experience and his eventual dismissal from the university. The first incident occurred during an argument at a Delta Phi fraternity party in the fraternity bar on January 27, 1989, when Hann, a white student, directed a racial epithet at a black student. Hann was rushing the fraternity to gain membership at the time. The incident was reported and Hann had to appear before the Undergraduate Disciplinary Council, a panel composed of five students and five faculty and administrators which metes out punishment for major offenses against the "University Community." For this offense, Hann was put on probation, required to attend a race relations workshop, and required to obtain counseling for a possible alcohol abuse problem. In retrospect, Hann would say it was "one of the most unfortunate incidents of my life."[8]

The second incident which, though completely unrelated to Hann, contributed to his eventual dismissal involved the appearance of anonymous racist and homophobic graffiti scrawled on several walls and doors in a dormitory on Brown's Pembroke Campus. Along with the graffiti, several pieces of white supremacist literature were circulated. Occurring just twenty days after he had taken office as Brown University's sixteenth president, the racist and homophobic graffiti and racist literature touched a nerve with Vartan Gregorian. He would later say, "The words and slogans scrawled anonymously on doors in one of our dormitories were vicious attacks threatening the well-being and security of Brown students."[9] It was the first incident that Gregorian, "a pot-bellied, goateed, septi-lingual emigré with mangled syntax and a mane of steel wool,"[10] had to address, and he did so in no uncertain fashion.

Amid stories describing Ku Klux Klan contacts at Brown and the threatened formation of a new Klan cell on College Hill, President Gregorian stood at

the center of a swirling maelstrom. Defiantly fixed on the steps of University
Hall on the college's main green, Gregorian issued the angry and bold procla-
mation which begins this chapter from a hand-held loudspeaker to an enormous crowd of students looking for direction from the new president. His
emotionally charged words and subsequent actions sent strong signals
throughout the university: he would not tolerate the slightest vestige of racism
on campus. He went so far as to threaten to consult the Federal Bureau of
Investigation for assistance in apprehending the culprits. Swift and sure punishment awaited any student who promoted racism on campus. Gregorian circulated a letter to this effect to all Brown students, faculty, alumni/ae and
parents.

As promised, one of his first acts following the mass meeting on the green
was to amend the offenses and penalties section of the Standards of Student
Conduct. This is a section of Brown's student handbook which sets out the
policies governing conduct for student members of the Brown community.
The two amendments to the Standards of Student Conduct reflect the president's anti-harassment rhetoric. These amendments will be considered later.

Douglas A. Hann was born on October 18, 1969. Twenty-one years later he
celebrated his birthday by becoming "visibly"[11] drunk at bars in Providence.
At 2:00 A.M. that night, Mr. Hann was walking home with friends past a freshman dormitory, Keeney Quadrangle. According to the account in the *Brown
Daily Herald*:

> [T]wo freshmen say they heard several voices in the street outside Keeney Quad
> shouting the word "nigger" and screaming "fuck you niggers." One of the fresh-
> men says he addressed three men on the street [one of whom was Hann] from his
> window, saying, "You should stop saying that. You're going to offend someone
> if you keep that up." One of the three men allegedly responded by yelling,
> "What's it to you? What are you, a faggot?" The freshman says he believes that
> the man then saw an Israeli flag hanging in the dorm room and the man began
> shouting, "Are you Jewish? Fucking Jew!"[12]

After this exchange, the unidentified freshman who responded from the
dormitory window, who was later confirmed to be Jewish, ran into the hallway
and asked two friends to join him in following the three men. The three students ran out of the dorm, telling others on their residence hall of the situation
as they went. The freshmen followed Hann's party to Wayland Arch, across
the street and half a block down from Keeney Quadrangle. A second confrontation, less clear in detail, ensued.

During this confrontation, Hann said "Happy Hanukkah"[13] to the student
he had yelled at in the window. One of the freshmen, a black woman, reported

that Hann yelled, "My parents used to own you people."[14] She responded by yelling "Asshole!"[15] at which point Hann had to be restrained by his companions from attacking the students. Upon questioning by the black woman, one of Hann's friends identified himself as being part Indian. The woman responded that she was surprised that someone who appeared to be an ethnic minority would stand up for a friend acting like Hann. He responded, "He's just drunk. He can't help it."[16] Hann and his friends left the Arch, still shouting racial epithets. One of Hann's friends, not quite as drunk as Hann, blocked the Arch, preventing pursuit by the freshmen. After this incident, the freshmen returned to Keeney Quadrangle and alerted Brown Police and Security, who sent an officer to take a report. Of the incident the freshman would say, "It went from something that just offended me, to something that offended me personally."[17]

Several days elapsed between the October 18 incident and Hann's introduction to the Brown student disciplinary system. The freshmen spoke to Dean of Student Life John Robinson and Dean of Students David Inman the next day and were encouraged to pursue the matter through the disciplinary system. Since none of the freshmen knew the identities of the men they had encountered that night, the freshman responsible for the confrontation and his roommate filled out witness statements at Police and Security headquarters and were given student "face" books, compilations of student pictures prepared for each freshman class, to review in hopes of making an identification. The "face" books were not helpful, though the students thought that they could identify the men in person.

After this effort, the case stagnated; there were no communications concerning the incident for over a week. Deans Robinson and Inman were silent and Director of Security John Kupervich maintained that he was waiting for the freshmen to come in and look through more face books. Of the administration's efforts on the case, the freshman observed, "It's not like they totally blew me off. But it wasn't like he said go down at a specific time. What I needed was for him to make an appointment . . . I did feel like they did not pursue it enough."[18]

The case was energized by the *Brown Daily Herald* reporters who covered the story for the paper and eventually the national media, Andy Bernstein and Smita Narula. In an interview, Ms. Narula said that Mr. Bernstein had heard about the incident from other students and encouraged her, then a freshman herself, to help with the reporting.[19] They met with the students involved and with another woman living in Keeney Quadrangle who had seen the incident. The woman believed that she had gotten Hann's first name and traced him through a picture in a face book. The freshmen were shown this picture, but were still unable to positively identify Hann. Ms. Narula characterized the offended freshman as still deeply shaken by the incident a week afterwards.[20] The resourceful *Herald* reporters then produced the university's fraternity "rush book" and sports media guide to offer more recent pictures. After positive confirmation using these sources, two of the freshmen and the *Herald* reporters went to Hann's room in Delta Phi and successfully identified him in person. The day after the identification, the freshmen contacted Police and Security again and pressed charges against Hann. The charges proceeded to the Office of Student Life, thus moving the case formally into the Brown University nonacademic disciplinary process.

The *Herald* reporters interviewed Hann soon after he was identified. He denied that he should be the subject of any charges. Beyond stating that he could not remember any such incident, he offered several excuses, "Are you serious or is this some kind of prank or something? . . . I have no idea what you are talking about."[21] In any event, he could not see the connection between calling someone a "fucking Jew" and anti-Semitism. A friend of Hann's would later comment, "Doug once went out with a Jewish woman, but said he was doing to her what the Jews had been doing to the American people for years."[22]

At the time of the Hann case, complaints were first dispatched to the Case Administration Group (CAG), which was charged with investigating to see if sufficient evidence existed to support a student conduct violation charge. The CAG was composed of the dean of students, who served as the chair, the director of Police and Security, three deans from the Office of Student Life, and a representative of the junior and senior classes, who were chosen from a list provided by the Undergraduate Disciplinary Council, exclusive of current UDC members. The CAG had almost complete control over the disposition of the charges, deciding whether and which offenses had been committed and whether they were of a major or minor character. Minor matters were channeled into various administrative offices as counseling problems. A major offense, as Hann's was ruled, was considered to have a significant impact on the university community and might warrant the expulsion of the offender. Upon an initial finding of evidentiary sufficiency for a major offense, the case would be transferred to the Undergraduate Disciplinary Council, the body which held hearings on such offenses.

The hearings were conducted by the chair of the Undergraduate Disciplinary Council, then Dean Robert Ripley. Only the UDC was allowed to have legal counsel at the hearing; the accused student was not allowed legal counsel. All hearing records were sealed until the university administration chose to make them public.[23] The accused and complaining students and any necessary parties were allowed to be in the room, but any other observers had to be approved by the chair. The Undergraduate Disciplinary Council arrived at its findings on the charges by vote. If the vote went against the accused, then one of the penalties listed in the student handbook would be chosen, also by a vote. The accused student's only appeal was to the university president.

After Dean Inman and the Case Administration Group's investigation, Hann was charged with violating Offenses II, III, and IV of the student disciplinary code. As they appear in the student handbook, these offenses include:

Offense II—Behavior which: causes or can reasonably be expected to cause physical harm to persons or shows flagrant disrespect for the well-being of others or is unreasonably disruptive of the University community or causes or can reasonably be expected to cause damage to property.

Offense III—Harassment: the subjection of another person, group, or class of persons to inappropriate, abusive, threatening, or demeaning actions, based on race, religion, gender, handicap, ethnicity, national origin, or sexual orientation.

Offense IV—Drugs and/or Alcohol: the illegal possession or use of drugs or alcohol, the illegal provision, sale, or possession with intent to sell of drugs and/or alcohol, drug and/or alcohol related behavior.[24]

The controversial anti-harassment offense, Offense III, formerly included only sexual harassment. The original Offense III was expanded by President Gregorian as one of his two amendments to the Standards of Student Conduct in the wake of the 1989 racist graffiti incident. Other types of harassment were not covered under specific university offenses, but were only alluded to under a more general statement of policy which preceded the actual student code. The statement read:

All members of the Brown University Community are entitled to the following basic rights: the rights of peaceful assembly, free exchange of ideas, and orderly protest, and the right to attend, make use of, or enjoy the facilities and functions of the University subject to prescribed rules. All members of the Brown University Community are also entitled to live in an environment free from harassment on the basis of such characteristics as race, gender, handicap, economic status, sexual orientation, ethnicity, national origin, or on the basis of position or function.[25]

The Case Administration Group sent the charges to the Undergraduate Disciplinary Council, which had its hearing on the Hann matter on Monday, November 19, 1990. Hann was present and admitted to making the statements in the complaint, but denied any harmful intent. Rather, he intended the statements as a warning that if he was attacked, he would file a lawsuit. The *Brown Daily Herald* reported that Hann handled himself poorly in the hearing. One member of the council who remained anonymous said, "He showed no remorse. He just said, 'All right, I fucked up.' "[26] At least six students who witnessed the alleged harassment were called to testify against Hann. He was able to cross-examine them. After taking testimony, the UDC found Hann guilty and unanimously agreed to immediate expulsion. The council decided to inform Hann of their decision by mail, but the story leaked and appeared in the *Brown Daily Herald* the next day.

Not only was Hann the first student to be found guilty under the harassment offense, he was also the first student to receive Brown University's ultimate penalty—expulsion. Expulsion is only one of the penalties available to the UDC in the student handbook. Others are: university sanction, suspension, community service, or university service. The expulsion penalty was the second amendment to the Standards for Student Conduct which President Gregorian changed in the wake of the 1989 racist and homophobic graffiti incident. Previously, the most severe penalty was suspension, which allowed the affected student to reapply to the university after the suspension period ended. Expulsion was simulated by extending the suspension period to ninety-nine years or more.[27]

Hann pursued his case to his only appeal, President Vartan Gregorian, who, two years earlier, had publicly promised the expulsion of any student who promoted racism on campus. The announcement of Hann's appeal appeared in the *Brown Daily Herald* on December 3, 1990.[28] On January 24, 1991, just after the winter vacation, the university made its first official comment in the matter of Douglas Hann, still without releasing his name. In a one-sentence memo tacked up outside Associate Dean of the College Robert Ripley's office, the administration announced, "The President has affirmed the decision of the UDC to expel a student for violation of Offenses II, III, and IV."[29] Hann would call the decision "a political statement by the University," maintaining that President Gregorian "just wanted to get someone."[30]

Campus reaction during this entire course of events was minimal. This quiet was interrupted when the *New York Times* picked up on the one-line university memo acknowledging the expulsion. A February 12, 1991, article was written for the *New York Times* by *Herald* editor and *Times* campus stringer Vernon Silver, entitled "Student at Brown Is Expelled Under a Rule Barring 'Hate Speech.' "[31] As one observer commented, "[s]uddenly the Free Speech pundits hopped on the Doug Hann bandwagon."[32]

Reactions from around the University

From its initial appearance in the *Brown Daily Herald* on November 2, 1990, through President Gregorian's decision to uphold the UDC verdict on January 24, 1991, there was a singular lack of campus concern for Hann's fate or its possible implications for free speech on campus. The number of articles written about Hann in the *Herald* was comparatively small and his case appeared in only one editorial in the campus newspaper—on November 28, 1990—prior to the expulsion.[33]

This editorial used Hann's case to support the hard university line on bias crimes and commented on the college's sexual assault policy:

> As a private institution, Brown can choose the standards it wants its students to uphold. Like many other universities across the country, Brown can theoretically discipline a student for pretty much anything, including "fighting words." The definition of "fighting words" is none too clear, but if anything falls into the category it is surely what Hann said on October 18th. We hope that definition doesn't expand to convict students who merely say or think things others don't want to hear, however. The UDC had adopted a hard line against bias crimes— even verbal harassment. Will it be hard on rapists? We hope so.[34]

The editorial offered Hann no quarter, and his UDC conviction was represented by the *Herald* editors as an improvement in the disciplinary system, symbolically communicating that the system was at least trying to respond to student concerns. The only publication where the free-speech implications of Hann's case were considered in detail was the December 1990 issue of the campus's libertarian publication, the *Brown Spectator*.[35] Prior to the attention in the popular press, even the Rhode Island ACLU, which had been aware of Hann's case for three months, said nothing.

Campus commentary on the expulsion after the case's appearance in the popular press fragmented into a shifting spectrum that ranged from the absolutist, free-speech faith to the "How did he get here in the first place?" school. One end of this spectrum is represented by then-senior Jeff Shesol, who spoke of the chilly atmosphere for free speech at Brown. "Unfortunately, I have to tell you that it all depends on your point of view. There are some things that are simply not discussed here and it's a frustrating thing as a student."[36] There were also more guarded comments that expressed the same concerns. Susan Leber, a freshman when Hann was expelled, offered her thoughts: "The ruling is in line with a student body . . . where my friends and I feel scared to stray from politically correct attitudes. . . . The problem is that abolishing words does not stop the thoughts behind them. I personally would rather know that someone is a racist, so I can watch my back, than stick my head in the sand and pretend that no such people exist."[37] While not condoning Hann's behavior, one of Hann's fraternity brothers commented to the *Times* that Brown students live under so many restrictions that great tension is created. He concluded, "It's like this place is some special world where there is no such thing as racism. Doug just got drunk and exploded."[38]

Nonetheless, many on campus supported the ruling. Indeed, the *Herald* editorial seemed to represent the majority sentiment among campus opinions. One observer commented, "On this issue, the University has drawn uncharacteristic support from the student body."[39] These views were captured by student Andrew Chen: "I'd like to think that there is a difference between free speech and free harassment. For any community there are conditions for membership. I think by joining the Brown Community, students agree to the kind of conduct that students want to see here."[40] Another student, Su Ming Yeh, echoed those thoughts: "Yes, there is free speech, but we've also got to take into consideration the rights of others to live in a comfortable and safe environment."[41]

At the far end of the spectrum were comments supporting Hann's expulsion as a necessary community purging, like the excision of a malignant growth. Sophomore Liber Della Piana said, "What Hann did was a direct personal assault on a student. But the New Right doesn't want you to see it that way. . . . In an atmosphere where racial harassment is tolerated, racist violence is not far off."[42] The *Herald*'s editorial stance increasingly reflected these opinions as the number of articles questioning the state of free speech at Brown increased in the popular press. In a February 13, 1991, editorial entitled "Good Riddance," the paper asserted that "Doug Hann is gone and the University is well to be rid of him. . . . [He was] a real jerk who got what he deserved."[43] The editorial also argued against the many who would try to raise Hann as a symbol of "political correctitude gone amuck."[44]

Brown University's alumni and alumnae also chimed in through the *Brown Alumni Monthly*. While the letters mirrored the range of student commentary on the expulsion, in some cases the letters offered interesting historical perspectives on free speech at Brown. Roger Vaughan, class of 1968, wrote: "In 1968 or thereabouts, I interviewed Barnaby Keeney, who was President of Brown University. Those were Vietnam War days, and antiwar sentiments were running high on all the campuses. On the day I met with Keeney, he had been handling a problem caused by the very radical pro–Viet Cong statements of a Brown professor. Here is what Keeney said when the press and alumni demanded to know what he was going to do about that professor. 'Every man has a right to make a damn fool of himself.' "[45]

James S. Dietz ('62) wrote:

I attended Brown during the conformist and repressive 1950s. Still I was allowed by the University to hear the divergent and sometimes explosive opinions of the American Nazi George Lincoln Rockwell, Fidel Castro, Malcolm X, a very young Martin Luther King Jr., and an assortment of bombastic beat poets. Regardless of the decade, this was an era of free speech at Brown. Drunk or sober, a lot of Brown men and Pembroke women and their guests exercised this basic American right. And for many of them it was the first time that they could do so without fear of banishment or expulsion. It was all a part of what some of us once called a "liberal education." Apparently, things are changing at Brown.[46]

Certainly not all of the alumni/ae comments assailed Gregorian's decision. Arthur Shippee ('79) wrote, "Freedom of speech? But he was not free to speak; he had given up his freedom—not his right to freedom, but the freedom itself—to drunkenness. He freely handed over his mind and tongue to a drug and to his hatred. That is not freedom. Freedom of opinion? I would certainly not grace that ejaculation of hate, 'nigger,' with the title of opinion. This is no opinion, no more than a squeaking door or jackhammer is, although they too are noises which should be stopped."[47] Lawrence Ross ('52) added, "How could a University, which prides itself on its selectivity, admit such a pathetic person?"[45]

The faculty itself was largely silent in the Hann case. Dean Edward N. Beiser, also a professor of political science, does not remember any strong faculty stands one way or the other on the issue.[49] Some, however, did comment. The professor who became most involved with the issue was William G. McLoughlin Jr., the controversial William Prescott and Annie McClelland Smith Professor of History and Religion. Though certainly not happy to defend Hann's choice of words, he took a strong libertarian stand on his right to say them: "As a libertarian, I'm not even sure that the government should be able to stop you from yelling 'fire' in a crowded theater."[50] His major concern was the extreme secrecy with which the university approached the case. "You had a unanimous vote, but you do not know why anyone voted the way they did. Some did it because they hate racism, some did it because they hate Hann's behavior."[51] Jacob Neusner, prominent Judaic scholar and professor, wrote in a letter to the *Herald*, "If Brown expels every student obnoxious by reason of bad thoughts, accompanied by unfriendly gestures, performed under the influence of liquor or drugs, the campus would be empty by reason of a single football weekend. The real question before us is . . . what is next? Who is going to compile the list of prohibited thoughts and deeds? Better to live with a little obnoxious bigotry than stifle under the blanket of permitted thought. . . ."[52] Despite this commentary, most of the faculty remained silent.

However, the president did not. Vartan Gregorian took a very public leadership role in presenting Brown's case to the world.

The Man at the Top

President Vartan Gregorian's public explanation and defense of the expulsion in the name of the offended student and the Brown Community began the day the *New York Times* article appeared. Rooted in his staunch commitment that universities are "partisans of heterodoxy" purveying a "rich and full range of opinions," his steadfast opposition to racist, anti-Semitic, and homophobic actions, and his commitment to First Amendment values, Gregorian differentiated Brown's disciplinary code from those of other universities by stating that Brown has no list of proscribed words or areas where speech is either more or less protected. Brown's code proscribes "actions," not "speech." The Brown code allows this important distinction to be drawn in a "hearing which considers the circumstances of each case. The student is entitled to an appeal, which includes review by a senior officer and a decision by the president."[53] He contended that he upheld the decision of the Undergraduate Disciplinary Council because it had passed judgment on Hann's actions, not on his speech.

A separate and more important part of Gregorian's defense of the expulsion was a reaffirmation of his commitment to the value of the free exchange of ideas at a university. This part of his defense begins with the following reaffirmation of his belief in free speech: "My commitment to the First Amendment . . . [is] well known. . . . Freedom of speech questions lie at the heart of any academic community."[54] He also recognized that speech codes on a college campus are problematic. "The world is throwing off shackles on free speech and we are on campus trying to set our own limitations, our own canon—what you can say, what you cannot say."[55] Yet Gregorian's reaffirmation of First Amendment values is modified from the traditional free-speech defense. Gregorian believes that the limits of free speech are circumscribed by his idea of community. He is convinced that "[i]ntellectual independence and social responsibility are not mutually exclusive."[56] Gregorian contended in a *Washington Post* article that the American college campus has changed:

> Students who represent a broad spectrum of our nation now expect to be welcomed and supported, not merely accommodated and tolerated. . . . We are striving to build communities where students can devote themselves to knowledge and personal growth without having to defend their personal dignity or that their right to privacy be respected. . . . The day when drunkenness was romanticized, when racial or sexual harassment could be winked at, condoned, or considered merely in poor taste, has long passed. In the nation's workplaces, a considerable corpus of federal and state laws protect the rights and dignity of employees.[57]

This argument is based on an idea of social development in the university community. Essential to this contention is the idea of the university as a community. A necessary corollary for Gregorian is the notion that a community is permitted to make demands on people as a price for membership. The "past," which Gregorian characterizes as tolerant of social stigmatization based on race, gender, and sexual orientation, is no longer appropriate and should not be protected under the rhetoric of free speech, because the composition of the American university community has changed. As diverse students move into these communities, they bring their individual and group identities and needs, which must be included in the composition of any membership requirements. Simple tolerance of various categories of diversity is insufficient. Rather, a university president self-consciously walks a value-laden tightrope between freedom and community. This appeared explicitly in Gregorian's introduction to the Brown University/*Providence Journal-Bulletin* Public Affairs Conference on "Free Expression After 200 Years," held at Brown in March 1991. In remarks loaded with irony, given Hann's expulsion, Gregorian "passionately quoted from Alexis de Tocqueville's observations on the inherent conflict between freedom and authority, the individual and community in a democracy."[58] In another context he would frame his dilemma explicitly as follows: "The university's most compelling challenge is to achieve a balance between the right of its individual members to operate and speak freely, and fostering the respect for and adherence to community values and standards of conduct."[59]

Gregorian's beliefs allowed others to present a dual image of him. Nat Hentoff of the *Village Voice* suggested there were two Vartan Gregorians—one speaking of free speech and one touting community values, principally equality.[60] Considering two of the interviews that Gregorian gave, Michael Gartner, commentator for *USA Today*, advised, "You should listen, Mr. Gregorian of the *Times*, to the Mr. Gregorian of *Rolling Stone*."[61]

For Vartan Gregorian, though, the First Amendment's value of untrammeled free speech is only *one* value to be balanced along with a range of others that face a community. His comments supporting either speech or community depend on which side of the balance he is talking about and what values are on the other side of the balance. On a larger scale, Gregorian offers a critically different taxonomy for deciding speech cases, one which fits comfortably into an emerging school of constitutional understanding that asserts a radically different agenda, at odds with more traditional conceptions of free speech and society. This taxonomy seems to agree with a newly developing constitutional scholarship about rights and liberties.[62] Balancing liberties like those embodied in the First Amendment against rights that can be read into

the Fourteenth leads one to a very different place than can be found in traditional First Amendment interpretations. Far from uncertain or ambivalent, the
offense and the penalty amendments and Hann's expulsion indicate that President Gregorian has moved Brown University away from the traditional parameters of discourse on free speech in America.

A New Orthodoxy and Brown

The most important implication of this new scholarship of rights and liberties
may not be its role in the expulsion of Douglas Hann, but instead its possible
manifestation as "political correctness," which might be described by some
as a "pall of orthodoxy"[63] chilling the educational environment. Debates rage
on campuses throughout America over the issues raised by the perceived need
to accommodate those who have traditionally been excluded. Many argue that
this new orthodoxy may create intellectual sterility by chilling the type of
thought-provoking challenges and exchanges that have traditionally proved
indispensable to the quest for knowledge and truth. That orthodoxy itself can
be a problem in education is clear. As long as educational institutions have
existed, there have been intense disputes about what to pass on, what not to
pass on, and how best to do it. There has not been a time when universities
have not been swept by one orthodoxy or another. The social and intellectual
conformity that characterized college campuses during the 1950s exudes some
of the same characteristics many see in the PC debates appearing today.
Though some may see the current debate as simply one more argument over
what to teach and how to teach it, it is probably something more than that,
given the changing nature of American society.

This changing nature has led to additional incidents at Brown, which support those who claim the existence of a PC orthodoxy. The weight of evidence
is considerable:

- Public speakers, both from within and without the university have had
  trouble completing speeches because of hecklers' protests. During the
  semester in which Hann was expelled, an El Salvadoran official received the "heckler's veto" at a lecture. Meetings concerning the reform of the university's sexual assault policy were disrupted and
  brought to a close by BASH (Brown Against Sexual Assault and Harassment) who opposed the university's perceived lax attitude toward
  date rape. Upon failing to prevent a lecture by the controversial writer
  P. J. O'Rourke, demonstrators packed the audience and disrupted the
  lecture by an angry mass exodus during the speech.

- Political Science Chair Nancy Rosenblum had to cajole her "Justice and Gender" class to start any discussion regarding Affirmative Action, despite her assertion that she was sure that there was an enormous range of opinions on the policy.
- Two weeks after President Gregorian addressed the assembled students on the green regarding the racist and homophobic graffiti incident, a Brown professor canceled the screening of "Birth of a Nation," after receiving criticism about the film's racist content.
- The Commencement issue of the *Brown Daily Herald* reported, "A professor of one of the editors of this [issue], in a small, informal discussion with five people following a section, confided that in class he had avoided discussing some research he had come across and some unpopular conclusions he had come to about a controversial topic—the problem of inner-city poverty. "It is a sensitive topic," he said, "and I don't want to get into it in front of a class of 150 Brown students."[64]

These are not isolated incidents. One former student notes that "Brown has had an oppressive PC orthodoxy at least since my time there, 1975–1979. I vividly recall students being silenced by professors when an 'objectionable' statement was made. One student was shouted down in class when he had the audacity to suggest that windfall profit taxes on oil companies were ill-advised. One really brave student once suggested that the native Africans the British found there in the 1800s benefited by learning about the alphabet and written language. The student survived—barely."[65]

A sense of a campus orthodoxy and the intolerant pall it casts is well captured by a letter to the *Brown Daily Herald* headed, "Hann Threatened Brown's Ideals." Jono Mainelli wrote:

> I would appreciate it if she [a woman who wrote an understanding letter about Douglas Hann] would restrain herself from instructing the community how to find the good core in those who are openly racist, anti-Semitic, and homophobic. Let them flaunt their elusive virtue somewhere else. I don't want to have to make an effort; it shouldn't be my responsibility to extract the goodness from someone like Hann if he's absolutely determined to hide it. While we're still in our insulated microcosm of college, we should take advantage of our ability to dismiss those who cripple the integrity of the community. Not enough people realize the importance of expelling people like Hann.[66]

Each year the *Brown Daily Herald* publishes a special issue for commencement exercises. The 1990 issue contained an editorial entitled "A Lesson in Liberalism," written by two of the paper's editors who were graduating seniors. After distinguishing the opinions of Brown University's student body from mainstream American ethics and politics, the editors wrote:

But in the process of defining our own somewhat leftist lifestyle, our community has labeled all other attitudes inferior. On this campus, only the "liberal" view is acceptable. Anyone who deviates from this Brown norm—be it on the pages of the *Herald* or the confines of a seminar room—is shot down and branded ignorant or insensitive. Brown is so immersed in defending leftist causes that it has become intolerant to opposing points of view. . . . It is sad that the full range of views on a topic cannot be heard, for whatever reason. Somehow, many Brown students have it in their heads that ideas themselves are dangerous, and that the student body at Brown is not capable of distinguishing between right and wrong for themselves. This is the antithesis of everything that academia should represent.[67]

Conclusion

It is clear in the law that Brown owes its students neither First Amendment rights nor due process as defined in the American legal tradition. Brown is a private educational institution and therefore not directly subject to First Amendment constraints. Perhaps, as a consequence, the Brown University disciplinary system, like that of other private colleges, lacks many of the safeguards that characterize the American judicial system. Nadine Strossen, president of the American Civil Liberties Union, observed that "Brown has no evidence that Mr. Hann engaged in harassment as we commonly understand it—the singling out of a particular individual for repeated intimidation. His isolated drunken outbursts can hardly be deemed such a clear instance of proscribable harassment to warrant the University's ultimate sanction."[68]

The Brown disciplinary system clearly would fail to meet the requirements of due process, were it subject to them. Beyond an apparent politicization by vocal, organized interests and the seemingly selective enforcement of rules to protect those interests, the process lacks accessibility, clearly stated rules, open hearings, and an equitable appeals process. One observer commented, "The number of cases that have been messed up procedurally [by the UDC] far outnumber those properly processed."[69] A defendant in a UDC hearing has few traditional rights. While Hann was able to cross-examine witnesses and retain an advisor, both of these privileges were undermined by the fact that the advisor could not be an attorney. Additionally, Brown has no subpoena power, which means that witnesses do not have to show up at a hearing.

Another procedural issue is the extreme secrecy that shrouds university action in the disciplinary process. University officials used claims of "confidentiality for the accused" and "potential pending litigation" to discourage inquiry into the case. Given the lack of official comment, it is surprising how much the *Herald* reporters were able to learn about the Hann case, though this was not without cost. Mr. Bernstein reported the attempts of several university administrators, including the dean of students and the dean of student life, to suppress the release of the story and Hann's name. Claiming the press attention would ruin the adjudicatory process, Dean Inman shouted, "If there's a case, you'll blow it" during an October 30, 1990, phone conversation before Hann's hearing.[70] Their efforts even included the preparation of charges against UDC members who were suspected of leaking information to the press, although no formal charges were ever lodged. In his letter to the editor in the *New York Times,* President Gregorian "regretted" that the *Herald* had printed any information on the case.[71]

Another flaw in the system is its lack of an authoritative interpretation of the clauses that the UDC is supposed to apply in major offense cases. Moreover, Mr. Bernstein identified a full range of opinion among the members of the UDC concerning the meaning of the harassment clause. At one end, student Chris Nugent was concerned with the potential for the limitation of speech, but added, "I don't think everyone on the UDC feels that way."[72] At the other end was the lone freshman member of the UDC, Robin Derosa, who said, "If someone feels personally offended [by something someone says], that's grounds for a case of harassment. . . . The nature of harassment depends intrinsically on the reaction of the harassee."[73] Without an authoritative interpretation, it is impossible to gainsay either of these opinions; one may be as correct as the other. No attempt is made in the text of the rule to distinguish speech from harassment or pure action. The potential for a prevalent campus orthodoxy to fill in for an authoritative understanding of the rule in this situation is always possible.

Douglas Hann's expressions of October 18, 1990, are reprehensible by virtually any standard. He is a symbol of insensitive ignorance tempered by fearful hatred that is all too common in America. Traditionally, we attempt to address ignorance through education. But Hann's education—and he may need it more than most—was cut short at Brown. Some fault a new orthodoxy that holds as paramount the elimination of the ideas Hann has come to represent, an orthodoxy that appears to cut short any possibility of rational discussion. Viewed from a different perspective, however, Douglas Hann's drunken invective should not be dignified as an exchange of ideas, but rather as a personal assault on another member of the university community. Brown— along with most other American universities—has yet to resolve the conflict in these two viewpoints.

Discussion Questions

1. Do you agree with President Gregorian's view that the notion of "community" sets limits on the exercise of free speech? The Brown University

"Tenets of Community Behavior" states in part that individual freedoms such as the freedom of expression are protected by the university only when they are not exercised so "self-indulgently that they threaten the rights or freedoms of other individuals or groups." Do you agree that offensive language tangibly threatens the rights of victims? What type of offensive speech would constitute such a threat? For instance, would shouting the word "nigger" at a black woman constitute the same type of threat as arguing with a black woman that the African-American race is genetically inferior to whites? In what ways are the two examples alike or different?

2. a. Does the fact that Douglas Hann was drunk at the time of the incident in any way contribute to the scenario? For instance, had Mr. Hann never shown evidence of racism prior to the incident, and had he apologized vigorously and convincingly immediately after it (explaining perhaps that he would never have made the racist remarks in a sober state), should the charges have been reduced to public drunkenness or disorderly conduct? Would this scenario somehow reduce the offense? Why or why not?

b. Mr. Hann claimed not only that his drunkenness contributed to his making the remarks, but that he could see no connection between calling someone a "fucking Jew" and the specter of anti-Semitism. In another speech code incident at the University of Pennsylvania, a white male student was charged with verbal harassment for calling a group of African-American women "water buffalo." In explaining his remark, the student claimed that the phrase "water buffalo" was an English translation of a Yiddish phrase meaning "dolt," and that any racial implications were unintended and regrettable. Does the fact that the Penn student did not intend anything racial by the remark reduce the offensiveness of the remark from the perspective of the women to whom it was directed? Should a lack of racist intent on the part of the speaker make him/her not responsible for alternative interpretations?

3. How do you assess the role of Brown's president, Vartan Gregorian, in this whole affair? Did his public statements, particularly those explaining or defending what Brown did, clarify matters or exacerbate feelings? How would you compare his commitment to First Amendment principles to those of the administrators at Duke described in a subsequent case study? Do you find credible President Gregorian's claim that only Hann's actions—his drunkenness—were being punished, and not his words?

4. In light of the cases you have read, do you think Hann could have been punished if Brown University were a state-supported public institution? Why or why not?

Notes

1. Jonathan Yardley, "At Brown, a Hard Lesson in Free Speech," *Washington Post,* 18 February 1991, at C2.

2. Andy Bernstein, "UDC Announces Hann's Appeal Denied," *College Hill Independent,* 31 January 1990, at 1.

3. Benno Schmidt Jr., "Universities Must Defend Free Speech," *Wall Street Journal,* 6 May 1991.

4. Office of Student Life, Brown University, *Tenets of Community Behavior, 1987–1988,* 1987.

5. *Ibid.*

6. *Ibid.*

7. Brown University Alma Mater.

8. Andy Bernstein and Narula Smita, "Student Charged with Violating Tenet Code," *Brown Daily Herald,* 2 November 1990, at 1.

9. Vartan Gregorian, Letter to the Editor, *New York Times,* 21 February 1991.

10. Norman Atkins, *The Making of the President,* Rolling Stone, 21 March 1991, at 63.

11. "Student at Brown is Expelled Under a Rule Barring 'Hate Speech'," *New York Times,* 12 February 1991.

12. Andy Bernstein and Narula Smita, *op. cit.,* note 8.

13. *Ibid.*

14. *Ibid.*

15. *Ibid.*

16. *Ibid.*

17. *Ibid.*

18. *Ibid.*

19. Telephone interview with Narula Smita, 23 April 1992.

20. *Ibid.*

21. Andy Bernstein and Narula Smita, *op. cit.,* note 8.

22. Andy Bernstein, "Harassment or Hate Speech?", *The Phoenix's New Paper,* 21 February 1991, at 6.

23. To date, the university has not unsealed the records of the investigation or hearing and still refuses to answer questions concerning the case.

24. Office of Student Life, Brown University, *Standards of Student Conduct,* Student Handbook, 1991.

25. *The Evolution of Brown's Anti-Harassment Clause,* Brown Alumni Monthly, May 1991, at 5.

26. Andy Bernstein and Narula Smita, *op. cit.,* note 8.

27. *op. cit.,* note 25.

28. Andy Bernstein and Narula Smita, "Hann Appeals Expulsion, Record Not Released," *Brown Daily Herald,* 3 December 1990, at 1.

29. Mark Nickel, Internal memo to University Relations Program Officers on Hann Case Materials, 21 February 1991.

30. *op. cit.,* note 11.

31. *Ibid.*

32. Andy Bernstein, *op. cit.,* note 22.

33. "Toughen Up," Editorial, *Brown Daily Herald,* 28 November 1990, at 10.

34. *Ibid.*

35. Noah Tratt, "Mixed Blessings," *Brown Spectator,* December 1990, at 5.

36. Robin Wilson, "The Debate on Campus Free Speech: Panelists Consider Wisdom of College's Policies to Fight Harassment," *Chronicle of Higher Education,* 20 March 1991, at A33.

37. Nat Hentoff, "In the Wake of the Banished Bigot," *Village Voice,* 2 April 1991.

38. Anthony DePalma, "Battling Bias: Campuses Face Free Speech Fight," *New York Times,* 20 February 1991, at B7.

39. Andy Bernstein, *op. cit.,* note 22.

40. *Ibid.*

41. Anthony DePalma, *op. cit.,* note 38.

42. Andy Bernstein, *op. cit.,* note 22.

43. "Good Riddance," Editorial, *Brown Daily Herald,* 13 February 1991, at 10.

44. *Ibid.*

45. Roger Vaughan, *Letter to the Editor,* Brown Alumni Monthly, May 1991, at 5.

46. James S. Dietz, *Letter to the Editor,* Brown Alumni Monthly, May 1991, at 5.

47. Arthur Shippee, *Letter to the Editor,* Brown Alumni Monthly, September 1991, at 4.

48. Lawrence Ross, *Letter to the Editor,* Brown Alumni Monthly, September 1991, at 4.

49. Telephone interview with Edward N. Beiser, 12 February 1992.

50. Interview with William G. McLoughlin Jr., 18 March 1992.

51. *Ibid.*

52. Jacob Neusner, Letters to the Editor, *Brown Daily Herald,* 14 February 1991, at 4.

53. Vartan Gregorian, *op. cit.,* note 9.

54. Norman Atkins, *op. cit.,* note 10, at 63.

55. *Ibid.*

56. Vartan Gregorian, "Free Speech? Yes. Drunkenness? No," *Washington Post,* 3 April 1991.

57. *Ibid.*

58. Charlotte Bruce Harvey, *When Free Speech and Community Collide,* Brown Alumni Monthly, May 1991, at 33.

59. Vartan Gregorian, *op. cit.,* note 9.

60. Nat Hentoff, "The Two Vartan Gregorians," *Village Voice,* 26 March 1991.

61. Michael Gartner, "The Right to Speak Belongs Even to the Outrageous and Hateful," *USA Today,* 26 March 1991.

62. See the introduction to this volume for a more complete discussion of this new approach to the First and Fourteenth Amendments.

63. *Keyishian* v. *Board of Regents,* 385 U.S. 586 (1967), at 603.

64. Amy Bach and Eric Emch, "A Lesson in Liberalism," Editorial, *Brown Daily Herald,* Commencement Edition, 1990, at 56.

65. John Grassi, *Letter to the Editor,* Brown Alumni Monthly, February 1991.

66. Jono Mainelli, Letter to the Editor, *Brown Daily Herald,* 20 March 1991.

67. Amy Bach and Eric Emch, *op. cit.,* note 64.

68. Charlotte Bruce Harvey, *The View from the Press Gallery,* Brown Alumni Monthly, May 1991, at 33.

69. Noah Tratt, *op. cit.,* note 35.
70. Andy Bernstein, *op. cit.,* note 2.
71. Vartan Gregorian, *op. cit.,* note 9.
72. Andy Bernstein, *op. cit.,* note 22.
73. *Ibid.*

PAVED WITH GOOD INTENTIONS: THE UNIVERSITY OF WISCONSIN SPEECH CODE

Kiki Jamieson
Rutgers University

It began with a party at the University of Wisconsin–Madison. A chapter of the Phi Gamma Delta fraternity held the party in May 1987. The Fiji Island theme was advertised with a large cardboard cutout of a black man, which was placed on the lawn. About the same time, another fraternity on the Madison campus held a party featuring a "Harlem Room," where guests could eat fried chicken and drink watermelon punch. Many of the students wore blackface. That fall, another episode involved racist name-calling that led to an altercation involving fraternity house members. As attention focused on these controversies, other incidents involving racial epithets and other verbal abuse were reported by minority students. The dramatic increase in instances of student-to-student discrimination alerted the university to the need for more specific guidelines for preventing these occurrences. As Patricia Brady, an attorney for the University of Wisconsin system, wrote, "Existing university rules and policies governing student conduct did not address harassing verbal conduct and offensive expressive behavior by students. Absent a threat of physical danger or harm to property, Wisconsin's student-conduct rules provided no mechanism for the redress of harassing verbal and expressive behavior."[1] It was clear to many in the university that a new policy was needed.

In early 1988 a committee was formed at the Madison campus to develop a strategy for handling discriminatory conduct by students. Although such a policy was too late to address the fraternity incidents, it would be designed to address the less publicized instances of discriminatory harassment, the reporting of which rose rapidly after events such as the Fiji Island party were publicized. At the same time, the Board of Regents of the twenty-six–campus University of Wisconsin system studied attempts to improve educational opportunities for minority students. The Regents found that the quality of the campus environment was an important part of attracting and retaining minority students. According to Brady, "The study also identified responding effectively to episodes of discriminatory harassment as an important element in assuring a hospitable environment. *Design for Diversity*, a comprehensive plan resulting from the Regents' study, addressed these issues by requiring that each University of Wisconsin campus prepare nondiscriminatory-conduct policies to address discriminatory harassment by faculty, staff, and students."[2] *Design for Diversity* was approved by the Regents in May 1988. In November 1988, then-Chancellor Donna Shalala emphasized that the university's response to incidents of discrimination must be measured and thoughtful. She gave enthusiastic support for freedom of speech at universities:

> The First Amendment is not something that we can honor when we choose and disregard when we do not like what we hear.
>
> It has been hard for those of us who believe passionately in the dignity of all, regardless of race or sex, to witness this affront to human dignity by young adults who should have known better. It has not been easy to withhold immediate action.
>
> But freedom is never easy, and a great university is not a place to play with constitutional rights. It is a laboratory for open debate, a haven for diverse opinions. It must be a special place where those rights are protected and where principles of freedom are taught to citizens.
>
> [U]niversity administrators cannot abandon those principles to satisfy the will of a few, or even of many, at the expense of civil rights guaranteed to us all.[3]

However, in the meantime, the Madison committee decided to propose amendments to the student-conduct rules to proscribe expressive discriminatory harassment. Efforts were centralized when University of Wisconsin–Madison Law School professors Gordon Baldwin, Richard Delgado, and Ted Finman were asked by the university administration to help devise a rule that would withstand constitutional scrutiny. Although Finman had been an ardent First Amendment supporter, he saw the value of a speech code on a campus fraught with tension. He said:

> I think initially if someone had come to me and said, "How about coming up with a code?" I would have said, "No." Later on I became quite convinced that the code, properly limited and very narrowly drawn, could serve some important functions without violating First Amendment provisions as I saw them. . . . There are really two [important functions]. One function is to communicate to the minority community that the rest of us do care and that we understand the hurt that is caused by malicious racial epithets inflicted on them. And the other function is to communicate to the campus community the sentiment that this [sort of behavior] is unacceptable. . . . Most of the people who use these epithets do so unthinkingly, not because they are deep-seeded racists but because they simply don't have the kind of background and experience that would teach them that this is bad and very hurtful conduct. There is symbolic value in telling people in the community what is accepted.[4]

In pursuit of this goal, revisions to the student-conduct code were drafted, circulated, and approved by the Faculty Senate. Having already decided not to promulgate the rule on an emergency basis, the Board of Regents met on June 9, 1989, to debate the code. The Regents first rejected an amendment that would have explained the legal principles underlying the rule. Instead, they asserted their own distinctions to bolster the rule's constitutionality. Regent Ness Flores said: "What we are regulating here is not free speech. It is conduct and speech as conduct which contributes absolutely nothing to the free exchange of ideas and has no value whatsoever to the university. . . . I think that when we hide behind the First Amendment on this issue, we are mistaken."[5] President of the Board of Regents Paul Schilling added that the rule "is only for those few rare instances where we are way beyond any expression or exchange of ideas and we are simply beyond insensitivity into mean-spirited conduct by one individual to another."[6] The amendments to the student-conduct code were approved by a vote of 12–5. The rules became effective September 1, 1989.[7] The new UW Rule stated:

UWS 17.06 Offenses defined. The university may discipline a student in nonacademic matters in the following situations. . . .

(2)(a) For racist or discriminatory comments, epithets or other expressive behavior directed at an individual or on separate occasions at different individuals, or for physical conduct, if such comments, epithets or other expressive behavior or physical conduct intentionally:
  1. Demean the race, sex, religion, color, creed, disability, sexual orientation, national origin, ancestry or age of the individual or individuals; and
  2. Create an intimidating, hostile or demeaning environment for education, university-related work, or other university-authorized activity.
(b) Whether the intent required under par. (a) is present shall be determined by consideration of all relevant circumstances.
(c) In order to illustrate the types of conduct which this subsection is designed to cover, the following examples are set forth. These examples are not meant to illustrate the only situations or types of conduct intended to be covered.
  1. A student would be in violation if:
    a. He or she intentionally made demeaning remarks to an individual based on that person's ethnicity, such as name calling, racial slurs, or "jokes"; and
    b. His or her purpose in uttering the remarks was to make the educational environment hostile for the person to whom the demeaning remark was addressed.
  2. A student would be in violation if:
    a. He or she intentionally placed visual or written material demeaning the race or sex of an individual in that person's university living quarters or work area; and
    b. His or her purpose was to make the educational environment hostile for the person in whose quarters or work area the material was placed.
  3. A student would be in violation if he or she seriously damaged or destroyed

private property of any member of the university community or guest because of that person's race, sex, religion, color, creed, disability, sexual orientation, national origin, ancestry or age.

4. A student would not be in violation if, during a class discussion, he or she expressed a derogatory opinion concerning a racial or ethnic group. There is no violation, since the student's remark was addressed to the class as a whole, not to a specific individual. Moreover, on the facts as stated, there seems no evidence that the student's purpose was to create a hostile environment.[8]

Penalties ranged from a written reprimand to expulsion from the university. As the attorney representing the university later explained, strict guidelines were to be used to identify punishable behavior. A violation of the rule had to meet four requirements: "[It] (1) must be discriminatory and demeaning; (2) must be directed at an individual; (3) must be intended to demean—on the basis of a protected characteristic [race, sex, religion, color, creed, disability, sexual orientation, national origin, ancestry, or age]—the person to whom it is directed; and (4) must be intended to interfere with education by creating a hostile environment for education and other university-related activities."[9] The university distributed the new rule to students and also circulated a brochure giving examples of fictional situations in which the UW Rule could or could not be applied. The brochure was designed to make clear what the words of the rule did not—that strict standards were to be used in determining violations. In the interests of demonstrating the clear distinctions between protected speech and punishable behavior, the university offered the following scenarios:

QUESTION 1. In a class discussion concerning women in the workplace, a male student states his belief that women are by nature better equipped to be mothers than executives, and thus should not be employed in upper management positions. Is this statement actionable under proposed S. UWS 17.06(2)?

ANSWER. No. The statement is an expression of opinion, contains no epithets, is not directed to a particular individual, and does not, standing alone, evince the requisite intent to demean or to create a hostile environment.

QUESTION 2. A student living in a university dormitory continually calls a black student living on his floor "nigger" whenever they pass in the hallway. May the university take action against the name-caller?

ANSWER. Yes. The word "nigger" is an epithet, and is directed specifically at an individual. Its use and continuous repetition demonstrate the required intent on the part of the speaker to demean the individual and create a hostile living environment for him.

QUESTION 3. Two university students become involved in an altercation at an off-campus bar. During the fight one student uses a racial epithet to prolong the dispute. May the university invoke a disciplinary action?

ANSWER. Perhaps. The use of the epithet, and its direction to an individual suggest a potential violation of proposed S. UWS 17.06(2); however, because the episode occurred off campus, the intent to create a hostile environment for university-authorized activities would be difficult to demonstrate. Additional facts would have to be developed if disciplinary action were to be pursued.

QUESTION 4. A group of students disrupts a university class, shouting discriminatory epithets. Are they subject to disciplinary action under the provisions related to regulation of expressive behavior?

ANSWER. Perhaps. It is clear that the students are subject to disciplinary action for disrupting a class under existing S. UWS 17.06(1)(c)3. The question is whether they have also violated the newly created provision concerning expressive behavior, because they shouted epithets while in the course of other misconduct. If the epithets were directed to individuals within the class, and were intended to demean them and create an intimidating environment, then the behavior might also be in violation of the provision concerning expressive misconduct.

QUESTION 5. A faculty member, in a genetics class discussion, suggests that certain racial groups seem to be genetically pre-disposed to alcoholism. Is the statement subject to discipline under Chapter UWS 17?

ANSWER. No. A faculty member is in no case subject to discipline under Chapter UWS 17, since that chapter applies only to students. The situation would not warrant disciplinary action under any other policy, either, since it is a protected expression of an idea.[10]

In retrospect, the brochure seems not to have clarified the rule but instead to have illustrated its overbreadth. Despite the university's arguments to the contrary, it seems clear that the rule would have covered racist and similar remarks directed at individuals in classrooms and other academic settings.

For a time the UW Rule seemed to fulfill the university's public relations aim—to demonstrate a commitment to diversity on its campuses. As one student editorialist later wrote retrospectively: "While many [student] activists hailed it [the speech code] as a victory, it was also a brilliant public relations move on the part of the administration. Not only did this enable the university to claim it was doing something about campus racism without actually doing much, it carried an implicit message of 'No racism here. Lookee here, we even have a law against it.' "[11] But dissent was brewing. Although there had been little debate while the rule was being approved, an editorial addressing the tension appeared in a Madison student newspaper, the *Daily Cardinal*, less than two months after the rule was instituted. It confirmed what some had suspected: a legal challenge was being planned. The American Civil Liberties Union had been following the enactment of the UW Rule and was preparing a constitutional challenge. The *Daily Cardinal* editorialized:

Last week the American Civil Liberties Union confirmed that it is currently searching for students to challenge the UW System's anti-racism rule, UWS 17.

Considering the ACLU's purported commitment to social justice, one must ask, why are they even bothering?

This is not a First Amendment issue at all. UWS 17 is an important step in stopping harassment, not free speech. It strives to create a safer environment for everyone regardless of race, gender, religion, creed, disability, sexual orientation, national ancestry or age.

It is also an issue of equal access to education. We pay dearly for our education at this University. And for those who are targets of a hostile environment, learning is unjustly impeded.

So, again, why [is the ACLU] working so hard to fight it? Instead of maintaining such an absolutist position, the ACLU should use this opportunity to make an intellectual jump and redefine free speech to account for the realities of current society. The Constitution was not written to be a stagnant document applicable only to a period 200 years ago—a period when the very fabric of U.S. society was based on slavery.

A shallow look at UWS 17 shows it to conflict with free speech. Yet the widespread use of certain words and the pain they inflict make such a rule necessary.

The debate must go beyond civil liberties—we must start defending human dignity.[12]

This argument was acceptable to many students, but others disagreed. A group of students on the University of Wisconsin–Milwaukee campus (as well as the student newspaper there, the *UWM Post*) stepped forward to meet the university's challenge. The students, most of whom were friends, were in general politically active in left-liberal causes (reproductive rights, environmental issues, art censorship issues, and so on). Unlike students who challenged speech codes at other institutions, they were attacking the code from the platform of progressive politics. As plaintiff Stephanie Bloomingdale said, "We really had to walk a very narrow rope—wanting to distinguish our argument from those of the right wing and those that were wanting to ban speech codes because they wanted to be able to say the things speech codes were banning."[13] The students took great pains to emphasize that although they opposed the rule, they were simultaneously supporting other efforts to improve the status of minorities on the University of Wisconsin's campuses. They believed that the rule was largely a symbolic measure, as plaintiff Michael Mathias explained:

There had been a number of appalling and highly publicized incidents involving fraternities on the Madison campus, and [the administration's] very public response to this was to pass a speech code. They didn't address minority recruitment and retention issues; they didn't address university funding that makes it difficult for students to complete their degrees in a reasonable amount of time; they didn't address funding of minority student groups; they didn't address funding of minority counseling or tutoring centers, or any of the things that would actually have made it a better environment [and] easier for minorities to go to a university that is so predominantly populated by majorities. But their very public response was to say "No. The problem is in the way we're talking to each other." And they never established that was in and of itself the problem. They didn't even try.[14]

But despite their frustrations with the speech code, the students also emphasized their belief that the university instituted the rule in good faith. They interpreted the rule as a thoughtful, though misguided, attempt to address the concerns of minority students and to improve campus climates more generally. Looking back on the rule, Bloomingdale reflected: "I don't think that the university did this to try to shut people up or be dictatorial. . . . I think they really had the best interests of all of us at heart. But the university administration used this as a Band-Aid solution. Racism, sexism, and homophobia are very complex problems that require many different levels of change. It frightened me that they could just blame the students for [campus tensions], saying in effect that it is the students' speech that is responsible for racism, sexism, and homophobia on campus."[15] These concerns helped to mobilize the students to challenge the speech code.

On March 29, 1990, the *University of Wisconsin–Milwaukee Post* and eleven students filed suit seeking to have the UW Rule declared unconstitutional. Again, the plaintiffs emphasized their political commitment to ending discrimination and its relationship to removing the rule. As stated in the plaintiffs' brief:

> The plaintiffs doubt neither the seriousness of the problems of racial, sexual, religious, and other forms of discrimination at the University of Wisconsin nor the sincerity of the Board of Regents' response to it. Invidious discrimination is reprehensible and intolerable, and the University has an obligation to promote equal educational opportunities for all of its students. The *only* issue raised by this case is whether the University, in an attempt to "protect" some of its students from offensive comments, has violated the First Amendment rights of all of its students.[16]

Their efforts were aided by the American Civil Liberties Union and its affiliated attorneys, Jeffrey Kassel and Brady Williamson. The plaintiffs claimed that the rule violated their First and Fourteenth Amendment rights and asked that the university be barred from enforcing the rule. Attorney Kassel explained that "[o]ne decision we made was not to make any attack political. We did not want to attack the university's good faith in attacking racism, sexism, homophobia. We made a clear decision to steer away from 'politically correct' arguments. We decided to restrict our challenge to pretty traditional legal doctrine."[17] And on those terms, many commentators seemed to support the students' claims. One month later, the *Milwaukee Sentinel*'s editorial page advanced the following view: "It remains for anyone's interpretation what constitutes the 'intentional' demeaning of an individual based on race, sex, religion . . . and it remains for anyone's interpretation exactly what constitutes creation of an intimidating, hostile or demeaning environment. Whoever makes such judgments becomes the arbitrar of speech on campus. And whoever decides the penalty becomes lord and master over a system with honorable objectives, but which must inevitably collapse."[18]

What explains the seachange in opinion? In the time between the filing of the case and the decision, even some of the authors of the UW Rule began to have doubts. Apparently, the rule in action was quite different from the rule at the drawing board. Professor Gordon Baldwin, one of the three primary architects of the rule, related that he began to question the legitimacy of the rule after learning how it had been applied on other campuses. The discovery process illuminated a few cases in which the UW Rule had been applied in ways that seemed clearly unconstitutional.[19]

In the twenty-five months from the inception of the rule to its review by the district court, there were nine cases in which University of Wisconsin students were sanctioned under the UW Rule. In one case, University of Wisconsin–Eau Claire student (and plaintiff) John Doe was found to have breached the UW Rule "by yelling epithets loudly at a woman for approximately ten minutes, calling her a 'fucking bitch' and 'fucking cunt.' . . . Doe was responding to statements the woman made in a university newspaper about the athletic department."[20] John Doe was put on probation for one semester and was required to perform community service (twenty hours) at a shelter for abused women. In another case, a University of Wisconsin–Stevens Point student was placed on probation for stealing a bank card and personal access number from his Japanese dormitory roommate. The student managed to steal $60 from the account and later "admitted that he was motivated by his resentment that his roommate is Japanese and does not speak English well."[21] To the outside observer, this instance would seem to be a clear example of the rule being misapplied. The sanctioned behavior, theft, could certainly have been punished without the help of the new rule. As Kassel explained, the disparate use of the rule on the various campuses[22] "supported our arguments that it would be applied [inconsistently] and that it left too much discretion to university administrators. It also showed that this was not just a theoretical/academic debate. [We saw] that it was being applied in a manner that supported our argument."[23]

Interestingly, none of those punished under UWS 17 was a student at the

Madison campus, the largest campus in the system.[24] Why was Madison different? One Madison-based university employee thought the differing use of the rule was due to overzealous administrators at other campuses. This source suggested that "a lot of student conduct officers follow the throw-the-book-at-people approach—charge the student with everything, with the idea that maybe the student will just *agree*."[25] Ted Finman, in contrast, thought the lack of sanctions on the Madison campus was due to its particular character. He cited the presence of the law school and its close relationship with the Dean of Students' Office as reasons why the rule was not used indiscriminately.[26] And the numbers at the system's largest campus seem to support his assertions. On the Madison campus, there were twenty-two instances of discriminatory harassment reported to the Dean of Students' Office from the beginning of 1989 until the court reached its decision. Only one of those circumstances met the rule's requirements, but the student involved was not subjected to the sanctions of the rule. The twenty-one others were outside the scope of UWS 17, most frequently because the conduct in question was not intended to interfere with university-related activities or it was not directed at an individual.[27]

Were there any significant practical effects of the rule's application? According to administrators, sanctions were less important to the university than educating students to prevent these incidents from occurring in the first place. In a proposal entitled "The 2% UW System Solution," publicized six months before the court case was decided, two members of the Madison administration—Dean of Students Mary K. Rouse and Associate Dean of Students Roger Howard—emphasized again their efforts to avoid using the rule. They wrote: "Unfortunately, the popular press has . . . portrayed the disciplinary rule as the 100% solution. From our perspective, by the time we have to apply the disciplinary rule, we have all failed."[28] The Madison administrators asserted their commitment to ending problems of discrimination on campus and bemoaned the way this serious issue had been reduced to a table of punishments.[29] Patricia Brady, Senior System Legal Counsel, who had helped institute the rule, also was troubled by the emphasis on the rule at the expense of other parts of *Design for Diversity*. She said, "[The UW Rule] was one more small piece of a much bigger effort . . . a little additional tool to be used to help educate students."[30] Still, the controversy continued.

The debate over speech codes on Wisconsin's campuses ended temporarily on October 11, 1991, when Senior District Judge Robert Warren for the Eastern District of Wisconsin decided that the rule was unconstitutional because of overbreadth and vagueness. Because the framers of the UW Rule as well as a university attorney had gone on record expressing their conviction that the UW Rule was constitutional and that it differed substantially from the University of Michigan code[31] previously found unconstitutional in federal court, it is necessary to detail the Wisconsin court's reasoning.

Judge Warren first tackled the issue of whether the regulation in question dealt with "fighting words." Warren wrote that since *Chaplinsky* v. *New Hampshire* (1942) the Supreme Court has narrowed the scope of the fighting words doctrine. "First, the Court has limited the fighting words definition so that it now only includes the second half ['words which by their very utterance tend to incite a breach of the peace']." The court then added, in a footnote, "The Board concurs that the first half of the fighting words definition ['words which by their very utterance inflict injury'] now constitutes protected speech."[32] But, "While the Board is correct that the language regulated by the UW Rule is likely to cause violent responses in many cases, the rule regulates discriminatory speech whether or not it is likely to provoke such a response. . . . Since the UW Rule covers a substantial number of situations where no breach of the peace is likely to result, the rule fails to meet the requirements of the fighting words doctrine."[33] That is, the UW Rule could apply to, and ultimately "chill," constitutionally protected speech. The court also agreed with the plaintiffs that, even on the university's own terms, the regulation was overbroad. The plaintiffs' brief stated:

> The University's own definition of "discriminatory comments" only emphasizes the Rule's impermissible viewpoint discrimination. . . . Demeaning expressions of opinion that do not "show prejudice" may be made with impunity, while demeaning expressions of opinion that "show prejudice" towards certain protected classes are prohibited by the Rule. The University has declared, in effect, that students may express opinions to other students only if those opinions do not "show prejudice."[34]

Ted Finman, who helped draft the UW Rule, granted in an interview that the language used in the regulation was a weak link. He said:

> The first part of the code speaks of "comments, epithets, or other expressive behavior," which has the effect of reaching didactic statements . . . which are expressions of opinion, which, while being inflammatory in the sense that they may cause hurt to the other person and could contribute to a violent reaction, are the sorts of expression of opinion that are entitled to protection.

> When the case was challenged, my first reaction was, "How the hell did we let this wording get through?" We should have known better. We should have seen the potential for attack there. I think the explanation is that in the process of political compromise, we had to come up with language that would satisfy the system-wide committee. . . . We did, incidentally, strongly urge the Attorney General's office to say, "Yes, this language is too broad, but it can be construed more narrowly and the court can limit the construction." . . . I don't know,

though, if it would have made any difference at all if he had taken a much stronger position.[35]

The district court agreed with the plaintiffs that the UW Rule was overbroad on its face.

The Board of Regents also asked the court to use *Chaplinsky*'s balancing test to show that the sanctioned speech (fighting words) "are no essential part of any exposition of ideas, and are of such slight social value as a step to the truth that any benefit that may be derived from them is clearly outweighed by the social interest in order and morality."[36] The Board of Regents asserted that the balance struck by the rule fell safely within the doctrine of *Chaplinsky*. The board claimed:

[T]he Rule's constitutionality flows logically and naturally from the fact that, as formulated and applied, it simply does not venture beyond the safe harbor of the *Chaplinsky* fighting words doctrine. The Rule is justified under the *Chaplinsky* balancing model because the slight social value of discriminatory harassment is far outweighed by its harm and the University's compelling interests in providing its students with equal educational opportunities, preventing disruption of educational activities and preserving an orderly, safe campus environment.[37]

However, the district court rejected the board's balancing approach because, among other reasons, the Seventh Circuit had stated previously (in *American Booksellers Association, Inc.* v. *Hudnut* [Seventh Cir. 1985]) that a balancing approach can be used only when the regulation in question deals with content-neutral speech. According to the court, "It is clear . . . that the UW Rule regulates speech based on its content. . . . Moreover, this Court finds that, even under the balancing test proposed by the Board of Regents, the rule is unconstitutional."[38]

The Board of Regents, in justifying its regulation, argued that the costs of restricting speech are outweighed by other compelling interests, which include: "(1) increasing minority representation; (2) assuring equal educational opportunities; (3) preventing interruption of educational activities; and (4) preserving an orderly and safe campus environment."[39] But the district court rebutted these arguments, point by point. Regarding the first assertion, Judge Warren wrote that the "UW Rule does as much to hurt diversity on Wisconsin campuses as it does to help it. By establishing content-based restrictions on speech, the rule limits the diversity of ideas among students and thereby prevents the 'robust exchange of ideas' which intellectually diverse campuses provide." Warren addressed the board's second point in the following terms: "Any inequality in educational opportunities addressed by the UW Rule is due to the discriminatory activity of students, not University of Wisconsin

System employees. Since students are generally not state actors, the board's Fourteenth Amendment equal protection argument is inapplicable to this case."[40] The court's responses to the third and fourth points had been made before. The court also dispensed with the board's appeals to *Meritor Savings Bank* v. *Vinson* (1986) by asserting a distinction between employment and educational settings. Judge Warren wrote: "Since employees may act as their employer's agents, agency law may hold an employer liable for its employees [*sic*] actions. In contrast, agency theory would generally not hold a school liable for its students' actions since students normally are not agents of the school."[41]

In sum, then, the court found the UW Rule to violate the First Amendment of the U.S. Constitution as overbroad and unduly vague. Judge Warren seemed sympathetic to the aims of the Board of Regents, but, in the end, their good intentions were not enough to overcome the constitutional difficulties. Warren wrote: "The problems of bigotry and discrimination sought to be addressed here are real and truly corrosive of the educational environment. But freedom of speech is almost absolute in our land and the only restriction the fighting words doctrine can abide is that based on fear of violent reaction. Content-based prohibitions such as that in the UW Rule, however well intended, simply cannot survive the screening which our Constitution demands."[42] Less than two weeks later, however, both sides were regrouping for another confrontation. The University of Wisconsin–Madison student newspaper, the *Daily Cardinal*, ran an editorial belittling the overturned speech code and urging that efforts to revive it be put aside: "[W]hy waste time and energy reworking a rule that is only part of a strategy designed to create a diverse campus free of harassment? Why not use these resources to help recruit and maintain minority faculty and students, to help create ethnic studies programs, *to better educate* students about the prejudices and bigotry which spawn the need for hate speech codes in the first place?"[43] But the University of Wisconsin administration had already begun to pursue revisions to the code. Ted Finman related that "[a]fter Warren's decision came down, [then-Chancellor] Donna Shalala asked us for advice on how to proceed. We agreed that we shouldn't just let it go. Having adopted the rule, it would be seen as a serious retreat from principle . . . if we just forgot about it."[44] While the university was unsure of its next step in the judicial arena, it was clear that some new measure would be put forward. The special assistant to the UW System President of Minority Affairs, James Sulton, said: "The Rule was a visible sign to prospective minority students and their parents that we are willing to do something. We are anxious to show that we will protect the rights of minorities on this campus."[45]

By February 1992, revisions to the code were written. Political science professor Joel Grossman explained that a new committee (including original members Finman and Baldwin) had agreed to the challenge issued by Judge Warren's opinion. Grossman said: "They came up with the draft, which tracked Warren's opinion and eliminated all of the points of contention, particularly with regard to the fighting words doctrine, and basically established a policy that was limited wholly to racial or ethnic epithets that occurred in a confrontational process. It was a much tighter document [which emphasized] confrontational speech imminently likely to bring about disorder."[46] The revised rule read as follows:

UWS 17.06 Offenses defined. The university may discipline a student in nonacademic matters in the following situations. . . .

(2)(a) *For directly addressing to a specific member* (or specific members) of the UW student body an epithet, as defined in subsection (b) below, that was
  1. *intended to demean* the race, sex, religion, color, creed, disability, sexual orientation, national origin, ancestry or age of the person addressed, and
  2. *intended to make the environment at the UW hostile or threatening* for the person addressed because of his or her race, sex, religion, color, creed, disability, sexual orientation, national origin, ancestry or age.

(b) *An "epithet" is a word, phrase or symbol that reasonable persons recognize to grievously insult or threaten persons because of their race, sex, religion, color, creed, disability, sexual orientation, national origin, ancestry or age*, and that
  1. would make the educational environment hostile or threatening for a person to whom the word, phrase or symbol is directly addressed, and
  2. *without regard to the gender or other physical characteristics involved, would tend to provoke an immediate violent response* when addressed directly to a person of average sensibility who is a member of the group that the word, phrase or symbol insults or threatens.

(c) The use of epithets in statements addressed to a general audience rather than directly to a specific individual (or specific individuals) shall not be a violation of this rule even though the speaker's intent is to demean and create a hostile environment and even though a member or members of the group demeaned by the epithet constitute part of that audience.

(d) The intent of a person charged with violating this rule shall be determined by consideration of all relevant circumstances.

(e) *No disciplinary action under this rule shall be instituted unless a person designated by the President of the University of Wisconsin System has determined that the conduct alleged to have occurred constitutes a violation of this rule.*[47]

The revision was much more tightly constructed than the original code. It relied significantly more on the letter of *Chaplinsky*'s "fighting words" doctrine. Other notable changes are the "reasonable person" standard and the requirement that disciplinary sanctions be cleared by the university president's office, which would reduce the haphazard enforcement of the original rule. But all were not appeased. Jeffrey Kassel, the Madison lawyer who had represented the plaintiffs in the *UWM Post* case, said the new rule was better than the previous version because it was more narrowly drawn. However, he added, "I'm still troubled by the notion of the university punishing speech, and punishing speech that is not punished elsewhere in society."[48] But proponents of the code were still optimistic. The *Daily Cardinal* editorialized:

> While the new code may be the most legally acceptable version possible, it may also be so narrowly written that prosecution under the code is almost impossible. So why have the hate speech code at all? Rules such as these are important in defining the university's commitment to equal educational opportunity. By having UWS 17 on the books, the university is saying that it takes racist and sexist hate speech seriously, that such speech will not be tolerated on campus, and that institutional recourse is available for the victims of this speech. . . . In isolation UWS 17 is a feel-good band-aid which is wholly inadequate in addressing the deplorable state of race relations on this campus . . . [but] UWS 17 is a small piece of what should be a much larger strategy.[49]

When the Faculty Senate approved the revised code on March 2, 1992, law professor Ted Finman, who helped write the original rule and the revisions, said, "I have consistently believed the primary function [of the code] is indeed symbolic." But at the same meeting others argued that a revised speech code was not the way to go. Political science professor Joel Grossman, the de facto spokesman for the opposition, requested a vote against the code but asked, too, for support for other methods of creating "a campus environment that promotes diversity and mutual respect for all students and other members of the university community. . . . There are adequate means to protect potential victims. . . . [The code's] chilling effect and symbolic implications are substantial."[50] Grossman emphasized that the symbolism ran high on both sides of the debate, and asked instead for a commitment to concrete means of improving the campus environment. But the Faculty Senate, by a margin of 89 to 70, approved the revised code.[51]

As the Board of Regents considered the revised code, the student newspaper again urged its approval. And Regent Paul Schilling echoed the students' belief in the benefits of the symbolic aspects of the code, telling the newspaper: "It's important to have a rule that demonstrates to minorities we're serious about the environment they have to contend with."[52] The Regents approved the revised code by a vote of 9 to 6. The board then sent the revisions, in the form of an administrative rule, to the state legislature for approval.

As the Wisconsin legislature considered the revisions, two unrelated cases were decided, which foreshadowed the revised code's demise. On June 22, 1992, the U.S. Supreme Court issued its opinion in *R.A.V.* v. *City of St. Paul, Minnesota* that overturned St. Paul's Bias-Motivated Crime Ordinance. This decision was widely heralded as the end of speech codes. Justice Scalia's argument about under-inclusiveness and the lack of viewpoint neutrality seemed, to the Wisconsin legislature, to doom the university's code. Around the same time, the Wisconsin Supreme Court found that the state's "hate crime" statute, providing for penalty enhancement for crimes in which the victim was selected because of race, was unconstitutional. The State Supreme Court in this case (to be called *Wisconsin* v. *Todd Mitchell*) relied on the decision in *R.A.V.*, finding that the hate crime statute "violates the First Amendment by punishing what the legislature has deemed to be offensive thought" and found the statute overbroad.[53] The legislature, feeling itself to be on shaky constitutional ground, remanded the revised code to the Board of Regents for reconsideration.

On September 12, 1992, the Board of Regents voted to repeal the hate speech code at the University of Wisconsin. Professor Ted Finman expressed disappointment, saying: "I think this is going to have some unfortunate symbolic consequences. . . . We're telling people there is less concern about the kind of conduct the rule prohibits." But Senior System Legal Counsel Patricia Brady had a different explanation: "After *R.A.V.* the Board of Regents became concerned we would be in a no-win situation with the rule. They were still committed to stopping harassment, but didn't want to be caught in a legal battle."[54] State senator Lynn Adelman, on the other hand, was pleased that the code was dead. "If the university wants to reassure minorities, laws and rules are not the way to do it," Adelman commented. "The way to achieve that goal is to sell the university based on the benefits it has to offer, not to pass rules which are arguably unconstitution[al] and clearly out of line with the mission of this university as a citadel of free expression." And Victor DeJesus, then co-president of the Wisconsin Student Association, said, "Even though I supported it at first, I think that instead of playing with the speech code, they should be doing more in terms of education. . . . We need to stop the divisiveness this has created."[55]

In the two years following the demise of the Wisconsin speech code, little changed. Instances of discriminatory harassment and assault reported to the Dean of Students' Office on the Madison campus declined to twenty-five cases in 1992, from thirty-seven the previous year. But, for the years in total, complaints that would have been actionable under the UW Rule decreased from 3 to 2—a minimal change.[56] However, the Dean of Students' Office hears anecdotally that instances of discriminatory harassment are as prevalent as ever.[57] One explanation for the decrease in reports may be that students are reluctant to pursue complaints when they know that there are no formal disciplinary guidelines in place. But it is hard to estimate nonreported instances of discrimination.

The numbers of minority students on the Madison campus have increased, however. In September 1991, before the *UWM Post* decision was reached, and while the speech code was still in effect, minority students accounted for 7 percent (3,047) of the 43,196 students at Madison. In September 1993, one year after the revised speech code had been repealed, minority students comprised 8.3 percent (3,397) of the 40,924 total.[58] These rising numbers of minority students indicate that the repeal of the speech code may not have meant the end of the goal of campus diversity. However, most of the increases in numbers of minority students were among non–African-Americans. In fact, from Fall 1983 to Fall 1993, enrollment of African-American students at the University of Wisconsin–Madison decreased 5 percent. During the same period, enrollment of Asian-American students increased 99 percent, Hispanic-American students increased 100 percent, and American-Indian students increased 90 percent.[59] The decreasing representation of African-American students is troubling, particularly as it occurred while other minorities were increasingly present on campus. The causes, however, cannot be determined definitively. The changing representation could be due to the speech code (or its repeal), but also could be a function of demographic shifts, the *Design for Diversity*, or cuts in financial aid in the 1980s. Still, the numbers tell a bittersweet story: diversity on campus is increasing, but still has far to go—particularly with regard to African-American students.

According to law professor Gordon Baldwin, the speech code issue has lost its cachet on the Madison campus.[60] The issue of discriminatory harassment remains, however. And even those like Ted Finman, who helped to draft both versions of the code and who was one of the rule's strong supporters, have begun to look outside the law for solutions. Finman said:

> Ultimately I've come to the conclusion that, although the codes we drafted are constitutionally defensible—I don't think they offend First Amendment principles—I've come to the conclusion that they're politically unwise because the unintended consequence is to encourage people and movements to censor their ideas themselves. . . . [A]doption of codes of this sort may have the effect of fostering a climate in which people think it is perfectly permissible and proper, not only to restrict speech in a fairly limited way, but to say that these are bad ideas and the ideas themselves should be subject to restriction or suppression, the First Amendment notwithstanding.[61]

Finman and others at the Madison campus have reevaluated their commitment to the speech code and have since focused their attention on pragmatic

steps to encourage campus diversity. More active measures, such as those
detailed in the Madison Plan, are getting renewed attention—for instance, recruitment of more minority faculty and students, providing funding for low-
income students, and encouragement of multicultural curricula, to name a
few.[62] In March 1994, the Faculty Senate at the University of Wisconsin–
Madison passed an update of the Madison Plan, which emphasized the continued commitment to diversity on campus. Included too was a "Statement on
Tolerance and Respect for All Individuals," adopted from the Regents' policy.
Its sentiments mirrored those that gave rise to the UW Rule, though the statement's language is more a statement of goals rather than a legal code. It read:

> True learning requires free and open debate, civil discourse, and tolerance of
> many different individuals and ideas. We are preparing students to live and work
> in a world that speaks with many voices and from many cultures. Tolerance is
> not only essential to learning, it is essential to be learned. The University of
> Wisconsin–Madison is built upon these values and will act vigorously to defend
> them. We will maintain an environment conducive to teaching and learning that
> is free from intimidation for all.
>
> In its resolve to create this positive environment, the UW–Madison will ensure
> compliance with federal and state laws protecting against discrimination. In addi-
> tion, the UW–Madison has adopted policies that both emphasize these existing
> protections and supplement them with protections against discrimination that are
> not available under either federal or state law.
>
> University policies create additional protections that prohibit harassment.[63]

The university's emphasis on tolerance and discourse underscores the system's real job, education. In addition to reading, writing, and arithmetic, universities must teach about diversity, liberty, and equality. As Ted Finman explained: "We have a lot of students who are simply ignorant about this
problem. They behave as other people in their communities behave—it is custom rather than deep-seeded hatred. They're educable. But there are a lot more
effective ways [to teach this] than speech codes at universities. . . . I think you
need to give white kids a sense of the emotional impact of discriminatory
harassment. They have to, in a sense, feel the hurt to understand what this is
all about."[64]

Discussion Questions

1. What differences do you see between the University of Michigan code,
   described in *Doe,* and the original University of Wisconsin code? The revised Wisconsin code? How would the various scenarios in the accompanying guidelines for each code be handled under each? Which codes seem

most protective of speech and/or academic freedom? Of the interests of
protected classes of individuals?

2. Do you think it was appropriate for the Wisconsin code to regulate student
   expression but to exempt faculty and staff from such rules? What are the
   political implications of this determination? What about issues of academic freedom?

3. To what degree do you think the Wisconsin code was a cynical attempt on
   the part of the administration to placate minority students and legislators
   rather than a good-faith attempt to address the problem within constitutional limits? How do the actions of the Wisconsin administrators compare
   with those of the University of Michigan on this dimension?

4. In his opinion, Judge Warren disagreed with university officials that the
   rule promoted diversity. Why? Were the university officials and the judge
   measuring diversity in the same way? Who is in a better position to evaluate the effectiveness of the rule on this dimension? Should the court have
   deferred to the "findings" of the university on this issue?

Notes

1. Patricia Brady (Hodulik), *Prohibiting Discriminatory Harassment by Regulating Student Speech: A Balancing of First-Amendment and University Interests*, 16
Journal of College and University Law 4 (1990), at 574.
   The nonacademic disciplinary guidelines specified only that: "A student would be
in violation if he or she attacked or otherwise physically abused, threatened to physically injure, or physically intimidated a member of the university community or a guest
because of that person's race, sex, religion, color, creed, disability, sexual orientation,
national origin, ancestry or age." Wis. Admin. Code § UWS 17.06(1)(a).

2. *Ibid.*, at 575.

3. *Wisconsin State Journal*, 13 November 1988, at 18A, cited in *Brief in Support
of Plaintiffs' Summary Judgment Motion*, 2 October 1990, at 49.

4. Telephone interview with Ted Finman, Emeritus Bascom Professor of Law,
University of Wisconsin Law School, 15 March 1994.

5. Minutes of meeting of Board of Regents, 9 June 1989, cited in *Brief in Support
of Plaintiffs' Summary Judgment Motion,* 2 October 1990, at 7.

6. *Ibid.*

7. The background for this comes primarily from Patricia Brady, *op. cit.*, note 1,
and the decision in *UWM Post* v. *Board of Regents of the University of Wisconsin
System*, 774 F. Supp. 1163 (E.D.Wis. 1991).

8. Wis. Admin. Code § UWS 17.06(2).

9. *Defendant's Combined Brief in Support of Its Motion for Summary Judgment
and in Response to the Plaintiff's Motion for Summary Judgment*, 28 December 1990,
at 2.

10. University of Wisconsin Brochure, *Discriminatory Harassment: Prohibited
Conduct Under Chapter UWS 17 Revisions.*

11. Derek Nystrom, Editorial, *Daily Cardinal*, 22 October 1991.

12. Editorial, *Daily Cardinal*, 25 October 1989, at 5.

13. Telephone interview with Stephanie Bloomingdale, plaintiff, 11 March 1994.

14. Telephone interview with Michael Mathias, plaintiff, 18 March 1994.

15. Telephone interview with Stephanie Bloomingdale, 11 March 1994.

16. *Brief in Support of Plaintiffs' Summary Judgment Motion*, 2 October 1990, at 2.

17. Telephone interview with Jeffrey Kassel, lawyer with LaFollette & Sinykin, Madison, Wis., and attorney for the plaintiffs, 22 February 1994.

18. *Milwaukee Sentinel*, 20 June 1989, part I, at 10.

19. Telephone interview with Gordon Baldwin, Professor, University of Wisconsin–Madison Law School, 20 December 1993.

20. *UWM Post*, at 1167.

21. *UWM Post*, at 1168. The student's penalty also required him to make restitution and to take a class in ethics or East Asian history.

22. The other seven cases in which students were sanctioned under the UW Rule were:

1. A UW–Parkside student entered another student's bedroom, used "inappropriate language," and then called the other student "Shakazulu." The student was given probation, was required to talk with a counselor about alcohol abuse, and had to "plan a project in conjunction with the Center for Education and Cultural Advancement to help sensitize [himself] to the issues of diversity" (p. 1167).

2. A UW–Osh Kosh student was placed on seven months' probation for telling an Asian-American student, "It's people like you—that's the reason this country is screwed up" and "You don't belong here." In addition, the student said, "Whites are always getting screwed by minorities and someday the whites will take over." The student was also required to undergo assessment and treatment for alcohol abuse.

3. A UW–Stevens Point student was placed on probation for eight months for harassing a Turkish-American student by pretending to be an immigration official and demanding to see immigration documents.

4. A student at UW–Stout became involved in a physical altercation with two dormitory staff members and called one of them "piece of shit nigger" and the other "South American immigrant." The student waived a hearing and was suspended for seven months.

5. A UW–Eau Claire student used the university computer system to send the message "Death to all Arabs!! Die Islamic scumbags!" to an Iranian faculty member. The student was placed on probation for the rest of the semester.

6. A UW–Osh Kosh student referred to a black female student as a "fat-ass nigger" during an argument. "The student, who was already on disciplinary probation, was required to view a video on racism and write an essay and a letter of apology and was reassigned to another residence hall" (p. 1168).

7. A male student at UW–River Falls was put on probation for shouting at a female student in public, "You've got nice tits." The student was also required to apologize, to refrain from further contact with her, and to get counseling.

(All details from *UWM Post*, at 1167 *et seq.*)

23. Telephone interview with Jeffrey Kassel, 22 February 1994. One particularly glaring example of the arbitrary enforcement of the code concerns the use of the epithet "nigger." A UW–Stout student was put on probation for using the term (see note 22, example 4). But a white student at UW–Whitewater who called a black student "nigger" was not punished. According to the university, the white student "was raised in a racially mixed neighborhood" where "it was common for both blacks and whites in this environment to refer to blacks who were not respected, liked, or appreciated as 'nigger.' " As the plaintiffs' attorney pointed out, "Under that interpretation of the rule, it is permissible for a white student to call a black student 'nigger' in a hostile manner—as long as he believes that blacks also use the term to insult blacks." *Brief in Support of Plaintiffs' Summary Judgment Motion*, 2 October 1990, at 45.

24. Nor were there any instances of students being sanctioned at the UW–Milwaukee campus.

25. Telephone interview with a university employee, not for attribution.

26. Telephone interview with Ted Finman, 15 March 1994.

27. *Discriminatory Harassment/Assault Complaints Reported to the Dean of Students Office, University of Wisconsin–Madison 1991*, Office of the Dean of Students, University of Wisconsin–Madison. One incident at the UW–Madison involved a student's complaint that he had been called a "redneck." The Dean of Students responded that "it would be very difficult to show that the term 'redneck' is by itself the equivalent of a discriminatory epithet." The student's complaint was not pursued. *Brief in Support of Plaintiffs' Summary Judgment Motion*, 2 October 1990, at 45.

28. Mary K. Rouse and Roger Howard, *The 2% UW System Solution*, 21 March 1991, at 2. [Memo distributed to university employees.]

29. Mary K. Rouse and Roger Howard, *op. cit.*, note 28, explain their position:

We have concluded that any effective strategy to change the climate of our community must have at least three essential elements:

1) Establish standards of interpersonal relationships for students, faculty and staff and articulate the kind of university community in which we want to live. In the simplest and most important terms, the hallmark of the community we yearn for is RESPECT. (*Setting and articulating community standards is 30% of our strategy.*)

2) Increase dramatically our efforts to educate our students about the beauty of diversity and the pain of racism. This is the critical step. (*Education about diversity is 68% of our strategy.*)

3) Identify conduct which so grossly and intentionally violates the standards we have articulated about RESPECT among students that we must use University disciplinary action to protect one individual from the intentional efforts of another to interfere with the victim's University education. . . . This disciplinary process is an important anchor for our efforts although it will only deal with a very small number of incidents. (*Discipline is 2% of our strategy.*)

30. Telephone interview with Patricia Brady, Senior System Legal Counsel, University of Wisconsin, 22 February 1994.

31. Brady wrote: "[There are] substantial differences between the Michigan policy and Wisconsin's regulation that make the application of the reasoning of [that] deci-

sion to Wisconsin's regulation unlikely. . . . The language of the Wisconsin rule is narrower . . . in terms of the conduct prohibited, the proof required to establish a violation, and the rule's application in the classroom setting." Patricia Brady, *op. cit.*, note 1, at 586.

But the plaintiffs had another perspective. They agreed that the Michigan and Wisconsin codes could be distinguished, but argued that the UW Rule was even broader. Unlike Michigan's code, the UW Rule was "unlimited in its application to students wherever they may be—even off campus. Student newspapers were not subject to regulation at all under the Michigan rule. They are subject to the UW Rule, however, and one student newspaper is a plaintiff in this case." *Brief in Support of Plaintiffs' Summary Judgment Motion*, 2 October 1990, at 12.

32. *UWM Post*, at 1170.

33. *UWM Post*, at 1173.

34. *Plaintiffs' Combined Reply Brief in Support of the Motion for Summary Judgment and Response Brief in Opposition to the Defendant's Motion*, 30 January 1991, at 4.

35. Telephone interview with Ted Finman, 15 March 1994.

36. *Chaplinsky*, at 769, cited in *UWM Post*, at 1173.

37. *Defendant's Combined Brief in Support of Its Motion for Summary Judgment and in Response to the Plaintiff's Motion for Summary Judgment*, 28 December 1990, at 4.

38. *UWM Post*, at 1174.

39. *UWM Post*, at 1176.

40. *UWM Post*, at 1176.

41. *UWM Post*, at 1177.

42. *UWM Post*, at 1181.

43. Peter Kafka, Editorial, *Daily Cardinal*, 22 October 1991, emphasis in the original.

44. Telephone interview with Ted Finman, 15 March 1994.

45. *Daily Cardinal*, 23 October 1991, at 5.

46. Telephone interview with Joel Grossman, Professor of Political Science, University of Wisconsin–Madison, 23 February 1994.

47. Wis. Admin. Code § UWS 17.06(2) Revised. The emphasis is mine and is designed to highlight the points at which the revised code differs from the original UW Rule.

48. *Wisconsin State Journal*, 23 February 1992, at 1C.

49. Editorial, *Daily Cardinal*, 2 March 1992.

50. *Daily Cardinal*, 3 March 1992. It is interesting to note, as law professor Gordon Baldwin observed, that the law and political science faculty seemed to be aligned on opposing sides of the debate. (Telephone interview with Gordon Baldwin, 20 December 1993.) In general, the law professors believed the speech code could improve campus diversity while the political scientists advocated other measures, such as improving minority recruitment and increasing educational efforts.

51. Telephone interview with Joel Grossman, 23 February 1994.

52. *Daily Cardinal*, 5 March 1992. It is interesting that the proponents of the speech code, acting in the name of "diversity," repeatedly assume hegemony of opinion among minority students. The assumption that all minorities support campus speech

codes runs through the rhetoric of the "politically correct" speech code advocates even as opponents emphasize diversity *within* groups.

53. Syllabus of Decisions, in *Wisconsin* v. *Todd Mitchell*, 124 L. Ed. 2d (1993), at 440. Note that the U.S. Supreme Court reversed the lower court decision on appeal.

54. Telephone interview with Patricia Brady, 22 February 1994.

55. *Capital Times*, 12 September 1992.

56. *Discriminatory Harassment/Assault Complaints Reported to the Dean of Students' Office, University of Wisconsin–Madison, 1991 and 1992.*

57. Telephone interview with Peggy Miezio, Assistant Dean, Office of the Dean of Students, University of Wisconsin–Madison, 20 December 1993.

58. Telephone interview with Bill Arnold, spokesperson, University of Wisconsin–Madison Office of News and Public Affairs, 20 December 1993. The percentage of women students declined, however, from 51% in 1991 to 49% in 1993.

59. From 1983 to 1993 the number of students of color increased 58% while the total number of students decreased 5%. (*A Profile of UW–Madison Diversity Initiatives and Data*, Spring 1994.)

60. Telephone interview with Gordon Baldwin, 20 December 1993.

61. Telephone interview with Ted Finman, 15 March 1994.

62. *New York Times*, 15 May 1988, section 1, at 26, cited in *Brief in Support of Plaintiffs' Summary Judgment Motion*, at 39.

63. *The Madison Commitment: A Reaffirmation of University Goals for Minority Programs*, UW–M Faculty Document 1064, 4 April 1994. I thank Joel Grossman for drawing my attention to this document.

64. Telephone interview with Ted Finman, 15 March 1994.

PRESERVING THE BASTION:
THE CASE OF THE *DARTMOUTH REVIEW*

Christopher McMahon
Dickinson College

Dartmouth College, located in the picturesque New England town of Hanover, New Hampshire, is a member of the Ivy League, and ranks among America's most prestigious and competitive educational institutions. Historically, Dartmouth was a bastion of white, male, liberal arts education from its founding in 1754 until the early 1970s. In 1972, the school attempted to change its conservative image and respond to changes in society by admitting women and minorities and attempting to encourage more diversity in the student body. Dartmouth College made diversity a priority in an attempt to transform the secluded New Hampshire college into a true university.

Along with the changes in student-body composition and college vision, a de-emphasis of the old western-centered "core" curriculum occurred at this time. Whether the change in curriculum came from radical feminists and minorities (as conservatives claim) or from a necessary broadening of the traditional curriculum in order to acknowledge the contributions of other groups that have been neglected (as supporters of the changes maintain), the result was a move away from a "core" curriculum and toward a fragmentation (or diversification) of the educational mission of the college. This diversification was viewed as either a positive move to deal with diversity in the world as well as on campus, or a perversion of the basic educational purpose of institutions of higher education, depending on the lenses through which the situation was viewed.

The debate over these changes at Dartmouth took on a degree of rancor, which made it the subject of national attention. The presence of a conservative independent school paper, founded in 1980 by a group of students and funded by a powerful national network of conservative groups, polarized and publicized the debate and made Dartmouth a testing ground for a conservative counterattack on the new trends in higher education.[1] The paper, the *Dartmouth Review,* mixed in with the usual college fare a weekly challenge to the foundations underlying the college's new mission.

The *Review* claimed it was fighting to preserve the underlying values that guided Dartmouth (and "true" liberal arts education) from its founding. The *Review* sought a return to the traditional western-dominated "core" curricu-

lum in order to give the students a shared foundation of knowledge felt to
be necessary to live in "our western society." One of the charges leveled at
Dartmouth was that there were nonwestern requirements but no traditional
western civilization course requirements. The *Review* labeled non-traditional
departments such as Black Studies and Women's Studies as "political indoctrination centers" rather than real sources of education.[2] The paper also criticized affirmative action programs that allowed for special admission standards
to be applied to certain groups based upon race or sex. To further this agenda,
the *Review* published critiques of courses and teachers who purportedly promoted a level of education commensurate with an Ivy League school. The
Review claimed that Dartmouth was hostile to its ideas and constantly trying
to intimidate it to the point where it would cease to publish.[3]

The school and many members of the Dartmouth community saw the *Review* in a different light. They pointed to the paper's notorious personal attacks
upon faculty, administrators, women, and minorities as evidence that the *Review* was not promoting academic quality, but rather was discouraging women
and minorities from attending or teaching at Dartmouth. Some members of
the Dartmouth community said it was these attacks, not the conservative views
of the paper, with which they disagreed. More importantly, some members of
the faculty pointed to the paper as a source of intimidation that prevented the
discussion of certain ideas. They claimed that it was not the school that chilled
free speech, but rather the *Review* that chilled the free exchange of ideas on
campus. This divergence of opinions led to a series of incidents involving the
Review and the Dartmouth community.

History of the Dartmouth Review

The *Dartmouth Review* has always been controversial. Soon after the *Review*
was founded, it ran a story on Music Professor Bill Cole that caused him to
sue the paper for libel. This incident, discussed in detail below, was only the
first confrontation between the *Review* and the greater Dartmouth community.
This chapter focuses primarily on the controversy surrounding the *Review* and
its treatment of Cole, but it is important to understand some of the history of
the *Review* as well, to place the case in its proper context. Two other incidents
illustrate the overall attitude and tactics of the *Review* and its staff.

The first incident concerned the taping of a meeting of the Dartmouth Area
Gay and Lesbian Organization (DAYGLO). DAYGLO claimed that the meeting (held on campus) was confidential and thus the taping was illegal. The
Review claimed that the meeting was advertised and open to all interested
students. In any event, the *Review* printed a story in which many of the people

in attendance were named, and staff members then sent copies of the paper to the relatives of these students. The *Review* maintained that it obtained a list of the organization's officers from the student government, only published those names, and only sent copies to individuals on the paper's subscription list.[4] The *Review* argued that any revelations concerning membership in the group were incidental and unintentional.

The second case involved a student group's protest against apartheid in South Africa and the college's alleged "complicity" in supporting the regime through investments of its endowment. The group erected shanties on the college green as a symbol to encourage the trustees of Dartmouth to divest their South African investments. The school repeatedly asked the students to remove the shanties, but they refused to do so. One evening, approximately a dozen students wielding sledgehammers, many of them *Review* staffers, took it upon themselves to demolish the structures in order to "beautify" the green before the traditional winter carnival.[5]

Dartmouth took disciplinary action against the students who destroyed the shanties, but refused to take action against those who built them. Moreover, the college later declined to discipline students who occupied the president's office as a protest of the destruction of the shanties. The *Review* pointed to this disparate treatment as evidence of a dual standard in force at the school in which harbingers of "diversity" were tacitly encouraged while supporters of the "traditions" and "legacy" of the college were punished. This clash of interpretations led to the incidents involving the *Review* and Professor Cole, raising the issues of racism, intolerance, and free speech.

Professor Bill Cole and the Review

The *Dartmouth Review* and Professor Cole first tangled in 1983. The catalyst was an article published by the *Review* entitled "Prof. Cole's Song and Dance Routine," in which the *Review* published a partial transcript of one of his classes. The article quoted Cole as saying, "A lot of you are racist or sexist or out to lunch. But that's your problem not mine."[6] The article made it clear that the *Review* considered Cole's class, Music II, as the most "outrageous gut" course on campus. The rest of the article detailed the lack of what the *Review* believed were adequate Ivy League academic standards in Cole's class. The article included carefully cloaked personal attacks, attributed to anonymous members of the class, such as one comment describing Cole as looking "like a used Brillo Pad."[7] The *Review* also used the article as an attack on the school's affirmative action policies, saying, "A goodly number of Cole's students are black. Some allege that these are 'affirmative action' kids looking for a course they can handle."[8] In this article, all of the *Review*'s trademarks were present: an attack on academic standards, an attack on "diversity," and a personal attack.

Professor Cole perceived the *Review* article as blatant racism and felt that he was singled out for criticism because he was one of the few black instructors at the college. The day after the article appeared, Professor Cole sought out the responsible *Review* reporter, appeared at her dorm room at 8:30 A.M., and hammered on her door, some say for as long as twenty minutes.[9] Cole was alleged to have yelled, "You cocksuckers [*Review* staffers] fuck with everybody."[10] The reporter's frightened roommate answered the door and told Cole that the reporter, Laura Ingraham, was not there. Later that day, Cole suspended his class after five minutes as a way of protesting the *Review* article and announced that the class would be suspended indefinitely until he received an apology from the *Review*. He was informed by the dean of faculty that he could be fired if he did not resume teaching his class, so Cole resumed his class.[11] Cole was later reprimanded by the administration for his actions in the dormitory.[12]

On March 17, 1983, Professor Cole filed a libel suit in U.S. District Court, alleging that the *Review* had acted "in a malicious, intentional, willful, wanton, reckless, scandalous, outrageous, and defamatory manner." He based his suit on the *Review* article and on comments made by some of the *Review* staffers to newspapers in Rutland, Vermont, and West Lebanon, New Hampshire. Several members of the Dartmouth faculty, led by Music Professor Jon Appleton, set up a fund to help pay Cole's legal expenses. The *Review* claimed that this was an attempt not only by Professor Cole but by Dartmouth College itself to bankrupt them, and cited the fund as evidence. What was left unsaid by the *Review* was that its legal services were being provided free of charge.[13]

Both the *Review* and Professor Cole asked the New Hampshire Civil Liberties Union (NHCLU) to represent them in the lawsuit. The NHCLU has a standing policy that regards all libel actions against public figures to be unconstitutional. Consequently, the NHCLU would not represent Cole, but were predisposed to take the case on behalf of the *Review*. However, they quickly became embroiled in a dispute with the *Review*. The *Review* claimed that although the NHCLU took the case, the organization was uncomfortable with the conservative nature of the paper, wanted to find a way to drop the case, and began placing conditions on its continued involvement. According to the *Review,* staff members were told, "If at any point there is evidence of intentional defamation the ACLU will withdraw from the case."[14] The *Review* believed that this caveat was unprecedented and was a "political out" used by

NHCLU to make conditions so untenable that the *Review* would have to refuse their help.[15]

On the other hand, the NHCLU contended that the *Review* wanted to expand the scope of the defense to include not just the NHCLU's traditional stand regarding the unconstitutionality of libel but also the issue of academic incompetence. The organization maintained that the *Review* was informed that the NHCLU was very selective in the issues it chose to litigate and that this was an area in which the NHCLU did not involve itself. When the NHCLU declined to become involved in the issue of Professor Cole's academic competence, the organization was, in essence, fired by the *Review*.[16]

In 1985 the lawsuit was settled out of court and a joint statement was issued as part of that settlement. In the statement, both sides reaffirmed their basic contentions—that is, Cole maintained that the article was a racially motivated attack on his teaching abilities, and the *Review* stood behind the accuracy of the story and its right to publish material relating to the curriculum at Dartmouth. The *Review* said that it offered Professor Cole a chance to reply to the article but that he refused to do so. Both sides acknowledged Professor Cole's right to teach in whatever manner he chose as well as the *Review*'s right to publish whatever it wished to publish.[17] Unfortunately, this was not the end of the battle. Yet to come was a confrontation that would rock the Dartmouth campus and send charges of racism, and countercharges of liberal intolerance, reverberating across the country.

Professor Cole v. *the* Review: *II*

The next shot was fired by the *Dartmouth Review* in an article that was intended as a follow-up to a "cultural literacy" poll published the previous week. In this poll, Dartmouth students were ranked at the bottom of the Ivy League. The *Review* article, published February 19, 1988, had a front-page photo of two professors, Cole and English Professor Richard Corum, altered to show them in Superman outfits, with a heading that read, "Dartmouth's Dynamic Duo of Mediocrity."[18] Inside the paper were stories detailing the alleged academic deficiencies of the two professors. The *Review* referred to Corum as "Clogs," a sixties reject who allegedly had no right to teach at any college, much less Dartmouth. In particular, the *Review* pointed out his failure to fulfill the college requirements for courses as specified in the course catalog.[19]

The article about Professor Cole went further. "Bill Cole in His Own Words—Sound and Fury Signifying Nothing" was based on a transcript of a tape recording of the February 16, 1988, session of Cole's Music II.[20] The recording was apparently made by a student who, at the time, was unaffiliated with the *Review* and disgruntled by Cole's class. The tape was provided to the *Review* based on the accurate prediction that the *Review* would use it to embarrass Cole.[21] The article argued that Cole's class was, in essence, a series of disjointed ramblings that bore little or no connection to the supposed subject matter of the course. In the same issue, the *Review* printed a transcript of a telephone conversation between Cole and John Sutter, who worked at the *Review*. Cole was quoted as calling members of the *Review* "racist dogs" and "scum of the earth."[22] According to Cole, the *Review* tried four times to illicit a comment from him, which he declined, and then continued to harass him until he finally lost his temper.

It is difficult to reconstruct accurately the events that occurred next, as accounts diverge depending on which party is telling the story. What follows is the author's attempt to decipher objectively the actions of both sides in the aftermath of the *Review*'s publication of the last article. But while opinions vary, it is universally agreed that four *Review* staffers—Christopher Baldwin, John Sutter, John Quilhot, and Sean Nolan—went to Cole's class on February 25, after the class session had concluded but while Professor Cole was still talking to some of his students. At this point, the facts become less clear.

The Review*'s Story:* The *Review* said that their lawyer advised them, based on their earlier problems with Professor Cole, to inform Cole of a *Review* policy allowing an unedited response to the articles. Four staffers were sent to Cole's class to "cover all the bases." Baldwin was there to give Cole a written copy of the policy; Sutter, to obtain an apology for Cole's remarks on the telephone; Quilhot, to photograph the "meeting"; and Nolan, to gather material for a follow-up story to run in the next edition of the *Review*.

The *Review* contended that when the four staffers walked in, Cole recognized at least one of them and asked what they wanted, at which point Baldwin offered Cole a copy of a memo detailing the editorial policy of the *Review*, which Cole refused to accept. Cole then began screaming that the *Review* members were invading his space. The staffers maintain that Cole jabbed his finger in Baldwin's eye a number of times, and that during this time Quilhot was taking pictures of the confrontation. Cole then turned to Quilhot, ordered him to stop taking pictures, and grabbed at the camera, dislodging the flash, which fell to the floor and broke. John Sutter then stepped in between Cole and Baldwin and asked Cole for an apology both for his language during the phone call and for comments made in his class on February 18 (prior to the *Review* article), when he called *Review* staffers "motherfucking racists."[23] At this point, Cole spotted a tape recorder, which was clearly visible, sticking out of Sutter's pocket. Cole grabbed for the recorder and Sutter said, "Get your hand out of my pocket."[24] Professor Cole then taunted Sutter, saying, "Take it [the apology] from me."[25] Sutter construed this as a challenge to fight. Cole then asked for the recorder to be turned off, which the *Review* did. Cole continued to scream at Sutter until the *Review* staffers left.[26]

Professor Cole's Story: Professor Cole claimed that the *Review* members were there to harass him until he reacted. He told *The Dartmouth* (the school's student newspaper), "When a student gets in the face of a professor, that in and of itself is provocative. . . . These people have nothing but the utmost contempt for me."[27] Cole went on to call the *Review* staff "bigots, racists, anti-Semites, and sexists, who are going to hell."[28]

According to a statement Cole gave to the campus police, the four *Review* staffers came into his class demanding that he read some sort of letter. He asked them to leave immediately; they refused and started taking pictures. He asked Quilhot to stop, and when he refused:

> I grabbed at the photographer's camera because he would not stop. One member of the *Review* [Sutter] grabbed me and prevented me from touching the camera. Then he stood right in my face and demanded I apologize for something I said to him on the phone. I asked if they were recording and they said no. The conversation got extremely heated and they continued to provoke me. . . . The man who had the tape recorder in his pocket [Sutter] stayed in my face and wanted me to put my hands on him so that some legal action could be taken against me.[29]

Fortunately, there were eighteen independent statements made to campus police after the incident. They range from those accusing the *Review* of provoking Professor Cole into a physical confrontation to those who said Cole accused the *Review* staff of being "bigots and motherfucking racists."

The inference to be drawn from the majority of the statements is that the *Review* staffers harassed Professor Cole, through both their words and the use of the camera. The students seem to base their conclusions on the fact that the *Review* staffers did not leave when asked, but continued to photograph and exchange heated words. One student's statement read: "The *Dartmouth Review* staff refused to leave and continued to harass Professor Cole by taking pictures. Professor Cole told the photographer to stop taking pictures of him. When he didn't stop Professor Cole tried to take the camera away from him. That's when Sutter said, 'Professor Cole, don't do it.' He said it like it was rehearsed, like this was all planned out in advance."[30] However, the support for Cole was not universal. One student supporting the *Review* stated: "Professor Cole was talking to another student when he recognized the *Review* staffers and asked, 'What do you want?' Baldwin told Cole why they were there and attempted to give Cole a letter. Cole became quite upset and told them he didn't want their 'racist bullshit.' . . . Cole yelled at the students to leave, Sutter continued to demand an apology, Cole called them 'motherfucking racists and bigots.' . . . At no time during the occurrence were there any racial or derogatory terms made by the *Review* members about Cole."[31]

The next day Professor Cole filed a complaint with the Dartmouth Committee on Standards against the *Review* and the four staffers.

The Aftermath

Over the next weekend (February 27–28), reports about the incident began to circulate around the campus. The Afro-American Society and other campus groups began organizing a rally for the following Monday. While it was not an official sponsor of the rally, the college administration lent tacit support when President Freedman agreed to address the crowd, and encouraged students to attend the gathering. A poster advertising the rally was printed, in which *Review* staffer Sutter was quoted as saying, "We've got to get rid of all you incompetent niggers." Sutter allegedly made this comment while leaving Cole's class after the confrontation.[32]

On Monday, February 29, the rally was held in front of Parkhurst Hall, the administration building. Prior to the rally, President Freedman met with about seventy-five members of the black community on campus, but throughout the day, he refused to meet with the *Review* or the four accused students. Freedman began his speech by stating that he would not address the specifics of the events surrounding the confrontation until a disciplinary hearing regarding the incident had been conducted. However, earlier that morning, Freedman had received a letter from the chairman of Dartmouth's Board of Trustees encouraging him to "get out front . . . to avoid a sit-in or a takeover" as had occurred during the shanty incident.[33]

The president's speech was a significant statement, designed to calm the tension that was building around the campus. In it Freedman explicitly supported the principle of free speech while at the same time recognizing that free speech, civility, and tolerance do not always easily mix.[34] All this being said, the president concluded that the *Review* was "unnecessarily and inappropriately provocative."[35]

Freedman found himself in a difficult position. On the one hand, he was sympathetic to the feelings of black students, saying, "These students say that the Cole incident is the straw that is breaking the students' backs. They say that if a small number of students can treat a full professor this way think how vulnerable the rest of us feel."[36] On the other hand, he had to be careful not to prejudice the upcoming disciplinary hearing. Freedman was not always successful at walking that fine line, as demonstrated by a comment made by college spokeswoman Cathy Wolff, who said, "Freedman's speech implicitly, if not explicitly, expressed his support of Professor Cole as a tenured member of the faculty."[37]

Students in the Afro-American Society advanced a series of demands for the college to meet in light of the incident. First, they called for the immediate suspension of the four *Review* staffers. Second, they called for a statement from the college reaffirming its confidence in Professor Cole and saying that the students had violated the code of conduct. Finally, they demanded an apology from the *Review* to Professor Cole.[38]

Demands were also made by a loosely affiliated group of faculty and students calling themselves the "Concerned People of the Dartmouth Community." In addition to supporting the demands of the Afro-American Society, this group wanted the trustees to initiate legal proceedings against the *Review* to have the word *Dartmouth* removed from its masthead. It also wanted President Freedman to write to the parents of all incoming freshmen, informing them that the college, in no uncertain terms, condemned the practices of the *Review*.[39] While Freedman was sympathetic to both groups, he refused to meet any of the demands.[40]

The Disciplinary Process

The courts have ruled that private universities are not bound directly by the provisions of the U.S. Constitution, but they are required to abide by their own codes of conduct, which serve as a contract between the schools and the students.[41] Students may thus claim that their relationship to a college is like a contract; as long as the students comply with the college's rules and regulations and satisfactorily complete its required course of study, they are entitled to the college's degree. The private college is obliged not to violate any of the contractual rights of its students or otherwise act arbitrarily or capriciously.[42]

In order to fulfill the criteria set out by the court, the Dartmouth disciplinary procedure must follow the rules and processes set forth in the Student Handbook and meet the requirements of basic fairness. The Student Code of Conduct, contained in the handbook, lays out the college's disciplinary process. It provides for a two-track system once charges have been laid. For lesser charges, an informal dean's hearing is conducted; for more serious charges, a hearing before the Committee on Standards (COS)[43] is held. The format of the hearings is the same in both cases. The hearing is a quasi-legal trial. The accused is not allowed legal representation, but can have an advisor from within the Dartmouth community. There is no cross-examination of witnesses. The accused can write questions for witnesses and have them submitted to the chair of the committee, who then asks the witnesses the questions. Witnesses are not required to be in attendance to present evidence, and the hearing is not open to the public unless all of the accused students request that it be so.

In this instance, the *Review* staffers requested an open meeting including both the Dartmouth community and select members of the media. The *Review* staffers were charged with disorderly conduct, harassment, and invasion of privacy. The hearing, which took two days and generated a transcript of over five hundred pages, was highlighted by Professor Cole's testimony, in which he referred to the *Review* staff as "bigots, racists, anti-Semites, and sexists."[44] He also testified that he believed the *Review* "viewed me as a nigger. These people [had] nothing but the utmost contempt for me."[45] Luzmilla Johnson and two other students testified that John Sutter uttered the racial epithet that was used on the posters to advertise the rally.[46] The chair of the committee, Dean of Students Shanahan, refused to allow the *Review* staffers to bring up the question of Ms. Johnson's potential bias (she presented the Afro-American Society demand that the staffers be immediately suspended). For their part, the *Review* staff members testified that they were just acting like journalists, but were interrupted by a frenzy of screamed obscenities.[47]

A key issue for the committee revolved around Sutter's tape recorder and whether it was concealed. The code of conduct has a provision wherein no student shall use any device for recording in any place where a person has a reasonable right to be "free from unwanted surveillance, eavesdropping, recording, or observation, unless the student has first obtained the consent of all persons involved."[48] According to the testimony at the hearing, Baldwin denied taping the event, going through a well-designed deception in which he emptied his pockets and opened his coat, while continually denying he was taping the incident. At the same time, Sutter had a tape recorder that Cole had not approved. Baldwin denied that the four students had invaded Cole's privacy, contending that the building in which the incident took place was a public place and Professor Cole could only expect privacy during class time.[49]

The students' advisor, English Professor Jeffrey Hart, summed up the *Review*'s position in this way: "I conclude that Professor Cole lives in a sort of mental nightmare populated by cliché demons." He justified the students' actions by pointing to Cole's past behavior, including the 1983 door-banging which, he contended, explained and excused the behavior of the *Review* staffers.[50]

The COS deliberated for three days before issuing its decision. In the meantime, one of the students on the committee voluntarily removed himself from the proceedings because he had written a fictional piece critical of the *Review* over the shanty-bashing incident.[51] On March 10, 1988, the committee released its decision suspending Baldwin and Sutter for eighteen months and Quilhot for six months, and placing Nolan on probation for one year.

The appeal of a Committee on Standards decision can be made on only two grounds. Reconsideration may be granted (1) when there has been a procedural error that has materially prejudiced the student or (2) when newly discovered facts that, had they been introduced at the proceeding, would likely have affected the outcome of the proceeding.[52]

The *Review* staffers filed an appeal on March 21, contending that several members of the committee were biased and that there were serious questions about the procedural integrity of the hearing. Specifically, they argued that Dean Shanahan was unfair in his decisions on what he would and would not allow into evidence, that some members of the committee were unfairly biased against the *Review*, and that the atmosphere on campus, especially the statements made by President Freedman at the rally, may have intimidated the committee.

From the *Review*'s point of view, Dean Shanahan—who had previously sent a letter to Professor Cole explaining that he had temporarily stepped down from the committee in order to become "personally involved in an attempt to develop the case" against one of the *Review* staffers—was biased.[53] As one of the *Review* members related, "We got screwed."[54] They maintained that it would have been almost impossible for Dean Shanahan, under these circumstances, to be a neutral judge. He reported directly to President Freedman who had, at the least, implicitly come out against the students. On March 25, 1988, Shanahan declined the students' request for reconsideration. The administration, particularly Dean Shanahan, reiterated that it could indeed be fair in handling this case. It cited the students' actions, not their speech or its content, as the sole reason for the actions taken against them. They continued to assert that all aspects of the process were fair.

Freedman's Speech to the Faculty

On March 28, President Freedman addressed an emergency faculty meeting called to discuss the crisis. His stance with regard to the *Review* was a departure from that of his predecessor, President McLaughlin, who had tried to remain above the fray and ignore the *Review*. However, Freedman's position was understandable in light of his stated goals for Dartmouth, and this speech was heralded as a major policy speech in support of those goals. In it, he reaffirmed both his personal commitment to freedom of speech and the college's commitment to diversity.

Freedman pointed out that the *Review*'s attacks on certain groups hurt the school's attempt to recruit qualified minorities. He argued that the *Review* was engaged in speech aimed at undercutting the school's attempt to maintain an atmosphere where all speech could compete in the "marketplace of ideas." The only way for this level of debate to be achieved was if all parties recognized and followed simple principles of civility. Only in this atmosphere could there truly be a marketplace open to all ideas where no individual was subject to the type of personal attacks that could chill his or her desire to freely express his or her ideas.

The Legal Battle

After their appeal was denied by the school, and after they had exhausted all of the school's administrative procedures for a reconsideration of their punishment, the *Review* staffers asked the NHCLU to represent them in a lawsuit alleging that Dartmouth had impinged upon both their First Amendment right to freedom of expression and their speech rights as set out in the Dartmouth Student Handbook.[55] The NHCLU reviewed the transcript of the COS hearing and refused to represent the students. This decision was based primarily on the presence of the concealed tape recorder, which was not only a clear violation of the code of conduct, but was in all likelihood a violation of the State of New Hampshire's wiretap laws as well. Moreover, the NHCLU concluded that the students were punished for their violations of the code of conduct, not for their speech. Clare Ebel, Director of the NHCLU, said, "The threshold question with which we had to deal was whether the record contained in the transcript supports the decision reached by the Committee on Standards. In our opinion the answer is yes."[56]

In the summer of 1988, the NHCLU, in conjunction with its parent group, the American Civil Liberties Union (ACLU), conducted an investigation of the free speech atmosphere at Dartmouth and the most recent incident involving Professor Cole. The ensuing report concluded that the school was not subject to the constitutional provisions applied by the courts to public institutions. Moreover, they reconfirmed their earlier determination that the *Review* staffers were punished for their actions rather than their speech. However, the ACLU was troubled by the conviction of the students based on "vexatious oral exchange" and the school's application of the harassment provision in its code of conduct. While the ACLU contended that this provision may have been used in this instance to punish speech, which the organization categorically opposes, it nevertheless concluded that the overall decision in the Cole case was appropriate.[57]

The *Review* pursued several other legal options. Letters were sent to alumni soliciting funds for the Dartmouth Defense Fund, set up by the *Review* to help defray its legal expenses. The students also received funding from the John Olin Foundation. With coffers beginning to swell, the students filed a complaint against the college with the National Endowment for the Humanities (NEH), which had provided Dartmouth with a total of $502,518 during the 1988 fiscal year. The action alleged that the judicial process used to suspend the students was discriminatory. NEH passed the complaint along to the Department of Education, which, under a delegation of powers arrangement, handled all civil rights complaints made to the NEH. The Department of Education found jurisdiction for its investigation in Title VI of the Civil Rights Act, which prohibits discrimination on the basis of race, color, or national origin in programs or activities receiving federal financial assistance. However, the Department of Education suspended its investigation pending the outcome of lawsuits that were soon to be filed by the students against the college.

On July 27, 1988, the students held a press conference in Washington, D.C., with United States Senator Gordon Humphrey to announce the beginning of legal proceedings against the school. Senator Humphrey referred to the events at Dartmouth as "nothing less than a crude assault on freedom of expression and political diversity on campus."[58] Two lawsuits were filed, one in the state court and the other in the Federal District Court for New Hampshire. The major contention in the state case was that the school violated its contract with the students by abridging their free speech rights.[59] Thus, the state case was based on a theory of contract law, that the student handbook operated as a contract between Dartmouth and its students.

The federal lawsuit, which the court subsequently summarily dismissed without comment, focused on the issue of discrimination. The students claimed that they were the victims of racial discrimination because they were denied a fair trial regarding a racial incident. They also claimed that they were treated differently when sentenced because they were white. The students cited several specific instances, especially those surrounding the shanty incident, where students (those opposing the regime in South Africa) who violated the school's code of conduct and were convicted by the COS were not disciplined because of the "strength of their convictions." Campus attitudes about the suit ranged from Dartmouth legal counsel Sean Gorman's calling the suits "frivolous and a waste of time," to college spokesman Alex Huppe's comment that the students' lawyer, Harvey Myerson, was "about as believable as his hairpiece."[60]

In late 1988, the state lawsuit was tried before Judge Bruce Mohl. The key issue in the case was whether the college had violated the provisions of the college handbook. Mohl found that a member of the COS, Professor Albert LaValley, had signed a letter characterizing the *Review* as sexist and racist prior to the hearing. At the COS hearing, LaValley mentioned signing the letter but said he could not remember its content, and no copy of the letter could be found prior to the hearing. LaValley felt that the letter was fairly general in its criticism of the *Review* and that he could be unbiased. Given these circumstances, Judge Mohl ruled that LaValley could not render an unbiased decision and, consequently, the COS hearing did not meet the requirements for "fundamental fairness."[61] The court also found, however, that it could find "no persuasive evidence that Dartmouth College [had] retaliated against or otherwise pursued disciplinary action against the plaintiffs on account of their association with the *Dartmouth Review*."[62]

In a later ruling, Mohl found that the president's speech did not have a prejudicial effect on the COS hearing. He also found that Dean Shanahan was an active participant in the planning and implementing of events relating to campus reactions over the Cole incident. Consequently, Mohl reinstated the *Review* staffers, pending a new COS hearing to be conducted absent the one biased member.

Dartmouth decided neither to hold a rehearing after the court's action nor to pursue an appeal of the decision. President Freedman and the trustees maintained that they did not want to disrupt the community any more than it had already been disrupted. As a result of the decision, Dartmouth changed its COS code to deal with the judge's objections to member bias. The school also added a section to its code of conduct explaining the impossibility of living up to judicial standards of impartiality in a small, insular community.[63]

The Fallout

In an article appearing in the Dartmouth Alumni Magazine, an alumnus of Dartmouth concluded, "The *Review* has not been censored. . . . But there is indeed a record of unequal sentencing over the past decade, and it poses troubling free-speech questions."[64] The unequal treatment was most apparent when considering that the students who put up the shanties repeatedly defied the school's orders to take them down and the school continually backed down from a confrontation. The students who engaged in a sit-in in the office of the college's president were found guilty of obstructing college activities but were not given any punishment because of their "strongly held convictions."[65]

In the fall of 1988, the Dartmouth College Committee on Diversity issued a report that savaged the *Review* as a source of "insinuations, vicious epithets, and personal attack." The report further explained that the *Review* had the effect of discouraging certain groups from attending Dartmouth. It characterized the *Review* as harassers of women, blacks, gays, and Hispanics, and criticized the penchant of the *Review* to engage in personal attacks. The *Review*'s editor, Harmeet Dhillon, responded by saying that she did not consider articles critical of particular groups to be harassment.

At least three former Dartmouth professors acknowledge that the *Dartmouth Review* was a significant factor in their decision to leave the college. One said, "By insisting that morality should be taught in the classroom, the Hopkins Institute [a conservative Alumni group] and the *Review* attempt to 'police the classroom' . . . and thus severely limit academic freedom."[66] Many teachers interviewed by the school paper, *The Dartmouth*, two months after the Cole incident indicated that they were actively looking for other teaching positions. They pointed to the *Review*'s repeated attacks on whole fields of scholarship as a strong force in limiting academic freedom. These professors expressed concern that all members of the faculty were aware of the *Review* and were constantly involved in self-censorship.[67] This was a climate that allegedly intimidated professors into changing lectures, ignoring controversial subjects, and carefully considering how, and even whether, to answer student questions.

At least one Dartmouth professor characterized the situation as a pervasive atmosphere that inhibited academic freedom and chilled professors' speech as a result of the intimidation levied by a well-financed, heavily endowed *Review*. William Cook, an English professor and chairman of the African and Afro-American Studies program, cited the *Review* as a definite disadvantage in the process of faculty recruitment. He was also sure that the *Review* intimidated professors to the point where they were afraid to speak out.[68]

For Professor Cole, the aftermath of the case was apparent from an interview he gave to the television program "60 Minutes," in which he said that the *Review* had treated him "like a dog, like shit underneath shoes."[69] Cole asserted that the incident had damaged his career to the point that he would have a very hard time finding work outside of Dartmouth. Professor Cole was bitter about the *Review* incident and also expressed anger that the school had not pursued action against the student who taped the class in the first place and gave the tape to the *Review*. In August of 1990, Professor Cole resigned from Dartmouth.

In a letter sent to Dartmouth alumni, alumnus and Visiting Professor Daniel Tompkins reached a conclusion similar to Cole's. After listing several instances where well-respected professors were the subject of the *Review*'s personal taunts, Professor Tompkins wrote: "I know of no other American college where this kind of cruel baiting and taunting goes on, much less one where it is endorsed by alumni. I've never seen a place where faculty are so contemptuously treated. I've never seen a publication that so blithely credits unfounded and unprovable rumors about professors."[70]

In the fall of 1988, *The Dartmouth* published an editorial in response to the NHCLU probe of the school, which stated that the "school does not censor papers, nor does it overtly repress the freedom to publish. But campus attitudes and misconceptions, along with tactics of individual faculty members and administrators, often translate into subtle attempts to control the campus press."[71] This editorial was superseded by another written during the Cole incident, which asked why it took charges of racism to bring out hostility toward the *Review*, and noted that no one ever came to the defense of those singled out by the *Review* unless they fit into "neat little victim boxes."[72]

The Dartmouth itself was involved in another free-speech debate. In 1987, the paper criticized a proposal for a Women's Resource Center in an editorial. Not only was it castigated for this view but it was also challenged over its right to publish that opinion. As one editor of the paper put it at the time, "A lot of people around here just have a basic lack of understanding of free speech."[73]

The problems of liberal and conservative intolerance were present at Dartmouth before the Cole incident, but the controversy served as a catalyst for the seeming breakdown of even a semblance of a marketplace of ideas. As an alumnus, *Newsweek* reporter Larry Martz observed that in the wake of the Cole incident, "feelings have become so polarized that they hamper communication." The conclusion to be reached is that both right-wing and left-wing demagogues gained control of the dialogue and made the middle ground untenable. In this atmosphere, both the *Review* and the hard-core left-wing faculty and students felt free to speak their minds while many moderates shied away from debate for fear of being personally castigated in the pages of the *Review* or facing some equally harrowing fate at the hands of the more liberal members of the community.[74]

In early 1989, a petition drive was started by a group of undergraduates condemning the *Review* for fostering an atmosphere of intolerance. The group had gathered over 1,400 signatures in February of 1989. According to the organizers of the drive, it was organized to counter the negative images that the school had received because of the *Review*. "The motivating force was a great deal of frustration over the fact that the *Review* is somewhat of a laughing stock in the community, but taken very seriously outside of it."[75]

The clash of individual freedoms and community values—in the context of diversity—generate disharmony, and a specific manifestation of that clash was evident at Dartmouth. The administration tried to balance as best it could these competing values and in the process satisfied almost no one. The faculty, outraged that a group of students, with support from powerful outsiders, could personally attack those it disagreed with, claimed that they engaged in self-censorship to avoid the attacks. The members of the *Review* claimed that they were victims of a liberal bias that subjected them to harsher disciplinary treatment based upon their conservative political viewpoint.

The incident involving Professor Cole and the students representing the *Review* went from an uncivil journalistic encounter to a national incident involving charges of racism and countercharges of suppression of speech. The presence of two competing values, individual freedom and diversity in the context of community, made the likelihood of true harmony seem utopic. The events at Dartmouth College are a poignant reminder of the potential costs—to academic freedom and freedom of expression, to the requirements of due process and fairness, as well as to the personal dignity of faculty and students—that are implicated in the hate speech controversy on college campuses.

Discussion Questions

1. The role of the press has loomed large in the development of American civil liberties. In a university community, are there limits that should be placed on newspaper coverage? Is the press "free" to write about matters that stigmatize by race? gender? sexual preference? academic ability? If Dartmouth had been utilizing a campus speech code similar to the one at Brown University when these events transpired, would or should the *Dartmouth Review* have been punished under it? Does the fact that the *Review* is a publication in any way influence your opinion?

2. Did the *Dartmouth Review*'s attack on Professor Cole have racial overtones? Should the presence of racial overtones in expression affect the level of its First Amendment protection? It may help to consider the Supreme Court's decisions in *Brandenburg* v. *Ohio, Beauharnais* v. *Illinois, Chaplinsky* v. *New Hampshire,* and *R.A.V.* v. *City of St. Paul* in answering this question.

3. How would you compare the role and leadership of Dartmouth's President

Freedman with those of Vartan Gregorian at Brown and the administration at Duke in handling campus hate speech issues?

Notes

1. Among the more notable sponsors of the *Review* have been presidential candidate Patrick Buchanan and syndicated columnist William F. Buckley.

2. Benjamin Hart, *Poisoned Ivy* (New York: Stein and Day, 1984), at 18.

3. The *Review* and the college were at odds on almost every level. The *Review* fought the change of the college's mascot from the Indian to the "Big Green." They ran an annual snow queen contest, replacing the event after the college canceled it on the grounds that it was insensitive to women. While all of these issues tended to raise the tension level between the *Review* and the college, for the purposes of this chapter we will focus on those issues that had First Amendment and PC implications.

4. Chris Witman, "Lies, Lies, and More Lies," *Dartmouth Review,* 9 March 1988, at 2.

5. Larry Martz, *When Dialogue Turns To Diatribe*, Dartmouth Alumni Magazine, May 1989, at 26.

6. Laura Ingraham, "Prof. Cole's Song and Dance Routine," *Dartmouth Review,* 17 January 1983, at 10.

7. *Ibid.*

8. *Ibid.*

9. Charles Sykes, *The Hollow Men* (Washington: Regenry Gateway, 1990), at 241.

10. *Ibid.*, at 242.

11. *Ibid.*

12. Confidential author interview with college administrator.

13. Roland Reynolds, "Professor Cole Drops Lawsuit," *Dartmouth Review,* 5 June 1985, at 5.

14. Aloke K. Mandel, "Bill Cole vs. the *Dartmouth Review*," *Dartmouth Review,* 2 May 1983, at 7.

15. *Ibid.*

16. Personal interview with Clare Ebel, Director, NHCLU.

17. "The Statement," *Dartmouth Review,* 5 June 1985, at 6.

18. *Dartmouth Review,* 24 February 1988, at 1.

19. John Sutter, "At the Movies with Professor Corum," *Dartmouth Review,* 24 February 1988, at 3.

20. Christopher Baldwin, "Bill Cole in His Own Words—Sound and Fury Signifying Nothing," *Dartmouth Review,* 24 February 1988, at 4.

21. Charles Sykes, *op. cit.*, note 9, at 280.

22. "Professor Cole Responds," *Dartmouth Review,* 24 February 1988, at 5.

23. Christopher Baldwin, Letter from the Editor, *Dartmouth Review,* 2 March 1988, at 3.

24. *Ibid.*

25. *Ibid.*

26. *Ibid.*

27. Jonathan Frankel, "*Review* Editor Baldwin Denies Charges," *The Dartmouth,* 7 March 1988, at 2.

28. *Ibid.*

29. Bill Cole, Statement to campus police, 25 February 1988.

30. Denise Chancy, Statement to campus police, 25 February 1988.

31. Jim Klug, Statement to campus police, 29 February 1988. This statement was given to the police a few days *after* the incident occurred.

32. Poster advertising rally. While this remark was not reported in the statements made after the incident, it was reported during testimony at the ensuing disciplinary hearing by Luzmilla Johnson, chairperson of the Afro-American Society.

33. *Dartmouth Review* v. *Dartmouth College*, New Hampshire Superior Court, 3 January 1989, at 8.

34. The president's statement included:

> But I do want to express my deep personal concern over the serious harm that is caused to the academic enterprise whenever any members of this community elect, for whatever reason, to introduce into the debate of the issues of this campus acts of disrespect, insensitivity, and personal attack. It is adherence to a set of principles of discourse that permits an academic institution to flourish. Civility, tolerance, and respect for others are at the heart of these principles, as are honesty and candor.
>
> The ultimate cost to an institution for a failure to abide by these principles is an atmosphere of inhibition and intimidation. Such an atmosphere undermines the important truth-seeking enterprise to which we are all dedicated. Racism, sexism, and other forms of ignorance and disrespect have no place at Dartmouth.
>
> It is the responsibility of the President of Dartmouth College to defend the principle of free speech vigorously and unambiguously, and the faculty and students of this university have every right to demand that he do so. The value of freedom of expression in creating and nurturing a marketplace of ideas depends centrally upon civility of expression and tolerance of diversity, two characteristic marks of a mature community. Personal attacks have the possibility of repressing ideas and inhibiting free expression.
>
> When freedom of speech strays from civility of expression and tolerance of diversity, colleagues have the responsibility to support colleagues by exercising their own First Amendment rights of expression. Because freedom of expression has the capacity to wound the feelings of members of the community, colleagues also have the responsibility to provide support for those who have been wounded. Earlier this morning there was a telephone call to my office which listed a number of demands from the "concerned people of the Dartmouth community." I would like to associate myself with the concerned people of the Dartmouth community. And in the course of doing that let me just briefly say, without going through this one by one, that I hope we will be able to respond in the appropriate way to each of these demands.

35. Allan Gold, "Racial Tension at Dartmouth as Teacher and Paper Clash," *New York Times*, 2 March 1988, Sec. I, at 16.

36. Charles Radin, "Racial Tensions Rekindled as Charges Fly at Dartmouth," *Boston Globe,* 2 March 1988, at 1.

37. Julie Cahalane, "College Does Not Meet Afro-Am Demands," *The Dartmouth,* 2 March 1988, at 7.

38. Flier distributed in Hinman box (Dartmouth's equivalent of the campus kiosks).

39. Rich Barlow, "200 Hold Rally for Professor," *Valley News,* 1 March 1988, at 1.

40. In his speech, Freedman rejected the notion of immediate suspension, and never commented or acted on any of the other suggestions.

41. *Stone* v. *Dartmouth College*, U.S. District Court for New Hampshire, 1 March 1988. This is the court decision handed down over the shanty incident mentioned above.

42. *Dartmouth Review* v. *Dartmouth College*, at 12 *et seq.*

43. The Committee on Standards is made up of faculty, students, and administrators. The students are upperclassmen who are elected. The faculty are chosen by the Committee on Organization and Policy, and the administrators are chosen by the president with the proviso that they are not part of the Office of the Dean of Students, the Freshman Office, or the Office of Residential Life. The dean of students acts as the nonvoting chairman.

44. Jonathan Frankel, *op. cit.*, note 27.

45. John Milne, "Sides Detain Confrontation at Dartmouth," *Boston Globe,* 6 March 1988, at 43.

46. Jonathan Frankel, *op. cit.*, note 27.

47. *Ibid.*

48. Dartmouth Student Handbook 1987–88, at 147.

49. Jonathan Frankel, *op. cit.*, note 27.

50. Transcript of Professor Jeffrey Hart's closing statement, 6 March 1988.

51. Jonathan Frankel, "COS Enters 4th Day of Talks," *The Dartmouth,* 10 March 1988, at 1.

52. Dartmouth Student Handbook 1987–88, at 141.

53. L. Gordon Crovitz, "Intolerance and the *Dartmouth Review*," *Wall Street Journal,* 28 December 1988, at A6.

54. Confidential personal interview with *Review* staffer.

55. Freedom of expression and dissent is protected by college regulations. Dartmouth College prizes and defends the right of free speech and freedom of the individual to make his or her own disclosures, while at the same time recognizing that such freedom exists in the context of the law and of responsibility for one's actions. The exercise of these rights must not deny the same rights to any other individual. Dartmouth Student Handbook 1991–92, at iii.

56. Kevin Acker, "ACLU Refuses to Take *Review* Case," *The Dartmouth,* 10 May 1988, at 1.

57. *Ibid.*

58. David Groff, "Staffers Announce Lawsuits," *The Dartmouth,* 29 July 1988, at 3.

59. *Supra* note 52.

60. David Groff, *op. cit.*, note 58.

61. *Dartmouth Review* v. *Dartmouth College*, at 21.

62. *Ibid.*, at 23.

63. There was a section added to the 1991–92 handbook relating to bias that was inserted after the state court ruling stating that, "Because Dartmouth is a small com-

munity, knowledge of or acquaintance with the charged student(s) and/or witnesses in a hearing, awareness of a case, participation as a consequence of one's official role in events surrounding a case and/or participation in the disciplinary process prior to the hearing of the case shall not automatically be grounds for disqualification. Any concern a charged student may have about the ability of any COS member or alternate to render an impartial decision in his or her case must be submitted in writing to the Chair. This submission must include any supporting material and must be submitted at least 72 hours in advance of the hearing." Dartmouth Student Handbook 1991–92, at 145.

64. Larry Martz, *op. cit.*, note 5, at 24.

65. *Ibid.*, at 27.

66. Debbi Wilgoren, "*Review* Spurs Profs. to Leave," *The Dartmouth,* 20 April 1988, at 9.

67. Confidential interview with Dartmouth professor.

68. Elene Tsakopoulos, "Ethics of Political Journalism: How Fair is the Review?" *The Fortnightly,* 28 October 1988, at 10.

69. Rosemund Hong, "60 Minutes Sizes up *Review* Case," *The Dartmouth,* 19 September 1988, at 2.

70. Daniel A. T. Tompkins, *A Letter to Dartmouth Alumni*, Paid advertisement in Dartmouth Alumni Magazine, November 1988, at 49.

71. Larry Martz, *op. cit.,* note 5, at 29.

72. Jeff Hoover, "Only When It Affects Us," *The Dartmouth,* March 1988, at 4.

73. Larry Martz, *op. cit.,* note 5, at 29.

74. Pro-choice activists have, on occasion, left soiled feminine products at the homes of their perceived opponents. *Ibid.*

75. Yawu Miller, "Over 600 Students Repudiate *Review*," *The Dartmouth,* 26 January 1988, at 1.

"WE DON'T NEED NO THOUGHT CONTROL": THE CONTROVERSY OVER MULTICULTURALISM AT DUKE

David P. Redlawsk
Rutgers University

> The traditional curriculum teaches all of us to see the world through the eyes of privileged, white European males and to adopt their interests and perspectives as our own. . . . It teaches all of us to use white male values and culture as the standard by which everyone and everything else is to be measured and found wanting. It defines "difference" as "deficiency" (deviance, pathology).
>
> —*Professor Paula Rothenberg, William Patterson College*[1]

> It is a time of lies on campus.
>
> —*A Duke University professor about multiculturalism*[2]

> We don't need no education. We don't need no thought control. No dark sarcasm in the classroom . . .
>
> —*Pink Floyd*[3]

The chapel at Duke University rises majestically over the Gothic campus, acting as the focal point for the entire university. *Eruditio et Religio*, Education and Religion, is the motto of Duke University, a relative latecomer to the ranks of nationally renowned schools. Duke was founded as a university in the 1920s, but did not rise to real prominence outside of the South until the 1970s and 1980s. While the chapel may be the physical focus of the university, the English department has been its intellectual focus since 1985. Critics of multiculturalism claim 1985 as the beginning point of a "takeover" in the English department, led by Professor Stanley Fish and Professor Frank Lentricchia.[4] Fish and Lentricchia were the first of a number of "academic stars" recruited by Duke's English department as part of an effort by the administration to increase Duke's presence in the humanities.[5] A year after his arrival, Fish became chair of the department. The effort to improve Duke's prominence apparently worked, because the English department at Duke became known in academic circles for its high quality, and "judging from the extraordinary demand for admission to the Humanities here and the exceptional quality of these students, [Duke has] succeeded in achieving this objective [in-

creasing Duke's presence]."[6] However, the English department also became
known as radical, rejecting conventional notions of literary scholarship in
favor of a postmodern view that literary texts must be judged within a context
of the culture and dynamic in which they were written. While university administrators claim not to have been surprised by the direction taken by the
English department,[7] there were suggestions that the university did not understand what it had wrought.[8] In an article highly critical of Duke's direction,
Dinesh D'Souza noted that the dean of the graduate school seemed mainly
impressed by the very fact that there was controversy: "These fellows are
cutting-edge. Whatever they're doing, they get attention. Our objective is to
stimulate debate."[9]

There is no question that debate was stimulated, although it initially remained within the walls of Duke University and the rarefied atmosphere of an
occasional academic conference.[10] It seemed to be an intramural debate, with
little relevance outside of Duke and a few other major universities. But, as
universities such as Stanford began to move in highly public and visible ways
to modify a curriculum being denounced as ethnocentric and western to the
exclusion of other "marginalized" cultures,[11] the debate at Duke began to take
on national tones as well. Once the popular press began to discover the alleged
evils of political correctness or the joys of multiculturalism, the debate at
Duke loomed large, especially after Duke began its Black Faculty Initiative,
intended to add additional black scholars to an overwhelmingly white faculty.[12] Soon, articles appeared in many mass-circulation magazines and newspapers, often with a specific focus on Duke or on Stanley Fish.[13] Even the
Wall Street Journal commented on events at Duke, quoting a former Duke
administrator as saying, "What's happened to Duke is the remaking of a mainstream university into a radical one—with terrible consequences—and I speak
as a man who campaigned for George McGovern."[14]

Has Duke become radical? I spent four days at Duke University in March
1992, in order to get an understanding of the current status of the debate on
campus. During that time, I interviewed a number of faculty, students, and
administrators about the major issues facing Duke today. In addition, I was
able to spend a great deal of time researching past issues of Duke's newspaper, the *Chronicle,* to get a perspective on what had been considered news
during the previous three years.[15] What I found was a campus on which the
main issue was no longer the curriculum in English, but the nature of a diverse
society. Three major events became the focus of my investigation: discussions
surrounding the possible implementation of a speech code beginning in spring
1989, the beginning of multicultural training as a part of freshman orientation
in fall 1989, and the extension of multicultural training to employees of the

university through the Diversity Awareness Program, which began in fall 1990. All three of these efforts, along with two controversies over student publications, speak to a university trying to come to grips with a perceived need to make the campus more inviting to minorities and women, while struggling with the liberal tradition of academic freedom and free and open speech.[16] The discussions that have resulted have grown far beyond Duke's original intent of getting noticed.

A Duke Speech Code?

If the numbers can be believed, the issue of implementing official restrictions on offensive speech has apparently not caused much controversy. One source suggests that perhaps 70 percent of all colleges and universities have adopted codes to prohibit offensive speech.[17] While it is not clear how many of these codes are of recent origin, there has been a clear trend toward implementation of restrictive codes at a number of major universities.[18] It appears that the impetus toward these codes often comes from the administration, in a response to some problem it perceives on the campus. Often the codes are a response to complaints by some students that they feel unwelcome on campus. This appears to be the case at Duke. As one Duke professor put it, the focus on speech codes and multiculturalism developed from administrators "running from trouble before it occurs. In effect, they tried to send a message to minority groups that 'we're on your side.' "[19] Yet, whatever message the Duke administration wanted to send, it was not done through a speech code. The one point stressed over and over again in interviews at Duke was the administration's pride that Duke does not have such restrictions. As Duke President H. Keith H. Brodie expressed in a letter to alumni, "[W]e have determined that the negative consequences which would come from efforts to define limits on freedom of speech would outweigh the benefits."[20]

That Duke would be able to trumpet its lack of a speech code was by no means certain in May 1989, when the campus first learned of a proposed addition to the Undergraduate Judicial Code[21] through an article in the *Chronicle*.[22] Vice President of Student Affairs William Griffith explained that "the proposal was a response to 'a couple of incidents we're attempting to identify, situations that have taken place involving racial or sexual harassment.' "[23] Dean of Student Life Suzanne Wasiolek expressed her view that "restricting certain types of expression would [not] necessarily be inconsistent with the University's commitment to learning."[24] The president of the Associated Students of Duke University (ASDU, the student government) suggested that Duke should consider "set[ting] a restrictive policy now and go[ing] from there with necessary changes" despite his concern about "gray areas."[25] Aligned against this initial enthusiasm for restrictions were two professors from the Duke Law School. One, William Van Alstyne, was quoted in an article in the *Chronicle* as vehemently objecting to the proposed policy as "totally unworthy of a major university" and inconsistent with "academic freedom and setting an example" of tolerance.[26] The other, Donald Horowitz, wrote a letter to the *Chronicle*, published in the May 25, 1989, edition: "The proposed regulation on verbal harassment described in last week's *Chronicle* has no place in this University. The purpose of a university is to subject thoughts and words to reasoned evaluations and not to cut them off in advance. It is not an adequate response to urge an exception for words that offend. A good many sound ideas have offended over the century, and no doubt more will continue to offend. The university cannot set its sights only on what is innocuous to the most readily offended of its students."[27]

The interesting thing is not that debate occurred, but that it did not become more public. The initial article appeared after most students had left campus for the summer break. On returning in the fall of 1989, the *Chronicle* ran a stinging editorial in opposition to the proposed code.[28] After that, only two more mentions of the code could be found in the *Chronicle*, both noting that the policy had not yet been adopted.[29] No specific announcement of the disbanding of the effort and the expressed intent not to adopt a code was found in subsequent issues of the newspaper. Something happened between May 1989 and December 1989 that led the administration to drop its efforts to put a code in place. The appropriate way to investigate this is in the context of the event that led to the decision to propose a policy.

The policy proposal began in the Office of Student Affairs under the guidance of Griffith. Its inspiration was a series of "demands" made in a public statement by the Women's Coalition and other student groups at Duke about safety and harassment on campus.[30] Among the demands was one that called for:

5. Revision of the Judicial code to address:
   A. Sexual Harassment
   B. Racial Harassment
   C. Rape and Sexual Assault[31]

In response, Griffith asked Wasiolek to develop a draft harassment proposal, telling Duke's president that:

A draft form (enclosed) has been developed by the Office of Student Life that speaks to the potential of addressing sexual harassment, racial harassment, and rape and sexual assault in our judicial structure. Further discussion concerning this matter will be taking place this Spring and appropriate students will be involved in those deliberations. One of the key concerns in addressing at least one of those areas is the first amendment freedom of speech aspect. There is a delicate balance involved here and we will be utilizing some of our best assistance from the law school.[32]

According to Griffith, events occurred in the following way in spring 1989.[33] Student groups pushed "very hard" to get some type of speech code in place. In addition to the Women's Coalition were the Black Student Alliance and the Duke Gay and Lesbian Association. They placed demands for judicial regulation of speech that offended minorities. Griffith formed a committee that included these groups as well as the student government, sorority presidents, and other student leaders. In addition, as he said he would in the memo to President Brodie, he invited an expert from the law school to sit in. In this way, William Van Alstyne was brought into the process.

Early on, it was clear that there were few problems with the issue of sexual assault. As Wasiolek put it, "[Van Alstyne] didn't have . . . many problems with the sexual assault issue. . . . [He] recommended we turn it over to our legal counsel's office and we did,"[34] but "the hate speech code was quite different."[35] So, from the beginning, the question of conduct was separated from the question of speech, and the committee focused on the question of speech. As noted earlier,[36] Van Alstyne expressed very strong public sentiments against the proposals. In addition, he expressed strong words against all speech codes to the committee. Wasiolek felt that Van Alstyne "went to town; he went nuts" over the speech code provisions[37] in a detailed memo he prepared for the committee citing a large number of freedom of speech concerns and concerns over the vagueness of the policy.[38] Apparently, Van Alstyne was successful in convincing the committee that a speech code could only be justified if there were very specific activities to be regulated. In order to find some specific incidents, Griffith sent a letter to student leaders requesting that they provide him with examples of discriminatory harassment[39] that could be used in formulating a policy, noting that it "is necessary to be able to identify actions that have taken place"[40] to justify a speech code that comports with the First Amendment.[41]

The first letter to the student groups generated only one response—from the Women's Coalition, the group that had been in the forefront of the initial stages of the process. Griffith made a second effort to get responses from the students with another letter on November 1, 1989,[42] requesting that the student groups reply by November 15 with their examples. This effort solicited one more response, from a coalition of minority groups called Spectrum. Spectrum noted that "in our meetings, we all agreed that we have experienced discrimination of one sort or another during our various Duke careers; however, with few exceptions, none of us were able to give very concrete descriptions of the discriminatory activities that we encountered."[43] The *Chronicle* noted that the president of the Black Student Alliance was one of those who had not responded.[44] "I've always heard about instances of harassment," Craig McKinney said, but he found it was difficult "getting people to put them in writing." McKinney received only two examples of harassment from his members.[45]

According to Wasiolek, the committee was ultimately convinced—by the difficulty of putting specific complaints on paper and by the sensitivity required toward the First Amendment expressed by Van Alstyne—that a speech code could not be justified. The examples of discrimination "didn't seem to rise to the level of screening out, to saying we need a judicial code, that we need the stick."[46] Griffith noted that the students "reluctantly agreed"[47] that the university did not need a speech code. So he "verbally" informed the students that there would be no speech code and communicated the same to President Brodie.[49] Whether, as Wasiolek infers, the students were truly converted to the cause of free speech, or whether they were brought along reluctantly, the result was that the administration believed that "[t]he kinds of things we would want to respond to in a judicial way were already covered [like disorderly conduct]. . . . [W]hile other schools were drawing the line with words like rude and obnoxious, we felt they ought to be dealt with in an educational way. We ought to bring the parties together. . . . [W]e ought to let the people who are speaking that language talk to the people who are hearing it, so that they know what effect it has. But it isn't really threatening, does not rise to the level of 'disorderly conduct.' "[49] Undoubtedly, some students were convinced and others were co-opted. Craig McKinney of the Black Student Alliance continued to profess a preference for sanctions.[50] But a representative of the Duke Gay and Lesbian Alliance told the *Chronicle* that "[a]n educational approach would be better . . . a pound of prevention to educate people before they do things that are obnoxious."[51]

Why was no speech code imposed at Duke? Administrators such as Griffith and Wasiolek, as well as President Brodie, insist that the university was never interested in putting such a code into place and that the process used caused students to be educated about the problems of speech codes. In both public and private statements, Griffith argued that he never supported a code. In fact, in an interview, he discussed talking with members of the Black Student Alliance about codes and pointing out that the same codes they were interested in putting into force in 1989 would have been used against them in the 1960s, and against those who supported civil rights. He told them that "some of the things I said in the 1960s in favor of civil rights could have been suppressed under current speech code proposals," warning that regulation of speech can "cut both ways."[52] However, it seems difficult to reconcile the initial evidence of support for a speech code expressed by administrators and students in the campus newspaper with the outcome and after-the-fact insistence that a code was never intended. Members of the faculty familiar with the speech code process attributed the lack of a code solely to the efforts of William Van Alstyne. For example, Lawrence Evans, professor and chair of physics at Duke, and a member of the Duke Association of Scholars, linked the lack of a speech code to Van Alstyne's public comments about the proposed code.[53] Van Alstyne was "astounded at the hostility" he felt at the meeting, according to Evans, so he asked that examples of incidents be supplied.[54] When such incidents were not forthcoming, it became clear that the proposed code could not be justified. The evidence does suggest that a speech code was anticipated by those who began the process. But the code was clearly derailed.

The fact that no speech code was forthcoming in the fall of 1989 is all the more interesting when other events that occurred at about the same time are taken into account. Duke's first attempt at a formal program to teach about multiculturalism was instituted for freshman orientation that fall. In addition, a major free speech issue overtook the campus late that fall semester when the Duke humor magazine, *Jabberwocky*, published two articles considered by most of the campus to be unfunny and racist. These two events would appear to have opposite impacts on any attempt to form a speech code. The orientation program, entitled *Duke's Vision*, could have bolstered the argument against the speech code, since its goal was to teach incoming freshmen about the need to be sensitive to diversity, thus presumably minimizing the amount of hate speech that would emanate from those freshmen. Perhaps the impending arrival of *Duke's Vision* was on the minds of administrators as they convened the committee to look at the speech code issue. The *Jabberwocky* incident discussed below, however, seemed tailor-made for those arguing in favor of a speech code, for no one could deny that what was published was offensive to minority groups. Although there is no evidence that this event had any effect on the deliberations over the speech code itself, it was an important part of the campus-wide debate over speech and sensitivity.[55]

Duke's Vision

The booklet *Duke's Vision* and the program surrounding it must have been in development some time before the beginning of the speech code process. However, there is no public information about when the planning for the program started. There was no announcement of the program and no information about it in the *Chronicle* prior to the first time it was used. The program was promulgated by the Office of Residential Life, under Dean Richard Cox. Residential Life reported to William Griffith. Griffith says that the program began as an internal project of the Office of Residential Life because of the "recognition that a lot of students came from nonintegrated backgrounds and communities. We felt there were a lot of unrecognized racial concerns. The goal was to get students to recognize the concerns and to address these attitudes."[56] The program was to be multifaceted. Incoming freshmen received the *Duke's Vision* booklet in the mail during the summer before their arrival at Duke, accompanied by a letter from President Brodie. They were told that the booklet would be the basis for discussions in their residence halls during one of the orientation evenings. Prior to the discussions, students would attend a speech by Maya Angelou, billed as a "nationally known writer, actress, and teacher."[57] After the speech, students would gather in their residence halls, in groups led by professors, to discuss the meaning behind *Duke's Vision*. During this discussion, they would take a "test" to assess their awareness of diversity. Group leaders would then discuss the answers to the test.

The *Duke's Vision* that went out to incoming freshmen in July 1989 represented Duke's statement about community and "multicultural equality."[58] In a letter introducing it, President Brodie said that the program's goal was "to help make Duke's diversity a resource for you rather than a barrier to community." He went on to say, "Because we are proud of the diversity of people who elect to come to Duke University to study, and because this diversity enriches the educational experience of all, we ask you to join us in confronting the racism, sexism, homophobia, and religious intolerance that threaten to diminish us all."[59] The *Duke's Vision* booklet was a slim document—no more than six pages of prose text, arranged in poetic-style paragraphs. The key statements about multiculturalism were on page 3:

> This vision of multicultural equality affirms
> the uniqueness and worth of each person
> and the need of human beings to live together in community.
> It calls for each of us to be sensitive and responsive to all others.

> Multicultural equality is not sameness.
> Therefore, we ought not to impose a unicultural perspective
> upon the diversity of persons who comprise the human family.

> Racism and sexism are two common expressions of uniculturalism.
> They, and any other expressions of a world view and value system

based solely on any one culture,
are a denial of the humanity of others.[60]

The *Chronicle* first noted the existence of *Duke's Vision* in an article about
Maya Angelou's speech to the freshmen. The article quoted Cox extensively
on the goals of the program: "[W]e are concerned that issues of racism, sexism, homophobia, and religious intolerance exist on campus but people don't
seem to be talking about it. . . . [The program is] intended to be a dream of
how the University community is going to be."[61] A follow-up article on August 28 showed that, generally, freshmen who had participated made positive
comments about the program. "Most students agreed with the messages of
Angelou's speech and *Duke's Vision*."[62] But the next day, an editorial calling
for changes in the program ran in the *Chronicle*:

> The program, however, could use some improvement if it is to fairly present the
> problems and provide realistic solutions. . . . Another booklet used in the pro-
> gram [the test booklet], which presented various discriminatory situations in quiz
> form, allowed participants to compare their own opinion with *Duke's Vision* by
> providing an answer key with right and wrong answers. However, the test booklet
> attempted to provide simplistic answers to complex problems. For example, the
> back of the test booklet reads "Numbers 7, 8, 9, and 13 represent attitudes consis-
> tent with *Duke's Vision*." The University's intent was to provide guidelines for
> discussion. Giving the answers to such questions does not allow people to come
> to their own conclusions. The test booklet also assumes a political bias. Fraternity
> members, for example, are portrayed in a one-dimensional McCarthyite light that
> is itself the result of a stereotype. Discrimination should be presented in an apolit-
> ical light, not as a product of a particular group's outlook. . . . [A] higher public
> profile would have allowed a more diverse group of students to develop the
> program.[63]

With that editorial, the *Chronicle* expressed many of the misgivings that
others on the campus came to have about *Duke's Vision.* The most prominent
complaint was that the vision expressed was being presented as if it were the
one and only vision of Duke University, when there had been little or no
consultation between the Office of Residential Life and any other organization
on campus. There seemed to be two strands to this argument. First, the most
basic complaint among faculty who became aware of the program was that
the faculty had not been involved. "If orientation . . . is going to have any
educational content, the faculty should be involved [as they have been in the
past]."[64] A second complaint was that the program "purports to speak for all
of Duke on controversial matters about which all of Duke has not been consulted and about which the University, in the end, cannot speak authoritatively
for its members."[65] And another faculty member noted that *Duke's Vision* "is

not diverse—it is particular. It is really rotten to tell students that they are identified by race and gender."[66]

Interestingly, given the apparent depth of feeling this program generated among some faculty, it caused little open controversy on the campus.[67] Beyond its editorial, the *Chronicle* took no particular note of the program. Freshmen who went through it often said that they found it interesting,[68] but there was some question about how much impact it really had.[69] One possibility is simply that the program was not widely known throughout the university. According to Lawrence Evans, Duke physics professor, the materials related to the program were never sent to the faculty; he found out about the program simply because a friend had a son in the 1989 freshman class and "I saw the book on his dining room table."[70] Another possibility is simply that few of those opposed believed that Duke freshmen could be "indoctrinated" by such a program. But, despite the limited public controversy, the private arguments apparently had some effect on the Office of Residential Life. The *Duke's Vision* booklet was rewritten and its title was changed to *A Vision for Duke* in order to show that it was never meant to be *the* university vision. According to Griffith, the name change indicates that it represents only one perspective.[71] However, one of the critics called it "Vision Lite," because "all they did was remove a few words here and there and change the title."[72] In addition, Duke President Brodie took note of controversy raised by *Duke's Vision* in his letter to alumni.[73] Brodie attributed the controversy to the title, expressing his "sense" that "had the title been *A Vision for Duke,* there would have been far less criticism—especially since much of it challenged *not* the principles espoused in the document but the process by which Duke's 'vision' was established" (emphasis in original).[74] With the changes made, the program continued to be held for each entering class.

Since the changes, *A Vision for Duke* has raised little controversy on the campus. However, it appears to have had an impact, judging from comments made in interviews and from articles and letters in the *Chronicle.* As early as September 4, 1989, only a week after the freshman orientation program, the new president of the Duke College Republican club was quoted in the *Chronicle* with a reference to *Duke's Vision*: "The new leader of the campus College Republicans said that their goals 'fit into Duke's vision as presented to the Freshman class during orientation. We want not only what benefits republicans, but what benefits the whole community.' "[75] While this might be explained simply by the fact that this new president was himself a freshman and had just gone through the program, the spread of *Duke's Vision* is even clearer in numerous references to it in later *Chronicle* articles, letters, and interviews on campus. In November 1989, the *Chronicle* noted that a group of upperclass students were preparing, with the help of the Office of Student Life, to extend the *Vision* to upperclass students in dormitories who had not gone through the program.[76] An unscientific sampling of issues of the newspaper since the fall of 1989 revealed a number of occasions in which writers of letters and columns invoked some form of *Duke's Vision* in order to emphasize a point about diversity at Duke. This was particularly true during controversies over *Jabberwocky* in 1989 and over an ad placed in the *Chronicle* in 1991, both of which are discussed below.

Generally, the invocation of *Duke's Vision* appeared most frequently as an admonition to the university that the "vision" was not being realized. As Wasiolek related, "I recently talked with a black student . . . who thought the booklet she received was 'nice,' but when she arrived at Duke she thought it was very hypocritical, and I asked her why. She said, 'I just don't see any manifestation of what that vision booklet is saying.' It's one thing to talk about it, it's another to practice it."[77] President Brodie talked about it a lot. One of the key parts of the program for freshmen is a talk by Brodie, in which he usually invoked the vision. In 1991, he told the entering class that "the ideals set forth in that booklet, ideals of justice, tolerance, and compassion, are goals that must serve the entire human community."[78] Other recent references indicate that the current program, while modified from the original, is still considered important by the university.[79]

Clearly, though, not everyone on campus has been happy with the program. Much like the speech code decision, the *Vision* program seems unlikely to satisfy all sides. In addition to the students who think that it is talk without action, criticism of the program can still be generated in discussions with Duke faculty members, some of whom not only object to the content of the program, but also continue to feel that the faculty should have had a role in designing and approving it.[80] The change of the title to *A Vision for Duke* and the revision of the text seem to have muted much of the direct criticism. Yet that cannot account for the failure of those opposed to it to make a more public argument against the program. As important as this program is to the Duke administration, its significance in the ongoing multicultural battle at Duke has been overshadowed by a newer program, designed to extend multicultural sensitivity to employees of the university.

Diversity at Duke

It seems a logical necessity that if an institution is going to focus on educational efforts to promote multiculturalism then those efforts must extend beyond each entering freshman class. That necessity was recognized at Duke in the form of the Diversity Awareness Program (DAP), begun in the fall of 1991.[81] The administrator initially in charge of the DAP was Leonard Beckum, university vice president and vice provost, and one of the few black senior administrators at Duke. Beckum's office sits directly above President Brodie's, in the main administration building. A short walk down the hall brings one to the offices of the Duke English Department. Somehow, the location seems appropriate. Beckum contracted the services of Lewis Bundy, director of Student Development Services at San Jose State University, to develop a program to enhance multicultural awareness on the campus. Bundy developed the DAP with two objectives:

1. to help individuals treat one another with understanding, dignity, and respect; and

2. to further the University's policies and procedures meant to value individual differences while maintaining standards of excellence.[82]

The program, according to Beckum, stemmed from a "philosophical position that says we see no reason for restricting speech. No desire to negate that right. But, if you don't restrict speech, what do you do? [You] work with people to recognize the value of having a diverse campus."[83] The program grew out of a concern that there might be discrimination in classrooms, based on concerns expressed in a report of a committee that was set up to investigate such allegations.[84] However, when asked why the Diversity Awareness Program was not focused on the faculty, Beckum replied that he decided to focus on the "larger community" because faculty make up only about 10 percent of the Duke population, and he wanted a "broad base on campus" for the program.[85]

The Diversity Awareness Program was designed as a voluntary program to be attended by university employees at the discretion of their supervisors. As Beckum described the session, people were asked to "think about things in their own life that were of a hurting nature—we didn't call it discrimination[86] . . . [but] we wanted people to understand the example of the 'out' person."[87] After the warm-up sessions to get the feeling of being left out, participants then discussed ways of defining diversity, "whether it represents a broad or narrow view. We also think about power relationships. Our goal was to activate awareness, not to develop a sense of value judgment. We had no intention of having a hierarchy of views."[88] In the course of a four-hour session, participants discussed "differential treatment," "stereotyping," and a "Cultural Competence Continuum."[89]

The Cultural Competence Continuum was perhaps the central part of the Diversity Awareness Program. The largest block of time in the workshop was devoted to the continuum. The results of each workshop's evaluation using the continuum were to be collated by the office of Training and Organizational Development, according to the DAP Handbook.[90] The continuum "represents a 'scale' for measuring the treatment of diversity issues at Duke. One (1) is the least preferred position and six (6) is the most preferred position."[91] The positions were labeled as:

Cultural Destructiveness: . . . practices that are destructive to cultures and consequently to individuals . . . Nazi Germany and apartheid [are examples].

Cultural Incapacity: . . . extremely biased attitudes and a fear of people who are different . . . belief in the supremacy of the dominant culture . . .

Cultural Blindness:[92] Values and behaviors of the dominant culture are presumed to be the "right" ones. . . . [Examples include statements like] "I don't understand why so many blacks remain on welfare."

Cultural Pre-competence: A desire to provide fair and equitable treatment with appropriate cultural sensitivity, combined with the frustration of not knowing exactly what is possible or how to proceed. For example, declaring a Black History Month . . .

Cultural Competence: Individuals demonstrate acceptance and respect for individual differences. . . . People go out of their way to accommodate differences.

Cultural Proficiency: The organization values differences. . . . The organization is committed to increasing the knowledge of others about culture and the dynamics of difference.[93]

Participants were told to rank Duke on the scale at the time of the workshop and to indicate what the ideal ranking would be for Duke. Then they were asked to suggest changes that could be made in their departments to achieve cultural competence. Finally, they were given a handout labeled "Guidelines for Valuing Diversity" and requested to adopt two or three of the eleven items as a personal "action plan" to improve their own handling of diversity. Suggestions included setting up seminars on the topic, taking time to learn of one's own ancestry, and learning to "celebrate" one's own "ethnicity, language, accent, skin color, gender, sexual orientation, [or] physical challenge."[94]

During the fall of 1991, only a few of the Diversity Awareness sessions were actually held. A number of resident advisors were trained, with the goal that they would train students in their dormitories. Several groups of staff employees and administrators went through the program. Dean Wasiolek found the workshops "excellent."[95] Beckum suggested that the administration was "pleased" with the way the initial program went.[96] But, on December 10, 1991, the *Chronicle* reported that the program had been put on "indefinite hold"[97] only three months after it had begun. "[Senior Vice President for Public Affairs John] Burness said that evaluations are normal at various stages of developmental programs. 'It is consistent with how Duke operates its programs,' he said. . . . '[T]here is nothing strange about it.' "[98] Leonard Beckum echoed that point, noting that "like anything new, it warrants review."[99] Others, like Dean Wasiolek, suggested that the program's suspension was due to pressure from faculty about the nature of the program. "Faculty uproar [caused the program's halt]. . . . I don't know how it happened, but somehow, they were able to influence the Academic Council to halt it."[100] The Academic Council appointed a two-person committee to investigate the program and to report back to the council. Despite Beckum's certainty that a decision to restart the program would be forthcoming by January 1992,[101] as of May 1992, the Academic Council had failed to release its report. According to the February 27, 1992, Academic Council meeting minutes, the investigating committee had turned its information over to the Executive Council of the Academic Council (ECAC) by that date, and "[t]he information that they provided ECAC is now the subject of discussion among ECAC, the President of the University, and Vice President Beckum *inter alia*."[102] While Beckum would not comment on the discussions, a *Chronicle* reporter hinted that the report would recommend that the program stand but that changes be made to parts of it, "especially the Lewis Bundy parts of the program. A lot of his ideas and the material he brought in were what caused the controversy."[103]

The suspension of the DAP represented a victory for a relatively new faculty group on campus, the Duke Association of Scholars (DAS). Founded in the fall of 1990 by James David Barber, a well-known professor of political science, the DAS quickly placed itself into the thick of the multiculturalism debate at Duke. As an affiliate of the National Association of Scholars, the DAS was certain to generate a reaction from those supporting the diversity programs at Duke, given the national organization's focus on preserving the prominence of western culture at the university.[104] The reaction was not long in coming; in fact, it predated the actual founding of the DAS.

Vision, Diversity, and Controversy

The University should know that there is currently an effort underway to establish a chapter of the National Association of Scholars at Duke. To date the effort has been a rather clandestine one. Envelopes marked confidential arrive at the desks of selected faculty members who are asked to remain silent until the chapter has been fully formed and is ready to act. The same letter gives as the goal of the Association the promotion of free and open scholarly discourse. Presumably the irony is unintended.

One reason for the semi-secrecy may be that the National Association of Scholars is widely known to be racist, sexist, and homophobic. This is not to say that those to whom the invitation has been tendered or those already listed as founding members are themselves racist, sexist, or homophobic. Many, if not most of them, are only seeking a forum for the expression of legitimate educational concerns. It is unfortunate that the forum they have chosen (if that is the word) is so tainted that it cheapens and damages their cause.[105]

The mystery to many seemed to be how someone of Barber's stature, a well-known liberal, former president of Amnesty International, and outspoken critic of the conservative agenda, could be involved with the National Association of Scholars. Barber was concerned about the lack of discourse over issues of importance and the tendency for programs with educational content to be approved without any involvement of the faculty. *Duke's Vision*, he argued, should have gone to the faculty, as should the other programs about multiculturalism. "We are like members of a law firm—all are owners."[106] As for the National Association of Scholars, "I like the Association's fundamental thrust—open discussion, faculty deliberation on how the recruitment of faculty should work, things like that."[107] Stanley Fish did not agree about the organization's basic thrust. He stated that because the National Association of Scholars is a right-wing, antiacademic group, members of it at Duke should not be allowed to sit on important faculty committees, like those that review faculty for promotion and tenure. In fact, he argued this in a letter to the provost that became public and that the provost rejected immediately.[108] Fish later denied suggesting that anyone be excluded from the committee.[109]

This exchange between Fish and Barber suggests the strength of feeling associated with the arrival of the Duke Association of Scholars chapter. President Brodie felt it necessary to assert a commitment to academic freedom in a statement to the Academic Council soon after the above exchange occurred: "[I]t is important that there be no ambiguity about Duke's position. We are absolutely committed, not only to ensure our faculty that they are free from possible outside interference in their teaching and research, but also to a structure of internal governance that adheres to the principles of free intellectual inquiry and respect for scholarship. . . . Let us continue to abide by [free speech and academic freedom] in a spirit of mutual civility and support for the open expression of differing viewpoints."[110] The *Chronicle* commented on the personal attacks in an editorial that called for calm, rational debate and condemned name calling as a substitute for rational discourse.[111] A second editorial was run two weeks later, calling the Fish letter to the provost "frightening" and noting the following:

> [Also frightening] is the notion of Barber asking the Gothic Bookshop to remove books that he felt were unsafe for impressionable University minds.[112]

> What is most disturbing is that students and faculty at the University still hold the belief that ideas we find distasteful or "politically incorrect" should be censored or hidden. One student at last week's Black Student Alliance meeting to discuss NAS said, "Duke is the one who came up with *Duke's Vision*. Duke made a statement and we expect Duke to stick with that statement."

> [I]t would be nice if [Provost] Griffiths could produce a blanket statement reaffirming academic freedom (and implicitly superseding the platitude-laden *Duke's Vision*).[113]

As the fall 1990 semester wore on, letters to the *Chronicle* from faculty and students supported and castigated the existence of the Duke Association of Scholars on campus.[114] The Black Student Alliance debated whether to "respond" to the organization.[115] The president of the National Association of Scholars visited Duke and defended his organization.[116] And in mid-November, a public faculty debate was held over the organization, with six members of the faculty expressing support or disapproval of the association.[117] The one common element in all of this activity was that it concerned the goals of the Duke Association of Scholars, not its actions. Ironically, perhaps, the DAS did not issue any statement of its policies and goals until much later.[118] When the goals statement was issued, it did not focus on western culture at all, stating instead that "[w]e have come together because we believe collectively in the highest principles of a liberal education."[119] A further irony is that once the goals were issued, they were attacked in the *Chronicle* as being nonspecific and "nebulous."[120] "No one on campus says much about the National Association of Scholars anymore," noted the newspaper, "and the Duke Association of Scholars, the group's campus affiliate, has finally issued a statement of policy that should continue that trend."[121]

If no one was saying much about the NAS by March 1991, did that mean that the Duke Association of Scholars failed to make a mark? Members of the organization felt that just the opposite was true. They noted that the DAS sponsored a number of speakers on campus since its founding, including Lynne Cheney, head of the National Endowment for the Humanities, Professor Glenn Loury of Boston University, and Professor James Coleman of the University of Chicago, to present a "different perspective" and to provide "public education."[122] More importantly to them, perhaps, are the "successes"— among them, halting the Diversity Awareness Program, raising the level of discourse about academic issues on campus, encouraging the anti–speech code attitude on campus, and "sensitizing" President Brodie to free speech issues.[123]

The level of discourse was raised, according to Barber, simply by the existence of the DAS. One problem with trying to debate issues on campus, according to Barber, is that "there are unprofessional professors who call people names and try to manipulate them. [They are] jackasses from the 60s . . . who lost any confidence they might have had in political discourse."[124] Barber saw the quality of the debate getting better, however, especially with the establishment of the *Faculty Newsletter*.[125] And while Lawrence Evans credited William Van Alstyne with stopping the speech code, he credited the DAS with the fact that no new proposal for a speech code had yet to be seriously considered.[126]

According to all DAS members who were interviewed, the greatest success of the DAS to date was the postponement and review of the Diversity Awareness Program. While public affairs Senior Vice President Burness characterized the review as "nothing strange,"[127] DAS member Lawrence Evans called the efforts against the program "a successful push, so far" to defeat a program designed for the "truly helpless."[128]

Evans's "truly helpless" are the Duke employees at whom the program was supposedly aimed. He pointed out that employees can be coerced into attending what is supposed to be a voluntary program. He argued that if an employee's supervisor suggests that the employee go, what recourse is there?[129] Beckum responded that nobody is coerced, that no supervisor would force employees to attend. Employees who object can "file a grievance. Lots of grievances get filed about lots of things."[130] The DAS also expressed frustration that this program, like *Duke's Vision*, was put into action without any faculty participation or approval.[131] But these points are relatively minor compared to the major concerns expressed about the program.

"The University has no business in this kind of mind-washing," was how Evans characterized the major complaint.[132] The Diversity Awareness Program was seen by those who opposed it as another attempt to indoctrinate—this time with employees instead of undergraduates. The most objectionable part of the program to many was the Cultural Competence Continuum. Professor

Donald Horowitz of the Duke Law School went so far as to write a column in the local Durham newspaper condemning the Diversity Awareness Program. Three threads make up his critique. First, the continuum was pseudo–social science; second, the program was run in an indoctrinating manner; and third, the program attempted to replace debate with an orthodoxy.

> To assert that the continuum is a "scale" is to suggest that it is a scientifically validated instrument. It is no such thing. It is a set of six arbitrarily labeled categories. . . . And it is changeable. An earlier version of the continuum condemned the liberal-egalitarian, "color-blind" position by ranking it third from the bottom.
>
> Nothing in the program is up for discussion; all discussions are to be manipulated. A section of the training manual[133] explains how to deal with "resistance" in a group session. Disagreement, such as "questioning of what (the discussion leaders) do," or "doubting the credibility of the results/data," are all branded as resistance.
>
> One source of "resistance" is described in the manual as "intellectualizing." . . . [Intellectualizing] would be regarded as "theorizing," a form of resistance to be overcome.
>
> It goes without saying—but needs to be said at Duke—that precisely such "resistance" should be found at every university.[134]

Horowitz went on to say, "The long and constructive Duke debate over a variety of subjects, including affirmative action, has been superseded by an authoritative declaration that one side of the debate is culturally incompetent."[135]

A graduate student in political science, Paul Ellenbogen, discussed his experience attending the workshop, which was extended beyond regular employees to include dormitory resident advisors (RAs). "[The continuum] perpetuates that multiculturalism and racial harmony and tolerance and respect for people are compatible—any other political orientation is not truly tolerant."[136] Ellenbogen, a member of the Duke Association of Scholars, characterized the continuum as a "correct ideology," as opposed to every other ideology. "This 'ism'—multiculturalism—is to me one of several 'isms, not necessarily the right one."[137] In expressing his discomfort over the program itself, Ellenbogen noted the existence of the procedures to eliminate "resistance" and "intellectualizing." "What I call 'academic exchange,' they call 'intellectualizing.' "[138]

The position of the Duke Association of Scholars on the Diversity Awareness Program was summed up by Evans. In addition to being an experience in indoctrination, "It's a remedy without an illness. . . . [T]here's been absolutely no evidence of racial problems or disrespect on campus. . . . [O]ne of the problems today [is that universities have] hired these people to solve a problem that isn't there so they have to first demonstrate there's a problem."[139] Leonard Beckum, however, argued that the fact that Duke has not had the problems other universities have reported is significant. "We have not had the kinds of problems that they have at Yale, Harvard, UNC, Michigan—we must be doing something right. . . . Our students are not naive and brainwashed. . . . [We are] giving an opportunity for open dialogue on issues that are critical to our country."[140] Beckum pointed to two incidents that involved student publications as examples of why the diversity programs are needed, even though Duke has not had direct racial or ethnic problems.

Jabberwocky *and the* Chronicle

Fall semester 1989 was a busy time for diversity issues on the Duke campus. While one group was studying the possibility of developing a speech code for Duke, another was implementing the first effort at educating students about multicultural issues, *Duke's Vision*. The speech code process had little publicity associated with it. The *Vision* program was noticed by some, especially the freshmen on its receiving end, but was mostly unknown to the Duke community. The *Jabberwocky* incident, however, was widely publicized and actively involved students, faculty, and administrators from throughout the university.

Jabberwocky is Duke's undergraduate humor magazine, funded by student fees that are allocated to publications by the Undergraduate Publications Board. The Pub Board serves as the publisher for the magazines within its purview. As publisher, it allocates funding, chooses editors, and exercises a broad policy control over publications. However, the Pub Board, by its own policy, does not get involved in the day-to-day operations of publications and does not exercise any prior restraint over what is printed. The board includes faculty, administrators, and students among its voting members, with students holding the majority of seats.[141]

Humor magazines at Duke have a history of offending people. There were instances when at least two different magazines were closed down in the past for printing items deemed offensive to either the university administration or the student body. The first instance was in the 1950s and the second during the 1979–80 school year.[142] *Jabberwocky* was the immediate successor to the 1979–80 magazine, first appearing in 1986. Apparently, it had managed to publish several issues without causing too much offense. But in November 1989, that changed.

The November 1989 issue of *Jabberwocky* featured two articles portraying black Duke University Food Services (DUFS) workers in an unflattering light. The first was entitled "The Grammar Primer to DUFS" and the second "A Day in the Life of Kenny, the DUFS Worker."[143] Both articles portrayed the DUFS workers as uneducated, lazy, and inarticulate, using black slang as well as made-up words to simulate the way the authors thought the DUFS workers spoke. As soon as the issue arrived on campus, concerns were expressed about it, first from the Black Student Alliance. Craig McKinney, president of that organization, said to the *Chronicle*, "We're not going to let it go without doing something . . . [even though] . . . I really don't think there was malicious intent, or even necessarily a racist intent, but it is beyond the bounds of what is acceptable. Apologies just won't do it."[144] Apparently, the editor responsible for the magazine, Marty Padgett, did not expect the reaction that developed. The point, he said, was "to satirize DUFS in general" and the "motivation wasn't to be demeaning." He claimed he was "trying to mitigate the DUFS stereotype."[145] The Black Student Alliance decided to try to stop the funding for *Jabberwocky* and to demand that the Publications Board fire Padgett.[146]

Under pressure from the Duke black community, as well as from the student government and other groups,[147] the Publications Board met to consider what to do. The result was a statement by the board that tried to support First Amendment principles while condemning what was printed. Padgett was censored by the board and ordered to give a public apology and meet with DUFS employees. The board also requested that he consider resigning, but it did not fire him, arguing that "it is against our principles to force the *Jabberwocky* staff to resign . . . [for fear] that the removal of the editorial staff would threaten the right of every other publication at Duke University to express their opinions."[148] Padgett agreed to apologize but refused to resign. "I think that in resigning I don't think that I'd be resolving anything. . . . We have to show that we can react to this criticism in a positive way."[149]

The criticism grew harsher, with the *Chronicle* itself calling for Padgett's removal in an editorial, arguing that while Padgett may have free speech rights, the student body had the right not to be forced to pay for an offensive publication.[150] The core of the argument by the *Chronicle* was that "[t]he U.S. Government has a responsibility to protect the expression of endangered or unpopular expression or speech. The publications board has no such charge."[151] During the controversy, several letters were written to the newspaper, all of which condemned Padgett and called for his ouster. Two columnists wrote columns claiming to support free speech, while condemning the actual content of the magazine and supporting the Publications Board. But the most important voice was that of President Brodie. Brodie purchased a full-page ad in the *Chronicle* on December 5, for an "Open Letter from the President to Members of the Duke Community," in which he expressed a "personal sense of shock and outrage" at the articles.[152] Brodie apologized to the food service workers and invoked the *Duke's Vision* credo.

> This painful event is a reminder of how essential it is that we respect and guard at all times the human dignity of every member of our community. At the beginning of the fall semester we addressed issues of intolerance together. We pledged that we would engage intolerance openly and publicly as a community at every opportunity. I regret the present necessity to confront attitudes of racism but it is my hope that this incident will further sensitize the Duke community and teach us how to build a community that is better for our efforts.[153]

That night the Publications Board met again and fired Marty Padgett on the grounds of "incompetence as an editor."[154] The chair of the Publications Board, Mona Amer, pointed out that even though the board had previously relied on the First Amendment, it was not really changing its approach. Instead, according to Amer, Padgett was fired for his failure to handle the situation appropriately, not for what he printed.[155]

Almost exactly two years later, the *Chronicle* itself became embroiled in a controversy, over its decision to print an advertisement denying that the Holocaust had occurred.[156] Ann Heimberger, editor-in-chief, explained that the ad ran because none of the normal "don't run it" issues were valid in this case, and because the newspaper should "err on the side of openness, rather than on the side of censorship. . . . I was uncomfortable . . . to start censoring things."[157] Was she prepared for a reaction on campus? "We knew there would be a backlash, but I was surprised at the extent of the backlash."[158]

The backlash included a vigil on the campus in memory of the Holocaust and in protest of the ad, attended by over 300 people,[159] denunciations of the newspaper and Heimberger by the undergraduate[160] and graduate student governments,[161] demands that Heimberger be fired by the newspaper's governing board,[162] a faculty debate over the issue,[163] and a torrent of letters to the newspaper, generally condemning what was done. The general manager of the *Chronicle* noted his surprise at what seemed to him to be a vicious campaign to "cruelly" humiliate and discredit the editor. "It took on McCarthyite tactics."[164] But, unlike Marty Padgett, Ann Heimberger kept her job.

Heimberger explained that the difference, from her point of view, was that the *Chronicle* ran an advertisement. This was not an issue over editorial content.[165] Running this ad was like running an ad that says "Pepsi Cola is better than Coke" while *Jabberwocky* printed its material as editorial content. If the material had been for a story like "new findings, Holocaust never happened,"

Heimberger said she never would have run it.[166] Lawrence Evans of the Duke Association of Scholars saw it differently. "I'll give the administration credit for their position on the Holocaust ads in the *Chronicle*. . . . [I]f a question is framed as free speech [Brodie] says the right thing."[167] The "right thing" that Brodie said in a statement issued the day after the ad appeared was, "[T]o have suppressed these outrageous claims, offensive as they are, would have violated our commitment to free speech and contradicted Duke's long tradition of supporting First Amendment rights."[168] Far from publishing a scathing open letter in the *Chronicle* as he did in the *Jabberwocky* incident, Brodie issued the statement and then stayed out of the controversy. Heimberger apparently appreciated this support. Commenting on it, she noted, "[A]t some other schools the president was wishy-washy. . . . [H]e could have said we shouldn't have done it. . . . [Brodie's] always stood up for freedom of speech and academic freedom on campus."[169]

That the editor of the *Chronicle* suggested that President Brodie has always supported free speech would be a surprise to members of the Duke Association of Scholars. Following the *Jabberwocky* incident, Law School Professor Donald Horowitz, along with other faculty, wrote a letter to the *Chronicle* raising questions about free speech at Duke.

> That tradition [of free speech] is now in jeopardy. The President of the University in a full-page advertisement in the *Chronicle* expressed his official disapproval of the *Jabberwocky* articles. The advertisement contained no reaffirmation of the value of free expression and was followed that very evening by the unfortunate action of the publications board.

> If this were a state university, the dismissal of an editor for his approval of an article, even an article in the worst of taste, would almost surely be an unlawful infringement on the right of free press. Since this is not a state university we need to rely upon the leadership of the university administration to promote rather than stifle an atmosphere of free discussion. We do not think the leadership of the University has met its responsibilities. It has missed a vital educational opportunity to prepare students for their role as citizens in a free society which tolerates even expressions of which it firmly disapproves.[170]

Jabberwocky occurred in an environment in which speech code issues were being discussed and the first effort to teach diversity sensitivity was under way. Within that context, the fact that Brodie strongly objected, and apparently influenced the removal decision, is consistent with the messages the university was trying to send to its members. The Holocaust ad controversy occurred in a different context. First, the ad was presented as a political and historical argument. Second, the *Chronicle* staff directly argued that it was a free speech issue. And third, the Duke Association of Scholars had been on campus for a year and had made previous public efforts to make the basis of discussion about offensive speech one of freedom of speech, rather than freedom from offense. The difference in context appears to have created the difference in outcome. One DAS member asked, "If the Holocaust ad was free speech to President Brodie, why wasn't the *Jabberwocky*? Brodie supported the *Chronicle*; a year and a half earlier he would not have done this."[171] Professor Evans suggested that President Brodie learned something about free speech from the DAS, explaining why, while Brodie supported firing the editor of *Jabberwocky,* he took a free speech stand when the *Chronicle* was denounced for running an ad questioning the reality of the Holocaust. "Our organization sensitized him to the problems of getting involved [in the Holocaust debate] like in the *Jabberwocky* case."[172] Dean Wasiolek agreed that Brodie's actions were contradictory. "I see a connection between these two events and there was an inconsistency. Frankly, if I had to choose a response I like best, although I didn't really like either of them, I would probably side with [the response made to the *Chronicle*]. . . . When we start putting bars on free speech we've got to be very careful."[173]

The Story of Duke

The picture painted of Duke University and its struggle to define itself in a diverse environment is one of an institution uncertain of the new rules of the game. Perhaps it would be even more appropriate to suggest that at Duke, as at major universities elsewhere, the new rules were being defined. Faculty spent as much time on *ad hominem* arguments as on rational discourse over the issues. Flamboyant personalities and scrutiny by the popular press combined to hide the real discussions taking place throughout the university. Duke attempted something few other institutions have tried—to reconcile the arguments for free speech and the arguments for sensitivity towards diverse groups. While these arguments may not be fully reconcilable within the existing liberal framework we take for granted, Duke did not resort to reconciliation through the use of speech codes. While several of those interviewed expressed doubts as to whether Duke would continue to remain speech-code–free, the institution expressed a firm commitment to free speech coupled with an intensive effort to educate students and staff about sensitivity toward others.

Thus the controversy at Duke was over multicultural training, over the effort to teach sensitivity. The DAS specifically stated that it was not concerned with western culture at Duke. As one member put it, "[W]estern culture is perfectly capable of defending itself—it doesn't need an organization to do it."[174] What concerned the traditional liberals on campus who joined the DAS was the possibility that the university was attempting to indoctrinate students and staff. Clearly, this motivated the formation of the Alumni Quorum, a group of Duke alumni dedicated to "diversity of mind" and the "pursuit of truth and knowledge through academic freedom unfettered by political indoctrination."[175] The attempt to maintain a balance between promoting diversity awareness and promoting free speech means that the university may, at times, appear to be contradictory. In this environment, we found the president promoting free speech, even when abhorrent, nearly every time he got the chance, while blasting the *Jabberwocky* editor and all but calling for his removal on the basis of something he published. And in his speech to the Class of 1995, Brodie invoked the Duke "Vision" of multicultural sensitivity, while simultaneously invoking James Madison to call for "support[ing] the rights of others to speak their conscience no matter how controversial their views."[176] Another administrator expressed strong support for free speech in an interview,[177] but was quoted in the *Chronicle* as saying that she "could definitely be convinced to pursue [a statutory solution]" (brackets in original).[178] The result may be a campus at which the advantage was always shifting. Sometimes those who wished to place restrictions on speech in order to promote diversity seemed to have the upper hand. At other times those who promoted classic liberalism and argued for the marketplace of ideas had control.

By combining a stand against speech codes with an attempt to use education to promote support for diversity, the university administration was unable to please many of the adherents to either side. Failure to implement a speech code was seen by some as a failure to put any real sanction behind the training that was done. The president of the Black Student Alliance was quoted in the *Chronicle* as saying, "[K]eeping in mind that harassment isn't right, I definitely favor a policy with sanctions."[179] Others, however, suggested that the *Vision* program and the Diversity Awareness Program showed that the university went too far in trying to appease groups, creating a *de facto* speech code on campus, if not a *de jure* one.[180] "[T]he absence of a speech code might be meant to appease a certain category. . . . [I]t allows them [the administration] to say there are no restraints on speech, but, in effect, they are trying to get people in another way. . . . I think there are [restraints] but I cannot say that people are punished for what they say."[181] On the other hand, a professor noted that "the [irony is] that the publicity over the speech code is making Duke a better place on speech issues these days."[182] Ultimately, university administrators argued, "[w]e have the best of all possible worlds—a focus on multiculturalism but no speech code."[183]

But there was also something else going on—something to do with power and the ability to shape this "best of all possible worlds" for the future. The visible controversy was over multiculturalism and sensitivity toward the oppressed, but the underlying foundation was the power to "symbolic[ly] control"[184] the Duke campus. In the traditional liberal university, ultimate control was expected to rest with the faculty, and even today universities exist throughout the world where all issues, great and small, are decided by the faculty. To many of the faculty at Duke University, however, it appeared that control was being taken over on more and more issues by the university administration. Certainly, to the outsider, the lack of faculty involvement in the *Duke's Vision* program as originally conceived, faculty reaction to the Diversity Awareness Program, and the minimal faculty participation in the speech code process all corroborate the impression that faculty were becoming less a part of the decision processes of the institution. While the original arguments over inclusion and diversity began in Duke's English department, within the context of literary criticism, the battle flag was picked up by administrators. The intra-faculty arguments over multicultural issues remained, but the real action took place in the offices of Brodie and Beckum, along with Student Affairs and Residential Life. All of the diversity-oriented programs discussed herein originated with administrators, and administrators played greater roles than faculty did in the controversies over publications at Duke. And while some faculty were content to allow this to happen and to withdraw from the public fray, others redirected the fight. What started out as an argument between professors in two of Duke's nationally renowned academic departments began to look more like a battle between traditionally liberal-egalitarian faculty members and an administration trying to keep itself in the good graces of the multicultural community.

A significant change has since occurred in the administration at Duke. As noted throughout this study, Duke President Brodie took different positions in the various controversies—positions that were, at times, contradictory. In 1992, Brodie announced his retirement, effective June 30, 1993. In his place, Duke appointed Nanerl Keohane, president of Wellesley College. Keohane met with members of the Duke Academic Council and student representatives soon after her appointment was announced. The minutes of the council's February 25, 1993, meeting reflect a discussion with Keohane over a number of issues, ranging from athletics at the university to health care as a fiscal challenge. And, in response to a question by the president of the Duke student government, Keohane stated, "I don't pretend that there are any easy answers" to the issues of balancing speech rights with abusive discourse.[185] The faculty secretary's summary of the Academic Council minutes reflected a lengthy

discussion on speech issues, focusing on the questions of balance that have
been the focal point for discussion at Duke all along.

> [The merits of espousing free speech result in] a balancing act. Free inquiry is at
> the heart of what we are about, a core value for the university. But it is easy to
> make that statement and then forget there are ways in which damage can be done
> by taking it too literally and too much in isolation. . . . We dampen down the
> effectiveness of our dialogue by not assuring that speech is not only free in the
> sense of being untrammeled and unconstrained, but also free in the sense of being
> genuinely open and inclusive. . . . If we take it rather to mean freedom in a more
> positive sense of making sure that people are included . . . then we might find
> the beginnings of some groundrules that would help us.[186]

Discussion Questions

1. Duke University administrators decided against implementing a campus
   speech code because they felt that issues of verbal harassment "ought to
   be dealt with in an educational way." Are campus speech codes antieduca-
   tional? In other words, do speech codes serve the purpose of teaching of-
   fenders the moral wrongs of verbal harassment, or is their aim simply to
   cleanse the university of opprobrious, valueless language? Do you consider
   Duke's *Vision* program to be an effective alternative to a campus speech
   code? Can you see any negative aspects of such a program that campus
   speech codes do not possess?
2. Duke refused to enact a speech code after minority students failed to provide specific examples of discrimination. What was the underlying premise
   of that decision—that the inability to describe specific examples meant that
   discrimination and harassment did not take place? That if discrimination
   was difficult to describe, it would be impossible to enforce a speech code?
   Is either premise necessarily true?
3. The introductory materials suggest an irony—that the private universities
   (Duke, Brown, and Dartmouth) are more protective of free speech than the
   public universities, to which the First Amendment actually applies. Do you
   agree? Are the private universities less sensitive to the values of diversity
   and equality?

Notes

The author would like to thank Milton Heumann, Susan Lawrence, Thomas Church,
and members of seminars at Rutgers University and the State University of New York
at Albany for their constructive comments on earlier drafts of this chapter. An earlier
version was presented at the 1993 annual meeting of the Law and Society Association,
Chicago, Ill.

1. Paula Rothenberg, "Critics of Attempts to Democratize the Curriculum Are Waging a Campaign to Misrepresent the Work of Responsible Professors," *Chronicle of Higher Education,* 10 April 1991, at B1.

2. Anonymous personal interview with a Duke University professor, 24 March 1992, Duke University, Durham, N.C. [hereinafter cited as Professor Interview].

3. Pink Floyd, The Wall.

4. Dinesh D'Souza, *Illiberal Education,* Atlantic Monthly, March 1991, at 52.

5. Letter by Philip Griffiths, Provost of Duke University, to William Whitworth, Editor of Atlantic Monthly, refuting claims made in the D'Souza article, *supra* note 4, 29 May 1991 [hereinafter cited as Provost letter]. The letter was never published.

6. *Ibid.* According to statistics from the Duke University Graduate School Admissions Office, dated 29 April 1991, applications to Duke's English department increased by 344 percent from 1981 to 1991, resulting in 22.4 applications for each offer of admission. During this same time, the political science department's applications increased by 369 percent, but, because of the larger number of offers made by that department, 1 out of every 5.6 applicants received an offer in 1991. Both of these results compare to an increase of only 68 percent in applicants, and an acceptance rate of 1 in 3, for the Graduate School as a whole.

7. Provost Letter *supra* note 5. Provost Philip Griffiths stated that Duke aimed to establish itself in the humanities "with full knowledge that many of the faculty we sought were at the cutting edge of literary scholarship which by definition means they would be controversial."

8. D'Souza *supra* note 4, at 62.

9. *Ibid.,* at 63.

10. See, e.g., L. Jarvik, "PC Atmosphere Reigns at Scholarly Convention," Letter, *Chronicle of Higher Education,* 22 January 1992, at B4; J. Berger, "Scholars Attack Academic 'Radicals,' " *New York Times,* 15 November 1988, at B12; and B. Vubejda, " 'New Orthodoxy' on Campus Assailed: Conservative Academicians Fault Studies of Pop Culture," *Washington Post,* 14 November 1988, at A3.

11. See, e.g., Nat Hentoff, *"Speech Codes" on the Campus,* Dissent, Fall 1991, at 546; also Ken Myers, *An Incident at Stanford Sparks More Dialogue on PC Speech,* National Law Journal, 9 March 1992.

12. See D'Souza, *supra* note 4, for one perspective on hiring initiative. While D'Souza presents a particular point of view that is an anathema to the Duke administration, the broad outlines of the program as he presents it appear to be accurate. The hiring initiative is also mentioned in Rabinowitz, *infra* note 14, and in S. Heller, "Duke Professors Back Plan to Require Each Academic Unit to Hire at Least One Black Faculty Member by 1993," *Chronicle of Higher Education,* 27 April 1988, at A17.

13. Recent articles in the general press about political correctness or multiculturalism include cover stories in Newsweek (24 December 1990), New York (21 January 1991), The Atlantic (March 1991), New Republic (8 July 1991), and McLeans (27 May 1991). Additional stories have run in all of the major daily newspapers, including the *New York Times,* the *Wall Street Journal,* and the *Washington Post.* For a perspective on the mass press approach to the subject, see "The Tyranny of the Media Correct," Extra!, May/June 1991, at 6. Extra! is published by Fairness and Accuracy in Reporting, which bills itself as a "national media watch group offering well-documented criticism in an effort to correct bias and imbalance." *Ibid.,* at 1.

14. D. Rabinowitz, "Vive the Academic Resistance," *Wall Street Journal,* 13 November 1990.

15. Interviews that were conducted were mostly on the record, although in one case a professor asked that his name not be used. Special thanks must be given to Ann Heimberger, editor-in-chief of the *Chronicle,* and her staff, for allowing me to use the newspaper's archives to get historical information. In addition, Carol Shumate of Duke's public relations office cheerfully provided me with copies of many articles that had appeared in the national press and letters written in response by Duke administrators. I must thank those who agreed to be interviewed on what is a sensitive subject, and while I recognize their contributions in helping me understand the details of events at Duke, any errors or misunderstandings certainly are my own. Notes for all interviews and tapes of those that were recorded, along with copies of all materials provided by members of the Duke community, are on file with the author.

16. Duke may seem an unlikely place for concern about diversity and groups in the student body, especially to the author, a 1980 graduate, who remembers very few minorities at Duke. According to now-retired Vice President of Student Affairs William J. Griffith, Duke has made aggressive efforts to recruit black students and other minorities. In 1992, about 14 percent of its 5,600 undergraduates were minority students, according to Griffith. As a consequence, the university has heightened its concern and sensitivity toward blacks. Personal interview with William J. Griffith, former vice president of student affairs, Duke University, Durham, N.C., 23 March 1992 [hereinafter cited as Griffith Personal Interview]. Griffith's comments were corroborated on an informal basis simply by walking around the Duke campus. The diversity of the student body, measured by variety of races and colors, was far greater than the author remembers from his undergraduate days fifteen years ago.

17. Carnegie Foundation, reported in D. F. McGowan and R. K. Tangri, *A Libertarian Critique of University Restrictions of Offensive Speech,* 79 California Law Review 825, note 26, at 830. Some argue that even though codes may be in place on campuses, their importance is minimal, since students are rarely sanctioned under them. See "Campus Codes that Ban Hate Speech Are Rarely Used to Penalize Students," *Chronicle of Higher Education,* 12 February 1992, at A35.

18. See *Doe* v. *University of Michigan,* 721 F. Supp. 852 (E.D. Mich. 1989), and *UMW Post, Inc.* v. *University of Wisconsin* 1991 LW 206819 (E.D. Wis.) for two U.S. District Court cases challenging recent speech codes at public universities. In both cases the codes were struck down as overly broad and unconstitutional restrictions on free speech.

19. Professor Interview *supra* note 2.

20. H. K. H. Brodie, M.D., *Letter to Alumni,* Duke University Office of the President, April 1991, at 3 [hereinafter cited as Alumni Letter].

21. The Undergraduate Judicial Code is the set of university rules and regulations that apply specifically to the Duke undergraduate community. There are additional codes that apply to graduate students, and policies that apply to faculty and staff. All of these codes note that they are elaborations of conduct that is unacceptable in the Duke community, while noting that state and federal laws also apply to all members of the community. Infractions of the Undergraduate Judicial Code are under the jurisdiction of the Undergraduate Judicial Board and of judicial boards of the various colleges and schools that make up the university. For the full text of the Undergraduate

Judicial Code and procedures followed in applying it, see the Bulletin of Duke University, 1991–92: Information and Regulations, Trinity College of Arts and Sciences, School of Engineering, July 1991, Durham, N.C., at 42 *et seq.* and at 82 *et seq.*

22. "Harassment Policy Considered," *Chronicle,* 18 May 1989, at 1.

23. *Ibid.* The proposed policy included a definition of discriminatory harassment as "includ[ing] conduct (oral, written, graphic, or physical) directed against any person or group of persons because of their race, color, national origin, religion, sex, sexual orientation, age, handicap, or veteran's status and that has the purpose or reasonably foreseeable effect of creating an offensive, demeaning, intimidating, or hostile environment for that person or group of persons. Such conduct includes, but is not limited to, objectionable epithets, demeaning depictions or treatment, and threatened or actual abuse or harm." Draft Policy on Discriminatory Harassment, Letter from William Griffith to John Burness, senior vice president for public affairs at Duke, 30 May 1991 [hereinafter cited as Griffith Letter], Enclosure #3.

24. *Ibid.* But see Wasiolek's comments *infra* note 30, where she notes that one must be very careful in putting bars on free speech. Three years elapsed between the *Chronicle* article in which she suggested some limits might be appropriate, and an interview in March 1992, during which Wasiolek expressed strong and continuing support for free speech.

25. *Ibid.*

26. "Harassment Policy Considered," *Chronicle,* 18 May 1989, at 1.

27. "Offensive Ideas Create Food for Thought," Letter by Donald Horowitz, professor of law, the *Chronicle,* 25 May 1989, at 10. Note that part of Horowitz's argument is couched in terms similar to those used by the Supreme Court in striking down an overly restrictive obscenity law that had the effect of requiring the authorities to consider the impact of purportedly obscene books on minors. *Butler* v. *Michigan,* 352 U.S. 380 (1957). The Court ruled that to do so would be "to reduce the adult population of Michigan to reading only what is fit for children."

28. "Fighting Words," Editorial, *Chronicle,* 8 September 1989, at 12.

29. "Harassment Code Still Not Formalized," *Chronicle,* 27 October 1989, at 1. "Student Delays Stall Harassment Policy," *Chronicle,* 7 December 1989, at 1.

30. Personal interview with Suzanne Wasiolek, dean of student life, Duke University, Durham, N.C., 24 March 1992 [hereinafter cited as Wasiolek Interview]. See also *Demonstration for Campus Safety,* flier attached as Enclosure #1 to Griffith Letter, *supra,* note 23.

31. *Demonstration for Campus Safety,* Enclosure #1 to Griffith Letter, *supra* note 23.

32. Memorandum from William Griffith to President H. Keith H. Brodie concerning *Response to the Women's Coalition, DARE, and other concerned students,* 7 February 1989, at 2, Enclosure #2 to Griffith Letter, *supra* note 23.

33. Telephone interview with William Griffith, Durham, N.C., 22 March 1992 [hereinafter cited as Griffith Telephone Interview]. The following discussion of the speech code process comes from this telephone interview except where otherwise noted.

34. Wasiolek Interview, *supra* note 30. The result was that the Undergraduate Judicial Code was quickly amended to include specific regulations regarding sexual assault and rape, as conduct. The relevant section reads:

II. Assault and/or Battery

C. Sexual Assault

1. Sexual Assault I. By stranger or acquaintance, rape, forcible sodomy, forcible sexual penetration, however slight, of another person's anal or genital opening with any object. These acts must be committed wither by force, threat, intimidation or through use of the victim's mental or physical helplessness of which the accused was aware or should have been aware.

2. Sexual Assault II. By stranger or acquaintance, the touch of an unwilling person's intimate parts (defined as genitalia, groin, breasts, or buttocks, or clothing covering them) or forcing an unwilling person to touch another's intimate parts. These acts must be committed wither by force, threat, intimidation or through use of the victim's mental or physical helplessness of which the accused was aware or should have been aware.

[Bulletin of Duke University, 1991–92: Information and Regulations, Trinity College of Arts and Sciences, School of Engineering, July 1991, Durham, N.C., at 43.]

35. *Ibid.*

36. See *supra* note 26.

37. Wasiolek Interview, *supra* note 30.

38. Griffith Letter, *supra* note 23, Enclosure #4, *Notes from William Van Alstyne.*

39. Griffith Letter, *supra* note 23, Enclosure #5, Memorandum dated 7 September 1989. The memorandum specifically quoted the proposed definition of discriminatory harassment described *supra* note 23.

40. *Ibid.*

41. Note that Duke University, as a private institution, is not directly subject to the First Amendment, which forbids state action against speech. Duke, as do many private universities, officially expresses a strong commitment to the principles of the First Amendment in making decisions about speech and academic freedom. U.S. Representative Henry Hyde of Illinois introduced in 1991 a bill that would have made the First Amendment apply to private colleges. Certainly there must be an irony in the fact that Hyde, champion of the Hyde Amendment, which made federal funding of abortions illegal, introduced the Collegiate Speech Protection Act of 1991 in the U.S. House of Representatives. The act would apply to private colleges and universities the requirements of the First Amendment that are currently applicable only to state institutions. For a detailed description of the proposed law, see, e.g., Henry Hyde and George Fishman, *The Collegiate Speech Act of 1991: A Response to the New Intolerance in the Academy,* 37 Wayne Law Review 1469 (1991). The proposed act was endorsed by the ACLU, ACLU Press Release, 12 March 1991, and the *Washington Post,* Editorial, 17 March 1991, at D6.

42. Griffith Letter, *supra* note 23, Enclosure #7, Memorandum dated 1 November 1989.

43. Griffith Letter, *supra* note 23, Enclosure #8, Letter from Deborah Hsu, Spectrum Chair, to William Griffith, dated 19 January 1990.

44. "Student Delays Stall Harassment Policy," *Chronicle,* 7 December 1989, at 1.

45. *Ibid.*

46. Wasiolek Interview, *supra* note 30.

47. Griffith Letter, *supra* note 23, at 3.

48. *Ibid.*, at 4.

49. Wasiolek Interview, *supra* note 30.

50. "Student Delays Stall Harassment Policy," *Chronicle,* 7 December 1989, at 1. The BSA president goes on to suggest, however, that "we have to be very careful on how we define harassment."

51. *Ibid.*

52. Griffith Personal Interview, *supra* note 16.

53. Personal interview with Lawrence Evans, professor and chair of the Department of Physics, Duke University, Durham, N.C., 24 March 1992 [hereinafter cited as Evans Interview].

54. *Ibid.*

55. As a finale of sorts to the speech code process, a lengthy article was published in the *Chronicle*'s feature magazine Currents on 25 July 1990, presenting the transcript of a discussion between William Griffith, Katherine Bartlett, a professor at the Law School, and several of the student leaders who had been involved in the speech code process. In the article, the participants discuss the need for speech codes and arrive at the final conclusion voiced by Matt Scalifani, editor-in-chief of the *Chronicle,* that "education is going to be the most effective route and it's certainly not going to end all forms of harassment, but, in terms of explaining to people why their behavior is unacceptable, it will have the most effect and . . . for the most part there is no need for, or it's too difficult to implement, a punitive solution." "Legislating Morality," *Chronicle,* Currents, 25 July 1990, at 18. It might be important to note that this issue of the *Chronicle* was the traditional summer "send-home" issue, which is mailed to all undergraduates, including incoming freshmen, at their home addresses. Thus, the reasoning behind the lack of a speech code was given wide circulation.

56. Griffith Personal Interview, *supra* note 16.

57. Letter from President Brodie to members of the class of 1993, 17 July 1989.

58. *Duke's Vision,* Office of Residential Life, Duke University, Durham, N.C., 1989, at 2.

59. Letter from President Brodie to members of the class of 1993, 17 July 1989.

60. *Duke's Vision, supra* note 58, at 3.

61. "Maya Angelou to Speak During Freshman Program on Humanity," *Chronicle,* 25 August 1989, at 3.

62. "Discrimination Discussed in Workshops," *Chronicle,* 28 August 1989, at 22.

63. "Black and White," Editorial, *Chronicle,* 29 August 1989, at 10.

64. Evans Interview, *supra* note 53.

65. Letter to Dean Richard L. Cox from Donald L. Horowitz, professor at Duke Law School, 19 September 1989.

66. Personal Interview with James David Barber, professor of political science, Duke University, Durham, N.C., 25 March 1992 [hereinafter cited as Barber Interview].

67. The *Duke's Vision* program was one of the issues noted by members of the Duke Association of Scholars that led to the creation of the group.

68. One student who went through the freshman orientation program in 1990, the second year of *Duke's Vision,* discussed his perspective on it. "I liked it, I enjoyed

reading [the booklet] and thought the ideas would be beneficial to the community."
On the question of indoctrination: "This program was an impetus to free discussion,
[but] it's possible some people would feel uncomfortable and inhibited . . . the way
some of the questions were framed and the atmosphere in which they were framed."
His overall evaluation of the program was positive, echoing the comments noted in the
Chronicle in 1989. "I heard of stories in these discussion sessions where a woman
stood up and said, 'I am a lesbian. Do I need to be discriminated against?' . . . Her
entire dorm had to confront that. I thought the reaction was beneficial. . . . We didn't
resolve anything at the end but it was beneficial." This student, while maybe not typical of Duke students in general, certainly represents what the administration hopes it
is getting out of the program—students interested in discussing and pursuing multicultural issues. [Personal interview with Michael Saul, Duke University sophomore, and
associate news editor for the *Chronicle,* Duke University, Durham, N.C., 24 March
1992.] Saul noted to the interviewer that "I'm not the average Duke student. . . . I
never feel inhibited about saying anything."

69. Griffith Personal Interview, *supra* note 16. See also a statement by Lawrence
Evans in R. J. Bliwise, *Are the Liberal Arts too Liberal?,* Duke Magazine [magazine
of the Duke Alumni Affairs Office], Summer 1991, at 16.

70. Evans Interview, *supra* note 53.

71. Griffith Personal Interview, *supra* note 16.

72. Professor Interview, *supra* note 2.

73. Alumni Letter, *supra* note 20, at 3.

74. *Ibid.*

75. "Freshman Leads Campus GOP," *Chronicle,* 4 September 1989, at 4.

76. "Program Extends *Duke's Vision* to Upperclassmen," *Chronicle,* 20 November
1989, at 3. It was not clear to this author whether this actually ever took place. Now
that the program has been in place for three freshman orientations (as of this writing),
there would be no more than one class remaining at Duke who had not gone through
it as freshmen. Therefore, the need to "extend" the program beyond orientation might
no longer be felt.

77. Wasiolek Interview, *supra* note 30.

78. H. Keith H. Brodie, M.D., Address to the Class of 1995, 29 August 1991, at 2
[hereinafter cited as Class of 1995 Speech].

79. Griffith Personal Interview, *supra* note 16. Wasiolek Interview, *supra* note 30.
See also " 'Vision for Duke' Program Reinstated for Fall," *Chronicle,* January 23,
1992, at 1.

80. Barber Interview, *supra* note 66. Evans Interview, *supra* note 53.

81. The Duke program was very clear about its role in promoting an understanding
of diversity throughout the Duke "workplace." A recent *New York Times* article provides a perspective on a program implemented in a nonuniversity setting. Some of the
reactions of those who went through the program reported in this article appear to be
very similar to reactions expressed by some Duke faculty and staff to the Diversity
Awareness Program. Timothy Egan, "Teaching Tolerance in Workplaces: A Seattle
Program Illustrates Limits," *New York Times,* 8 October 1993, at A18.

82. Lewis Bundy, *Draft Statement of Purpose for the Diversity Awareness Program,* Duke University, Durham, N.C., 10 September 1991.

83. Personal Interview with Leonard Beckum, university vice president and vice

provost, Duke University, Durham, N.C., 25 March 1992 [hereinafter cited as Beckum Interview].

84. *Ibid.* This report was unavailable to the author. Beckum cited it as the driving force behind the plan to develop the Diversity Awareness Program. Faculty members who mentioned it, however, characterized the findings as nonexistent, despite every effort of the committee to find a problem. Personal interview with Allan Kornberg, chair and professor of political science, Duke University, Durham, N.C., 24 March 1992 [hereinafter cited as Kornberg Interview]. Also, Professor Interview, *supra* note 2.

85. *Ibid.*

86. While Beckum insists that the word "discrimination" was not used in the program, the actual handbook used by those leading the program does specifically ask participants to think about "[h]ow your ethnic group has been disciminated against/ excluded" [at 7] or "how you have been discriminated against or excluded as an individual or as a member of a group" [at 8] as warm-up sessions to get the program started. Diversity Awareness Program Handbook, Duke University, Durham, N.C., 1991 [hereinafter cited as DAP Handbook]. Beckum's secretary told the author that no written materials could be made available from Beckum's office about the Diversity Awareness Program. A copy of the handbook was provided to the author by another source. It is presumed to be an accurate copy of the program in use in the fall of 1991.

87. Beckum Interview, *supra* note 83.

88. *Ibid.*

89. DAP Handbook, *supra* note 86, at 2.

90. *Ibid.,* at 24.

91. *Ibid.,* at 20.

92. The text accompanying the label "Cultural Blindness" on page 20 of the DAP Handbook follows. However, in an addendum to the handbook, the text following all of the labels differs from that on page 20. It is not clear from the materials why there is a difference. The labels referenced on page 20 of the handbook were for the workshop leader's use, while those in the addendum were the pages to be duplicated and handed out to participants. Most of the differences are minimal in content, but the text following the "Cultural Blindness" label differs significantly. The addendum speaks of "Cultural Blindness" as "the belief that color or culture makes no difference and that all people are the same. . . ." DAP Handbook Addendum, at 2. Arguments that centered on the continuum as antiliberal were made by a number of members of the Duke Association of Scholars and appear to be related specifically to this phrase.

93. DAP Handbook, *supra* note 86, at 20–21.

94. DAP Handbook Addendum, *supra* note 86, at 5.

95. Wasiolek Interview, *supra* note 30.

96. Beckum Interview, *supra* note 83.

97. "Diversity Programs Put on Indefinite Hold," *Chronicle,* 10 December 1991, at 1. The article also notes that the *Vision for Duke* program had also been put on hold, as it was linked to the DAP. A later *Chronicle* article noted that the Vision program had been reinstated because it was not linked to DAP. " 'Vision for Duke' Program Reinstated for Fall," *Chronicle,* 23 January 1992, at 1.

98. *Ibid.*

99. Beckum Interview, *supra* note 83.

100. Wasiolek Interview, *supra* note 30. The Academic Council is the governing body of the Duke faculty. The faculty response included a meeting between President Brodie, several faculty members, and a graduate student who had become aware of the program. According to one faculty member who was aware of this meeting, it was the proximate cause of the order to suspend and study the program. Professor Interview, *supra* note 2.

101. "Vision for Duke Program Reinstated for Fall," *Chronicle,* 23 January 1992, at 1.

102. Academic Council Meeting Minutes, reported in the Faculty Newsletter, Duke University, Durham, N.C., March 1992, at 4.

103. Personal Interview with Michael Saul, Reporter for the *Chronicle,* Durham, N.C., 24 March 1992.

104. See, e.g., "NAS Head Defends Group on Campus," *Chronicle,* 16 October 1990, at 1.

105. Stanley Fish, letter, "Clandestine Faculty Group Is Coming," *Chronicle,* 19 September 1990, at 8.

106. Barber Interview, *supra* note 66.

107. "Fish and Barber, the Loose Cannons Behind the Canon: Barber Doesn't Hold Back Criticism," *Chronicle,* 19 October 1990, at 12.

108. "Fish Asks Provost to Exclude NAS Members from Committees," *Chronicle,* 5 October 1990, at 1.

109. *Ibid.*

110. H. Keith H. Brodie, *A Statement Addressing Concerns in Regard to Academic Freedom,* The Academic Council, 18 October 1990, at 2.

111. Editorial, *Chronicle,* 26 September 1990.

112. Apparently, at some point during the conversations between Stanley Fish and James David Barber over the black faculty hiring initiative, Barber walked into one of Duke's bookstores and turned on its side any book that had "Marx" in the title. Though this incident attained the level of campus legend at Duke, I found no specific reference to it other than in this editorial. However, several individuals mentioned the event, and it does seem likely that it occurred.

113. "Voices of Reason," Editorial, *Chronicle,* 11 October 1990, at 6.

114. See "Letters," *Chronicle,* 18 October 1990, at 6, for an assortment of views about the DAS at Duke.

115. "BSA Debates Over NAS," *Chronicle,* 11 October 1990, at 1.

116. "NAS Head Defends Group on Campus," *Chronicle,* 16 October 1990, at 1.

117. "Faculty Weigh Judgment of NAS," *Chronicle,* 16 November 1990, at 1.

118. "University NAS Chapter Outlines Policy and Goals," *Chronicle,* 1 March 1991, at 1.

119. *Ibid.*

120. "Take a Stand, NAS," Editorial, *Chronicle,* 6 March 1991, at 8.

121. *Ibid.*

122. Evans Interview, *supra* note 53.

123. *Ibid.*

124. Barber interview, *supra* note 66.

125. A review of the March 1992 issue of the Faculty Newsletter shows several articles about the multicultural debate, couched generally in terms of scholarly dis-

course, rather than employing the name-calling and invectives that characterized the earlier debates between Fish and Barber. The lead article is entitled "Exorcising Euro-centrism," while a second one calls on readers to "Drop the Term 'PC.' " Of course, the newsletter also has other functions, including reporting minutes of the Academic Council and providing a forum for faculty versus administration concerns. The news-letter is published monthly by the Academic Council.

126. Evans Interview, *supra* note 53.

127. See *supra* note 97.

128. Evans Interview, *supra* note 53.

129. *Ibid.*

130. Beckum Interview, *supra* note 83.

131. Professor Interview, *supra* note 2.

132. "University Chapter Denounces Program," *Chronicle,* 12 September 1991, at 1.

133. The DAP Handbook contains a section to help workshop leaders manage the workshop process. Included in that section are several pages entitled "Three Steps for Handling Resistance." *Supra* note 86.

134. Donald Horowitz, "Duke Program Quashes Debate," *Herald-Sun,* Durham, N.C., 3 November 1991, at G6.

135. *Ibid.*

136. Personal Interview with Paul Ellenbogen, graduate student in political science, Duke University, Durham, N.C., 23 March 1992 [hereinafter cited as Ellenbogen Interview].

137. *Ibid.*

138. *Ibid.*

139. Evans Interview, *supra* note 53.

140. Beckum Interview, *supra* note 83.

141. The author served on the Publications Board for two years while a student at Duke, chairing the board's finance committee in his second year. At that time, the board oversaw all undergraduate publications, including the *Chronicle.* The newspaper became independent of the Publications Board in 1982, and now operates under the aegis of its own publishing board. In 1991, the *Chronicle* became independent of student fees at Duke, funding its daily publication schedule through advertising.

142. In the 1979–80 school year, the Publications Board chartered a new humor magazine—the first in many years—under the name *Harlequin,* and funded it for the school year. The first issue of that magazine was never published. Instead, the editors changed the name to *Duke Pravda* and published an issue that contained a photograph on its cover of a female Duke student sitting on the shoulders of the statue of James B. Duke in the Chapel Quadrangle, apparently engaged in a sex act. The uproar caused by this picture resulted in the firing of the editors by the Publications Board and the withdrawal of funding for the magazine by the student body in a referendum. As business manager for Undergraduate Publications in 1979–1980, the author was in-volved in this incident as a nonvoting member of the Publications Board.

143. "Magazine Story Sparks BSA Concern," *Chronicle,* 13 November 1989, at 1.

144. *Ibid.*

145. *Ibid.*

146. "BSA to Seek *Jabberwocky* Defunding," *Chronicle,* 16 November 1989, at 1.

147. "*Jabberwocky* Editors Asked to Resign," *Chronicle,* 21 November 1989, at 1.

148. "Editor Censored by Board: Declines Request to Resign," *Chronicle,* 21 November 1989, at 1.

149. *Ibid.*

150. "What's So Funny," Editorial, *Chronicle,* 21 November 1989, at 8.

151. *Ibid.*

152. *Chronicle,* 5 December 1989, at 16.

153. *Ibid.*

154. "Pub Board Removes Padgett from *Jabberwocky* Position," *Chronicle,* 6 December 1989, at 1.

155. *Ibid. Jabberwocky* has never published since the incident. It was noted in spring 1991 that the new editor was having a difficult time acquiring publishable material for the magazine. Perhaps this was due to a "chilling" effect from the controversy, but it may also have simply been a typical problem for Duke humor magazines, given the short life spans of previous incarnations. See, e.g., "*Jabberwocky* Remains Dormant," *Chronicle,* 25 March 1991, at 1.

156. *Chronicle,* 5 November 1991.

157. Personal interview with Ann Heimberger, editor-in-chief, the *Chronicle,* Duke University, Durham, N.C., 24 March 1992 [hereinafter cited as Heimberger Interview].

158. *Ibid.* Contrast this with Padgett, who appeared completely surprised by the reaction of the campus toward the *Jabberwocky* articles.

159. "Ad Protesters Remember Holocaust," *Chronicle,* 11 November 1991, at 1.

160. "ASDU to *Chronicle:* Acknowledge Wrong," *Chronicle,* 20 November 1991, at 1.

161. "GPSC Denounces *Chronicle,* Falls Short on Resignation Measure," *Chronicle,* 12 November 1991, at 1.

162. "*Chronicle* Board Says Its Staff Acted Properly," *Chronicle,* 18 November 1991, at 1.

163. "Faculty Debate Decision to Run Ad," *Chronicle,* 20 November 1991, at 1. Interestingly, the Holocaust issue split members of the Duke Association of Scholars. Two of its more prominent members, Professor Kornberg and Professor Horowitz, took opposite sides during the debate, with Horowitz arguing that by making the issue public it could be debated and refuted, and Kornberg calling the ad "vicious and racist," suggesting that it added nothing to public debate about the Holocaust.

164. Personal interview with Barry Eriksen, General Manager, the *Chronicle,* Duke University, Durham, N.C., 25 March 1992. The general manager position is a full-time university staff position. Eriksen has been with the newspaper since 1983.

165. An interesting point here is that many of those who objected vehemently to the ad did so because it was a paid advertisement. In his interview, Kornberg noted this as the main reason for his opposition. From his perspective, a column would have been a legitimate expression of free speech, but taking money for the ad was wrong. [Kornberg Interview, *supra* note 84.] The student government resolution condemning the newspaper specifically noted the choice to run a paid advertisement rather than to run it on the editorial page. ["ASDU to *Chronicle:* Acknowledge Wrong," *Chronicle,* 20 November 1991, at 1.] Later in the semester the student government attempted, but failed, to pass a resolution that would have barred student-government–funded groups from advertising in the *Chronicle* unless the money made from the ads was put to some Holocaust remembrance use. ["Resolution Against *Chronicle* Dropped," *Chron-*

icle, 11 December 1991, at 1.] Dean of Students Wasiolek noted, "What deeply disturbed me the most about that ad was that there was money involved." [Wasiolek Interview, *supra* note 30.]

166. Heimberger Interview, *supra* note 157.

167. Evans Interview, *supra* note 53.

168. Statement from H. Keith H. Brodie, president, Duke University, 6 November 1991, press release from Duke University News. It is important to note that the statement also forthrightly condemns the content of the ad while supporting the right of the newspaper to publish it.

169. Heimberger Interview, *supra* note 157. The Holocaust ad was submitted to other student newspapers throughout the country for publication. Many schools did not publish it; others did, and similar uproars ensued.

170. Donald Horowitz et al., Letter, *Chronicle,* 11 January 1990, at 6.

171. Professor Interview, *supra* note 2.

172. Evans Interview, *supra* note 53.

173. Wasiolek Interview, *supra* note 30.

174. Evans Interview, *supra* note 53.

175. Alumni Quorum, Statement of Purpose, November 1991, provided to the author by the Duke University Office of Public Relations. A report in the *Chronicle* describing the formation of the group quoted its founder, James McFarlane, as planning to "get the university out of the business of what we call political indoctrination." "Unhappy Alumni Start Group Protesting PC at the University," *Chronicle,* 26 November 1991, at 1.

176. Class of 1995 Speech, *supra* note 78, at 8.

177. Wasiolek Interview, *supra* note 30.

178. "Harassment Code Still Not Formalized," *Chronicle,* 27 October 1989, at 18.

179. "Student Delays Stall Harassment Policy," *Chronicle,* 7 December 1989, at 1.

180. Kornberg Interview, *supra* note 84; Heimberger Interview, *supra* note 157; Wasiolek Interview, *supra* note 30.

181. Ellenbogen Interview, *supra* note 136.

182. Professor Interview, *supra* note 2.

183. Griffith Telephone Interview, *supra* note 33. This sentiment is routinely expressed by university administrators, including Leonard Beckum [Beckum Interview, *supra* note 83], whose office is responsible for the Diversity Awareness Program and is cited by members of the Duke Association of Scholars as the hub of multiculturalism on campus, and President Brodie, who told alumni in his letter to them, "We try to address issues such as possible hate speech through educating young people to be more sensitive to the impact of their *behavior* on others rather than by curtailing their freedom of speech" (Emphasis in original). [Alumni Letter, *supra* note 20, at 3.]

184. Professor Interview, *supra* note 2.

185. Duke Dialogue/Faculty Newsletter, March 1993, at 8.

186. *Ibid.*

COMMENTARY

INTRODUCTION

What are we to make out of the preceding set of legal and case study materials? Does current constitutional doctrine permit *any* limitations on hate speech on state-supported university campuses? Should it? What should be the stance of private institutions where constitutional considerations are not determinative? What values are advanced and which are diminished by efforts to limit campus hate speech? How is one to balance the latter against the former? Answers to these questions can be implied from the case study and legal case material in the preceding sections of this book. The legal materials provide the basis for arguments regarding constitutional limitations on efforts to regulate hate speech on campus. The case studies suggest real-world lessons from descriptions of how different institutions attempted to address this problem.

This final section of the book includes commentary that provides a variety of competing perspectives on the general issues raised in previous sections. The first two readings are not directed specifically at the problem at hand, but rather are general discussions of the social and individual values served by freedom of expression. These philosophical discussions set the broad bounds within which the issue of hate speech on college campuses must be assessed. Careful readers will find the general arguments made here to be critical underpinnings of the discussions found in the cases, the case studies, and the commentary focused more directly on the issue of campus hate speech.

The first excerpt is from *On Liberty*, the classic defense of freedom and tolerance of ideas by the nineteenth-century English philosopher John Stuart Mill. While Mill's writings postdate the framing of the First Amendment to the U.S. Constitution, his defense of freedom of speech is based on the liberal ideas of Locke, Montesquieu, and other influential contemporaries of the framers of the Bill of Rights. His discussion of the specific issue of free speech is more comprehensive and well developed than what is found in the earlier texts. Mill's justification of freedom of expression is largely instrumental; the maximum amount of free expression should be permitted to individuals in society because it benefits society as a whole. Mill's discussion can be usefully compared to the defense of free expression by Justice Brandeis in *Whitney* v. *California*, reprinted in Part I, "Cases."

While Mill's defense of freedom of expression is widely cited, there are other voices that argue about the value of freedom of speech from quite different perspectives. Herbert Marcuse, a radical thinker who was especially influential on university campuses during the protest movements of the 1960s and 1970s, argues that the "marketplace of ideas" that underlies the defense of freedom of expression is not a free market; its rules are rigged in favor of the powerful, moneyed interests in society. Thus, Marcuse argues, the "pure tolerance" supported by liberals like Mill leads to repression and perpetuates inequality.

The themes raised in the first two readings are explicitly related to the area of campus hate speech in the final excerpts. These excerpts are drawn from a symposium on campus speech printed in the *Duke Law Review*. Charles Lawrence, a law professor at Georgetown University, argues that at least some categories of hate speech can be addressed within the constraints of existing constitutional restrictions. While specifically defending the hate speech ordinance adopted at Stanford, his former university, Professor Lawrence sets out a much broader defense—phrased in terms of both law and politics—for the prohibition of certain types of hate speech. Nadine Strossen, a law professor at New York Law School and general counsel and president of the American Civil Liberties Union, strongly disagrees. Her assault on Professor Lawrence's proposals are a clear indication of the tensions raised by the hate speech issue among traditional "liberals"—the same people who, prior to this debate, were allies in battles over expansion of both freedom of expression and racial, sexual, and ethnic equality.

FROM *ON LIBERTY*

John Stuart Mill

Of the Liberty of Thought and Discussion

The time, it is to be hoped, is gone by when any defense would be necessary of the "liberty of the press" as one of the securities against corrupt or tyrannical government. No argument, we may suppose, can now be needed against permitting a legislature or an executive, not identified in interest with the people, to prescribe opinions to them and determine what doctrines or what arguments they shall be allowed to hear. This aspect of the question, besides, has been so often and so triumphantly enforced by preceding writers that it needs not be specially insisted on in this place. Though the law of England, on the subject of the press, is as servile to this day as it was in the time of the Tudors, there is little danger of its being actually put in force against political discussion except during some temporary panic when fear of insurrection drives ministers and judges from their propriety; and, speaking generally, it is not, in constitutional countries, to be apprehended that the government, whether completely responsible to the people or not, will often attempt to control the expression of opinion, except when in doing so it makes itself the organ of the general intolerance of the public. Let us suppose, therefore, that the government is entirely at one with the people, and never thinks of exerting any power of coercion unless in agreement with what it conceives to be their voice. But I deny the right of the people to exercise such coercion, either by themselves or by their government. The power itself is illegitimate. The best government has no more title to it than the worst. It is as noxious, or more noxious, when exerted in accordance with public opinion than when in opposition to it. If all mankind minus one were of one opinion, mankind would be no more justified in silencing that one person than he, if he had the power, would be justified in silencing mankind. Were an opinion a personal possession of no value except to the owner, if to be obstructed in the enjoyment of it were simply a private injury, it would make some difference whether the injury was inflicted only on a few persons or on many. But the peculiar evil of silencing the expression of an opinion is that it is robbing the human race,

John Stuart Mill's *On Liberty* was first published in London in 1859.

posterity as well as the existing generation—those who dissent from the opinion, still more than those who hold it. If the opinion is right, they are deprived of the opportunity of exchanging error for truth; if wrong, they lose, what is almost as great a benefit, the clearer perception and livelier impression of truth produced by its collision with error.

It is necessary to consider separately these two hypotheses, each of which has a distinct branch of the argument corresponding to it. We can never be sure that the opinion we are endeavoring to stifle is a false opinion; and if we were sure, stifling it would be an evil still.

First, the opinion which it is attempted to suppress by authority may possibly be true. Those who desire to suppress it, of course, deny its truth; but they are not infallible. They have no authority to decide the question for all mankind and exclude every other person from the means of judging. To refuse a hearing to an opinion because they are sure that it is false is to assume that *their* certainty is the same thing as *absolute* certainty. All silencing of discussion is an assumption of infallibility. Its condemnation may be allowed to rest on this common argument, not the worse for being common.

Unfortunately for the good sense of mankind, the fact of their fallibility is far from carrying the weight in their practical judgment which is always allowed to it in theory; for while everyone well knows himself to be fallible, few think it necessary to take any precautions against their own fallibility, or admit the supposition that any opinion of which they feel very certain may be one of the examples of the error to which they acknowledge themselves to be liable. Absolute princes, or others who are accustomed to unlimited deference, usually feel this complete confidence in their own opinions on nearly all subjects. People more happily situated, who sometimes hear their opinions disputed and are not wholly unused to be set right when they are wrong, place the same unbounded reliance only on such of their opinions as are shared by all who surround them, or to whom they habitually defer; for in proportion to a man's want of confidence in his own solitary judgment does he usually repose, with implicit trust, on the infallibility of "the world" in general. And the world, to each individual, means the part of it with which he comes in contact: his party, his sect, his church, his class of society; the man may be called, by comparison, almost liberal and large-minded to whom it means anything so comprehensive as his own country or his own age. Nor is his faith in this collective authority at all shaken by his being aware that other ages, countries, sects, churches, classes, and parties have thought, and even now think, the exact reverse. He devolves upon his own world the responsibility of being in the right against the dissentient worlds of other people; and it never troubles him that mere accident has decided which of these numerous worlds is the object of his reliance, and that the same causes which make him a churchman in London would have made him a Buddhist or a Confucian in Peking. Yet it is as evident in itself, as any amount of argument can make it, that ages are no more infallible than individuals—every age having held many opinions which subsequent ages have deemed not only false but absurd; and it is as certain that many opinions, now general, will be rejected by future ages, as it is that many, once general, are rejected by the present.

The objection likely to be made to this argument would probably take some such form as the following. There is no greater assumption of infallibility in forbidding the propagation of error than in any other thing which is done by public authority on its own judgment and responsibility. Judgment is given to men that they may use it. Because it may be used erroneously, are men to be told that they ought not to use it at all? To prohibit what they think pernicious is not claiming exemption from error, but fulfilling the duty incumbent on them, although fallible, of acting on their conscientious conviction. If we were never to act on our opinions, because those opinions may be wrong, we should leave all our interests uncared for, and all our duties unperformed. An objection which applies to all conduct can be no valid objection to any conduct in particular. It is the duty of governments, and of individuals, to form the truest opinions they can; to form them carefully, and never impose them upon others unless they are quite sure of being right. But when they are sure (such reasoners may say), it is not conscientiousness but cowardice to shrink from acting on their opinions and allow doctrines which they honestly think dangerous to the welfare of mankind, either in this life or in another, to be scattered abroad without restraint, because other people, in less enlightened times, have persecuted opinions now believed to be true. Let us take care, it may be said, not to make the same mistake; but governments and nations have made mistakes in other things which are not denied to be fit subjects for the exercise of authority: they have laid on bad taxes, made unjust wars. Ought we therefore to lay on no t⌐xes and, under whatever provocation, make no wars? Men and governments must act to the best of their ability. There is no such thing as absolute certainty, but there is assurance sufficient for the purposes of human life. We may, and must, assume our opinion to be true for the guidance of our own conduct; and it is assuming no more when we forbid bad men to pervert society by the propagation of opinions which we regard as false and pernicious.

I answer, that it is assuming very much more. There is the greatest difference between presuming an opinion to be true because, with every opportunity for contesting it, it has not been refuted, and assuming its truth for the purpose of not permitting its refutation. Complete liberty of contradicting and disproving our opinion is the very condition which justifies us in assuming its truth for purposes of action; and on no other terms can a being with human faculties have any rational assurance of being right.

When we consider either the history of opinion or the ordinary conduct of human life, to what is it to be ascribed that the one and the other are no worse than they are? Not certainly to the inherent force of the human understanding, for on any matter not self-evident there are ninety-nine persons totally incapable of judging of it for one who is capable; and the capacity of the hundredth person is only comparative, for the majority of the eminent men of every past generation held many opinions now known to be erroneous, and did or approved numerous things which no one will now justify. Why is it, then, that there is on the whole a preponderance among mankind of rational opinions and rational conduct? If there really is this preponderance—which there must be unless human affairs are, and have always been, in an almost desperate state—it is owing to a quality of the human mind, the source of everything respectable in man either as an intellectual or as a moral being, namely, that his errors are corrigible. He is capable of rectifying his mistakes by discussion and experience. Not by experience alone. There must be discussion to show how experience is to be interpreted. Wrong opinions and practices gradually yield to fact and argument; but facts and arguments, to produce any effect on the mind, must be brought before it. Very few facts are able to tell their own story, without comments to bring out their meaning. The whole strength and value, then, of human judgment depending on the one property, that it can be set right when it is wrong, reliance can be placed on it only when the means of setting it right are kept constantly at hand. In the case of any person whose judgment is really deserving of confidence, how has it become so? Because he has kept his mind open to criticism of his opinions and conduct. Because it has been his practice to listen to all that could be said against him; to profit by as much of it as was just, and to expound to himself, and upon occasion to others, the fallacy of what was fallacious. Because he has felt that the only way in which a human being can make some approach to knowing the whole of a subject is by hearing what can be said about it by persons of every variety of opinion, and studying all modes in which it can be looked at by every character of mind. No wise man ever acquired his wisdom in any mode but this; nor is it in the nature of human intellect to become wise in any other manner. The steady habit of correcting and completing his own opinion by collating it with those of others, so far from causing doubt and hesitation in carrying it into practice, is the only stable foundation for a just reliance on it; for, being cognizant of all that can, at least obviously, be said against him, and having taken up his position against all gainsayers—knowing that he has sought for objections and difficulties instead of avoiding them, and has shut out no light which can be thrown upon the subject from any quarter—he has a right to think his judgment better than that of any person, or any multitude, who have not gone through a similar process. . . .

Let us now pass to the second division of the argument, and dismissing the supposition that any of the received opinions may be false, let us assume them to be true and examine into the worth of the manner in which they are likely to be held when their truth is not freely and openly canvassed. However unwilling a person who has a strong opinion may admit the possibility that his opinion may be false, he ought to be moved by the consideration that, however true it may be, if it is not fully, frequently, and fearlessly discussed, it will be held as a dead dogma, not a living truth.

There is a class of persons (happily not quite so numerous as formerly) who think it enough if a person assents undoubtingly to what they think true, though he has no knowledge whatever of the grounds of the opinion and could not make a tenable defense of it against the most superficial objections. Such persons, if they can once get their creed taught from authority, naturally think that no good, and some harm, comes of its being allowed to be questioned. Where their influence prevails, they make it nearly impossible for the received opinion to be rejected wisely and considerately, though it may still be rejected rashly and ignorantly; for to shut out discussion entirely is seldom possible, and when it once gets in, beliefs not grounded on conviction are apt to give way before the slightest semblance of an argument. Waiving, however, this possibility—assuming that the true opinion abides in the mind, but abides as a prejudice, a belief independent of, and proof against, argument—this is not the way in which truth ought to be held by a rational being. This is not knowing the truth. Truth, thus held, is but one superstition the more, accidentally clinging to the words which enunciate a truth.

If the intellect and judgment of mankind ought to be cultivated, a thing which Protestants at least do not deny, on what can these faculties be more appropriately exercised by anyone than on the things which concern him so much that it is considered necessary for him to hold opinions on them? If the cultivation of the understanding consists in one thing more than in another, it is surely in learning the grounds of one's own opinions. Whatever people believe, on subjects on which it is of the first importance to believe rightly, they ought to be able to defend against at least the common objections. . . .

If, however, the mischievous operation of the absence of free discussion, when the received opinions are true, were confined to leaving men ignorant of the grounds of those opinions, it might be thought that this, if an intellectual, is no moral evil and does not affect the worth of the opinions, regarded in their influence on the character. The fact, however, is that not only the grounds of the opinion are forgotten in the absence of discussion, but too often the meaning of the opinion itself. The words which convey it cease to suggest ideas, or suggest only a small portion of those they were originally employed to communicate. Instead of a vivid conception and a living belief, there remain only a few phrases retained by rote; or, if any part, the shell and husk only of the meaning is retained, the finer essence being lost. The great chapter in human history which this fact occupies and fills cannot be too earnestly studied and meditated on. . . .

It still remains to speak of one of the principal causes which make diversity of opinion advantageous, and will continue to do so until mankind shall have entered a stage of intellectual advancement which at present seems at an incalculable distance. We have hitherto considered only two possibilities: that the received opinion may be false, and some other opinion, consequently, true; or that, the received opinion being true, a conflict with the opposite error is essential to a clear apprehension and deep feeling of its truth. But there is a commoner case than either of these: when the conflicting doctrines, instead of being one true and the other false, share the truth between them, and the nonconforming opinion is needed to supply the remainder of the truth of which the received doctrine embodies only a part. Popular opinions, on subjects not palpable to sense, are often true, but seldom or never the whole truth. They are a part of the truth, sometimes a greater, sometimes a smaller part, but exaggerated, distorted, and disjointed from the truths by which they ought to be accompanied and limited. Heretical opinions, on the other hand, are generally some of these suppressed and neglected truths, bursting the bonds which kept them down, and either seeking reconciliation with the truth contained in the common opinion, or fronting it as enemies, and setting themselves up, with similar exclusiveness, as the whole truth. The latter case is hitherto the most frequent, as, in the human mind, one-sidedness has always been the rule, and many-sidedness the exception. Hence, even in revolutions of opinion, one part of the truth usually sets while another rises. Even progress, which ought to superadd, for the most part only substitutes one partial and incomplete truth for another; improvement consisting chiefly in this, that the new fragment of truth is more wanted, more adapted to the needs of the time than that which it displaces. Such being the partial character of prevailing opinions, even when resting on a true foundation, every opinion which embodies somewhat of the portion of truth which the common opinion omits ought to be considered precious, with whatever amount of error and confusion that truth may be blended. No sober judge of human affairs will feel bound to be indignant because those who force on our notice truths which we should otherwise have overlooked, overlook some of those which we see. Rather, he will think that so long as popular truth is one-sided, it is more desirable than otherwise that unpopular truth should have one-sided assertors, too, such being usually the most energetic and the most likely to compel reluctant attention to the fragment of wisdom which they proclaim as if it were the whole. . . .

We have now recognized the necessity to the mental well-being of mankind (on which all their other well-being depends) of freedom of opinion, and freedom of the expression of opinion, on four distinct grounds, which we will now briefly recapitulate:

First, if any opinion is compelled to silence, that opinion may, for aught we can certainly know, be true. To deny this is to assume our own infallibility.

Secondly, though the silenced opinion be an error, it may, and very commonly does, contain a portion of truth; and since the general or prevailing opinion on any subject is rarely or never the whole truth, it is only by the collision of adverse opinions that the remainder of the truth has any chance of being supplied.

Thirdly, even if the received opinion be not only true, but the whole truth; unless it is suffered to be, and actually is, vigorously and earnestly contested, it will, by most of those who receive it, be held in the manner of a prejudice, with little comprehension or feeling of its rational grounds. And not only this, but, fourthly, the meaning of the doctrine itself will be in danger of being lost or enfeebled, and deprived of its vital effect on the character and conduct: the dogma becoming a mere formal profession, inefficacious for good, but cumbering the ground and preventing the growth of any real and heartfelt conviction from reason or personal experience.

Discussion Questions

1. As discussed in the Duke University case study, an organization has tried to promulgate on university campuses the theory of "Holocaust revisionism," the notion that the murder of three million Jews by Nazi Germany in World War II either did not occur as a matter of historical fact, or has at the least been grossly exaggerated in historical accounts. Several campus newspapers have refused to publish this group's paid advertisements. If you were editor of a campus daily, would this selection from Mill convince you that such ads should be run? What if a sizable portion of your readership were Jewish and would certainly be hurt and offended by such ads? What if you feared that the ads might worsen an already serious problem of anti-Semitism on campus? Would your response be different if your campus were a state-supported institution?

2. The Declaration of Independence includes in its second paragraph the statement: "We hold these truths to be self-evident, that all men are created equal, that they are endowed by their Creator with certain unalienable Rights, that among these are Life, Liberty, and the pursuit of Happiness." To what degree, if any, should these "self-evident" truths be set outside the realm of debate in a regime founded upon them? Should equality trump free speech if the notion of human equality, whether objectively true or not, undergirds the very framework of our government? Consider this question in light of the next reading, by Herbert Marcuse.

3. To what degree is Mill's defense of freedom of expression confined to the realm of scientific truth? Does it include politics and realms of social policy where "truth" is far more difficult to ascertain or even define? What about artistic endeavors? What, if any, aspects of campus "hate speech" would be included within Mill's notion?

4. Mill's basic defense of freedom of expression is utilitarian: freedom of expression is important because it serves important social goals related to the search for truth. Can you think of any types of expression—perhaps from the cases or case studies set out earlier in this book—in which this justification has less relevance? Are there nonutilitarian arguments supporting freedom of expression in these contexts? What do you think Mill would say to the assertion that freedom of expression is good in and of itself, as an essential component of human self-realization, regardless of its usefulness to society at large?

FROM "REPRESSIVE TOLERANCE"

Herbert Marcuse

Generally, the function and value of tolerance depend on the equality prevalent in the society in which tolerance is practiced. Tolerance itself stands subject to overriding criteria: its range and its limits cannot be defined in terms of the respective society. In other words, tolerance is an end in itself only when it is truly universal, practiced by the rulers as well as by the ruled, by the lords as well as by the peasants, by the sheriffs as well as by their victims. And such universal tolerance is possible only when no real or alleged enemy requires in the national interest the education and training of people in military violence and destruction. As long as these conditions do not prevail, the conditions of tolerance are "loaded": they are determined and defined by the institutionalized inequality (which is certainly compatible with constitutional equality), i.e., by the class structure of society. In such a society, tolerance is *de facto* limited on the dual ground of legalized violence or suppression (police, armed forces, guards of all sorts) and of the privileged position held by the predominant interests and their "connections."

These background limitations of tolerance are normally prior to the explicit and judicial limitations as defined by the courts, custom, governments, etc. (for example, "clear and present danger," threat to national security, heresy). Within the framework of such a social structure, tolerance can be safely practiced and proclaimed. It is of two kinds: (1) the passive toleration of entrenched and established attitudes and ideas even if their damaging effect on man and nature is evident; and (2) the active, official tolerance granted to the Right as well as to the Left, to movements of aggression as well as to movements of peace, to the party of hate as well as to that of humanity. I call this non-partisan tolerance "abstract" or "pure" inasmuch as it refrains from taking sides—but in doing so it actually protects the already established machinery of discrimination.

The tolerance which enlarged the range and content of freedom was always partisan—intolerant toward the protagonists of the repressive status quo. The

From Robert Paul Wolff, Barrington Moore, and Herbert Marcuse, *A Critique of Pure Tolerance* (Boston: Beacon Press, 1965). Reprinted by permission of Beacon Press.

issue was only the degree and extent of intolerance. In the firmly established liberal society of England and the United States, freedom of speech and assembly was granted even to the radical enemies of society, provided they did not make the transition from word to deed, from speech to action.

Relying on the effective background limitations imposed by its class structure, the society seemed to practice general tolerance. But liberalist theory had already placed an important condition on tolerance: it was "to apply only to human beings in the maturity of their faculties." John Stuart Mill does not only speak of children and minors; he elaborates: "Liberty, as a principle, has no application to any state of things anterior to the time when mankind have become capable of being improved by free and equal discussion." Anterior to that time, men may still be barbarians, and "despotism is a legitimate mode of government in dealing with barbarians, provided the end be their improvement, and the means justified by actually effecting that end." Mill's often-quoted words have a less familiar implication on which their meaning depends: the internal connection between liberty and truth. There is a sense in which truth is the end of liberty, and liberty must be defined and confined by truth. Now in what sense can liberty be for the sake of truth? Liberty is self-determination, autonomy—this is almost a tautology, but a tautology which results from a whole series of synthetic judgments. It stipulates the ability to determine one's own life: to be able to determine what to do and what not to do, what to suffer and what not. But the subject of this autonomy is never the contingent, private individual as that which he actually is or happens to be; it is rather the individual as a human being who is capable of being free with the others. And the problem of making possible such a harmony between every individual liberty and the other is not that of finding a compromise between competitors, or between freedom and law, between general and individual interest, common and private welfare in an *established* society, but of *creating* the society in which man is no longer enslaved by institutions which vitiate self-determination from the beginning. In other words, freedom is still to be created even for the freest of the existing societies. And the direction in which it must be sought, and the institutional and cultural changes which may help to attain the goal are, at least in developed civilization, *comprehensible*, that is to say, they can be identified and projected, on the basis of experience, by human reason.

In the interplay of theory and practice, true and false solutions become distinguishable—never with the evidence of necessity, never as the positive, only with the certainty of a reasoned and reasonable chance, and with the persuasive force of the negative. For the true positive is the society of the future and therefore beyond definition and determination, while the existing positive is that which must be surmounted. But the experience and understanding of the existent society may well be capable of identifying what is *not* conducive to a free and rational society, what impedes and distorts the possibilities of its creation. Freedom is liberation, a specific historical process in theory and practice, and as such it has its right and wrong, its truth and falsehood.

The uncertainty of chance in this distinction does not cancel the historical objectivity, but it necessitates freedom of thought and expression as preconditions of finding the way to freedom—it necessitates *tolerance*. However, this tolerance cannot be indiscriminate and equal with respect to the contents of expression, neither in word nor in deed; it cannot protect false words and wrong deeds which demonstrate that they contradict and counteract the possibilities of liberation. Such indiscriminate tolerance is justified in harmless debates, in conversation, in academic discussion; it is indispensable in the scientific enterprise, in private religion. But society cannot be indiscriminate where the pacification of existence, where freedom and happiness themselves are at stake; here, certain things cannot be said, certain ideas cannot be expressed, certain policies cannot be proposed, certain behavior cannot be permitted without making tolerance an instrument for the continuation of servitude. . . .

Tolerance of free speech is the way of improvement, of progress in liberation, *not* because there is no objective truth, and improvement must necessarily be a compromise between a variety of opinions, but because there *is* an objective truth which can be discovered, ascertained only in learning and comprehending that which is and that which can be and ought to be done for the sake of improving the lot of mankind. This common and historical "ought" is not immediately evident, at hand: it has to be uncovered by "cutting through," "splitting," "breaking asunder" . . . the given material—separating right and wrong, good and bad, correct and incorrect. The subject whose "improvement" depends on a progressive historical practice is each man as man, and this universality is reflected in that of the discussion, which a priori does not exclude any group or individual. But even the all-inclusive character of liberalist tolerance was, at least in theory, based on the proposition that men were (potential) *individuals* who could learn to hear and see and feel by themselves, to develop their own thoughts, to grasp their true interests and rights and capabilities, also against established authority and opinion. This was the rationale of free speech and assembly. Universal toleration becomes questionable when its rationale no longer prevails, when tolerance is administered to manipulated and indoctrinated individuals who parrot, as their own, the opinion of their masters, for whom heteronomy has become autonomy.

The telos of tolerance is truth. It is clear from the historical record that the authentic spokesmen of tolerance had more and other truth in mind than that of propositional logic and academic theory. John Stuart Mill speaks of the truth which is persecuted in history and which does *not* triumph over persecution by virtue of its "inherent power," which in fact has no inherent power "against the dungeon and the stake." And he enumerates the "truths" which were cruelly and successfully liquidated in the dungeons and at the stake: that of Arnold of Brescia, of Fra Dolcino, of Savonarola, of the Albigensians, Waldensians, Lollards, and Hussites. Toleration is first and foremost for the sake of the heretics—the historical road toward *humanitas* appears as heresy: target of persecution by the powers that be. Heresy by itself, however, is no token of truth.

The criterion of progress in freedom according to which Mill judges these movements is the Reformation. The evaluation is *ex post*, and his list includes opposites (Savonarola too would have burned Fra Dolcino). Even the ex post evaluation is contestable as to its truth: history corrects the judgment—too late. The correction does not help the victims and does not absolve their executioners. However, the lesson is clear: intolerance has delayed progress and has prolonged the slaughter and torture of innocents for hundreds of years. Does this clinch the case for indiscriminate, "pure" tolerance? Are there historical conditions in which such toleration impedes liberation and multiplies the victims who are sacrificed to the status quo? Can the indiscriminate guaranty of political rights and liberties be repressive? Can such tolerance serve to contain qualitative social change?

I shall discuss this question only with reference to political movements, attitudes, schools of thought, philosophies which are "political" in the widest sense—affecting the society as a whole, demonstrably transcending the sphere of privacy. Moreover, I propose a shift in the focus of the discussion: it will be concerned not only, and not primarily, with tolerance toward radical extremes, minorities, subversives, etc., but rather with tolerance toward majorities, toward official and public opinion, toward the established protectors of freedom. In this case, the discussion can have as a frame of reference only a democratic society, in which the people, as individuals and as members of political and other organizations, participate in the making, sustaining, and changing policies. In an authoritarian system, the people do not tolerate—they suffer established policies.

Under a system of constitutionally guaranteed and (generally and without too many and too glaring exceptions) practiced civil rights and liberties, opposition and dissent are tolerated unless they issue in violence and/or in exhortation to and organization of violent subversion. The underlying assumption is that the established society is free, and that any improvement, even a change in the social structure and social values, would come about in the normal course of events, prepared, defined, and tested in free and equal discussion, on the open marketplace of ideas and goods. Now in recalling John Stuart Mill's passage, I drew attention to the premise hidden in this assumption: free and equal discussion can fulfill the function attributed to it only if it is *rational*—expression and development of independent thinking, free from indoctrination, manipulation, extraneous authority. The notion of pluralism and countervailing powers is no substitute for this requirement. One might in theory construct a state in which a multitude of different pressures, interests, and authorities balance each other out and result in a truly general and rational interest. However, such a construct badly fits a society in which powers are and remain unequal and even increase their unequal weight when they run their own course. It fits even worse when the variety of pressures unifies and coagulates into an overwhelming whole, integrating the particular countervailing powers by virtue of an increasing standard of living and an increasing concentration of power. Then, the laborer, whose real interest conflicts with that of management, the common consumer whose real interest conflicts with that of the producer, the intellectual whose vocation conflicts with that of his employer find themselves submitting to a system against which they are powerless and appear unreasonable. The ideas of the available alternatives evaporates [*sic*] into an utterly utopian dimension in which it is at home, for a free society is indeed unrealistically and undefinably different from the existing ones. Under these circumstances, whatever improvement may occur "in the normal course of events" and without subversion is likely to be improvement in the direction determined by the particular interests which control the whole.

By the same token, those minorities which strive for a change of the whole itself will, under optimal conditions which rarely prevail, be left free to deliberate and discuss, to speak and to assemble—and will be left harmless and helpless in the face of the overwhelming majority, which militates against qualitative social change. This majority is firmly grounded in the increasing satisfaction of needs, and technological and mental coordination, which testify to the general helplessness of radical groups in a well-functioning social system.

Within the affluent democracy, the affluent discussion prevails, and within the established framework, it is tolerant to a large extent. All points of view can be heard: the Communist and the Fascist, the Left and the Right, the white and the Negro, the crusaders for armament and for disarmament. Moreover, in endlessly dragging debates over the media, the stupid opinion is treated with the same respect as the intelligent one, the misinformed may talk as long as the informed, and propaganda rides along with education, truth with falsehood. This pure toleration of sense and nonsense is justified by the democratic argument that nobody, neither group nor individual, is in possession of the truth and capable of defining what is right and wrong, good and bad. Therefore, all contesting opinions must be submitted to "the people" for its deliberation and choice. But I have already suggested that the democratic argument implies a necessary condition, namely, that the people must be capable of deliberating and choosing on the basis of knowledge, that they must have access to authentic information, and that, on this basis, their evaluation must be the result of autonomous thought.

In the contemporary period, the democratic argument for abstract tolerance tends to be invalidated by the invalidation of the democratic process itself. The liberating force of democracy was the chance it gave to effective dissent, on the individual as well as social scale, its openness to qualitatively different forms of government, of culture, education, work—of the human existence in general. The toleration of free discussion and the equal right of opposites was to define and clarify the different forms of dissent: their direction, content, prospect. But with the concentration of economic and political power and the integration of opposites in a society which uses technology as an instrument of domination, effective dissent is blocked where it could freely emerge: in the formation of opinion, in information and communication, in speech and assembly. Under the rule of monopolistic media—themselves the mere instruments of economic and political power—a mentality is created for which right and wrong, true and false are predefined wherever they affect the vital interests of the society. This is, prior to all expression and communication, a matter of semantics: the blocking of effective dissent, of the recognition of that which is not of the Establishment which begins in the language that is publicized and administered. The meaning of words is rigidly stabilized. Rational persuasion, persuasion to the opposite is all but precluded. The avenues of entrance are closed to the meaning of words and ideas other than the established one—established by the publicity of the powers that be, and verified in their practices. Other words can be spoken and heard, other ideas can be expressed, but, at the massive scale of the conservative majority (outside such enclaves as the intelligentsia), they are immediately "evaluated" (i.e. automatically understood) in terms of the public language—a language which determines "a priori" the direction in which the thought process moves. Thus the process of reflection ends where it started: in the given conditions and relations.

Discussion Questions

1. What does Marcuse mean by "pure" tolerance? Is it the same thing that Mill means by freedom of expression? In Marcuse's view, is pure tolerance *always* a bad social practice? Are there circumstances in which it might be appropriate?

2. The key to Marcuse's critique of freedom of expression is his view of the marketplace of ideas and the role of "monopolistic media." Do you agree that Mill's supposedly free market is rigged in the United States today? How might Mill respond to Marcuse's observations? Were the means of communication necessarily less concentrated in nineteenth-century England than in the waning days of the twentieth century in America?

3. Even if you disagree with Marcuse's Marxist interpretation of the power of moneyed interests in influencing public opinion and democratic debate, you might agree that the growing power of business and the accelerating concentration of all forms of media in a small number of hands poses a problem for democratic self-government. What kind of social policies might address this problem?

4. A solution to the problems of free expression that Marcuse poses might be easier to address on a university campus than in society at large. What kind of campus policies regarding hate speech would Marcuse's theories support? Do you think these policies would be (a) consistent with the First Amendment? (b) beneficial to free exchange of ideas or the search for truth? (c) supportive of the equality of dispossessed minorities—be they political, religious, racial, or ethnic?

FROM "IF HE HOLLERS LET HIM GO: REGULATING RACIST SPEECH ON CAMPUS"

Charles R. Lawrence III

Introduction

In recent years, American campuses have seen a resurgence of racial violence and a corresponding rise in the incidence of verbal and symbolic assault and harassment to which blacks and other traditionally subjugated groups are subjected. There is a heated debate in the civil liberties community concerning the proper response to incidents of racist speech on campus. Strong disagreements have arisen between those individuals who believe that racist speech . . . should be regulated by the university or some public body and those individuals who believe that racist expression should be protected from all public regulation. At the center of the controversy is a tension between the constitutional values of free speech and equality. Like the debate over affirmative action in university admissions, this issue has divided old allies and revealed unrecognized or unacknowledged differences in the experience, perceptions, and values of members of long-standing alliances. It also has caused considerable soul-searching by individuals with longtime commitments to both the cause of political expression and the cause of racial equality.

I write this article from within the cauldron of this controversy. I make no pretense of dispassion or objectivity, but I do claim a deep commitment to the values that motivate both sides of the debate. As I struggle with the tension between these constitutional values, I particularly appreciate the experience of both belonging and not belonging that gives to African-Americans and other outsider groups a sense of duality. W.E.B. Du Bois—scholar and founder of the National Association for the Advancement of Colored People—called the gift and burden inherent to the dual, conflicting heritage of all African-Americans their "second-sight."

The "double consciousness" of groups outside the ethnic mainstream is particularly apparent in the context of this controversy. Blacks know and value the protection the First Amendment affords those of us who must rely upon our voices to petition both government and our neighbors for redress of grievances. Our political tradition has looked to "the word," to the moral power of

From *Duke Law Journal*, 1990, at 431 *et seq.* Reprinted by permission of Charles R. Lawrence III. Footnotes omitted.

ideas, to change a system when neither the power of the vote nor that of the gun is available. This part of us has known the experience of belonging and recognizes our common and inseparable interest in preserving the right of free speech for all. But we also know the experience of the outsider. The Framers [of the Constitution] excluded us from the protection of the First Amendment. The same Constitution that established rights for others endorsed a story that proclaimed our inferiority. It is a story that remains deeply ingrained in the American psyche.

We see a different world than that which is seen by Americans who do not share this historical experience. We often hear racist speech when our white neighbors are not aware of its presence.

It is not my purpose to belittle or trivialize the importance of defending unpopular speech against the tyranny of the majority. There are very strong reasons for protecting even racist speech. Perhaps the most important reasons are that it reinforces our society's commitment to the value of tolerance, and that, by shielding racist speech from government regulation, we will be forced to combat it as a community. These reasons for protecting racist speech should not be set aside hastily, and I will not argue that we should be less vigilant in protecting the speech and associational rights of speakers with whom most of us would disagree.

But I am deeply concerned about the role that many civil libertarians have played, or the roles we have failed to play, in the continuing, real-life struggle through which we define the community in which we live. I fear that by framing the debate as we have—as one in which the liberty of free speech is in conflict with the elimination of racism—we have advanced the cause of racial oppression and have placed the bigot on the moral high ground, fanning the rising flames of racism. Above all, I am troubled that we have not listened to the real victims, that we have shown so little empathy or understanding for their injury, and that we have abandoned those individuals whose race, gender, or sexual orientation provokes others to regard them as second-class citizens. These individuals' civil liberties are most directly at stake in the debate.

I have set two goals in constructing this article. The first goal is limited and perhaps overly modest, but nonetheless extremely important. I will demonstrate that much of the argument for protecting racist speech is based on the distinction that many civil libertarians draw between direct, face-to-face racial insults, which they think deserve First Amendment protection, and all other fighting words, which they concede are unprotected by the First Amendment. I argue that the distinction is false, advances none of the purposes of the First Amendment, and that it is time to put an end to the ringing rhetoric that condemns all efforts to regulate racist speech, even when those efforts take the form of narrowly drafted provisions aimed at racist speech that results in direct, immediate, and substantial injury.

I also urge the regulation of racial epithets and vilification that do not involve face-to-face encounters—situations in which the victim is a captive audience and the injury is experienced by all members of a racial group who are forced to hear or see these words; the insulting words, in effect, are aimed at the entire group.

My second goal is more ambitious and more indeterminate. I propose several ways in which the traditional civil liberties position on free speech does not take into account important values expressed elsewhere in the Constitution. Further, I argue that even those values the First Amendment itself is intended to promote are frustrated by an interpretation that is contextual and idealized, by presupposing a world characterized by equal opportunity and the absence of societally created and culturally ingrained racism. . . .

Brown *v.* Board of Education:
A Case About Regulating Racist Speech

The landmark case of *Brown* v. *Board of Education* is not a case we normally think of as a case about speech. As read most narrowly, the case is about the rights of black children to equal educational opportunity. But *Brown* can also be read more broadly to articulate a principle central to any substantive understanding of the equal protection clause, the foundation on which all antidiscrimination law rests. This is the principle of equal citizenship. Under that principle, "every individual is presumptively entitled to be treated by the organized society as a respected, responsible, and participating member." Furthermore, it requires the affirmative disestablishment of societal practices that treat people as members of an inferior or dependent caste, as unworthy to participate in the larger community. The holding in *Brown*—that racially segregated schools violate the equal protection clause—reflects the fact that segregation amounts to a demeaning, caste-creating practice.

The key to this understanding of *Brown* is that the practice of segregation, the practice the Court held inherently unconstitutional, was speech. *Brown* held that segregation is unconstitutional not simply because the physical separation of black and white children is bad or because resources were distributed unequally among black and white schools. *Brown* held that segregated schools were unconstitutional primarily because of the message segregation conveys—the message that black children are an untouchable caste, unfit to be educated with white children. Segregation serves its purpose by conveying an idea. It stamps a badge of inferiority upon blacks, and this badge communicates a message to others in the community, as well as to blacks wearing the badge, that is injurious to blacks. Therefore, *Brown* may be read as regulating the content of racist speech. As a regulation of racist speech, the decision is an exception to the usual rule that regulation of speech content is presumed unconstitutional.

The Conduct/Speech Distinction

Some civil libertarians argue that my analysis of *Brown* conflates speech and conduct. They maintain that the segregation outlawed in *Brown* was discriminatory conduct, not speech, and the defamatory message conveyed by segregation simply was an incidental by-product of that conduct. . . . This objection to my reading of *Brown* misperceives the central point of the argument. I have not ignored the distinction between the speech and conduct elements of segregation by mistake. Rather, my analysis turns on that distinction. It asks the question whether there is a purpose for outlawing segregation that is unrelated to its message, and it concludes the answer is "no." . . .

Properly understood, *Brown* and its progeny require that the systematic group defamation of segregation be disestablished. Although the exclusion of black children from white schools and the denial of educational resources and association that accompany exclusion can be characterized as conduct, these particular instances of conduct are concerned primarily with communicating the idea of white supremacy. The non-speech elements are by-products of the main message rather than the message simply a by-product of unlawful conduct. . . .

Another way to understand the inseparability of racist speech and discriminatory conduct is to view individual racist acts as part of a totality. When viewed in this manner, white supremacists' conduct or speech is forbidden by the equal protection clause. The goal of white supremacy is not achieved by individual acts or even by the cumulative acts of a group, but rather by the institutionalization of the ideas of white supremacy. The institutionalization of white supremacy within our culture has created conduct on the societal level that is greater than the sum of individual racist acts. The racist acts of millions of individuals are mutually reinforcing and cumulative because the status quo of institutionalized white supremacy remains long after deliberate racist actions subside.

It is difficult to recognize the institutional significance of white supremacy or how it acts to harm, partially because of its ubiquity. We simply do not see most racist conduct because we experience a world in which whites are supreme as simply "the world." Much racist conduct is considered unrelated to race or regarded as neutral because racist conduct maintains the status quo, the status quo of the world as we have known it. Catherine MacKinnon has observed that "to the extent that pornography succeeds in constructing social reality, it becomes invisible as harm." Thus, pornography "is more act-like than thought-like." This truth about gender discrimination is equally true of racism. . . .

Racism is both 100% speech and 100% conduct. Discriminatory conduct is not racist unless it also conveys the message of white supremacy—unless it is interpreted within the culture to advance the structure and ideology of white supremacy. Likewise, all racist speech constructs the social reality that constrains the liberty of nonwhites because of their race. By limiting the life opportunities of others, this act of constructing meaning also makes racist speech conduct.

The Public/Private Distinction

There are critics who would contend that *Brown* is inapposite because the equal protection clause only restricts government behavior, whereas the First Amendment protects the speech of private persons. They say, "Of course we want to prevent the state from defaming blacks, but we must continue to be vigilant about protecting the speech rights, even of racist individuals, from the government. In both cases, our concern must be protecting the individual from the unjust power of the state."

At first blush, this position seems persuasive, but its persuasiveness relies upon the mystifying properties of constitutional ideology. In particular, I refer to the state action doctrine. By restricting the application of the Fourteenth Amendment to discrimination implicating the government, the state action rule immunizes private discriminators from constitutional scrutiny. In so doing, it leaves untouched the largest part of the vast system of segregation in the United States. . . .

In the abstract, the right to make decisions about how we will educate our children or with whom we will associate is an important value in American society. But when we decontextualize by viewing this privacy value in the abstract, we ignore the way it operates in the real world. We do not ask ourselves, for example, whether it is a value to which all persons have equal access. And we do not inquire about who has the resources to send their children to private school or move to an exclusive suburb. The privacy value, when presented as an ideal, seems an appropriate limitation on racial justice because we naively believe that everyone has an equal stake in this value.

The argument that distinguishes private racist speech from the government speech outlawed by *Brown* suffers from the same decontextualizing ideology. If the government is involved in a joint venture with private contractors to engage in the business of defaming blacks, should it be able to escape the constitutional mandate that makes that business illegal simply by handing over the copyright and the printing presses to its partners in crime? I think not. And yet this is the essence of the position that espouses First Amendment protection for those partners. . . .

When a person responds to the argument that *Brown* mandates the abolition of racist speech by reciting the state action doctrine, she fails to consider that the alternative to regulating racist speech is infringement of the claims of blacks to liberty and equal protection. The best way to constitutionally protect these competing interests is to balance them directly. To invoke the state action doctrine is to circumvent our value judgment as to how these competing interests should be balanced.

The deference usually given to the First Amendment values in this balance is justified using the argument that racist speech is unpopular speech—that, like the speech of civil rights activists, pacifists, and religious and political dissenters, it is in need of special protection from majoritarian censorship. But for over 300 years, racist speech has been the liturgy of America's leading established religion, the religion of racism. Racist speech remains a vital and regrettably popular characteristic of the American vernacular. It must be noted that there has not yet been satisfactory retraction of the government-sponsored defamation in the slavery clauses, the Dred Scott decision, the black codes, the segregation statutes, and countless other group libels. The injury to blacks is hardly redressed by deciding the government must no longer injure our reputation if one then invokes the First Amendment to ensure that racist speech continues to thrive in an unregulated private market.

Consider, for example, the case of *McLaurin* v. *Oklahoma State Regents*, where the University of Oklahoma graduate school, under order by a federal court to admit McLaurin, a black student, designated a special seat, roped off from other seats, in each classroom, the library, and the cafeteria. The Supreme Court held that this arrangement was unconstitutional because McLaurin could not have had an equal opportunity to learn and participate if he were humiliated and symbolically stigmatized as an untouchable. Would it be any less injurious if all McLaurin's classmates had shown up at the class wearing blackface? Should this symbolic speech be protected by the Constitution? Yet, according to a *Time* magazine report, last fall at the University of Wisconsin "members of the Zeta Beta Tau fraternity staged a mock slave auction, complete with some pledges in blackface." More recently, at the same university, white male students trailed black female students, shouting,

"I've never tried a nigger before." These young women were no less severely injured than was Mr. McLaurin simply because the university did not directly sponsor their assault. If the university fails to protect them in their right to pursue their education free from this kind of degradation and humiliation, then surely there are constitutional values at stake. . . .

The Supreme Court also has indicated that Congress may enact legislation regulating private racist speech. In upholding the public accommodations provisions of Title II of the Civil Rights Act of 1964 in *Heart of Atlanta Motel* v. *United States*, the Court implicitly rejected the argument that the absence of state action meant that private discriminators were protected by First Amendment free speech and associational rights. Likewise, in *Bob Jones University* v. *United States*, the court sustained the Internal Revenue Service's decision to discontinue tax exempt status for a college with a policy against interracial dating and marriage. The college framed its objection in terms of the free exercise of religion, since their policy was religiously motivated, but the Supreme Court found that the government had "a fundamental, overriding interest in eradicating racial discrimination in education" that "substantially outweighs whatever burden denial of tax benefits" placed on the college's exercise of its religious beliefs. It is difficult to believe that the university would have fared any better under free speech analysis or if the policy had been merely a statement of principle rather than an enforceable disciplinary regulation. Regulation of private racist speech also has been held constitutional in the context of prohibition of race-designated advertisements for employees, home sales, and rentals.

Thus *Brown* and the antidiscrimination law it spawned provide precedent for my position that the content regulation of racist speech is not only permissible but may be required by the Constitution in certain circumstances. This precedent may not mean that we should advocate the government regulation of all racist speech, but it should give us pause in assuming absolutist positions about regulations aimed at the message or idea such speech conveys. If we understand *Brown*—the cornerstone of the civil rights movement and equal protection doctrine—correctly, and if we understand the necessity of disestablishing the system of signs and symbols that signal blacks' inferiority, then we should not proclaim that all racist speech that stops short of physical violence must be defended.

Racist Speech as the Functional Equivalent of Fighting Words

Much recent debate over the efficacy of regulating racist speech has focused on the efforts by colleges and universities to respond to the burgeoning inci-

dents of racial harassment on their campuses. At Stanford, where I teach, there
has been considerable controversy over the questions whether racist and other
discriminatory verbal harassment should be regulated and what form that regulation should take. Proponents of regulation have been sensitive to the danger
of inhibiting expression, and the current regulation . . . manifests that sensitivity. It is drafted somewhat more narrowly than I would have preferred, leaving
unregulated hate speech that occurs in settings where there is a captive audience, speech that I would regulate. But I largely agree with this regulation's
substance and approach. I include it here as one example of a regulation of
racist speech that I would argue violates neither First Amendment precedent
nor principle. The regulation reads as follows:

Fundamental Standard Interpretation:
Free Expression and Discriminatory Harassment

1. Stanford is committed to the principles of free inquiry and free expression.
   Students have the right to hold and vigorously defend and promote their opinions, thus entering them into the life of the University, there to flourish or
   wither according to their merits. Respect for this right requires that students
   tolerate even expression of opinions which they find abhorrent. Intimidation
   of students by other students in their exercise of this right, by violence or
   threat of violence, is therefore considered to be a violation of the Fundamental Standard.
2. Stanford is also committed to principles of equal opportunity and non-dis-
   crimination. Each student has the right to equal access to a Stanford education, without discrimination on the basis of sex, race, color, handicap, religion, sexual orientation, or national and ethnic origin. Harassment of students
   on the basis of any of these characteristics contributes to a hostile environment that makes access to education for those subjected to it less than equal.
   Such discriminatory harassment is therefore considered to be a violation of
   the Fundamental Standard.
3. This interpretation of the Fundamental Standard is intended to clarify the
   point at which protected free expression ends and prohibited discriminatory
   harassment begins. Prohibited harassment includes discriminatory intimidation by threats of violence, and also includes personal vilification of students
   on the basis of their sex, race, color, handicap, religion, sexual orientation, or
   national and ethnic origin.
4. Speech or other expression constitutes harassment by personal vilification
   if it:
   a) is intended to insult or stigmatize an individual or a small number of indi-
      viduals on the basis of their sex, race, color, handicap, religion, sexual
      orientation, or national and ethnic origin; and
   b) is addressed directly to the individual or individuals whom it insults or
      stigmatizes; and
   c) makes use of insulting or "fighting" words or non-verbal symbols.

In the context of discriminatory harassment by personal vilification, insulting or "fighting" words or non-verbal symbols are those "which by their very utterance inflict injury or tend to incite to an immediate breach of the peace," and which are commonly understood to convey direct and visceral hatred or contempt for human beings on the basis of their sex, race, color, handicap, religion, sexual orientation, or national and ethnic origin.

This regulation and others like it have been characterized in the press as the work of "thought police," but it does nothing more than prohibit intentional face-to-face insults, a form of speech that is unprotected by the First Amendment. . . .

Face-to-face racial insults, like fighting words, are undeserving of First Amendment protection for two reasons. The first reason is the immediacy of the injurious impact of racial insults. The experience of being called "nigger," "spic," "Jap," or "kike" is like receiving a slap in the face. The injury is instantaneous. There is neither an opportunity for intermediary reflection on the idea conveyed nor an opportunity for responsive speech. The harm to be avoided is both clear and present. The second reason that racial insults should not fall under protected speech relates to the purpose underlying the First Amendment. If the purpose of the First Amendment is to foster the greatest amount of speech, then racial insults disserve that purpose. Assaultive racist speech functions as a preemptive strike. The racial invective is experienced as a blow, not a proffered idea, and once the blow is struck, it is unlikely that dialogue will follow. Racial insults are undeserving of First Amendment protection because the perpetrator's intention is not to discover truth or initiate dialogue but to injure the victim. . . .

The subordinated victim of fighting words also is silenced by her relatively powerless position in society. Because of the significance of power and position, the categorization of racial epithets as "fighting words" provides an inadequate paradigm; instead one must speak of their "functional equivalent." The fighting words doctrine presupposes an encounter between two persons of relatively equal power who have been acculturated to respond to face-to-face insults with violence. The fighting words doctrine is a paradigm based on a white male point of view. In most situations, minorities correctly perceive that a violent response to fighting words will result in a risk to their own life and limb. Since minorities are likely to lose the fight, they are forced to remain silent and submissive. This response is most obvious when women submit to sexually assaultive speech or when the racist name-caller is in a more powerful position—the boss on the job or the mob. Certainly, we do not expect the black women crossing the Wisconsin campus to turn on their tormentors and pummel them. Less obvious, but just as significant, is the effect of pervasive racial and sexual violence and coercion on individual members of subordinated groups who must learn the survival techniques of suppressing and disguising rage and anger at an early age. . . .

The proposed Stanford regulation, and indeed regulations with considerably broader reach, can be justified as necessary to protect a captive audience from offensive or injurious speech. Courts have held that offensive speech may not be regulated in public forums such as streets and parks where a listener may avoid the speech by moving on or averting his eyes, but the regulation of otherwise protected speech has been permitted when the speech invades the privacy of the unwilling listener's home or when the unwilling listener cannot avoid the speech. Racist posters, fliers, and graffiti in dorms, classrooms, bathrooms, and other common living spaces would fall within the reasoning of these cases. Minority students should not be required to remain in their rooms to avoid racial assault. Minimally, they should find a safe haven in their dorms and other common rooms that are a part of their daily routine. I would argue that the university's responsibility for ensuring these students receive an equal educational opportunity provides a compelling justification for regulations that ensure them safe passage in all common areas. A black, Latino, Asian, or Native American student should not have to risk being the target of racially assaulting speech every time she chooses to walk across campus. The regulation of vilifying speech that cannot be anticipated or avoided would not preclude announced speeches and rallies where minorities and their allies would have an opportunity to organize counterdemonstrations or avoid the speech altogether.

Knowing the Injury and Striking the Balance: Understanding What is at Stake in Racist Speech Cases

I argued [above] that narrowly drafted regulations of racist speech that prohibit face-to-face vilification and protect captive audiences from verbal and written harassment can be defended within the confines of existing First Amendment doctrine. [Now,] I will argue that many civil libertarians who urge that the First Amendment prohibits any regulation of racist speech have given inadequate attention to the testimony of individuals who have experienced injury from such speech—these civil libertarians fail to comprehend both the nature and extent of the injury inflicted by racist speech. I further urge that understanding the injury requires reconsideration of the balance that must be struck between our concerns for racial equality and freedom of expression.

The argument most commonly advanced against the regulation of racist speech goes something like this: We recognize that minority groups suffer pain and injury as the result of racist speech, but we must allow this hate-mongering for the benefit of society as a whole. Freedom of speech is the lifeblood of our democratic system. It is a freedom that enables us to persuade others to our point of view. Free speech is especially important for minorities because often it is their only vehicle for rallying support for redress of their grievances. We cannot allow the public regulation of racist invective and vilification because any prohibition precise enough to prevent racist speech would catch in the same net forms of speech that are central to a democratic society.

Whenever we argue that racist epithets and vilification must be allowed, not because we would condone them ourselves but because of the potential danger that precedent would pose for the speech of all dissenters, we are balancing our concern for the free flow of ideas and the democratic process [with] our desire to further equality. This kind of categorical balance is struck whenever we frame any rule—even an absolute rule. It is important to be conscious of the nature and extent of injury to both concerns when we engage in this kind of balancing. In this case, we must place on one side of the balance the nature and extent of the injury caused by racism. We also must be very careful, in weighing the potential harm to free speech, to consider whether the racist speech we propose to regulate is advancing or retarding the values of the First Amendment.

Understanding the Injury Inflicted by Racist Speech

There can be no meaningful discussion about how to reconcile our commitment to equality and our commitment to free speech until we acknowledge that racist speech inflicts real harm and that this harm is far from trivial. I should state that more strongly: To engage in a debate about the First Amendment and racist speech without a full understanding of the nature and extent of the harm of racist speech risks making the First Amendment an instrument of domination rather than a vehicle of liberation. Not everyone has known the experience of being victimized by racist, misogynist, and homophobic speech, and we do not share equally the burden of the societal harm it inflicts. Often we are too quick to say we have heard the victims' cries when we have not; we are too eager to assure ourselves we have experienced the same injury, and therefore we can make the constitutional balance without danger of mismeasurement. For many of us who have fought for the rights of oppressed minorities, it is difficult to accept that—by underestimating the injury from racist speech—we too might be implicated in the vicious words we would never utter. Until we have eradicated racism and sexism and no longer share in the fruits of those forms of domination, we cannot justly strike the balance over the protest of those who are dominated. My plea is simply that we listen to the victims. . . .

Again, *Brown* v. *Board of Education* is a useful case for our analysis. *Brown* is helpful because it articulates the nature of the injury inflicted by the racist message of segregation. When one considers the injuries identified in the *Brown* decision, it is clear that racist speech causes tangible injury, and it is the kind of injury for which the law commonly provides, and even requires, redress.

Psychic injury is no less an injury than being struck in the face, and it often is far more severe. *Brown* speaks directly to the psychic injury inflicted by racist speech in noting that the symbolic message of segregation affected "the hearts and minds" of Negro children "in a way unlikely ever to be undone." Racial epithets and harassment often cause deep emotional scarring, and feelings of anxiety and fear that pervade every aspect of a victim's life. Many victims of hate propaganda have experienced physiological and emotional symptoms ranging from rapid pulse rate and difficulty in breathing, to nightmares, posttraumatic stress disorder, psychosis, and suicide.

A second injury identified in *Brown* . . . is reputational injury. "[L]ibelous speech was long regarded as a form of personal assault . . . that government could vindicate . . . without running afoul of the Constitution." Although *New York Times* v. *Sullivan* and its progeny have subjected much defamatory speech to constitutional scrutiny—on the reasoning that "debate on public issues should be uninhibited, robust and wide-open" and should not be "chilled" by the possibility of libel suits—these cases also demonstrate a concern for balancing the public's interest in being fully informed with the competing interest of defamed persons in vindicating their reputation.

Brown is a case about group defamation. The message of segregation was stigmatizing to black children. To be labeled unfit to attend school with white children injured the reputation of black children, thereby foreclosing employment opportunities and the right to be regarded as respected members of the body politic. An extensive discussion on the constitutionality or efficacy of group libel laws is beyond the scope of this essay. However, it will suffice to note that whereas *Beauharnais* v. *Illinois*, which upheld an Illinois group libel statute, has fallen into ill repute, and is generally considered to have been overruled implicitly by *Sullivan*, *Brown* remains an instructive case. By identifying the inseparability of discriminatory speech and action in the case of segregation, where the injury is inflicted by the meaning of the message,

Brown limits the scope of *Sullivan*. *Brown* reflects that racism is a form of subordination that achieves its purposes through group defamation.

The third injury identified in *Brown* is the denial of equal educational opportunity. *Brown* recognized that black children did not have an equal opportunity to learn and participate in the school community if they bore the additional burden of being subjected to the humiliation and psychic assault that accompanies the message of segregation. University students bear an analogous burden when they are forced to live and work in an environment where, at any moment, they may be subjected to denigrating verbal harassment and assault. The testimony of nonwhite students about the detrimental effect of racial harassment on their academic performance and social integration in the college community is overwhelming. A similar injury is recognized and addressed in Title VII's requirement that employers maintain a nondiscriminatory (nonhostile) work environment, and in federal and state regulations prohibiting sexual harassment on campuses as well as in the workplace.

All three of these very tangible, continuing, and often irreparable forms of injury—psychic, reputational, and the denial of equal educational opportunity—must be recognized, accounted for, and balanced against the claim that a regulation aimed at the prevention of these injuries may lead to restrictions on important First Amendment liberties.

The Other Side of the Balance:
Does the Suppression of Racial Epithets Weigh for or Against Speech?

In striking a balance, we also must think about what we are weighing on the side of speech. Most blacks—unlike many white civil libertarians—do not have faith in free speech as the most important vehicle for liberation. The First Amendment coexisted with slavery, and we still are not sure it will protect us to the same extent that it protects whites. It often is argued that minorities have benefited greatly from First Amendment protection and therefore should guard it jealously. We are aware that the struggle for racial equality has relied heavily on the persuasion of peaceful protest protected by the First Amendment, but experience also teaches us that our petitions often go unanswered until they disrupt business as usual and require the self-interested attention of those persons in power. . . .

Blacks and other people of color are equally skeptical about the absolutist argument that even the most injurious speech must remain unregulated because in an unregulated marketplace of ideas the best ideas will rise to the top and gain acceptance. Our experience tells us the opposite. We have seen too many demagogues elected by appealing to America's racism. We have seen too many good, liberal politicians shy away from the issues that might brand them as too closely allied with us. The American marketplace of ideas was founded with the idea of the racial inferiority of nonwhites as one of its chief commodities, and ever since the market opened, racism has remained its most active item in trade.

But it is not just the prevalence and strength of the idea of racism that makes the unregulated marketplace of ideas an untenable paradigm for those individuals who seek full and equal personhood for all. The real problem is that the idea of the racial inferiority of nonwhites infects, skews, and disables the operation of the market (like a computer virus, sick cattle, or diseased wheat). Racism is irrational and often unconscious. Our belief in the inferiority of nonwhites trumps good ideas that contend with it in the market, often without our even knowing it. In addition, racism makes the words and ideas of blacks and other despised minorities less salable, regardless of their intrinsic value, in the marketplace of ideas. It also decreases the total amount of speech that enters the market by coercively silencing members of those groups who are its targets. . . .

The disruptive and disabling effect on the market of an idea that is ubiquitous and irrational, but seldom seen or acknowledged, should be apparent. If the community is considering competing ideas about providing food for children, shelter for the homeless, or abortions for pregnant women, and the choices made among the proposed solutions are influenced by the idea that some children, families, or women are less deserving of our sympathy because they are not white, then the market is not functioning as either John Stuart Mill or Oliver Wendell Holmes envisioned it. In John Ely's terms, there is a "process defect." . . .

Mill's vision of truth emerging through competition in the marketplace of ideas relies on the ability of members of the body politic to recognize "truth" as serving their interest and to act on that recognition. As such, this vision depends upon the same process that James Madison referred to when he described his vision of a democracy in which the numerous minorities within our society would form coalitions to create majorities with overlapping interests through pluralist wheeling and dealing. Just as the defect of prejudice blinds the white voter to interests that overlap with those of vilified minorities, it also blinds him to the "truth" of an idea or the efficacy of solutions associated with that vilified group. And just as prejudice causes the governmental decision-makers to misapprehend the costs and benefits of their actions, it also causes all of us to misapprehend the value of ideas in the market.

Prejudice that is unconscious or unacknowledged causes even more distortions in the market. When racism operates at a conscious level, opposing ideas may prevail in open competition for the rational or moral sensibilities of the market participant. But when an individual is unaware of his prejudice, neither reason nor moral persuasion will likely succeed.

Racist speech also distorts the marketplace of ideas by muting or devaluing the speech of blacks and other nonwhites. . . . An obvious example of this type of devaluation would be the black political candidate whose ideas go unheard or are rejected by white voters, although voters would embrace the same ideas if they were championed by a white candidate. Racial minorities have the same experiences on a daily basis when they endure the microaggression of having their words doubted, misinterpreted, or assumed to be without evidentiary support, or when their insights are ignored and then appropriated by whites who are assumed to have been the original authority.

Finally, racist speech decreases the total amount of speech that reaches the market. I noted earlier in this article the ways in which racist speech is inextricably linked with racist conduct. The primary purpose and effect of the speech/conduct that constitutes white supremacy is the exclusion of nonwhites from full participation in the body politic. Sometimes the speech/conduct of racism is direct and obvious. When the Klan burns a cross on the lawn of a black person who joined the NAACP or exercised his right to move to a formerly all-white neighborhood, the effect of this speech does not result from the persuasive power of an idea operating freely in the market. It is a threat, a threat made in the context of a history of lynchings, beatings, and economic reprisals that made good on earlier threats, a threat that silences a potential speaker. The black student who is subjected to racial epithets is likewise threatened and silenced. Certainly she, like the victim of a cross-burning, may be uncommonly brave or foolhardy and ignore the system of violence in which this abusive speech is only a bit player. But it is more likely that we, as a community, will be denied the benefit of many of her thoughts and ideas.

Again, MacKinnon's analysis of how First Amendment law misconstrues pornography is instructive. She notes that in concerning themselves only with government censorship, First Amendment absolutists fail to recognize that whole segments of the population are systematically silenced by powerful private actors. "As a result, [they] cannot grasp that the speech of some silences the speech of others in a way that is not simply a matter of competition for airtime."

Asking Victim Groups to Pay the Price

Whenever we decide that racist hate speech must be tolerated because of the importance of tolerating unpopular speech, we ask blacks and other subordinated groups to bear a burden for the good of society—to pay the price for the societal benefit of creating more room for speech. And we assign this burden to them without seeking their advice or consent. This amounts to white domination, pure and simple. . . .

If one asks why we always begin by asking whether we can afford to fight racism rather than asking whether we can afford not to, or if one asks why my colleagues who oppose all regulation of racist speech do not feel that the burden is theirs (to justify a reading of the First Amendment that requires sacrificing rights guaranteed under the equal protection clause), then one sees an example of how unconscious racism operates in the marketplace of ideas.

Well-meaning individuals who are committed to equality without regard to race, and who have demonstrated that commitment in many arenas, do not recognize where the burden of persuasion has been placed in this discussion. When they do, they do not understand why. . . .

Derrick Bell has noted that often in our constitutional history the rights of blacks have been sacrificed because sacrifice was believed necessary to preserve the greater interests of the whole. It is not just the actual sacrifice that is racist but also the way the "whole with the greater interests" gets defined. Today, in a world committed to the ideal of equality, we rarely notice the sacrifice or how we have avoided noticing the sacrifice by defining the interests of whites as the whole. . . . When we think this way, when we see the potential danger of incursions on the First Amendment but do not see existing incursions on the Fourteenth Amendment, our perceptions have been influenced by an entire belief system that makes us less sensitive to the injury experienced by nonwhites. Unaware, we have adopted a world view that takes for granted black sacrifice. . . .

Which Side Are (We) On?

However one comes out on the question of whether racist hate speech should be artificially distinguished from other fighting words and given First Amendment protection, it is important to examine and take responsibility for the effects of how one participates in the debate. It is important to consider how our voice is heard. We must ask ourselves whether, in our well-placed passion for preserving our First Amendment freedoms, we have been forceful enough in our personal condemnation of ideas we abhor, whether we have neglected our alliances with victims of the oppressive manifestations of the continuing dominance of these ideas within our communities and within ourselves. . . .

There is much about the way many civil libertarians have participated in the debate over the regulation of racist speech that causes the victims of that speech to wonder which side they are on. Those who raise their voices in protest against public sanctions of racist speech have not organized private protests against the voices of racism. It has been people of color, women, and gays who have held vigils at offending fraternity houses, staged candlelight marches, counterdemonstrations, and distributed fliers calling upon their classmates and colleagues to express their outrage at pervasive racism, sexism, and homophobia in their midst and to show their solidarity with victims.

Traditional civil libertarians have been conspicuous largely in their absence from these group expressions of condemnation. Their failure to participate in this marketplace response to speech with more speech is often justified, paradoxically, as concern for the principle of free speech. When racial minorities or other victims of hate speech hold counterdemonstrations or engage in picketing, leafleting, heckling or booing of racist speakers, civil libertarians often accuse them of private censorship, of seeking to silence opposing points of view. When both public and private responses to racist speech are rejected by First Amendment absolutists as contrary to the principle of free speech, it is no wonder that the victims of racism do not consider them allies.

Blacks and other racial minorities also are made skeptical by the resistance encountered when we approach traditional civil liberties groups like the ACLU with suggestions that they merely reconsider the ways they engage in this complex debate concerning speech and equality. Traditional civil liberties lawyers typically have elected to stand by while universities have responded to the outbreak of hate speech by adopting regulations that often are drafted with considerable attention to appeasing various, widely diverging political constituencies and only passing concern for either free speech or equality. Not surprisingly, these regulations are vague and overbroad. They provide easy prey for the white-hatted defenders of the First Amendment faith who dutifully march into court to have them declared unconstitutional. . . .

The recent outbreak of racism on our campuses in its most obvious manifestations provides an opportunity to examine the presence of less overt forms of racism within our educational institutions. But the debate that has followed these incidents has focused on the First Amendment freedoms of the perpetrators rather than the university community's responsibility for creating an environment where such acts occur. The resurgence of flagrant racist acts has not occurred in a vacuum. It is evidence of more widespread resistance to change by those holding positions of dominance and privilege in institutions, which until recently were exclusively white. Those who continue to be marginalized in these institutions—by their token inclusion on faculties and administrations, by the exclusion of their cultures from core curricula, and by commitments to diversity and multiculturalism that seem to require assimilation more than any real change in the university—cannot help but see their colleagues' attention to free speech as an avoidance of these larger issues of equality.

When the ACLU enters the debate by challenging the University of Michigan's efforts to provide a safe harbor for its black, Hispanic, and Asian students (a climate that a colleague of mine compared unfavorably with Mississippi in the 1960s), we should not be surprised that nonwhite students feel abandoned. When we respond to Stanford students' pleas for protection by accusing them of seeking to silence all who disagree with them, we paint the harassing bigot as a martyred defender of democracy. When we valorize bigotry, we must assume some responsibility for the fact that bigots are encouraged by their newfound status as "defenders of the faith." We must find ways to engage actively in speech and action that resists and counters the racist ideas the First Amendment protects. If we fail in this duty, the victims of hate speech rightly assume we are aligned with their oppressors.

Discussion Questions

1. Lawrence argues that *Brown* v. *Board of Education*, the landmark Supreme Court decision that outlawed state-imposed racial segregation in public schools, was a case about "regulating racist speech," that what is wrong with the state's discrimination against African-Americans is the "discriminatory message" of segregation, not its actual operation. Do you agree with this characterization of the evils of state-imposed discrimination? If a state were to impose segregation among the races not because of a notion of the inferiority of one, but rather because of a good-faith belief that the races were simply "different" and needed different educational environments, would the asserted lack of a racist "message" make the practice constitutional? Should it?

2. There is a suggestion in this article that the private racist speech of individuals may itself be a violation of the Constitution—that "content regulation of racist speech is not only permissible but may be required by the Constitution in certain circumstances." What might these circumstances be? Do you agree? Might universities be violating the Constitution by *not* imposing speech codes?

3. Lawrence argues that racist speech is not addressable through Mill's "marketplace of ideas"—that it needs special regulation because it has a "disruptive and disabling effect on the market of an idea [racism] that is ubiquitous and irrational." Do you agree? Can you think of any other ideas that might be put into the same category? Would such a potential exception to

Mill's marketplace metaphor cast doubt on this entire justification for freedom of expression?

4. Lawrence sets out an early version of the Stanford University speech code in this article. How does this compare to the codes adopted at the University of Michigan and the University of Wisconsin? Is it more or less protective of freedom of expression? More or less protective of the rights of protected minorities? Does this limited code respond adequately to the broader concerns for protecting equality and the harm caused by racist ideas expressed by Professor Lawrence? Can you think of examples of destructive racist, sexist, or homophobic speech or expressive behavior that might cause equal harm to the victim but that are not reachable under this code? What about a general speech by a Ku Klux Klan member discussing the alleged racial inferiority of African-Americans? A speech by a Holocaust revisionist alleging that Hitler never tried to exterminate millions of Jews in World War II? A cross-burning to celebrate "Confederate Revival Day"?

FROM "REGULATING RACIST SPEECH ON CAMPUS: A MODEST PROPOSAL?"

Nadine Strossen

Introduction

Professor Lawrence has made a provocative contribution to the perennial debate concerning the extent to which courts and civil libertarians should continue to construe the Constitution as protecting some forms of racist expression. This recurring issue resurfaced most recently in connection with the increase of racial incidents at colleges and universities around the country. In response, many of these institutions have adopted, or are considering, regulations that curb "hate speech"—i.e., speech that expresses hatred or bias toward members of racial, religious, or other groups.

Civil libertarians are committed to the eradication of racial discrimination and the promotion of free speech throughout society. Civil libertarians have worked especially hard to combat both discrimination and free speech restrictions in educational institutions. Educational institutions should be bastions of equal opportunity and unrestricted exchange. Therefore, we find the upsurge of both campus racism and regulation of campus speech particularly disturbing, and we have undertaken efforts to counter both.

Because civil libertarians have learned that free speech is an indispensable instrument for the promotion of other rights and freedoms—including racial equality—we fear that the movement to regulate campus expression will undermine equality, as well as free speech. Combating racial discrimination and protecting free speech should be viewed as mutually reinforcing, rather than antagonistic, goals. A diminution in society's commitment to racial equality is neither a necessary nor an appropriate price for protecting free speech. Those who frame the debate in terms of this false dichotomy simply drive artificial wedges between would-be allies in what should be a common effort to promote civil rights and civil liberties. . . .

Insofar as Professor Lawrence advocates relatively narrow rules that apply traditionally accepted limitations on expressive conduct to the campus setting, his position should not be alarming (although it is debatable). In portions of his article, Professor Lawrence seems to agree with traditional civil libertari-

From *Duke Law Journal,* 1990, at 484 *et seq.* Reprinted by permission of *Duke Law Journal.* Footnotes omitted.

ans that only a small subset of the racist rhetoric that abounds in our society should be regulated. Although we may disagree about the contours of such concepts as "captive audience," "fighting words," or "intentional infliction of emotional distress" in the context of racist speech on campus, these differences should not obscure strong common goals. Surely our twin aims of civil rights and civil liberties would be advanced more effectively by fighting together against the common enemy of racism than by fighting against each other over which narrow subset of one symptom of racism—namely, verbal and symbolic expressions—should be regulated.

What is disquieting about Professor Lawrence's article is not the relatively limited Stanford code he defends, but rather his simultaneous defense of additional, substantially more sweeping, speech prohibitions. The rationales that Professor Lawrence advances for the regulations he endorses are so open-ended that, if accepted, they would appear to warrant the prohibition of all racist speech, and thereby would cut to the core of our system of free expression.

Although Professor Lawrence's specific proposed code appears relatively modest, his supporting rationales depend on nothing less immodest than the abrogation of the traditional distinctions between speech and conduct and between state action and private action. He equates private racist speech with governmental racist conduct. This approach offers no principled way to confine racist speech regulations to the particular contours of the Stanford code, or indeed to any particular contours at all. Professor Lawrence apparently acknowledges that, if accepted, his theories could warrant the prohibition of all private racist speech. Moreover, although he stresses the particular evils of racism, he also says that "much of my analysis applies to violent pornography and homophobic hate speech." Thus, Professor Lawrence himself demonstrates that traditional civil libertarians are hardly paranoiac when we fear that any specific, seemingly modest proposal to regulate speech may in fact represent the proverbial "thin edge of the wedge" for initiating broader regulations.

As just explained, the relatively narrow Stanford code that Professor Lawrence endorses is incongruous with his broad theoretical rationale. The Stanford code also is at odds with Professor Lawrence's pragmatic rationale. The harms of racist speech that he seeks to redress largely remain untouched by the rule. . . .

Two problems arise from the disharmony between the breadth of the racist speech regulations endorsed by Professor Lawrence and the harm that inspires them. First, this disparity underscores the rules' ineffectiveness. The regulations do not even address much of racist speech, let alone the innumerable other manifestations of racism which—as Professor Lawrence himself stresses—pervade our society. Second, this disharmony encourages the proponents of hate speech regulations to seek to narrow the gap between the underlying problem and their favored solution by recommending broader regulations. . . .

This article attempts to bridge some of the gaps that Professor Lawrence believes separate advocates of equality from advocates of free speech. It shows that—insofar as proponents of hate speech regulations endorse relatively narrow rules that encompass only a limited category of racist expression—these gaps are not that significant in practical effect. It also demonstrates that the First and Fourteenth Amendments are allies rather than antagonists. Most importantly, this article maintains that equality will be served most effectively by continuing to apply traditional, speech-protective precepts to racist speech, because a robust freedom of speech ultimately is necessary to combat racial discrimination. Professor Lawrence points out that free speech values as well as equality values may be promoted by regulating certain verbal harassment, and retarded by not regulating it. But it also must be recognized that equality values may be promoted most effectively by not regulating certain hate speech, and retarded by regulating it. . . .

Some Limited Forms of Campus Hate Speech May Be Regulable Under Current Constitutional Doctrine

General Constitutional Principles Applicable to Regulating Campus Hate Speech

To put in proper perspective the specific points of disagreement between Professor Lawrence's analysis and traditional civil libertarian views, the points of agreement should be noted first. Professor Lawrence usefully rehearses the many shared understandings between advocates of a traditional doctrine, which protects much racist speech, and advocates of various less protective regulations. Professor Lawrence acknowledges that there are strong reasons for sheltering even racist speech, in terms of reinforcing society's commitment to tolerance and mobilizing its opposition to intolerance. Consequently, he recognizes that to frame the debate in terms of a conflict between freedom of speech and the elimination of racism poses a false dichotomy. Accordingly, he urges civil libertarians to examine not just the substance of our position on racist speech, but also the way in which we enter the debate, to ensure that we condemn racist ideas at the same time as we defend the right to utter them. . . .

Consistent with Professor Lawrence's free speech concerns, the category of racist speech he seeks to regulate under the Stanford code is relatively narrow compared to other campus hate speech rules. In important respects, this proposal overlaps with the traditional civil libertarian position. On the end of the spectrum where speech is constitutionally protected, Professor Lawrence agrees with courts and traditional civil libertarians that the First Amendment should protect racist speech in a Skokie-type context. The essentials of a Skokie-type setting are that the offensive speech occurs in a public place and the event is announced in advance. Hence, the offensive speech can be either avoided or countered by opposing speech. Traditional civil libertarians recognize that this speech causes psychic pain. We nonetheless agree with the decision of the Seventh Circuit in Skokie that this pain is a necessary price for a system of free expression, which ultimately redounds to the benefit of racial and other minorities. Professor Lawrence apparently shares this view.

On the other end of the spectrum, where expression may be prohibited, traditional civil libertarians agree with Professor Lawrence that the First Amendment should not necessarily protect targeted individual harassment just because it happens to use the vehicle of speech. The ACLU maintains this nonabsolutist position, for example, with regard to sexually harassing speech on campus or in the workplace. The ACLU recently adopted a policy that specifically addresses racist harassment on campus, and it previously had adopted analogous policies concerning sexual harassment on campus and in the workplace. These earlier policies recognize that unlawful sex discrimination can consist of words specifically directed to a particular individual— words that undermine the individual's continued ability to function as a student or employee. With regard to sexual harassment on campus, ACLU policy provides:

> College[s] and universities should take those steps necessary to prevent the abuse of power which occurs . . . where a pattern and practice of sexual conduct or sexually demeaning or derogatory comments is directed at a specific student or gender [and] has definable consequences for the student that demonstrably hinders her or his learning experience as a student. This policy does not extend to verbal harassment that has no other effect on its recipient than to create an unpleasant learning environment.

> As the last sentence of this policy emphasizes, the ACLU demands evidence that harassing speech causes verifiable harm that directly interferes with a student's education in a more tangible, specific manner than creating an "unpleasant environment."

These ACLU policies recognize that conduct that infringes on the right to equal educational (or employment) opportunities, regardless of gender (or other invidious classifications), should not be condoned simply because it includes expressive elements. . . .

The captive audience concept in particular is an elusive and challenging one to apply. As Professor Tribe cautioned, this concept "is dangerously encompassing, and the Court has properly been reluctant to accept its implications whenever a regulation is not content-neutral." Noting that we are "often 'captives' outside the sanctuary of the home and subject to objectionable speech," the Court has ruled that, in public places, we bear the burden of averting our attention from expression we find offensive. Otherwise, the Court explained, "a majority [could] silence dissidents simply as a matter of personal predilections." The Court has been less reluctant to apply the captive audience concept to private homes. However, the Court has held that even in the home, free speech values may outweigh privacy concerns, requiring individuals to receive certain unwanted communications. . . .

The foregoing principles that govern the permissibility of speech regulations in general should guide our analysis of the permissibility of particular speech regulations in the academic setting. The Supreme Court has declared that within the academic environment freedom of expression should receive heightened protection and that "a university campus . . . possesses many of the characteristics of a traditional public forum." These considerations would suggest that hate speech should receive special protection within the university community. Conversely, Professor Mari Matsuda argues that equality guarantees and other principles that might weigh in favor of prohibiting racist speech are also particularly important in the academic context.

The appropriate analysis is more complex than either set of generalizations assumes. In weighing the constitutional concerns of free speech, equality, and privacy that hate speech regulations implicate, decision makers must take into account the particular context within the university in which the speech occurs. For example, the Court's generalizations about the heightened protection due free speech in the academic world certainly are applicable to some campus areas, such as parks, malls, or other traditional gathering places. The generalizations, however, may not be applicable to other areas, such as students' dormitory rooms. These rooms constitute the students' homes. Accordingly, under established free speech tenets, students should have the right to avoid being exposed to others' expression by seeking refuge in their rooms.

Some areas on campus present difficult problems concerning the appropriate level of speech protection because they share characteristics of both private homes and public forums. For example, one could argue that hallways, common rooms, and other common areas in dormitory buildings constitute extensions of the individual students' rooms. On the other hand, one could argue that these common areas constitute traditional gathering places and should be regarded as public forums, open to expressive activities at least by all dormitory residents if not by the broader community. . . .

Even in the areas of the university reserved for academic activities, such as classrooms, the calculus to determine the level of speech protection is complex. On the one hand, the classroom is the quintessential "marketplace of ideas," which should be open to the vigorous and robust exchange of even insulting or offensive words, on the theory that such an exchange ultimately will benefit not only the academic community, but also the larger community, in its pursuit of knowledge and understanding.

On the other hand, some minority students contend that in the long run, the academic dialogue might be stultified rather than stimulated by the inclusion of racist speech. They maintain that such speech not only interferes with equal educational opportunities, but also deters the exercise of other freedoms, including those secured by the First Amendment. Professor Lawrence argues that, as a consequence of hate speech, minority students are deprived of the opportunity to participate in the academic interchange, and that the exchange is impoverished by their exclusion. It must be emphasized, though, that expression subject to regulation on this rationale would have to be narrowly defined in order to protect the free flow of ideas that is vital to the academic community; thus, much expression would remain unregulated—expression which could be sufficiently upsetting to interfere with students' educational opportunities.

Another factor that might weigh in favor of imposing some regulations on speech in class is that students arguably constitute a captive audience. This characterization is especially apt when the course is required and class attendance is mandatory. Likewise, the case for regulation becomes more compelling the more power the racist speaker wields over the audience. For example, the law should afford students special protection from racist insults directed at them by their professors.

Even if various areas of a university are not classified as public forums, and even if occupants of such areas are designated captive audiences, any speech regulations in these areas would still be invalid if they discriminated on the basis of a speaker's viewpoint. Viewpoint-based discrimination constitutes the most egregious form of censorship and almost always violates the First Amendment. Accordingly, viewpoint discrimination is proscribed even in regulations that govern nonpublic forum government property and regulations that protect captive audiences.

Many proposed or adopted campus hate speech regulations constitute unconstitutional discrimination against particular views, either as they are written or as they are applied. This is a constitutional defect of the rule advocated by Professor Lawrence, for example. He endorsed a variation on the Stanford regulation that expressly would have excluded speech directed at "dominant majority groups." Despite the absence of explicit viewpoint discrimination in the rule that Stanford adopted, the chair of the committee that propounded this rule indicated that, as applied, it would effect viewpoint discrimination. Professor Lawrence concedes that the Stanford code is facially content-discriminatory, and, as applied, probably viewpoint-discriminatory as well.

As the foregoing discussion illustrates, the question whether any particular racist speech should be subject to regulation is a fact-specific inquiry. We cannot define particular words as inherently off limits, but rather we must examine every word in the overall context in which it is uttered.

Particular Speech-Limiting Doctrines Potentially Applicable to Campus Hate Speech

In addition to the foregoing general principles, Professor Lawrence and other proponents of campus hate speech regulation invoke three specific doctrines in an attempt to justify such rules: the fighting words doctrine, the tort of intentional infliction of emotional distress, and the tort of group defamation. As the following discussion shows, the Supreme Court has recognized that each of these doctrines may well be inconsistent with free speech principles. Therefore, these doctrines may not support any campus hate speech restrictions whatsoever. In any event, they at most would support only restrictions that are both narrowly drawn and narrowly applied.

Fighting Words. The fighting words doctrine is the principal model for the Stanford code, which Professor Lawrence supports. However, this doctrine provides a constitutionally shaky foundation for several reasons: it has been substantially limited in scope and may no longer be good law; even if the Supreme Court were to apply a narrowed version of the doctrine, such an application would threaten free speech principles; and, as actually implemented, the fighting words doctrine suppresses protectable speech and entails the inherent danger of discriminatory application to speech by members of minority groups and dissidents. . . .

In *Gooding* v. *Wilson,* the Court substantially narrowed *Chaplinsky*'s definition of fighting words by bringing that definition into line with *Chaplinsky*'s actual holding. In *Gooding,* as well as in every subsequent fighting words case, the Court disregarded the dictum in which the first prong of *Chaplinsky*'s definition was set forth and treated only those words that "tend to incite an immediate breach of the peace" as fighting words. Consistent with this narrowed definition, the Court has invalidated regulations that hold certain words to be per se proscribable and insisted that each challenged utterance be evaluated contextually. Thus, under the Court's current view, even facially valid laws that restrict fighting words may be applied constitutionally only in circumstances where their utterance almost certainly will lead to immediate violence. . . .

Even if there were a real danger that racist or other fighting words would cause reflexive violence, and even if that danger would be reduced by the threat of legal sanction, the fighting words doctrine still would be problematic in terms of free speech principles. As Professor Chafee observed, this doctrine "makes a man a criminal simply because his neighbors have no self-control and cannot refrain from violence." In other contexts, the Court appropriately has refused to allow the addressees of speech to exercise such a "heckler's veto."

The fighting words doctrine is constitutionally flawed for the additional reasons that it suppresses much protectable speech and that the protectable speech of minority group members is particularly vulnerable. . . . [T]he record of the actual implementation of the fighting words doctrine demonstrates that—as is the case with all speech restrictions—it endangers principles of equality as well as free speech. That record substantiates the risk that such a speech restriction will be applied discriminatorily and disproportionately against the very minority group members whom it is intended to protect. . . .

Intentional Infliction of Emotional Distress. A committee report that the University of Texas is currently considering recommends the common law tort of intentional infliction of emotional distress as a basis for regulating campus hate speech. This doctrinal approach has a logical appeal because it focuses on the type of harm potentially caused by racist speech that universities are most concerned with alleviating—namely, emotional or psychological harm that interferes with studies. In contrast, the harm at which the fighting words doctrine aims—potential violence by the addressee against the speaker—is of less concern to most universities.

Traditional civil libertarians caution that the intentional infliction of emotional distress theory should almost never apply to verbal harassment. A major problem with this approach is that "the innate vagueness of the interest in preventing emotional injury to listeners suggests that any attempt at judicial enforcement will inevitably result in the imposition of judges' subjective linguistic preferences on society, discrimination against ethnic and racial minorities, and ultimately the misuse of the rationale to justify the censorship of the ideological content of the speaker's message."

Again, as was true for the fighting words doctrine, there is a particular danger that this speech-restrictive doctrine also will be enforced to the detriment of the very minority groups whom it is designed to protect. . . .

Group Defamation. Professor Lawrence does not elaborate on either the constitutionality or efficacy of the group defamation concept, yet he approvingly notes others' alleged support for it. The group defamation concept, however, has been thoroughly discredited by others.

First, group defamation regulations are unconstitutional in terms of both Supreme Court doctrine and free speech principles. To be sure, the Supreme Court's only decision that expressly reviewed the issue, *Beauharnais* v. *Illinois,* upheld a group libel statute against a First Amendment challenge. However, that 5–4 decision was issued almost forty years ago, at a relatively early point in the Court's developing free speech jurisprudence. *Beauharnais* is widely assumed no longer to be good law in light of the Court's subsequent speech-protective decisions on related issues, notably its holdings that strictly limit individual defamation actions so as not to chill free speech. . . .

In addition to flouting constitutional doctrine and free speech principles, rules sanctioning group defamation are ineffective in curbing the specific class of hate speech that Professor Lawrence advocates restraining. . . .

One additional problem with group defamation statutes as a model for rules sanctioning campus hate speech should be noted. As with the other speech-restrictive doctrines asserted to justify such rules, group defamation laws introduce the risk that the rules will be enforced at the expense of the very minority groups sought to be protected. The Illinois statute upheld in *Beauharnais* is illustrative. According to a leading article on group libel laws, during the 1940s, the Illinois statute was "a weapon for harassment of the Jehovah's Witnesses," who were then "a minority . . . very much more in need of protection than most." Thus, a rule based on the group defamation theory provides no guarantee that it will not be used against minorities.

Even a Narrow Regulation Could Have a
Negative Symbolic Impact on Constitutional Values

Taking into account the constraints imposed by free speech principles and doctrines potentially applicable to the regulation of campus hate speech, it might be possible—although difficult—to frame a sufficiently narrow rule to withstand a facial First Amendment challenge. The federal judge who invalidated the University of Michigan's anti–hate speech regulation as overbroad and vague expressly noted this possibility. ACLU affiliates that have challenged particular campus hate speech restrictions have proposed alternative policies that might pass constitutional muster as a facial matter. However, it bears reemphasizing that, as the University of Texas report stressed, "[T]here can be no guarantee as to the constitutionality of any university rule bearing on racial harassment and sensitive matters of freedom of expression."

Even assuming that a regulation could be crafted with sufficient precision to survive a facial constitutional challenge, several further problems would remain, which should give any university pause in evaluating whether to adopt such a rule. Although these inherent problems with any hate speech regulation are discussed in greater detail below, they are summarized here. First, because of the discretion entailed in enforcing any such rule, they involve an inevitable danger of arbitrary or discriminatory enforcement. Therefore, the rule's implementation would have to be monitored to ensure that it did not exceed the bounds of the regulations' terms or threaten content- and viewpoint-neutrality principles. The experience with the University of Michigan's rule—the only campus hate speech rule that has an enforcement record—graphically illustrates this danger.

Second, there is an inescapable risk that any hate speech regulation, no matter how narrowly drawn, will chill speech beyond its literal scope. Members of the university community may well err on the side of caution to avoid being charged with a violation. For example, there is evidence that the rule which the University of Wisconsin implemented in 1989 has had this effect, even though it has not yet been directly enforced. A third problem inherent in any campus hate speech policy, as Professor Lawrence concedes, is that such rules constitute a precedent that can be used to restrict other types of speech. As the Supreme Court has recognized, the long-range precedential impact of any challenged governmental action should be a factor in evaluating its lawfulness.

Further, in light of constitutional constraints, any campus hate speech policy inevitably would apply to only a tiny fraction of all racist expression, and accordingly it would have only a symbolic impact. Therefore, in deciding whether to adopt such a rule, universities must ask whether that symbolic impact is, on balance, positive or negative in terms of constitutional values. On the one hand, some advocates of hate speech regulations maintain that the regulations might play a valuable symbolic role in reaffirming our societal commitment to racial equality (although this is debatable). On the other hand, we must beware of even a symbolic or perceived diminution of our impartial commitment to free speech. Even a limitation that has a direct impact upon only a discrete category of speech may have a much more pervasive indirect impact—by undermining the First Amendment's moral legitimacy. . . .

Professor Lawrence's Conception of Regulable Racist Speech Endangers Free Speech Principles

The preceding discussion of relevant constitutional doctrine points to several problems with the Stanford regulations, as well as other regulations adopted or advocated by other universities. As previously explained, the Stanford regulations violate the cardinal principles that speech restrictions must be content- and viewpoint-neutral. Moreover, although these regulations purportedly incorporate the fighting words doctrine, they in fact go well beyond the narrow bounds that the Court has imposed on that doctrine, and, as the University of Michigan example demonstrates, they threaten to chill protected speech.

The Proposed Regulations Would Not Pass Constitutional Muster

The Regulations Exceed the Bounds of the Fighting Words Doctrine. As discussed above, the fighting words doctrine is fraught with constitutional problems. As a result, it either has been abrogated *sub silentio* or probably should be. In any event, even assuming that the doctrine is still good law, it has been severely circumscribed by Supreme Court rulings. Because those limits are necessitated by free speech principles, they must be strictly enforced. Professor Gard's thorough study of the law in this area summarizes the Court's limitations on the fighting words doctrine: "The offending language (1) must constitute a personally abusive epithet, (2) must be addressed in a face-to-face manner, (3) must be directed to a specific individual and be descriptive of that individual, and (4) must be uttered under such circumstances that the words have a direct tendency to cause an immediate violent response by the average recipient. If any of these four elements is absent, the doctrine may not justifiably be invoked as a rationale for the suppression of the expression. . . ."

A comparison of the Stanford code to the Supreme Court's four criteria for constitutional fighting words restrictions reveals that the code clearly does not satisfy one of the Court's criteria, and it may not satisfy the other three. Most importantly, as outlined above, since *Gooding* v. *Wilson,* the Court consistently has invalidated fighting words definitions that refer only to the content of words. Instead, it has insisted that these words must be evaluated contextually, to assess whether they are likely to cause an imminent breach of the peace under the circumstances in which they are uttered. Yet, the Stanford code punishes words which are commonly understood to convey "group-based hatred." By proscribing certain words, without considering their context, the Stanford code violates Gard's fourth criterion, and for that reason alone falls afoul of the First Amendment.

The Stanford code also may fail to satisfy the Court's strict parameters for the fighting words doctrine in other respects. First, it does not expressly require that the prohibited speech "must constitute a personally abusive epithet." . . .

Although the Stanford code may comply with the Court's second and third requirements, by prescribing that the prohibited speech be "addressed directly to the individual or individuals whom it insults or stigmatizes," both of these elements have been construed so strictly that they may not be satisfied by this provision. Some judicial rulings indicate that the second requirement, the face-to-face element, "is not satisfied by mere technical physical presence, but contemplates an extremely close physical proximity." The third requirement has been interpreted to mean that "the offensive words must be descriptive of a particular person and addressed to that person." The Stanford code does not require that the prohibited words describe the individual to whom they are addressed. Instead, under the Stanford code, the words may convey hatred for broad groups of people.

The Regulations Will Chill Protected Speech. Beyond its facial problems of violating neutrality principles and fighting words limitations, the Stanford code will also dampen academic discourse. This inevitable outcome is indicated by the experience under the University of Michigan hate speech regulation.

Even though the Michigan regulation was in some respects broader than its Stanford counterpart, the latter rule also suffers from facial overbreadth and ambiguity. One of the key terms in the Stanford regulation, the term "stigmatize," also was contained in the Michigan regulation and was specifically ruled unconstitutionally vague. Accordingly, the Stanford code appears to be as constitutionally suspect as the Michigan rule, contrary to Professor Lawrence's assumption. As discussed in the preceding section, all the alternative theories that have been offered—the fighting words doctrine, the intentional infliction of emotional distress tort, and group defamation—also pose significant threats to free speech principles. . . .

In the recent wave of college crackdowns on racist and other forms of hate speech, examples abound of attempts to censor speech conveying ideas that clearly play a legitimate role in academic discourse, although some of us might find them wrong-headed or even odious. For example, the University of Michigan's anti–hate speech policy could justify attacks on author Salman Rushdie because his book, *The Satanic Verses,* was offensive to Muslims.

Such incidents are not aberrational. Any anti–hate speech rule inescapably entails some vagueness, due to the inherent imprecision of key words and concepts common to all such proposed rules. For example, most regulations employ one or more of the following terms: "demeaning," "disparaging," "harassing," "hostile," "insulting," "intimidating," and "stigmatizing." Therefore, there is real danger that even a narrowly crafted rule will deter some expression that should be protected—especially in the university environment. In particular, such a rule probably will "add to the silence" on "gut issues" about racism, sexism, and other forms of bias that already impede interracial and other intergroup dialogues. . . .

In addition to their chilling effect on the ideas and expressions of university community members, policies that bar hate speech could engender broader forms of censorship. As noted by Professor William Cohen of Stanford Law School, an anti–hate speech rule such as the one adopted by his university "purports to create a personal right to be free from involuntary exposure to any form of expression that gives certain kinds of offense." Therefore, he explains, such a rule "could become a sword to challenge assigned readings in courses, the showing of films on campus, or the message of certain speakers."

The Proposed Regulations Would Endanger Fundamental Free Speech Principles

The various proposed campus hate speech regulations, including the Stanford code that Professor Lawrence endorses, are inconsistent with current Supreme Court doctrine prescribing permissible limits on speech. More importantly, they jeopardize basic free speech principles. Whereas certain conduct may be regulable, speech that advocates such conduct is not, and speech may not be regulated on the basis of its content, even if many of us strongly disagree with—or are repelled by—that content. . . .

It is important to place the current debate about campus racist speech in the context of earlier efforts to censor other forms of hate speech, including sexist and anti-Semitic speech. Such a broadened perspective suggests that consistent principles should be applied each time the issue resurfaces in any guise. Every person may find one particular type of speech especially odious and one message that most sorely tests his or her dedication to free speech values. But for each person who would exclude racist speech from the general proscription against content-based speech regulations, recent experience shows that there is another who would make such an exception only for anti-choice speech, another who would make it only for sexist speech, another who would make it only for anti-Semitic speech, another who would make it only for flag desecration, and so on.

The recognition that there is no principled basis for curbing speech expressing some particular ideas is reflected in the time-honored prohibition of any content-based or viewpoint-based regulations. . . .

In light of the universal condemnation of racial discrimination and the worldwide regulation of racist speech, it certainly is tempting to consider excepting racist speech from First Amendment protection. Episodes of racist speech, such as those cited by Professor Lawrence and others, make a full commitment to free speech at times seem painful and difficult. Civil libertarians find such speech abhorrent, given our dedication to eradicating racial discrimination and other forms of bigotry. But experience has confirmed the truth of the indivisibility principle articulated above: History demonstrates that if the freedom of speech is weakened for one person, group, or message, then it is no longer there for others. The free speech victories that civil libertarians have won in the context of defending the right to express racist and other anti–civil libertarian messages have been used to protect speech proclaiming anti-racist and pro–civil libertarian messages. . . .

To attempt to craft free speech exceptions only for racist speech would create a significant risk of a slide down the proverbial "slippery slope." . . .

First, we must think hard about the groups that should be protected. Should we regulate speech aimed only at racial and ethnic groups? . . . Or should we also bar insults of religious groups, women, gays and lesbians, individuals with disabilities, Vietnam War veterans, and so on? . . .

Second, we must carefully define proscribable harassing speech to avoid encompassing the important expression that inevitably is endangered by any hate speech restriction. Censorial consequences could result from many proposed or adopted university policies, including the Stanford code, which sanctions speech intended to "insult or stigmatize" on the basis of race or other prohibited grounds. For example, certain feminists suggest that all heterosexual sex is rape because heterosexual men are aggressors who operate in a cultural climate of pervasive sexism and violence against women. Aren't these feminists insulting or stigmatizing heterosexual men on the basis of their sex and sexual orientation? . . .

Once we acknowledge the substantial discretion that anti–hate speech rules will vest in those who enforce them, then we are ceding to the government the power to pick and choose whose words to protect and whose to punish. Such discretionary governmental power is fundamentally antithetical to the free speech guarantee. Once the government is allowed to punish any speech based upon its content, free expression exists only for those with power. . . .

Professor Lawrence's Rationales for Regulating Racist Speech Would Justify Sweeping Prohibitions, Contrary to Free Speech Principles

Although Professor Lawrence actually advocates regulating only a relatively narrow category of racist speech, his rationales could be asserted to justify broader rules. Indeed, he himself appears to recognize that, if accepted, his approach could lead to outlawing all racist speech, as well as other forms of hate speech. Since many universities and individuals now advocate broader-ranging regulations—and since Professor Lawrence also endorses restrictions that have a "considerably broader reach" than the Stanford code—it is important to consider the problems with Professor Lawrence's more expansive rationales. His general theories about racist speech entail substantial departures from traditional civil libertarian and constitutional law positions.

Brown and Other Cases Invalidating Governmental Racist Conduct do not Justify Regulating Nongovernmental Racist Speech

Professor Lawrence intriguingly posits that *Brown* v. *Board of Education, Bob Jones University* v. *United States,* and other civil rights cases justify regulation of private racist speech. The problem with drawing an analogy between all of these cases and the subject at hand is that the cases involved either government speech, as opposed to speech by private individuals, or conduct, as opposed to speech. Indeed, *Brown* itself is distinguishable on both grounds. . . .

First, the governmental defendant in *Brown*—the Topeka, Kansas, Board of Education—was not simply saying that blacks are inferior. Rather, it was treating them as inferior through pervasive patterns of conduct, by maintaining systems and structures of segregated public schools. To be sure, a by-product of the challenged conduct was a message, but that message was only incidental. Saying that black children are unfit to attend school with whites is materially distinguishable from legally prohibiting them from doing so, despite the fact that the legal prohibition may convey the former message.

Professor Lawrence's point proves too much. If incidental messages could transform conduct into speech, then the distinction between speech and conduct would disappear completely, because all conduct conveys a message. To take an extreme example, a racially motivated lynching expresses the murderer's hatred or contempt for his victim. But the clearly unlawful act is not protected from punishment by virtue of the incidental message it conveys. And the converse also is true. Just because the government may suppress particular hate messages that are the by-product of unlawful conduct, it does not follow that it may suppress all hate messages. Those messages not tightly linked to conduct must still be protected. . . .

Even if *Brown* involved only a governmental message of racism, without any attendant conduct, that case still would be distinguishable in a crucial way from a private individual's conveyance of the same message. Under the post–Civil War constitutional amendments, the government is committed to eradicating all badges and incidents of slavery, including racial discrimination. Consistent with the paramount importance of this obligation, the Supreme Court has held that the equal protection clause bars the government from loaning textbooks to racially discriminatory private schools, even though the Court had held previously that the establishment clause does not bar the government from loaning textbooks to private religious schools. In this respect, the government's constitutional duty to dissociate itself from racism is even greater than its constitutional duty to dissociate itself from religion. The government's supreme obligation to counter racism clearly is incompatible with racist speech promulgated by the government itself. Private individuals have no comparable duty. . . .

The Nonintellectual Content of Some Racist Speech does not Justify its Prohibition

In addition to his principal argument that private racist speech can be regulated because it is indistinguishable from governmental racist conduct, Professor Lawrence offers a second justification. He contends that "[a] defining attribute of speech is that it appeals first to the mind of the hearer who can evaluate its truth or persuasiveness," and that because certain racist speech lacks this quality, it should not be viewed as speech. This position is inconsistent with fundamental free speech values. . . .

Together, *Terminiello* and *Cohen* recognize that speech often expresses the speaker's emotions and appeals to the audience's emotions. This generalization applies not only to the ugly words of racist vituperation, but also to the beautiful words of poetry. Indeed, much indisputably valuable language, as well as expressive conduct, has the intention and effect of appealing not directly, or not only, to the mind. Such language also seeks to, and does, engage the audience's emotions. If emotion-provoking discourse were denied protected status, then much political speech—which is usually viewed as being at the core of First Amendment protection—would fall outside the protected realm. . . .

Prohibiting Racist Speech Would Not Effectively Counter, and Could Even Aggravate, the Underlying Problem of Racism

Civil Libertarians Should Continue to Make Combating Racism a Priority

Despite Professor Lawrence's proffered justifications for regulating a broader spectrum of racist speech, he in fact advocates regulating only a limited category of speech. Thus, even Professor Lawrence's views of regulable speech, although broader than those of the Supreme Court or traditional civil libertarians, would allow most racist speech on campus.

I do not think it is worth spending a great deal of time debating the fine points of specific rules or their particular applications to achieve what necessarily will be only marginal differences in the amount of racist insults that can be sanctioned. The larger problems of racist attitudes and conduct—of which all these words are symptoms—would remain. Those who share the dual goals of promoting racial equality and protecting free speech must concentrate on countering racial discrimination, rather than on defining the particular narrow subset of racist slurs that constitutionally might be regulable. . . .

Punishing Racist Speech Would not Effectively Counter Racism

This article emphasizes the principle reasons, arising from First Amendment theory, for concluding that racist speech should receive the same protection as other offensive speech. This conclusion also is supported by pragmatic or strategic considerations concerning the efficacious pursuit of equality goals. Not only would rules censoring racist speech fail to reduce racial bias, but they might even undermine that goal.

First, there is no persuasive psychological evidence that punishment for name-calling changes deeply held attitudes. To the contrary, psychological studies show that censored speech becomes more appealing and persuasive to many listeners merely by virtue of the censorship.

Nor is there any empirical evidence, from the countries that do outlaw racist speech, that censorship is an effective means to counter racism. . . .

Banning Racist Speech Could Aggravate Racism

For several reasons, banning the symptom of racist speech may compound the underlying problem of racism. Professor Lawrence sets up a false dichotomy when he urges us to balance equality goals against free speech goals. Just as he observes that free speech concerns should be weighed on the pro-regulation, as well as the anti-regulation, side of the balance, he should recognize that equality concerns weigh on the anti-regulation, as well as the pro-regulation, side.

The first reason that laws censoring racist speech may undermine the goal of combating racism flows from the discretion such laws inevitably vest in prosecutors, judges, and the other individuals who implement them. One ironic, even tragic, result of this discretion is that members of minority groups themselves—the very people whom the law is intended to protect—are likely targets of punishment. . . . History teaches us that anti–hate speech laws regularly have been used to oppress racial and other minorities. . . .

Professor Lawrence himself recognizes that rules regulating racist speech might backfire and be invoked disproportionately against blacks and other traditionally oppressed groups. Indeed, he charges that other university rules already are used to silence antiracist, but not racist, speakers. Professor Lawrence proposes to avoid this danger by excluding from the rule's protection "persons who were vilified on the basis of their membership in dominant majority groups." Even putting aside the fatal First Amendment flaws in such a radical departure from content- and viewpoint-neutrality principles, the proposed exception would create far more problems of equality and enforceability than it would solve.

A second reason why censorship of racist speech actually may subvert, rather than promote, the goal of eradicating racism is that such censorship measures often have the effect of glorifying racist speakers. Efforts at suppression result in racist speakers receiving attention and publicity which they otherwise would not have garnered. As previously noted, psychological studies reveal that whenever the government attempts to censor speech, the censored speech—for that very reason—becomes more appealing to many people. Still worse, when pitted against the government, racist speakers may appear as martyrs or even heroes. . . .

There is a third reason why laws that proscribe racist speech could well undermine goals of reducing bigotry. As Professor Lawrence recognizes, given the overriding importance of free speech in our society, any speech regulation must be narrowly drafted. Therefore, it can affect only the most blatant, crudest forms of racism. The more subtle, and hence potentially more invidious, racist expressions will survive. Virtually all would agree that no law could possibly eliminate all racist speech, let alone racism itself. If the marketplace of ideas cannot be trusted to winnow out the hateful, then there is no reason to believe that censorship will do so. The most it could possibly achieve would be to drive some racist thought and expression underground, where it would be more difficult to respond to such speech and the underlying attitudes it expresses. . . .

The positive effects of racist speech—in terms of making society aware of and mobilizing its opposition to the evils of racism—are illustrated by the wave of campus racist incidents now under discussion. Ugly and abominable as these expressions are, they undoubtedly have had the beneficial result of raising public consciousness about the underlying societal problem of racism. If these expressions had been chilled by virtue of university sanctions, then it is doubtful that there would be such widespread discussion on campuses, let alone more generally, about the real problem of racism. . . .

Means Consistent with the First Amendment Can Promote Racial Equality More Effectively than Can Censorship

The Supreme Court recently reaffirmed the time-honored principle that the appropriate response to speech conveying ideas that we reject or find offensive is not to censor such speech, but rather to exercise our own speech rights. In *Texas* v. *Johnson,* the Court urged this counter-speech strategy upon the many Americans who are deeply offended by the burning of their country's flag: "The way to preserve the flag's special role is not to punish those who feel differently about these matters. It is to persuade them that they are wrong." In addition to persuasion, the types of private expressive conduct that could be invoked in response to racist speech include censure and boycotts.

In the context of countering racism on campus, the strategy of increasing speech—rather than decreasing it—not only would be consistent with First Amendment principles, but also would be more effective in advancing equality goals. . . .

If universities adopt narrowly framed rules that regulate racist expression, then these rules should constitute one element of a broader program that includes the more positive, direct strategies outlined above. Many universities appear to be responding constructively to the recent upsurge in campus hate speech incidents by adopting some of the measures suggested here. This development demonstrates the positive impact of racist speech, in terms of galvanizing community efforts to counter the underlying attitudes it expresses.

It is particularly important to devise antiracism strategies consistent with the First Amendment because racial and other minority groups ultimately have far more to lose than to gain through a weakened free speech guarantee. History has demonstrated that minorities have been among the chief beneficiaries of a vigorous free speech safeguard. . . .

Conclusion

Some traditional civil libertarians may agree with Professor Lawrence that a university rule banning a narrowly defined class of assaultive, harassing racist expression might comport with First Amendment principles and make a symbolic contribution to the racial equality mandated by the Fourteenth Amendment. However, Professor Lawrence and other members of the academic community who advocate such steps must recognize that educators have a special responsibility to avoid the danger posed by focusing on symbols that obscure the real underlying issues.

The recent exploitation of the American flag as a symbol of patriotism, to distort the true nature of that concept, serves as a sobering reminder of this risk. Joseph S. Murphy, Chancellor of the City University of New York, recently offered lessons for educators from the flag-related controversies. His cautionary words apply even more powerfully to the campus hate speech controversy, since the general responsibility of academics to call for an honest and direct discourse about compelling societal problems is especially great within our own communities: "As educators, we should be somewhat concerned [about the manipulation of such symbols as the flag for partisan political purposes]. At our best, we convey ideas in their full complexity, with ample appreciation of the ambiguity that attaches to most important concepts. We use symbols, but we do so to illuminate, not to obscure. . . . The real question is how we use our position in the university and in society to steer national discourse away from an obsessive fixation on the trivial representation of ideas, and toward a proper focus on the underlying conflicts that define our era."

An exaggerated concern with racist speech creates a risk of elevating symbols over substance in two problematic respects. First, it may divert our attention from the causes of racism to its symptoms. Second, a focus on the hateful message conveyed by particular speech may distort our view of fundamental neutral principles applicable to our system of free expression generally. We should not let the racist veneer in which expression is cloaked obscure our recognition of how important free expression is and of how effectively it has advanced racial equality.

Discussion Questions

1. Strossen suggests that the "viewpoint discrimination" inherent in many speech codes constitutes "the most egregious form of censorship [that] almost always violates the First Amendment." Are there grounds for ar-

guing that a prohibition of racist or sexist insults is not viewpoint discrimination? (You may find help in the excerpt from Charles Lawrence.) Do you agree with this assertion?

2. Strossen argues that even a narrowly drawn campus hate speech regulation may "chill" otherwise protected speech because "[m]embers of the university community may well err on the side of caution to avoid being charged with a violation." Is this a legitimate fear in light of the case studies you have read? *Should* this "chilling effect" on potentially discriminatory speech be regarded as a danger, or as a bonus from hate speech regulation?

3. Do you agree with Strossen that even the relatively modest Stanford hate speech code is unconstitutional, and that, even if constitutional, is likely to be ineffective in reaching the most hurtful forms of hate speech?

4. Strossen emphasizes the dangers to freedom of expression posed by *any* attempt to regulate speech. Indeed, according to Strossen, hate speech regulation poses perhaps the most serious dangers to precisely the minority groups it is supposed to help. Lawrence, on the other hand, emphasizes the very real hurt inflicted on the victims of hate speech. Is Strossen, as Lawrence suggests, "asking victim groups to pay the price" for freedom of expression exercised primarily by the more privileged groups in society? Is she necessarily siding with the racists and bigots? How effective do you think her proposed "means consistent with the First Amendment" would be in combating the evils of hate speech on campus? You might usefully refer to the Duke University case study in considering your answer to this final query.